Erik Jobstl 10b
Lisa Briewig 10c

D1671893

English G21 Klasse 10
Ansch.J. 2017

20544

English G | 21

B6
für Realschulen

English G 21 • Band B 6

Im Auftrag des Verlages herausgegeben von
Prof. Hellmut Schwarz, Mannheim
Wolfgang Biederstädt, Köln

Erarbeitet von
Susan Abbey, Nenagh, Irland
Roderick Cox, Freudenstadt
Laurence Harger, Wellington, Neuseeland
Claire Lamsdale, Llangybi, Wales

unter Mitarbeit von
Wolfgang Biederstädt, Köln
Joachim Blombach, Herford
Helmut Dengler, Limbach
Jennifer Seidl, München
Andrea Ulrich, Berlin

in Zusammenarbeit mit der Englischredaktion
Dr. Christiane Kallenbach (Projektleitung);
Dr. Philip Devlin (verantwortlicher Redakteur);
Susanne Bennetreu (Bildredaktion); Britta Bensmann;
Bonnie S. Glänzer; Stefan Höhne; Renata Jakovac;
Anne Linder; Kathrin Spiegelberg; Uwe Tröger;
Klaus G. Unger *sowie* Ulrike Berendt; Maike Horoba;
Sarah Silver

Beratende Mitwirkung
Anja Bersch, Waldstetten; Peer Brändel, Gütersloh;
Uwe Chormann, Einselthun; Matthew George, Frankfurt
(Main); Prof. Dr. Liesel Hermes, Karlsruhe; Bernhard
Hunger, Dettingen; Helge Kipp, Mülheim an der Ruhr;
Gabriele Künstler, Altlußheim; Ulrike Rath, Aachen;
Lutz Salvi, Braunschweig; Michael Semmler, Lünen;
Karl Starkebaum, Diekholzen; Elke Storz, Freiburg i. Br.

Illustrationen
Silke Bachmann, Hamburg; Roland Beier, Berlin;
Carlos Borrell, Berlin; Dylan Gibson, Pitlochry;
Alfred Schüssler, Frankfurt/Main

Layoutkonzept
Aksinia Raphael; Korinna Wilkes

Technische Umsetzung
Aksinia Raphael; Korinna Wilkes;
Stephan Hilleckenbach; Rainer Bachmaier

Umschlaggestaltung
Klein & Halm Grafikdesign, Berlin

www.cornelsen.de
www.EnglishG.de

Die Internetadressen und -dateien, die in diesem
Lehrwerk angegeben sind, wurden vor Drucklegung
geprüft. Der Verlag übernimmt keine Gewähr für die
Aktualität und den Inhalt dieser Adressen und Dateien
oder solcher, die mit ihnen verlinkt sind.

Dieses Werk berücksichtigt die Regeln der reformierten
Rechtschreibung und Zeichensetzung.

1. Auflage, 1. Druck 2011

Alle Drucke dieser Auflage sind inhaltlich unverändert
und können im Unterricht nebeneinander verwendet
werden.

Druck: CS-Druck CornelsenStürtz, Berlin

ISBN 978-3-06-031315-0 – broschiert
ISBN 978-3-06-031365-5 – gebunden

 Inhalt gedruckt auf säurefreiem Papier aus nachhaltiger Forstwirtschaft.

Dein Englischbuch enthält folgende Teile:

Units **1** **2** **3**	die drei Kapitel des Buches
Getting ready for a test	Hier kannst du dich gezielt auf einen Test vorbereiten.
Extra: English for jobs	Hier kannst du typische Situationen des Berufsalltags üben.
Extra: Exam File	vielfältige Prüfungsaufgaben zur Vorbereitung auf die Abschlussprüfung
Extra: Text File	viele interessante Texte zum Lesen (passend zu den Units)
Skills File (SF)	Beschreibung wichtiger Lern- und Arbeitstechniken
Grammar File (GF)	Zusammenfassung der wichtigsten Grammatikthemen der Bände 1–6; Übersichten über die Zeitformen (*present, past, future*)
Vocabulary	Wörterverzeichnis zum Lernen der neuen Wörter jeder Unit
Dictionary	alphabetisches englisch-deutsches Wörterverzeichnis

Die Units bestehen aus diesen Teilen:

Lead-in	Einstieg in das neue Thema
Part A, B (Unit 1: Part C)	neuer Lernstoff mit vielen Aktivitäten
Practice	Übungen
How am I doing?	Hier kannst du dein Wissen und Können überprüfen.

In den Units findest du diese Überschriften und Symbole:

Dossier	Schöne und wichtige Arbeiten kannst du in einer Mappe sammeln.
EVERYDAY ENGLISH	Hier übst du wichtige Alltagssituationen.
MEDIATION	Hier vermittelst du zwischen zwei Sprachen.
VIEWING	Aufgaben zu Filmausschnitten
Now you	Hier sprichst und schreibst du über dich selbst.
REVISION	Übungen zur Wiederholung
WORDS	Übungen zu Wortfeldern und Wortverbindungen
👥 👥👥	Partnerarbeit / Gruppenarbeit
🎧 🎧	nur auf CD / auf CD und im Schülerbuch
🎥	Filmausschnitte auf DVD
>	Textaufgaben
Extra	zusätzliche Aktivitäten und Übungen

Contents

Love life!

The world we live in

Have your say!

Love life!   The world we live in   Have your say!

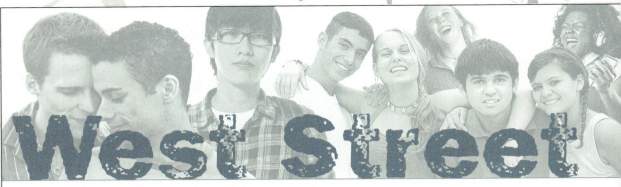

West Street

The characters

an exciting drama series for young people

Toby

He's very confident, very charming and very good-looking. Girls fancy him and he knows it. Some people think he's arrogant – and he is a bit. But he's a loyal friend too. He's been together with his girlfriend for eight months.

Minty

(real name Katy Minton) Everyone respects Minty. She's serious, full of confidence and isn't afraid to say what she thinks. She's the class rep. She's attractive, but she doesn't care very much about her appearance. She's very different from her brother, Toby.

Ed

(real name James Ford) The first things you notice about Ed are his size – he's really tall – and his bright red curly hair. He has a great sense of humour and is very easy-going. Hasn't got a girlfriend but would really like one. He and Peanut are old friends.

Bex

(also known as Becky) Minty's best friend. Unlike Minty she's relaxed and laughs all the time. And you never see Bex without her make-up. Bex fancies Ed a lot, but he hasn't noticed and she hasn't told him – yet.

The episodes

Episode 1:
Just be cool

Peanut is excited. He has met a girl and she has said she'll go out with him. But now there's a problem.

[»]

Peanut

(real name Philip Nutt)
A lovable geek. He's thin with big glasses. He knows everything about everything, from science to football to music. He's quite shy, but he's popular. Lots of people, girls and boys, like him because he's very cool in an uncool kind of way.

Episode 2:
Top chat-up lines

Ed wants to ask a girl out, but he doesn't know how. Peanut has some suggestions.

[»]

1   The characters

Read about the people in the series. Then copy and complete the chart.

Name	Appearance	Character	Relationships
Toby	good-looking	confident	girlfriend
	...	...	...
Minty	...		

2   Just be cool (Episode 1)

a) *Listen and answer the questions.*
1 What does Peanut want from Toby?
2 Does Toby give it to him?
3 Who has Peanut called? How often?
4 What does Toby advise Peanut to do?

b) 👥 *Do you agree with Toby? Why (not)?*

3   Top chat-up lines (Episode 2)

a) *Listen to part 1 and answer the questions.*
1 What two tips does Peanut give Ed?
2 What does Toby think of Peanut's advice?
3 Who could Ed speak to next and why?

b) 👥 *Discuss what you think will happen next. Then listen to part 2 and check if your ideas were right.*

c) *Which statement sums up best what happens in part 2?*
1 Minty thinks Ed is interested in Bex, so she advises Bex to ask him out.
2 Ed asks Bex about her favourite pizza because he wants to go out with her.
3 When Ed asks Bex about her favourite pizza, she asks him out.

d) **Extra** 👥👥 *Think of good ways to start a conversation with someone you fancy. Report your best idea to the class.*

▶ SF Having a conversation (p. 139)

4   👥 Now you

Did you like the West Street *series? Why (not)? Make an appointment with two partners. Say what you think about the characters and the story.*

▶ WB 1–3 (p. 2)

REAL-LIFE RELATIONSHIPS

1

Hey Jake

Got a problem? **Email Jake** ⚪

>> Your comments

I don't want to go to Spain

I don't know what to do. My mum died three years ago. My dad now has a girlfriend and wants to make a new start – in Spain! He's found a job in a holiday place and he's found a school for me and my sister. My sister (she's 13, I'm 16) thinks it's a great idea. But I really don't want to go. I have a girlfriend here and our relationship is important to me. And I hate the idea of having to make new friends. I could stay here and live with my granny, but I don't want to do that either. Whatever happens, I'm not going to Spain. I think it's really unfair of my dad. We argue all the time. What can I do?   Sam

Jake says:

This is a hard one, Sam. If I were you, I'd try to talk to your dad in a calm way. You should listen to what he has to say. He probably thinks that he's doing the best thing for your family. Perhaps you could go to Spain for a year and see if you like it. Only you can decide what to do, but you should talk to your dad and try to understand his reasons.   Good luck!

Ally

What about going to Spain for the school term? You could come back in the holidays and see your friends and spend time with your girlfriend then. Could your girlfriend go and visit you in the holidays?   Ally x

Dani

Your dad shouldn't put you in this situation. I think it's really mean of him.   Dani

JC

I think you should go to Spain – it might be fun! And with the internet and cheap phone calls you can stay in touch with your friends.   JC

First ⏮ ◀ **1–3** 4–6 … ▶ ⏭ **Last**

a) Answer the questions.
1 Why doesn't Sam want to go to Spain? Give two reasons.
2 What advice does he get from Jake, Ally, Dani and JC? Do you agree? Why (not)?

b) Look at the answers to Sam's problem. Write down at least four phrases you can use to make suggestions or give advice.
If I were you, I'd …
…

c) Imagine you are Sam's sister. Tell him how you feel about going to Spain and why. Then give him some advice about what he should do.

More problems for Jake

We have the same friends

I like this girl, but she hangs out with the same group of friends as me. Some people in the group have been out with each  other, but usually they break up and stop speaking to each other. And then one of the two people stops hanging out with the group. I don't want to mess things up like that. But I do like her a lot. Should I ask her out or not?   Matty

She doesn't hang out any more

My best friend spends all her time with her new boyfriend and doesn't hang out with her old friends any more. I've talked to her  about it, but she says I'm just jealous. I think she's stupid. Her relationship with her boyfriend probably won't last, and then she'll need her friends. But I don't know whether I'll want to spend time with her after this.   Nikki

My girlfriend's best friend flirts with me

My girlfriend and I have been together for 11 months. Recently her best friend told me that if I get bored with my girlfriend,  she'll always be there for me. She texts me all the time and stands really close to me whenever she gets a chance. She's really attractive, but I love my girlfriend. I don't know what to do. Should I tell my girlfriend about her friend or not? They've been friends for 12 years.   Mel

2   More comments from Jake

Match Jake's comments to the problems on the left. There is one comment that doesn't fit. Explain your choice.

1   When people start a new relationship, they often forget to find time for old friends.

2   If you want to stay with your girlfriend, you should explain this clearly to the other girl.

3   If your girlfriend has decided to leave you, you'll have to learn to live without her.

4   Why not tell her you'd like to be more than 'just friends' and see how she feels?

3   Now you

a) 👥 *With your partner, choose one of the problems on the left. Discuss answers.*

b) 👥 *Together write a comment for the problem. Put it up on the wall.*

c) Walk around and read all the comments for the problem that you wrote about. Choose your favourite comment. Report to the class.

d) **Extra** *Work on your own. Choose one of the problems and write a detailed answer.*

▶ *SF Writing course (pp. 143–144)*

4   👥 Role play

Partner B: Go to p. 99.
Partner A: Explain your problem and ask for advice.

You did badly in your last exams. Your parents say you spend too much time with your friends and not enough on school work. They want you to change schools, but you don't want to.

Then listen to your partner's problem and try and give him/her some advice.

▶ **Text File 1** *(pp. 104–109)* • *WB 4 (p. 3)*

>> Post your comments

P1 WORDS Describing people

I'm short and a bit fat, with green eyes and short, straight, black hair. I've got two lip piercings. (I also want a tattoo, but I'll have to wait until I'm 18 for that.) I'm not a very serious or hard-working person – actually I'm a bit silly and VERY lazy. (But of course I don't mention that in my CV!)

a) *Read the description above. Find words for describing people's appearance and character (e.g. fat, serious, ...). Organize them in a chart or network.*

b) *Add more words to your chart or network. Try to think of synonyms (e.g. easy-going/relaxed) or opposites (e.g. rude/polite).*

c) *Write a short description of yourself. Collect all the descriptions. Someone should read them out loud. Guess who each text is about.*

d) **Extra** *Describe one of the people below:*
– your best friend.
– someone from your family.
– a dream (or nightmare) girlfriend or boyfriend.

P2 REVISION A group of friends (Present tenses)

a) *Complete the text with the correct form of the verbs in brackets. Use the simple present or the present progressive.*

▶ *GF 3: Talking about the present (p. 154)*

1 These people ... (be) at a summer camp in the US.
2 The sun ... (shine) and everyone ... (have) a good time.
3 The girl who ... (play) the guitar is Rose. On her right is her boyfriend Seb, the guy with the curly brown hair and the white T-shirt.
4 He ... (not smile). That's typical of Seb. He always ... (look) very serious.
5 Rose's brother Jake ... (sit) behind her.
6 Usually he ... (not wear) hats. I ... (not know) why he ... (wear) one in this photo.
7 The girl on Jake's left is Ruby. She ... (come) from South Africa, but she ... (spend) the summer in the US.
8 The guy with the yellow T-shirt is Josh. As you can see, he ... (kiss) his girlfriend Kate. They ... (like) each other very much.

9 And the others? The two guys on the left ... (come) from Germany, but I ... (not remember) their names. And the good-looking guy with the short hair and the big smile? Well, that's me.

b) **Extra** *Find a photo of you and your friends and write about it.*

▶ *SF Describing pictures (p. 125–126) • WB 5–6 (pp. 3–4)*

P3 **EVERYDAY ENGLISH** **SPEAKING Keeping a conversation going** 🎧

a) Listen to the first conversation between Ed and Nadia. Ed is finding it difficult to keep the conversation going. What could he do better? ▶ *SF Having a conversation (p. 139)*

b) Look at the dialogue between Ed and another girl, Holly. What do you think he should say? Write down your ideas. If you need help, look at the box below.

*Ed*____ Hi I'm Ed.

*Holly*__ Hi.

*Ed*____ Er ... (1)

*Holly*__ Oh right. I'm Holly.

*Ed*____ Hi Holly. Er ... (2), Holly?

*Holly*__ It's not really my kind of music.

*Ed*____ Really? ... (3)?

*Holly*__ Well, I don't know really. Not this kind. I only came because Peanut wanted to come.

*Ed*____ Oh ... (4)?

*Holly*__ Yes, he's my cousin.

*Ed*____ Oh that's a surprise, ... (5)

*Holly*__ Really? Well, he has.

*Ed*____ So ... (6)?

*Holly*__ No, I'm from Scotland.

*Ed*____ From Scotland. Wow! That's why you have that great accent. ... (7)?

*Holly*__ You wouldn't know the place.

*Ed*____ I might. I've been to Scotland a few times and ... (8)

*Holly*__ Really? Well, do you know Fort William?

*Ed*____ Of course.

*Holly*__ Well, it's not far from there.

*Ed*____ Wow, ... (9)

c) Now listen to Ed and Holly. Compare what Ed says with your suggestions. Are his conversation skills better this time?

How to keep a conversation going

Find out the person's name, where he/she is from, etc.

Hi, I'm ... And what's your name?
Sorry, I didn't catch your name. / Sorry, what was your name?
So do you live around here?
Where exactly is that?

Ask lots of open questions (what, where, when, why, how, ...).

What do you think of this music/the weather?
Where do you go to school?
So, who do you know here?

If one topic isn't working, change it!

By the way, do you like ...?
Anyway, there's something I really wanted to ask you ...

Encourage the person to talk about his/her interests.

You know, I really like your mobile. How long have you had it?
So you like films. What's your favourite film?
What kind of films/music/... do you like?
I see you're reading ... What's it like?

Show surprise or interest.

No! I don't believe it.
Really? That's amazing. / That's a surprise. / I didn't know ...
That sounds great.
I've been there too! I love it there.
I love your jacket. Is it new?

d) 👥 Imagine you meet someone at a party for the first time. Start a conversation and talk to each other for as long as you can.

▶ *WB 7–8 (pp. 5–6)*

ON-SCREEN RELATIONSHIPS

1   The best films on TV this week

▶ *What was the last film you watched on TV?*
What do you look for in a film?

(500) Days of Summer ★★★★★

(Wednesday 8.00 pm, Sky 1)

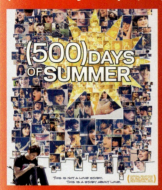

Boy meets girl. Boy falls in love. Girl doesn't. This anti-love story about a 500-day relationship between two young people, Tom and Summer, is not your typical Hollywood romantic comedy. In fact, Tom is dumped by Summer at the start, so we know the ending first. The film is set in LA and was directed by Marc Webber. It stars Joseph Gordon-Levitt as Tom and Zooey Deschanel as Summer and there is an interesting soundtrack with a good mix of old and new songs.

Bend it like Beckham ★★★★★

(Friday 9.00 pm, Virgin 1)

You've probably seen it already, but this comedy is one that everyone will enjoy watching again and again. Football-mad Jess (Parminder Nagra) is 18 and lives in London. She wants to play for a top women's football team. The problem is that her traditional Indian parents want her to find a nice Indian husband, learn how to cook and study law! Although it's a very funny film, it also looks at serious topics (like racism, parent-teenager relationships and homophobia) and there is an important message: Don't be afraid to be yourself.

Twilight ★★★★★

(Friday 9.40 pm, Film 4)

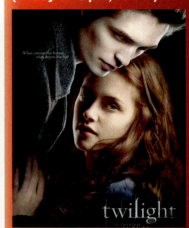

Twilight is a drama, fantasy, love story and thriller based on Stephenie Meyer's bestseller. Kristen Stewart plays Bella, who has just moved to a small town in the north-west of the US. At her new school, Bella fancies Edward, played by Robert Pattinson. But there's a problem: unfortunately Edward is a vampire! He's worried about what could happen if he and Bella get together. But the problem is not that she could get pregnant. There's a different danger: he might lose control and bite her! Fans of the book will love this film. But even if you don't think it's your kind of film, you should try it. The special effects are amazing.

a) *True or false?*
All the films are ...   1   romantic comedies.   2   set in America.   3   about young people.

b) *What does each film review mention? Copy the chart and tick (✓) the right boxes.*

Title	Kind of film	Plot and characters	Actors	Who will like it	Soundtrack	Special effects
(500) Days						
Bend it						
Twilight						

c) *Which of the films would/wouldn't you watch? Say why.*
I like/don't like thrillers/..., so I'd watch/I wouldn't watch ...
I think ... sounds good/boring/... because the review says ...

2 VIEWING A review of *Juno*

a) *Make a chart like the one in 1b) on p. 12. Then watch the review. Which points about the film does the reviewer mention? Tick (✓) the right boxes.*

b) *Watch the review again. Which of these things does the reviewer say?*
1 He is a big fan of romantic films.
2 Juno is an unattractive character.
3 Juno wants to find perfect parents for her baby.
4 Juno talks to her dad about relationships.
5 Paulie Bleaker is nervous and uncool through the whole film.
6 4 out of 5 is the right score for the film.

c) *What did you find good (or bad) about the review?*

3 The perfect partner

a) *In the film, Juno is trying to find out what makes a relationship successful. What would you look for in a partner? Write down five things.*
I think it's important that a partner ...

> is good-looking • is fashionable •
> has a good sense of humour •
> has a lot of money • is relaxed •
> has the same interests as me •
> has the same religion • is very intelligent •
> is patient and kind • is confident •
> comes from a good family •
> is a happy, positive person •
> has/doesn't have tattoos/piercings

b) *Make appointments with three partners. Tell each other about the things that are important to you in a relationship.*
– To me it's important that a partner is ...
– I agree, but I think it's more/less important that a partner ...
– I disagree. I don't think that's important because ...

c) *Report back to the class. What things do most people think are important in a relationship?*

4 Extra SONG All I want is you

a) *Read the first two verses of the song from the film* Juno. *Then listen.*

If I was a flower growing wild and free,
All I'd want is you to be my sweet honey bee.
And if I was a tree growing tall and green,
All I'd want is you to shade me and be my
    leaves.

All I want is you, will you be my bride?
Take me by the hand and stand by my side.
All I want is you, will you stay with me?
Hold me in your arms and sway me like the
    sea.

by Barry Louis Polisar

b) *Say what you think of the song.*
The song makes me want to laugh/sing along/ run away/...
The music is energetic/old-fashioned/...
The lyrics are easy to understand/silly/ romantic/...
The singer's voice is beautiful/painful/...

c) *Do you think the song fits the film? Why (not)?*
▶ **Text File 2** *(pp. 110–112)* • *WB 9 (p. 6)*

P1   WORDS   Describing films

a) *Organize the words and phrases from the box in a chart or network. Use headings like these.*

special things	film people	plot

kind of film	reviewer's opinion

action film • actor • boring • brilliant •
cartoon • character • costumes • (to) direct •
director • exciting • famous • happy ending •
hero • historical drama • horror film •
music • (to) play • scene •
science fiction film • sentimental • (to) star •
strange • western • (to) win an Oscar

b) *Add more words to your chart or network.*

c) 👥 *Compare your words with a partner.*

d) *Choose a word to complete the sentences. Put the verbs in the correct form.*

1 The film ... Julia Roberts and George Clooney. (play/star)
2 This exciting ... is set in 18th century England. (historical drama/western)
3 It's a typical ... with a happy ending. (horror film/love story)
4 In *Twilight*, Robert Pattinson ... Edward the vampire. (direct/play)

5 The ... is played by Brad Pitt. (actor/hero)
6 My favourite ... in the film is where the hero kisses Elizabeth. (plot/scene).
7 The ... on the soundtrack go well with the story. (songs/special effects)
8 I'd recommend the film because it's really ... (boring/exciting)

e) **Extra** 👥 *Decide on a film that you and your partner have both watched. Work on your own and write at least three sentences about the film. Use words that you have collected in your chart or network. Then compare your sentences.*

P2   SPEAKING   About a film

a) *Give a talk on a film you have seen. The ideas below can help you to structure your talk.*

Introduction
– title of the film
– kind of film
– names of main actors
– name of director

Plot
– where the film is set
– when it takes place
– what happens
– kind of ending

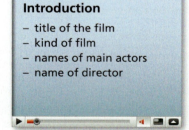

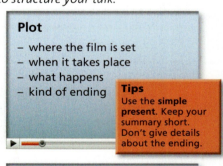

Tips
Use the **simple present**. Keep your summary short. Don't give details about the ending.

Main characters
– names
– age
– appearance
– what they're like

Special information
– soundtrack
– special effects
– costumes
– awards

Personal opinion
– reasons why you liked/didn't like the film
– favourite/least favourite scenes
– if you can recommend the film
– who you think would like it

b) **Extra** *Record your talk.*

▶ *SF Giving a presentation (p. 130) • WB 10–13 (pp. 7–9)*

P3 WRITING A film plot (Creative writing)

Chaz

Tyler

Hailey

Alexis

a) Read the film plot on the right. Then think about what might happen when Hailey and Chaz meet next time.

– How will Hailey feel about the bet? Will she be upset or not?
– Will Hailey talk to Chaz about it? If so, how will Chaz react?
– Will they stop seeing each other or will they go to the prom together?

Note down some of your ideas.

b) 👥👥👥 *In a group, brainstorm your ideas.*

c) Working on your own, write the dialogue between Chaz and Hailey.

Chaz⎯⎯⎯ Hey Hailey!
Hailey⎯⎯⎯ Sorry, Chaz. I'm in a hurry. I have to catch a bus.
Chaz⎯⎯⎯ Hey, what's wrong, Hailey?
Hailey⎯⎯⎯ ...

d) In your group read the different dialogues and vote for the best one.

Just before the school prom, Chaz, the most popular guy in school, is dumped by his girlfriend, Alexis. He has a bet with his best friend, Tyler. He says that he can change even the most boring and unattractive girl so that she can become the most popular girl in school and win the election for prom queen[1]. Tyler chooses Hailey, a quiet, unpopular girl who is interested in art, politics and the environment. First Chaz finds her boring, but as he gets to know her better he starts to like her more and more. But then Tyler tells Hailey about the bet ...

[1] prom queen *girl chosen by her classmates to be the queen of the formal party (prom) at American high schools*

P4 👥👥 MEDIATION What's this film about?

Partner B: Go to p. 98.
Partner A: Partner B visits you with a friend from England. You want to watch a film together.
a) Read about Crazy. *Explain in English what the film is about.*

crazy

Der 16-jährige Benni (Robert Stadlober) wird von seinen Eltern wegen seiner schlechten Mathe-Noten in ein Internat geschickt. Es ist nicht sein erster Schulwechsel, und meist war es für den halbseitig gelähmten Jungen schwer, Freunde zu finden. Diesmal geht es einfacher – zunächst. Benni teilt sich das Zimmer mit Janosch (Tom Schilling), der sich mehr für Mädchen und Spaß als für die Schule interessiert. Die Jungen freunden sich an – bis sich beide in ihre Klassenkameradin, die schöne Malen (Oona-Devi Liebich), verlieben. Dass das zu Konflikten führt, ist klar, und die Freundschaft zwischen Benni und Janosch wird auf eine echte Probe gestellt. In diesem Film über die schwierige Zeit des Erwachsenwerdens und das Spannungsfeld zwischen Freundschaft und Liebe kommen aber auch Spaß und Abenteuer nicht zu kurz.

b) Partner B will talk about a different film. Listen carefully.

▶ SF Mediation (p. 149) • WB 14–16 (pp. 9–10)

c) The English visitor can't decide which film to watch. You and Partner B have to choose. Say which film you *think is better and why. Then listen to Partner B's opinion and agree on a film.*

Extra The Absolutely True Diary of a Part-time[1] Indian
(Extracts from the novel by Sherman Alexie, adapted and abridged)

The story so far

Arnold lives and goes to school on the Spokane Indian Reservation in Wellpinit, Washington State. The Indians on the reservation are very poor, and Arnold can see that most of them have no hope for the future. He makes a brave decision. He leaves the reservation school and starts at Reardan High School. Reardan is an all-white school in a town 22 miles outside of the reservation. Arnold is the odd one out:
5 *a poor Indian boy in a rich, racist town. But slowly he starts to make friends at his new school. He even starts to go out with the beautiful Penelope.*

▶ *SF Reading literature (p. 137)*

Me (drawn by me)   Penelope in her dad's old hat (drawn by me)

BIG DREAMS

Everybody is absolutely shocked that Penelope chose me to be her new friend. I am an absolute stranger at the school.

10 And I am an Indian. And Penelope's father, Earl, is a racist. The first time I met him, he said, "Kid, she's only dating you because she knows it will piss me off[2]. So I ain't going to get pissed. And if I ain't pissed then she'll stop
15 dating you."

BLEEEEATHPGH!

← Earl: #1 candidate for the Father-of-the-Year Award

slime

Okay, so you're probably thinking that Penelope was dating me ONLY because I was the worst possible choice[3] for her. She was probably dating me ONLY because I was an Indian boy. And, okay, so she wasn't seriously
20 dating me. We held hands sometimes and we kissed once or twice, but that was it. I don't know how important I was to her. I think she was bored of being the prettiest, smartest and most popular girl in the world. She wanted to
25 do something a little crazy, you know?

But, hey, I was kind of using her too. After all, I suddenly became popular. Penelope had shown that she thought that I was cute[4], and so all of the other girls in school decided that
30 I was cute too. I was allowed to hold hands with Penelope, and kiss her goodbye when she jumped on the school bus to go home, and so all of the other boys in school decided that I was cool. I was different.
35

I looked and talked and dreamed and walked differently than everybody else. I was new.

So okay, those are all the obvious[5] reasons why Penelope and I were friends. But what about the bigger and better reasons?
40

"Arnold," she said one day after school, "I hate this little town. It's so small, too small. Everything about it is small. The people here have small ideas. Small dreams. They all want to marry each other and live here forever."
45

"What do you want to do?" I asked.

"I want to leave as soon as I can. I think I was born with a suitcase."

Yeah, she talked like that. All big and dramatic. I wanted to laugh, but she was so
50 serious.

"Where do you want to go?" I asked.

"Everywhere. I want to walk on the Great Wall of China. I want to walk to the top of

---

[1] part-time *Teilzeit-* [2] (to) piss sb. off *(infml, vulgär) jn. wütend machen, jn. ankotzen* [3] choice [tʃɔɪs] *(Aus-)Wahl* [4] cute [kjuːt] *niedlich, süß; (AE infml auch:) sexy* [5] obvious [ˈɒbvɪəs] *offensichtlich, naheliegend*

55 pyramids in Egypt. I want to swim in every
ocean. I want to climb the highest mountain.
I want to go on an African safari. I want to do
everything and see everything."

Her eyes had this strange, dreamy look.
60 I laughed.

"Don't laugh at me," she said.

"I'm not laughing at you," I said. "I'm
laughing at your eyes."

"That's the problem," she said. "Nobody
65 takes me seriously."

"Well, come on, it's kind of hard to take you
seriously when you're talking about China and
Egypt and stuff. Those are just big, crazy
dreams. They're not real."

70 "They're real to me," she said.

"Why don't you tell me what you really want
to do with your life," I said. "Make it simple."

"I want to be an architect."

"Wow, that's cool," I said. "But why an
75 architect?"

"Because I want to build something
beautiful. Because I want to be remembered."

And I couldn't laugh at that dream. It was
my dream too. But Indian boys shouldn't
80 dream like that. And white girls from small
towns shouldn't dream big either. We should
be happy with what we have. But there was no
way Penelope and I were going to sit still. No,
we both wanted to fly.

This bird is an
Australian Arnelope.
It is good at flying
long distances.

PANCAKES[1] OF DOOM[2]

Arnold often hitchhikes[3] between Reardan and 85
home. But he doesn't tell his classmates because he
doesn't want them to know how poor he is. One
night after a school dance, Arnold plans to wait
until everybody has gone, and then hitchhike home
in the dark. But Penelope's friend, Roger, has a 90
different idea.

Roger and a few of the other popular guys
decided they were going to drive into Spokane
and have pancakes at a twenty-four-hour diner
and Roger invited us to come along. 95

Penelope was very excited about the idea.
I was so scared that I felt sick. I had five bucks[4]
in my pocket. What could I buy with that?
Maybe one plate of pancakes. Maybe. What
a nightmare[5]. 100

"What do you say, Arnie?" Roger asked. "Do
you want to come with us?"

"What do you want to do, Penelope?" I asked.

"Oh, I want to go, I want to go," she said.
"Let me go and ask Daddy." 105

Oh, man, I saw my only chance to escape.
I could only hope that her father wouldn't let
her go. Only Earl could save me now.

I needed Earl to save me. That's how bad my
life was at that moment. 110

"Hey, I'll go with you," Roger said. "I'll tell
him you guys are going with me."

As they walked together towards the car,
I saw that Roger and Penelope looked good
together. They looked natural. They looked like 115
they should be a couple.

And after everyone found out I was a poor
Indian, I knew they would be a couple.

Come on, Earl! Come on, Earl! Break your
daughter's heart! 120

---

[1] pancake ['pænkeɪk] *Pfannkuchen*   [2] doom [duːm] *Verderben, Verhängnis, Untergang*   [3] (to) hitchhike ['hɪtʃhaɪk] *trampen, per Anhalter fahren*   [4] buck [bʌk] *(bes. AE, infml) Dollar*   [5] nightmare ['naɪtmeə] *Albtraum*

But Earl loved Roger. Everybody loved Roger. He was the best football player. Of course they loved him. All real Americans love the best football player.

Me being absolutely terrified

125 I was angry and jealous and absolutely terrified.

"I can go! I can go!" Penelope said, as she ran 130 back to me and hugged[1] me hard.

An hour later, about twenty of us were sitting in Denny's in Spokane.

Everybody ordered pancakes.

135 I ordered pancakes for Penelope and me. I ordered orange juice and coffee and toast and hot chocolate and French fries too, even though I knew I wouldn't be able to pay for any of it.

140 I decided it was my last meal before my death, and I was going to have a feast[2].

Halfway through our meal, I went to the bathroom. I thought maybe I was going to throw up. Roger came into the bathroom.

145 "Hey, Arnie," he said. "Are you okay?"

"Yeah," I said, "I'm just tired."

"All right, man," he said. "I'm happy you guys came tonight."

"Hey, listen," I said.

150 I thought about telling him the whole truth[3], but I just couldn't.

"The thing is," I said, "I, er, forgot my wallet[4]. I left my money at home, man."

"Dude[5]!" Roger said. "Man, don't worry 155 about it. You should have said something earlier."

He opened his wallet and gave me forty bucks.

I couldn't believe it.

160 What kind of kid can just give someone forty bucks like that?

"I'll pay you back man," I said

"Whenever man. Just have a good time, all right?"

165 We walked back to the table together, finished our food and Roger drove me back to the school. I told them my dad was going to pick me up there.

"Dude," Roger said, "it's three in the morning." 170

"It's okay," I said. "My dad works nights. He's coming here from work."

"Are you sure?"

"Yeah, everything is cool."

So Penelope and I got out of Roger's car to 175 say goodbye.

"Roger told me he lent you some money," she said.

"Yeah," I said. "I forgot my wallet."

"Arnold." 180

"Yeah."

"Can I ask you something big?"

"Yeah. I guess[6]."

"Are you poor?"

I couldn't lie[7] to her any more. 185

"Yes," I said, "I'm poor."

I thought she was going to march out of my life right then. But she didn't. Instead she kissed me. On the cheek. I guess poor guys don't get kissed on the lips. At first I was 190 annoyed[8] at her for not kissing me properly[9]. But then I understood that she was being my friend. Being a really good friend in fact.

"Roger guessed you were poor," she said

"Oh, great ... now he's going to tell 195 everybody."

"He's not going to tell anybody. Roger likes you. He's a great guy. He's like my big brother. He can be your friend too."

That sounded pretty good to me. I needed 200 friends.

"Is your Dad really coming to pick you up?" she asked.

"Yes," I said.

"Is that true?" 205

"No," I said.

"How will you get home?" she asked.

---

[1] (to) hug (-gg-) [hʌg] *umarmen* [2] feast [fiːst] *Festessen, Festmahl* [3] truth [truːθ] *Wahrheit* [4] wallet [ˈwɒlɪt] *Brieftasche* [5] dude [djuːd] *(bes. AE, infml) Mann* [6] I guess. *Ich schätze schon.* [7] (to) lie [laɪ] *lügen* [8] annoyed [əˈnɔɪd] *verärgert* [9] properly [ˈprɒpəli] *richtig*

"I usually walk home. I hitchhike. Somebody usually picks me up. I've only had to walk the
210 whole way a few times."

She started to cry.

FOR ME!

I didn't know that a girl could look so sexy when she cried.

215 "Oh, my God, Arnold, you can't do that," she said. "I won't let you do that. Roger will drive

you home. He'll be happy to drive you home."

Penelope ran over to Roger's car and told him the truth.

And Roger drove me home that night.   220

And he drove me home lots of other nights too.

If you let people into your life a little bit, they can be pretty damn amazing.

Working with the text

1 The story
Finish these sentences about the story.
1 Penelope's father thinks she's dating Arnold because …
2 Arnold thinks Penelope started dating him because …
3 Penelope hates living in Reardan because …
4 As soon as she can, Penelope wants to …
5 Penelope and Arnold have the same dream: they both want to …
6 Arnold hopes that Penelope's father won't let her go to the diner in Spokane because …
7 Penelope's father likes Roger because …
8 Arnold tells Roger that he has forgotten his wallet, and Roger …
9 After the evening at the diner Arnold is afraid that Roger …
10 When Penelope tells Roger that Arnold usually hitchhikes home, …

2 What do they mean?
Who says this? Explain what exactly they mean.
1 "But, hey, I was kind of using her too." (l. 27)
2 "Nobody takes me seriously." (ll. 64–65)
3 "No, we both wanted to fly." (ll. 83–84)
4 "Break your daughter's heart!" (ll. 119–120)
5 "Man, don't worry about it." (ll. 154–155)
6 "If you let people into your life a little bit, they can be pretty damn amazing." (ll. 223–224)

3 The characters
What kind of people do you think Arnold, Penelope and Roger are? The adjectives in the box can help you. Find examples in the story to support your opinion.

> ambitious • attractive • charming • cheeky • confident • cool • crazy • easy-going • friendly • funny • helpful • jealous • likeable • loyal • patient • popular • proud • romantic • sentimental • serious • shy • successful • …

4 Writing a character description
Imagine you are Penelope or Roger. Write an email to a friend about Arnold, the new boy at your school. What is he like? What do you think of him?
or
Imagine you are Arnold. Write an email to a friend about Penelope or Roger.

5 Giving a summary
Prepare a summary of the extract from the novel. You could use these phrases:
The extract is from a novel about/by …
The story is set in …
The main character is …
He seems to be a funny/likeable/proud/… person. You can see this in line … where …
At the beginning of the story, Arnold describes/explains …
I enjoyed/didn't enjoy the story because …

▶ *SF Summarizing texts (p. 142)* • *WB 17 (p. 11)* • **Exam Check** *WB (pp. 12–21)*

1 Outdoor holidays (Simple present: questions)

a) *Sharon often goes on outdoor holidays. Her friend Lucy has some questions for her.*
Make Lucy's questions in the simple present. Use the verbs in brackets.

1 ... you ... to sleep in tents or caravans?
   (prefer)
   Do you prefer to sleep in tents or caravans?
2 ... you ... a big caravan? (have got)
3 ... there a shower in your caravan? (be)
4 ... you ... a good place to camp? (know)

5 Who usually ... camping with you? (go)
6 How many people ... in your tent? (fit)
7 ... your tent ... a window? (have got)
8 What gear ... I ... when I go camping?
   (need)
9 How much ... cooking equipment ...? (cost)

b) *You want to ask a friend about a theme park/hotel or shop/magazine/... Make questions.*
Do you know a good theme park? How ... ▶ *GF 2: Making questions (p. 153)* • *GF 3: Talking about the present (p. 154)*

2 A holiday by the sea is more exciting (Comparison of adjectives)

Copy and complete the sentences. Use the words in brackets. Give your opinion in each sentence.

1 A holiday by the sea ... a holiday in the
   mountains. (exciting)
   ... is more exciting than ...
   ... is/isn't as exciting as ...
2 Travelling by train ... travelling by car.
   (comfortable)
3 A sports holiday ... a holiday on the beach.
   (cool)
4 Beaches in Spain ... beaches in Germany.
   (crowded)

5 A camping holiday ... staying at a B&B.
   (expensive)
6 A day at a theme park ... a day at the zoo.
   (interesting)
7 Going on holiday with lots of friends ...
   going with your partner. (exciting)
8 Cooking your own food ... going to
   a restaurant for meals. (good)
9 In Germany, temperatures in June ...
   temperatures in September. (high)

▶ *GF 12: Adjectives: comparison (p. 167)*

3 👥 SPEAKING Likes and dislikes

*Ask your partner what he/she thinks about
a topic, e.g. camping holidays, sports, music,
fashion, ...*
The phrases below will help you.

So do you like hip hop?

Hip hop's OK. But it isn't as cool as ...

like	love	hate	not mind
I prefer ... to ...	I like ... a lot/very much.	I can't stand ...	... is OK/all right.
I like ... better than ...		I like ... least.	I don't care about ...
... is pretty/quite good.	I like ... best.	... is terrible/awful.	It's all the same to me.
	... is great/fantastic.	I'm afraid/scared/ terrified of ...	
I'm looking forward to ...	I can't wait to ...		I'm easy-going/ relaxed about ...

4   WORDS A teenage magazine

a) Zink! *is a teenage magazine with six sections:*

| COMPUTER | SPORT | THEATRE | MUSIC | BOOKS | CINEMA & TV |

Make lists of typical words for each section.
First use the words from the box.
Then add more words.

COMPUTER	SPORT	...
install	athletics	...
...	...	

anchorwoman • athletics • ballet • cable •
comic • install • label • link • menu •
narrator • novel • pitch • playlist • poem •
prime time • rehearsal • release •
repeat (*n*) • save • scene • sound file •
stage • train

b) You want to tell your friend about some of the things you have read in Zink!.
Choose the right word for each sentence.

1 A new ballet is starting soon at the theatre.
   Zink! went to the rehearsals/repeats/
   research.

2 The Huddersfield Half Pipes did pretty
   well, but they just can't comment/compete/
   impress with a team like the South London
   Skaters.

3 Helsinki Motel have just installed/released/
   reviewed their new album. *Zink!* thinks it's
   hot.

4 *Zink!* says the new software is cheap and
   easy to install/join/repair.

5 Don't miss tonight's rehearsal/repeat/
   revision of *The English Patient* if you haven't
   seen it yet. *Zink!* loves it.

6 *Zink!* recommends a concert/playlist/tune
   of religious music at Bath Abbey tomorrow.

▶ *You could now do tasks 1 and 2 in the Practice*
   test on p. 24.

5   WORDS Talking about religions

a) Which word doesn't fit in each group?
1 Jewish • English • Hindu • Muslim
2 Catholic • cathedral • Christian • Protestant
3 church • mosque • palace • synagogue
4 minister • nun • priest • technician
5 bell • funeral • mass • service
6 believe • bell • cathedral • tower

b) Complete the sentences with a word from each
group in a).
1 Our friend Murat is Turkish. Like most
   Turkish people, he's a ...
2 My wife and I are both Christians, but she's
   a Catholic and I'm a ...
3 Our Jewish friends go to the ... on Saturdays.
4 My uncle is a Catholic ... but we don't go to his church. It's too far from where we live.
5 You can hear the church ... a mile away.
6 Jews, Muslims and Christians all ... in one God.

6   WORDS The world of soap opera

a) *Who's who in this soap opera? Read these statements.*
Then complete sentences 1 to 6 with a word from the box.

– Amy and Bill are a couple, but they aren't
  married.
– Chris fancies Amy, but he's married to
  Diana.
– Ella's mother is Fay. She's single.
– Gary is Ella's grandfather. His wife died.
– Hanif is Layla's brother. He has a secret
  relationship with Diana.
– Layla is Ella's aunt. She's divorced from Bill.

> ex-husband • father • granddaughter •
> lover • uncle • wife

1 Gary is Fay's ...
2 Hanif is Ella's ...
3 Ella is Gary's ....
4 Diana is Chris' ...
5 Hanif is Diana's ...
6 Bill is Layla's ...

b) *Fay and Layla are at a café. Complete their conversation with words from the box.*

> baby • divorced • father • love •
> relationship • single

Fay   Hi, Layla. Guess what! I've just heard
        that Chris and Diana are getting (1) ...
Layla   What? Is that because Chris has fallen
        in (2) ... with Amy?
Fay   Well, either that or he's heard about
        Diana's (3) ... with Hanif.
Layla   Actually, I saw her today. I think she's
        going to have a (4) ...
Fay   No! But who's the (5) ...? Her husband
        or her lover?
Layla   Well, let's hope it's Hanif so they can
        get married quickly. Who wants to be
        a (6) ... mum? Oh – sorry, Fay!

7   Tell me it isn't true (Simple present: negatives)

Complete the dialogue with the negative form of
the verbs in brackets.

Jack   Hey, Sam! I hear that Phil and Tina
        have broken up. Tell me it (1) *isn't* (be)
        true.
Sam   I'm afraid it is, Jack. Lucy told me. She
        thinks it's because they (2) ... (have) the
        same interests.
Jack   Oh, I see. So Tina (3) ... (like) football?
Sam   No, and Phil (4) ... (care) much about
        ballet either.
Jack   By the way, I (5) ... (can) go to the
        theatre tomorrow. I've got too much
        work.
Sam   That's no problem. I've heard the actors
        (6) ... (be) great anyway. Let's do
        something on Saturday instead.

Jack   I (7) ... (know). I've really got a lot of
        work to do.
Sam   But that (8) ... (mean) you can't have a
        break, does it?

▶ *GF 3: Talking about the present (p. 154)*

8   I'd never fall in love ...   (Prepositions)

Complete the sentences with the correct prepositions.

1   I'd never fall in love ... a boy my age! (in/ with)
2   It won't work. We're just too different ... each other. (from/of)
3   You can't judge a person ... the clothes they wear. (after/by)
4   How do your parents feel ... your new boyfriend? (about/over)
5   If I had known he'd be so upset ... what I said, I would have been more careful. (about/across)

6   ... my point of view, he's just jealous. (From/Out of)
7   The best thing ... my parents is that they aren't prejudiced. (about/at)
8   His parents are so strict. He has to be home ... 10 o'clock – always! (by/for)
9   What do you mean ... 'jealous'? I'm just angry, that's all! (by/with)
10   We're so fed up ... our parents. They never understand! (of/with)

▶ *You could now do tasks 3 and 4 in the Practice test on p. 25.*

9   Teenage mums   (Adverbs, conjunctions and prepositions)

Which of the two words in brackets fits the sentences?

1   ... girls don't want to be teenage mums, it happens all the time. (Although/Also)
2   Lots of girls think it couldn't happen to them, ... girls who aren't in a relationship. (definitely/especially)
3   They don't believe that it ... can happen so quickly. (always/really)
4   ... they just don't want to think about it? (Even/Perhaps)

5   ... if they aren't careful, it might be too late. (However/While)
6   ... just hoping that everything will be OK, they should talk to the boy! (Because of/Instead of)
7   And ..., boys should also remember what can happen when they have sex. (of course/unfortunately)

10   👥 SPEAKING Expressing opinions

a) *Read the dialogue about teenage mums. Then practise it with your partner. Use alternatives for the phrases in blue.*

A: I feel young girls shouldn't be mothers. ——→ | I think (that) ... • If you ask me ...

B: It's true that it's not an ideal situation, but it's not impossible. ——→ | You're right (that) ..., but ... • I agree that ... However, ...

A: In my view, it isn't good for the baby, and it's kind of hard for the mother too. ——→ | In my opinion, ... • From my point of view, ...

B: Well, I definitely think you're wrong there. It isn't too bad, especially if the mother gets enough help. ——→ | I really believe (that) ... • I honestly think (that) ...

b) *Choose a topic for discussion or agree on a different topic. Use phrases from a) to express your opinion.*

| Online magazines are better than print magazines. | | The best age to get married? | | You can judge people by their clothes. |

▶ *SF Having a discussion (p. 140)*

1　LISTENING　What can we do this weekend?

Listen carefully to two girls on the phone. You will hear the recording only once. Take notes on what you hear. Then give a summary of the discussion between the two friends.

2　👥 SPEAKING　Holiday plans

a) *Choose a role and read the information.*

Partner A: Role card	**Partner B: Role card**

• You and your best friend have just finished your exams. You are planning a holiday.
• Your friend has found information about a camp in the mountains. You have some information about a youth hostel by the sea:
  – costs 15 euros a night
  – opportunities for swimming, surfing, beach volleyball
  – 500 metres from railway station and beach
• Your friend wants to go on holiday in a group. You want to go just with your friend.
Reasons:
  – fun to spend time with your best friend
  – easier to agree what to do
  – easier to plan a holiday for two
	• You and your best friend have just finished your exams. You are planning a holiday.
	• Your friend has found information about a youth hostel by the sea. You have some information about a camp in the mountains:
	  – costs 35 euros a night
	  – opportunities for hiking, mountain biking, swimming in lakes
	  – 60 km from nearest town
	
	• Your friend wants to go on holiday just with you. You want to go in a group.
	Reasons:
	  – more fun in a group
	  – everybody can do what they like
	  – group holiday could be cheaper

b) *Act out a conversation with a partner. Try and agree on a holiday plan.*

3   LISTENING Living together 🎧

You will hear a radio phone-in about relationships between people of different religions. Look at the tasks below for 30 seconds. Then listen and choose the correct answers (A, B, C or D). You will hear the phone-in twice.

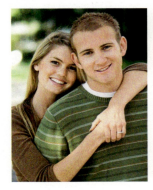   

1 *All about me* is about …
   A life 50 years ago.
   B English cities.
   C married people with problems.
   D a successful mixed relationship.

2 Sharon's …
   A parents are both Muslims.
   B mum is a Muslim.
   C dad is a Muslim.
   D parents have lots of problems.

3 Sean …
   A has a girlfriend who is a Catholic.
   B has a girlfriend who often goes to church.
   C is a Protestant.
   D tries to go to church every week.

4 Afra …
   A is no longer with her boyfriend.
   B is a Hindu.
   C has children.
   D says mixed relationships aren't a problem.

5 Bob …
   A met his girlfriend in England.
   B has an Italian girlfriend.
   C is Irish.
   D is English.

6 Bob says that …
   A he plays rugby.
   B he's a rugby fan.
   C his girlfriend is a rugby fan.
   D his team always wins.

4   LISTENING Radio adverts 🎧

Listen to three radio adverts. You will hear the recordings twice.
Are the following statements true or false?

1 Although the woman is on a diet, the man has bought her chocolates.
2 *Her World* sells flowers and special chocolates for women.
3 The second advert is for unmarried couples.
4 *A lifetime's love* is the title of a book.
5 The third advert is for men.
6 The main topic of the third advert is magazines.

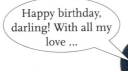

Happy birthday, darling! With all my love …

5   SPEAKING Too young to be a mum?

Talk about the pictures. The following questions can help you.
1   Do you think the girls in the photos are happy? Why (not)?
2   How do you think their parents and friends reacted to the news that they were pregnant?
3   How do you think that being a mother can change a teenager's life?
4   Who can help teenage mothers, and how?
5   What role should the baby's father play?
6   What do you think is the best age to have a baby? Why?

6   PRESENTATION My lifestyle

Tell the class how careful (or not!) you are about looking after yourself and keeping well.

Include the following points:
Food: likes/dislikes • healthy/unhealthy food
Exercise: keeping fit • the role of sport
Social life: friends • free-time activities

Prepare your presentation before you talk to the class. Use good, clear notes in English.

How am I doing?

In the Practice test you did some typical exam (Abschlussprüfung) tasks. If you found some tasks difficult, the questions below will help you to find out what you need to practise.

Listening

Tasks 1, 3 and 4 were listening tasks. Check your answers on pp. 226–227 and decide how easy/hard you found them.

1　How easy or hard was each task?

	easy	OK	quite hard	very hard
Task 1				
Task 3				
Task 4				

If you found any of the tasks quite hard or very hard, look at 2 and say why.

2　What was difficult about the listening tasks?
a) I didn't understand the task.
b) People spoke too quickly.
c) I found the accents difficult.
d) There was a lot of information. I couldn't find the exact answers.
e) There were words and phrases that I just couldn't understand.
f) I didn't have time to finish all the tasks.

3　How did you do the tasks?
a) I looked quickly at the tasks first but only read them carefully while I was listening.
b) I read the tasks carefully first so I knew what I had to do.
c) (Tasks 3 and 4) I wrote as many answers as I could the first time I heard the text and checked them the second time.
d) There were lots of things that I couldn't understand and I panicked.

▶ *SF Listening (p. 132)*

▶ *You will find more LISTENING tasks in the Exam File, pp. 87–89.*

▶ *You will find more SPEAKING tasks in the Exam File, pp. 80–82.*

Speaking

Tasks 2, 5 and 6 were speaking tasks. Decide how easy/hard you found them.

4　How easy or hard was each task?

	easy	OK	quite hard	very hard
Task 2				
Task 5				
Task 6				

If you found any of the tasks quite hard or very hard, look at 5 and say why.

5　What was difficult about the speaking tasks?
a) I felt very nervous.
b) I didn't know what to say.
c) I didn't know enough about the topic.
d) I couldn't think of the right words.

Ask your teacher for a copy of the assessment sheet and fill it in.

Assessment sheet	☹	☺	☺		
Name ...	1	2	3	4	5
2 SPEAKING Holiday plans					
a) We listened to each other and tried to agree on a holiday plan.					
b) Our answers were long enough.					
c) We both showed interest in what our partner said.					
d) We were able to keep the conversation going.					
5 SPEAKING Too young to be a mum?					
e) I understood the message of the pictures and explained my ideas well.					
f) I used the questions to get ideas and to structure my talk.					
g) I said enough about the topic.					
h) I spoke clearly and loudly.					
6 PRESENTATION My lifestyle					
i) I spoke clearly and loudly.					
j) I included all the important points.					
k) I used visual materials (posters, ...) and explained them well.					
l) I looked at the audience and not at my notes most of the time.					

▶ *SF Speaking course (pp. 139–140)*

Unit 2 The world we live in

7:15

7:45

8:00

9:45

1 Technology in your life

a) *Find examples of modern technology in the pictures above. Think of more examples for each situation. The words in the box may help you.*

central heating • coffee machine •
double glazing • DVD player •
electric kettle • games console •
insulation • interactive whiteboard •
microwave • OHP • remote control •
toaster • tram • video projector • ...

b) *Make a diary like this for part of your day.*

> 7:15   A cold winter's morning: I wake up in
> a warm flat. We have insulation,
> central heating, ...
>
> 7:45   A modern kitchen: Breakfast is easy
> to make with all our modern gadgets
> – electric kettle, ... And if I need to
> contact friends before school, ...
>
> 8:00   ...

2 What is it? 🎧

a) *Listen and guess what things the people are talking about.*

b) 👥 *Choose an example of technology you often use. Make notes about it. Without naming it, say what it does and why you use it. Can the others guess what it is?*
– It's a gadget that .../that you get ...   – It's something you use to .../they put in ...

MODERN TECHNOLOGY ... WHAT IS IT DOING TO THE WORLD?

YOUR CARBON FOOTPRINT

■ Most scientists agree that releasing huge amounts of carbon dioxide (CO_2) into the atmosphere is one of the causes of global warming, perhaps the biggest problem of today's world.

■ Modern technology allows you to have comfortable living conditions. It keeps you warm, it lets you communicate with your friends, it lets you travel. But almost everything you do causes CO_2 emissions: like making yourself some tea, turning your heating up when you're cold, watching TV, taking the bus to school, texting your friends, buying a bottle of lemonade, or flying to Antalya or Majorca on holiday.

■ The amount of CO_2 you personally produce every year is known as your **carbon footprint**.

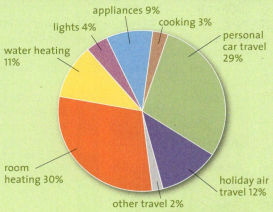

appliances 9%
cooking 3%
lights 4%
personal car travel 29%
water heating 11%
room heating 30%
holiday air travel 12%
other travel 2%

Source: The Open University

Average carbon footprints in tonnes of CO_2 per person per year (2009)

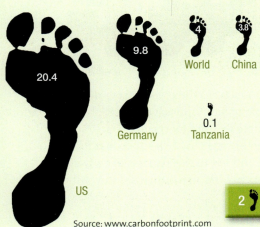

20.4
US

9.8
Germany

4
World

3.8
China

0.1
Tanzania

Source: www.carbonfootprint.com

The average person in the UK produces 9.8 tonnes of CO_2 per year, so that's their carbon footprint. The pie chart above shows how the average footprint in the UK is made up.

> *Which use of energy in the home is the biggest cause of carbon emissions? About how many tonnes of CO_2 does the average person in the UK produce through flying on holiday?*

2 ❯ Target for the world to stop climate change

---

3 CO_2 – how you produce it

a) 👥 *Take examples of everyday activities in the text above. Discuss how you think they release carbon dioxide into the atmosphere.*

A: We heat water for tea with an electric kettle at home. That uses electricity.

B: Yes, and they burn oil and gas to produce electricity. That releases CO_2 into the atmosphere.

b) **Extra** *Use the carbon footprint calculator at www.englishg.de/footprint to calculate your own carbon footprint. Are you above or below the German average? How far are you from the world target?*

▶ SF Having a discussion (p. 140) • **Text File 3** (p. 113) • WB 1–3 (pp. 22–23)

CHANGING THE FUTURE

1 Greatest inventions

On its 100th anniversary, London's Science Museum chose what it thinks are some of the most important inventions in human history. The timelines below show some of the milestones that changed the future for earlier generations – and also asks what the future may bring us.

ENERGY

MOBILITY

COMMUNI-CATION

1712 ENERGY

Steam engine

Steam power led to the Industrial Revolution. How? Steam engines made it possible to pump water from coal mines and to mine lots of coal. Coal then gave the new factories energy for their steam-powered machines.

1800 ENERGY

Electric battery

Alessandro Volta – the volt is named after him – invented the first electric battery. Batteries make it possible to carry energy around with you. Without them, you couldn't use your laptop, MP3 player, mobile phone …

1829 MOBILITY

Stephenson's *Rocket*

Rocket was the first modern steam train. After its success, railways grew quickly. Earlier, most people never travelled far from where they were born. Now trains could move huge numbers of people across countries and continents, many looking for a new life.

1837 COMMUNICATION

Electric telegraph

Two hundred years ago, people had to wait days, weeks or even months for letters. They arrived by horse or ship. The electric telegraph changed all that. Soon, anyone in a large town could send a message hundreds of miles in just a few minutes.

a) *Match the inventions to the correct sentence endings on the right.*

1 The steam engine
2 Volta's electric battery
3 Stephenson's *Rocket*
4 The electric telegraph
5 The Model T Ford
6 The Pilot ACE computer

a was so cheap it started the age of mass motoring.
b allowed people to send messages faster than ever before.
c made it possible to store electric power.
d was a big step towards today's super-fast PCs.
e pulled trains and led to the success of railways.
f was the power behind the Industrial Revolution.

b) ***Think*** *about the inventions in a). Which are most important? Make a list of your Top 3. Give reasons for your choices.*

👥 ***Pair***: *Compare lists with a partner and agree on your Top 3.*

👥👥 ***Share***: *Agree on your Top 4 in your group.*

c) *Present your Top 4 to the class. Explain each choice in two or three sentences.*

– We think … is the most important … because for the first time …
– Next we chose … We think this is important because … But it isn't as important …
– Our third choice …
– Finally, we …

d) *Look at the future sections of the timelines on p. 31. What effect would the inventions/discoveries have on you if they became reality during your lifetime? Would you welcome these changes?*

e) **Extra** *Think of an invention – or possible future invention – you could add to a timeline on pp. 30–31. Describe it in one or two sentences.*

Pilot ACE

2025

ENERGY
Clean energy?
Burning coal and other fossil fuels like oil and gas gives us lots of energy, but also a big problem: climate change. What could be the source of carbon-free energy? Waves, wind power or solar energy? Or will nuclear fusion give us endless clean energy one day?

1905
MOBILITY

The Model T
Henry Ford made the first car that everyone could afford.

1950
COMMUNICATION

Pilot ACE
The first computer that could do more than one thing and the first step on the road to your laptop. So now you can write letters, send them by email in a few seconds, surf the internet …

MOBILITY
Pod cars?
How will you get around town in the future? Driverless pods might be one way. Your personal 'pod car' will take you where you want to go, with fewer traffic jams and much less pollution.

COMMUNICATION
Voice only?
Keyboards will disappear. We'll talk to our computers, which will always be connected to the web – and maybe even to our brains. Then, when we 'think' a question, we'll get an answer immediately.

▶ **Text File 4** *(pp. 114–116)*

2 VIEWING *Human Power Station* 🎥

In *Human Power Station*, a programme shown on BBC television, the Collins family are invited to take part in a special experiment. For just one day, they move into another house, but they don't know what the experiment is about.

a) 👥 *Describe the picture. How is it connected with the title of the TV programme? What could the experiment be about?*

b) 👥 *Look at a scene from the programme. What's the link between the cyclists and the man in the shower? Why do people cheer at the end?*

c) *Watch another scene and answer the questions.*
1 What is the presenter doing in the house and what does she discover?
2 How much a year does this cost?
3 How does the programme show how much money is wasted?

d) **Extra** *Would this programme make you change your behaviour? Discuss.*

P1 WORDS Science and technology

a) *Make a network or word chart on science and technology. Choose your own headings, e.g.* inventions, communication, household gadgets, transport, how technology helps us, *etc.*
First collect words/phrases from pp. 28–31 and the box below. Then add your own ideas.
If necessary, choose more headings.

> antibiotics • discovery • effect •
> fight infectious diseases • medicine •
> penicillin • remote control • (to) test

b) 👥 *Compare your results with a partner. Add more words and phrases if you can.*

c) *Use verbs from the box to write five sentences about the effects (good or bad) of technology.*

> cause(s) ... • lead(s) to ... •
> allow(s) us to ... • keep(s) us ... • ...

... causes a lot of air pollution.
Modern communication technology allows us to ...

P2 REVISION Then and now (Simple past and simple present)

a) *Complete the text with the correct form of the verbs in brackets.*
When Grandpa was a boy he ... (had to/have to) stand up to change channels because they ... (didn't have/don't have) a remote control for the TV. The family ... (sat/sits) together in one room to watch TV because it ... (is/was) the only one in the house. They often ... (argue/argued) about which channel to watch. All programmes ... (are/were) in black and white. Today we ... (had/have) three TVs in our house, and I (watch/watched) TV programmes on the computer too. There ... (are/were) no more arguments, but we ... (didn't sit/don't sit) together as a family very often. In Grandpa's opinion, this ... (is/was) a shame.

b) *Think of a gadget that you use and what you do with it. Then think about what people did before it was invented – say 50 or 100 years ago. Describe the difference between then and now.*

Modern technology allows us to ...
Today I can text or email a friend in the US in seconds. A hundred years ago, people...

▶ *GF 4: Talking about the past (pp. 155–156) • GF 3: Talking about the present (p. 154)*

P3 REVISION Revolutions for medicine (Simple past)

Use the simple past of the verbs in brackets and complete the texts.
Be careful – you will need two passive forms.

The X-ray machine ... (change) the future in 1895:
Before Wilhelm Röntgen ... (discover) X-rays, if you ... (break) a bone in your arm, doctors ... (have to) cut it open to see inside it. With X-rays, for the first time we ... (be able to) see bones and other things inside the living body. It ... (be) a revolution for medicine.

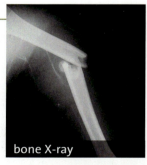
bone X-ray

Penicillin ... (change) the future in 1928:
The discovery of penicillin ... (make) it possible to win the fight against infectious disease and ... (save) millions of lives around the world. The first of our modern antibiotics ... (discover) by Alexander Fleming, but it ... (not test) successfully until 1940. Thanks to penicillin and other antibiotics, people ... (be able to) lead longer, healthier lives.

penicillin

▶ *GF 4: Talking about the past (pp. 155–156) • GF 7: The passive (p. 160)*

P4   LISTENING *Realize the dream* 🎧

a) 👥👥 *New Zealand high school student Jake Martin won an award for a gasifier that he built in the 'Realize the dream' science competition. Look at the picture. What do you think his gasifier does? Then listen and see if you were right.*

– I think it looks like some kind of engine. Perhaps it goes in a boat, or a …
– It might be a car engine.
– It's called a gasifier, so maybe it changes something into gas.
– Yes, like a 'Vergaser' in German, in a car.
…

b) 👥 *Listen again and answer these questions. Check with a partner.*
1 How much did Jake win?
2 What does he burn in his machine?
3 How long does it have to run to give a house power for a day?
4 How did he get the idea?
5 What is he going to do with the money?
6 What is he going to do after he leaves school?

Jake Martin and his gasifier

P5   👥 **EVERYDAY ENGLISH**   **MEDIATION** Smartphone application

An American exchange student asks you about the application you're using on your smartphone. Explain in English what you can use the application for.

Mit der neuen Anwendung **AllAroundYou**
AllAround**You** von *MobiSoft* bist du immer auf dem Laufenden – egal, wo du gerade bist.

Du willst wissen, wo du in deiner Stadt coole Outfits kaufen kannst? Oder du bist in einer fremden Stadt und suchst ein Kino oder das nächste Internetcafé?

Mit **All**Around**You** findest du alles – und das blitzschnell. Wähle aus den verschiedenen Kategorien die gesuchte Location aus und **All**Around**You** zeigt dir, wo sie ist und wie weit sie von dir entfernt ist. Du kannst dir die ausgewählte Location auf einer Karte anzeigen lassen, die Route dorthin anschauen, die Infos an deine Freunde schicken und vieles mehr. Du bist noch ohne **All**Around**You** unterwegs? Lade dir **All**Around**You** heute noch auf dein Smartphone!

▶ *SF Mediation (p. 149)*

SAVING THE PLANET

1 Welcome to the future (Abridged and adapted from *The Carbon Diaries 2015* by Saci Lloyd)

On page 29, you read about the causes of climate change. But what effects could the fight against climate change have on you and your lifestyle? Saci Lloyd's novel paints one possible picture:
It's 2015. The UK government is introducing carbon rationing to reduce the country's carbon footprint. From 8th January everyone will have a carbon allowance of 200 points a month. Everything you do, like driving the car, listening to music, having a shower, will cost carbon points. What will this mean for 16-year-old Laura Brown, her older sister Kim and their family?

Sat, Jan 3rd

Dad sat down with us tonight and took us through a stupid government online form to work out what our family CO allowance is. It's
5   heavy. We've each got a carbon allowance of 200 Carbon Points per month to spend on travel, heat, food. All other stuff like clothes and technology and books have already got the Carbon Points in the price, so if you want to
10 buy a PC but it's from China and they used dirty fossil fuel to build it, then you're going to pay a lot more for it in euros – cos you're paying for all the energy needed to make it.

   The worst thing is, me and Kim have to give
15 up lots of our points for the family carbon allowance. That leaves us almost nothing for travel, college, going out ... The car is going to be used much less, all of us can use the PC, TV, stereo for only two hours a day, heating is
20 down to 16 °C in the living room and 1 hour a day for the rest of the house, 5-minute showers, baths only at weekend. We have to choose – hairdryer, toaster, microwave, smartphone, kettle, lights, fridge or cooker and
25 on and on.

   Flights are a real no-no and shopping and going out are not much better. It's all kind of a *choice*.

Mon, Jan 5th

30 Carbon cards came today ...
They've got these little blocks down the side going from green to red and as you use your year's ration they disappear one by one till you're at your last red and then you're all
35 alone, crying in the dark. Kim doesn't want to open her card, she says if she touches it then that's all her youth gone. I feel pretty nervous

when I open mine, not that I really have a youth in my family. My sister's got it.

40

Thurs, Jan 8th – Rationing.

Back to college, and I got in late cos I had to
45 take Mum to her bus stop. Her eyes filled with tears as we walked past the Saab. She whispered, 'It's not for ever,' and softly touched it. I pretended not to see.

   We missed the first bus, so we had to wait
50 15 minutes in the rain till the next one. When it finally came I jumped on, swiped my carbon card and started running upstairs. Mum was going through her purse, bag and pockets. She looked up at me.
55
   'Laura, I can't find my card. Can you lend me some ...'
   The driver shook his head. 'No carbon card, no ride, love.'
   'But, please ...'
60
   A woman out in the rain shouted: 'Get off, you stupid cow! You're holding us up.'
And then Mum started to cry. I went back down and helped her off the bus. 'We'll have to go home and get your card, Mum.'
65
   'Found it! In my coat! Bastards!' Mum shook her green plastic card at the bus as it disappeared into the traffic. 'Oh, I shouldn't get so upset. Sweetie, let's go to Alfredo's and have a cup of tea.'
70
   'I'm so sorry, Laura.' Mum picked up her tea cup. 'I know I should be strong, but I feel so responsible for my generation – we're the ones who've messed it all up for you.' ...

75 When I finally got to college there was a huge queue cos everyone had to swipe their CO cards at the gate and the machine kept breaking down. I don't know what we were swiping for anyway – the building was 80 freezing cold.

'Welcome to the future,' said Adisa, my best mate. 'They're ripping us off already.'

Tues, Jan 13th

My family has disappeared. Dad spends all 85 night on his laptop, Mum is always lost on a bus somewhere and Kim just lives in her room – an evil ball of silence. I feel sick being in the same atmosphere, I feel so much evil energy. She's definitely got the TV on 24/7 in 90 her room. I can hear it through the wall.

Weds, Jan 14th

I woke up this morning and it was freezing, freezing cold. I'm only allowed heat on in my room between 7 and 8. I went and looked at the Smart Meter in the hall. It's this thing that 95 tells you everything that's happening with energy in the house. Even for our one hour of heat Dad keeps the bedroom temperature at 15 °C. What a joke – it's not even enough to melt the ice on the windows. 100

Thurs, Jan 15th

There's heavy snowstorms all over the south of Europe.

Mon, Jan 19th

The snowstorms in Europe are getting worse 105 – and moving north. Italy has just lost all its electricity. The news showed the Vatican going black, window after window.

Tues, Jan 20th

We had a power cut in the night. The house is 110 so cold now, it feels like 200 years of cold in my bones. Cuts give me the creeps – you know when you go to turn the light on and it's dead?

2   The carbon rationing system
Are these statements true? Find proof in the text.
1 Everybody gets a card which shows how much of their carbon allowance they use.
2 Adults are given a bigger carbon allowance than children.
3 People must use their cards for travel or heat, but not for things like books or clothes.
4 Under-18s don't have to use their carbon points for household energy.
5 If you use up your year's ration too quickly, you can buy new points.

3   What do they think about it?
a) *Which phrases or sentences show how Laura, Kim and their mum feel about carbon rationing? Choose what you think are the best six and write them down.*
stupid government online form ...

b) 👥 *Compare your results with a partner and explain your choices.*
Do you share the Brown family's attitude?

4   How did they say it?
Read these sentences. Then find the parts in the text which express the same idea.
1 There's no way we can go by plane. (l. 26)
2 She started to cry. (ll. 46–47)
3 You need a CO_2 card to get on a bus. (ll. 58–59)
4 We will be late because of you. (l. 62)
5 We all had to put our cards through the machine. (ll. 76–77)
6 She never turns off the television. (l. 89)
7 Our electricity went off. (l. 110)
8 Cuts are scary. (l. 112)

5   Now you
a) *Would you like to read the whole novel? Why (not)?*
Is the story just science fiction? Or could this happen in the future? Why do you think so?

b) **Extra** *Look at ll. 14–28. Which of the things could you give up most easily? Which couldn't you give up? Explain why.*

6   SPEAKING A cartoon

a) 👥 *Describe the cartoon to your partner. Then discuss what you think its message is.*

b) 👥👥 *Join up with another pair. Compare your ideas about the cartoon. Then give your opinion of the cartoon and its message.*

▶ *SF Describing cartoons (p.126)*

SINGER

7   👥   You can make a difference

a) *Partner B: go to p. 99.*
Partner A: You and your partner have different tips under each heading in Go Green. Read your tips. Make notes and use them to tell your partner what you've read. Then listen to his/her tips. Together, think of at least one more tip for each heading.

> My text says low-energy light bulbs save lots of electricity.

> Here it says newer fridges use much less energy.

GO Green!

Climate change is a problem for the whole world.
But don't just sit around and wait for governments to act.
Here are some simple things you can do to help to stop global warming:

Heat less water
Showers cause over 65 per cent of home water-heating costs. Try taking shorter showers to save energy.

Think trees
Why not plant a tree? Trees use CO_2 and produce clean air that we can breathe. More trees mean less CO_2 in the atmosphere.

Use low-energy products
Producing electricity is a big cause of CO_2. Compact fluorescent light bulbs use almost four times less energy than traditional bulbs. And their lifetime is much longer too.

Eat for the environment
Modern agriculture uses chemicals, and producing them uses energy. Organic food production uses no chemicals, so it releases less CO_2. Whenever you can, buy organic!

Don't waste energy
Take out the plug of your MP3 player charger as soon as the batteries are full. Or even better: get one of the new solar chargers.

Reduce rubbish
Try to buy products with less packaging. More packaging means more rubbish, and collecting rubbish costs energy.

b) *Make a copy of the chart. Decide where to put the tips from* Go Green *and your own ideas.*

Things I already do	Things I could do	Things I couldn't do	Things I wouldn't want to do
...	...	...	...

Make appointments with three students. At each appointment, exchange information about the content of your charts. Give reasons for your decisions. How different or similar are your attitudes?

P1 WORDS The environment

a) *Complete the sentences with words from the box.*

carbon footprint • cars • chemicals • coal • emissions • gadgets • gas • global • insulation • recycle rubbish • solar energy • turn off • wind power

1 If there were fewer ... on the roads, we could reduce carbon ...
2 Good ... keeps a house warm and saves energy.
3 ... and ... are examples of green energy.
4 Organic farms don't use ... to grow food.
5 We should all ... like glass, paper and cans.
6 Burning ..., ... and oil is one of the main causes of ... warming.
7 To save energy we can ... electric lights and ... when we aren't using them.
8 The average ... of someone in Europe is much larger than of someone in Africa.

b) *Find nouns that go with the verbs in each list.*

reduce the use of petrol, ...
use wind power, ...
clean up beaches, ...
plant/grow trees, ...
save energy, ...
recycle glass, ...

cause CO_2 emissions, ...
burn coal, ...
pollute the environment, ...
destroy forests, ...
waste energy, ...
produce rubbish, ...

For each list, write three sentences.
We should try to reduce the use of petrol, because ...

If we don't stop causing CO2 emissions, we'll ...

P2 WRITING No driving on Sundays (A written discussion)

Produce a written discussion on the topic below or on a similar topic:
Banning driving on Sundays is a good way to reduce pollution

a) *Collect and organize your ideas*
– *Brainstorm your ideas and make notes (alone or with partners).*
– *Organize your ideas into arguments **for** and **against** the topic.*
– *Decide your opinion on the topic.*
– *Write an outline.*

b) *Write your text*
Introduction Say what the written discussion is about and why the question is important.

Points of view Write about each point of view in separate paragraphs.
List the arguments for each view and give examples. Tip: It's often better to start with the view you disagree with.

Conclusion Sum up the arguments and give your own view.

c) *Read your text when it's finished and correct it. You can put your text in your DOSSIER.*

I am going to discuss/write about ...
Most people agree that ... is a big problem.
So the important question is ...

Some/Other people think/believe/... that ...
First, .../Second, .../
On the one hand, .../On the other hand, ...
For example, .../Finally, ...

To sum up, it is clear that ...
In my opinion, ...

► *SF From outline to written discussion (p. 148)*

1   WORDS Mobility

a) *Make lists of words about travel under these headings: air, railway, road, sea. Use words from the box and add more if you can.*

> airport • boat • cab • carriage • (to) cycle •
> (to) drive • ferry • flight • gate •
> harbour • (to) land • motorway •
> petrol station • plane • platform •
> rush hour • ship • traffic jam • train •
> truck • the Tube • underground • ...

b) *All the verbs in sentences 1–6 are mixed up. Find the right verb for each sentence.*

1 Bob and I **drive** on a trip to Brighton last year.   *... went ...*
2 At 6 in the morning, I **went** him up at his house.
3 We had planned to **ask** on the early train.
4 But the train **travel** and the line was closed for the rest of the day.
5 So I phoned mum and she offered to **picked** us to Brighton.
6 We had to **broke down** a policeman for directions and then we were on our way. We had a great day!

2   London's underground   (Simple past or present perfect?)

*Complete the sentences in the correct tense: **simple past** or **present perfect**. Use the passive for two verbs.*

When London's underground – the Tube – (1) *opened* (open) in 1863, there (2) ... (be) only one line, just six km long. Since then many more lines (3) ... (add), and today's network is over 400 km. The first trains (4) ... (pull) by steam engines, but electric trains (5) ... (come) into use in 1890. Back in 1863, 30,000 people (6) ... (travel) on the underground on the first day. But of course the number of passengers (7) ... (grow) enormously in the last 150 years and over three million people now use the system every day. The famous logo, which you can see in the picture, first (8) ... (appear) in 1908.

▶ *GF 4: Talking about the past (pp. 155–156)* • *GF 7: The passive (p. 160)*

3   Customers' mails   (Word order)

Read these statements about public transport in London. Choose the right place for the words in brackets.

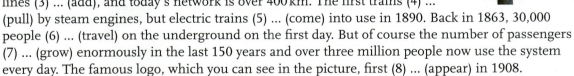

1 Julie___I love buses. I always try ? to sit ? so I can enjoy the view. (at the top)
2 Maria__I was ? in a terrible traffic jam ? . (yesterday)
      It took one hour ? from Piccadilly to Tower Bridge ? ! (to drive)
      I don't think that I'll go ? into London by car ? . (again)
3 Jack___I want to reduce my carbon footprint, so I ? my car a long time ago ? . (sold)
4 Paul___Bus drivers can give you information about travel times if you ? them ? . (ask)
5 Mike___When I got to the stop, the last bus had ? left ? . I was really angry. (early)
6 Sue___My husband and I always use ? the Tube ? when we go shopping. (on Saturdays)

▶ *You could now do task 1 in the Practice test on p. 42.*   ▶ *GF 1: Word order (p. 152)*

4   WORDS After the accident

Complete the dialogue with words from the box.

| alcohol • ambulance • drunk • headache • |
| healthy • hurts • operation • sweat • |
| threw up • unconscious |

Doctor Mike, can you hear me? You had an accident on your motorbike. Your friend Julie is still (1) *unconscious*. Both of you have broken arms and legs. You'll have to have an (2) ... But first we have to ask you some questions. Did you drink any (3) ... today?

Mike No, I didn't. Julie had one or two glasses of wine, but she wasn't (4) ...

Doctor Have you or Julie had a cold recently?

Mike No, we've been really (5) ... actually.

Doctor Good. Do you feel any pain right now?

Mike Yes, I do. My leg (6) ... terribly and I've got quite a bad (7) ... and stomach ache too.

Doctor Well, maybe you've forgotten, but you (8) ... after the accident. You were in shock.

Mike I only remember feeling really weak. I was shivering all the time and felt cold (9) ... on my face. Doctor, who called the (10) ...?

Doctor Luckily, there was a nurse in the car behind you. He gave you first aid too.

5   Reporting what people said (Indirect speech)

Later Mike told a friend what the doctor had said. Complete Mike's sentences. Remember to change the tense of the verb.

1 **Doctor** You had an accident.
   Mike He told me I had had an accident.

2 **Doctor** Julie is still unconscious.
   Mike He said that Julie ...

3 **Doctor** You'll have to have an operation.
   Mike He added that we ...

4 **Doctor** Did you drink any alcohol?
   Mike He asked if we ...

5 **Doctor** Have you or Julie had a cold recently?

6 **Doctor** Do you feel any pain?

7 **Doctor** You threw up after the accident.

▶ You could now do task 2 in the Practice test on p. 43.   ▶ *GF 11: Indirect speech (pp. 165–166)*

6   STUDY SKILLS Writing   (The 5 Ws and 'how')

a) Use the phrases in the box to complete the report.

b) Match each phrase from a) to one of the 5 Ws. Which phrase tells us 'how'?

| driving at over 80 miles per hour • hit by |
| broken glass • in the late afternoon • |
| one of the worst accidents • St Pauls and |
| Eastville Park • 23-year-old truck driver |

Young dad loses left eye in accident

Yesterday a (1) ... was badly hurt in (2) ... in the Bristol area this year. The father of two sons had been (3) ... (where only 60 are allowed) and wasn't able to stop in time when he saw a traffic jam in front of him. Martin Smith from St Pauls in Bristol lost his left eye, which was (4) ... from the windscreen of his truck. Fortunately doctors were able to save the other eye. The accident happened (5) ... as rush hour commuters were travelling home. The M32 was blocked for two hours between (6) ..., causing traffic chaos in the centre of Bristol. Police said it was lucky that Mr Smith hadn't been killed.

▶ *SF Writing a report (p. 144)*

7   WORDS For a greener world

a) *For each group, find the word that doesn't fit.*
1 sun • plastic • paper • glass
2 oil • coal • wind • gas
3 waste • recycle • reduce • save
4 help • pollute • protect • save
5 climate change • solar power •
   global warming • air pollution
6 trees • electricity • cars • heating

b) *Match the sentence beginnings (1–7) to the endings (a–g).*

1 Organic food is grown	a than to produce vegetables.
2 Locally grown products	b are usually better for the environment.
3 You need more energy to produce meat	c than to throw it into the dustbin.
4 You can buy cool clothes cheaply	d of plastic ones.
5 Use a cotton shopping bag instead	e at second-hand shops.
6 Buying recycled paper can	f without using chemicals.
7 It's much better to recycle glass	g help to save trees.

8   Our green holiday   (Simple past: questions)

Read the dialogue. Then use the verbs in brackets
to complete the questions in the simple past.

Lucy   So (1) ...? (enjoy)
         So did you enjoy your holiday?
Sharon   Yes, I did. I think it was the best
         holiday I've ever had.
Lucy   Where (2) ...? (stay)
Sharon   At a 'Green Hotel' in the south of
         France, near Marseille.
Lucy   A 'Green Hotel'! That sounds
         interesting. How (3) ...? (find out)
Sharon   Our neighbours told us about it. They
         were there last year.
Lucy   So what (4) ...? (be)
Sharon   Special? Well, the food was delicious – all locally grown.
Lucy   And (5) ...? (be)
Sharon   Of course it was organic. One hundred per cent! And we were allowed to help in the
         garden. That was great fun.
Lucy   Fun? I'm not sure if I'd enjoy that. Anyway, what (6) ...? (do)
Sharon   What else? Well, we went down to the beach every day.
Lucy   That sounds more like a holiday. How (7) ...? (be)
Sharon   It wasn't too far. Just over half a mile.
Lucy   And (8) ...? (have)
Sharon   Yes, we had fantastic weather. Twenty-five degrees and lots of sun every day!

▶ GF 2: Making questions (p. 153) • GF 4: Talking about the past (pp. 155–156)

9   Ben's blog   (Simple past: negative statements)

*Ben has started to 'shop green'. Read his blog. Complete the sentences with the **simple past** negative form of the verbs in brackets.*

Friday	:-)	Went shopping in town by bike today. I (1) … (take) the bus because it uses too much energy.
	:-(	Asked for recycled paper. Unfortunately, they (2) … (have) any.
	:-)	Bought some fruit. I (3) … (choose) the big red apples from Italy. Instead I chose small, locally grown ones. Cheaper too.
	:-(	Got some eggs for mum. Parents! (4) … (be allowed to) buy organic ones just because they're a bit more expensive!
Sunday	:-(	Went to town again. Can you believe it? (5) … (can find) a second-hand clothes shop anywhere!
	:-(	Bought a T-shirt made in China. I just (6) … (be able to) find one made in this country.

▶ *You could now do tasks 3 and 4 in the Practice test on pp. 43–44.*

▶ *GF 4: Talking about the past (pp. 155–156)*

10   WRITING A written discussion

a) *Put these paragraphs in the right order (introduction, first point of view, opposite point of view, conclusion).*

A   On the other hand, there are arguments against buying clothes from the Third World, at least if the label has no reliable information about their background. First, fashion isn't everything. Second, conditions in clothes factories can be cruel. For example, one report mentions young children who work for no pay, and who are beaten if they don't produce enough.

B   You often hear people say that there is a problem with clothes from Third World countries. Here in Europe, these clothes can be very cheap. But the people who produce them for western markets often have to work very hard for very little. So the question is: should teenagers buy these clothes or not?

C   After looking at both sides, I think it is safer not to buy clothes from Third World countries if you know nothing about conditions in the factories. For me, fashion is very important, but human rights are even more important.

D   On the one hand, you can argue that it is not wrong to buy clothes from the Third World. First, most teenagers are interested in fashion, but they do not have much money. So it is an advantage to be able to buy clothes cheaply. Second, you cannot know the background to all the clothes you buy. And buying clothes from Third World countries helps people there to make some money.

b) *Write down phrases that are used to structure the discussion. What other phrases could you use?*

▶ *SF From outline to written discussion (p. 148)*

1   LANGUAGE

Read the text. Choose A, B or C below to complete the text.

They said it would never work!

It was getting worse from day to day. There were just too many cars in the centre of London. Nobody ... (1) get anywhere on time because of all the traffic. When Ken Livingstone, the mayor of London, decided to do something about this, everybody said it would never work, but it did! In 2003, London ... (2) the first city in the world to introduce a 'congestion charge'. Drivers now have to pay £8 a day to enter the centre of London. At first people said it would cause lots of problems because the technology used for paying the charge would ... (3). It didn't! The prime minister at that time, Tony Blair, was also very worried, but he soon had to admit that he was wrong. People began to realize that traffic jams weren't something that couldn't be changed.

The congestion charge has to ... (4) from Monday to Friday from 7 am to 6.30 pm. *Transport for London* say that since the introduction of the congestion charge, the number of cars per day in the centre of London ... (5) by 50,000 and traffic jams by a third. Another positive effect is that ... (6) in the congestion charge zone between Piccadilly and Tower Bridge has started to move faster. However, the managers of big ... (7) are less happy because they ... (8) fewer customers since the congestion charge was introduced.

And many people said that it was unfair that only people with money could ... (9) into London, since both the congestion charge and parking had to be paid for.

And there are other problems too. *Transport for London* ordered hundreds of new ... (10) for all the extra passengers they expected. ... (11), however, people used the Tube instead, which was already very full. But *Transport for London* think that, ... (12), the congestion charge has been a big success. Now comes the $64,000 question: Would it work in other cities too?

1 A can   B could   C couldn't
2 A became   B become   C has become
3 A break down   B break up
   C cut down
4 A pay   B paid   C be paid
5 A goes down   B has gone down
   C went down
6 A the motorway   B the rush hour
   C traffic

7 A airports   B stations
   C department stores
8 A had   B have had   C will have
9 A drive   B cycle   C travel
10 A buses   B cabs   C trucks
11 A Fortunately   B Luckily
   C Unfortunately
12 A altogether   B although   C always

2   WRITING

a) A dialogue

*You are at the doctor's. You fell off your bike
yesterday evening. Your left arm hurts terribly and
you have a headache and stomach ache. You
threw up after the accident and felt weak. You
were shivering all the time and felt cold. You want
to know if your arm is broken.*
*In your exercise book, complete your part of the
dialogue. Use about 80 words.*

Doctor___ Good morning. And how can I help
            you today?
You_____ (1) ...
Doctor___ Poor you! Do you feel any pain at the
            moment?
You_____ (2) ...
Doctor___ Hmm. And do you have pain in other
            parts of your body?
You_____ (3) ...
Doctor___ Can you remember what happened
            after the accident?
You_____ (4) ...
Doctor___ That can't have been very nice for
            you. But don't worry about it. You
            were probably in shock. Did you feel
            weak?
You_____ (5) ...
Doctor___ OK. So let me have a look at your
            arm. Does that hurt?

You_____ No, it doesn't. (6) ...?
Doctor___ No, it isn't. You were lucky. You must
            have been wearing a thick jacket.
            Your arm will feel better in a couple
            of days' time. Try not to use it too
            much. And here, take this to the
            chemist's and they'll give you
            something for your head and
            stomach. You should be able to go
            back to school tomorrow.
You_____ (7) ...

b) An email

You have just come home from the doctor's. Write an email to your best friend.
In your email tell your friend:
- how long you had to wait.
- what the doctor asked you.
- what you told her.
- what the doctor advised you to do.

3   WRITING   A report

Choose one of the following topics and write a report about it. Write about 100 words altogether.
a) You missed a flight because you couldn't get to the airport on time.
b) You saw an accident between a bus and somebody on a bike.
c) You spent a 'green holiday' in the country with your parents.

4   WRITING A shopping survey

Answer the questions below.

Shopping – for myself and my world

1 Do you help to write your family shopping list? Why (not)?
2 Do you think it's a good idea to buy organic food? Why (not)?
3 Do you agree it's better to eat less meat and more vegetables? Why (not)?
4 Do you think it's a good idea to buy recycled paper? Why (not)?
5 Do you try not to buy products with lots of packaging? Why (not)?
6 Do you use plastic shopping bags more than once? Why (not)?

7 Have you ever bought clothes at second-hand shops? Why/Why not?

5   WRITING A letter to a newspaper

Child slaves work for western fashion companies

Two journalists have discovered a factory in Delhi where clothes for western markets were being produced by children between the ages of eight and fifteen.

The reporters were able to enter the factory by pretending to represent a large British fashion company. They described the conditions they saw inside as unbelievable. 'The children were working in dark and dirty rooms. Most of them were wearing almost nothing. They looked very tired and very hungry.'

Later the journalists returned with the police and the children were taken to the local police station, where they answered questions. They described how they worked for long hours for almost no money and said they were often beaten by the factory owners. Most of them came from poor families who could not afford to support them.

One of the reporters, Julian Thomson, commented: 'This shows that it's really important for shoppers in the West to ask where clothes were made before they buy them.'

Read the newspaper article. Then write to the newspaper and say
– how you felt when you read it
– what you think about children working and why
– how you and other shoppers in your country could react.

6   WRITING Opinions

Choose one of the following statements and write your opinion about it. Write about 100 words.
a) City centres would be nicer places if there were fewer cars there.
b) The most important thing about food is that it is cheap.
c) I can't worry about what clothes workers earn. I don't have enough money myself.

How am I doing?

In the Practice test you did some typical exam (Abschlussprüfung) tasks.
If you found some tasks difficult, the questions below will help you to find out what you need to practise.

1 How easy or hard was each task?

	easy	OK	quite hard	very hard
Task 1				
Task 2a				
Task 2b				

Language (Task 1) _____

Check your answers on p. 228

2 Why was the language task difficult?
a) I didn't understand the task.
b) I found the multiple choice format difficult.
c) I couldn't decide which answer was correct.
d) I didn't understand all the text and panicked.

Writing (Tasks 2–6) _____

3 Why were the writing tasks difficult?
a) I felt nervous.
b) I didn't know what to write.
c) I couldn't find the right words.
d) I wasn't sure about the rules for writing different kinds of text (e. g. email, report, etc.).
e) The texts I wrote weren't clear enough.
f) I made a lot of spelling and grammar mistakes.
g) I didn't have time to finish all the tasks.

▶ *SF Writing course (pp. 143–144)*

4 👥 How did your partner do?

Ask your teacher for a copy of the assessment sheet on the right.
Use it to assess your partner's work.

▶ You will find more WRITING tasks in the Exam File, pp. 83–86.

You will find more WRITING tasks in the Exam File, pp. 83–86.

Assessment sheet ☹ ☺ ☺						
Name ...	1	2	3	4	5	Comr
2 a) WRITING A dialogue: Did your partner ...						
a) answer all the doctor's questions?						
b) use all the ideas in the instructions and write enough?						
2 b) WRITING An email: Did your partner ...						
c) use all the ideas in the instructions?						
d) use indirect speech?						
3 WRITING A report: Did your partner ...						
e) structure the report and say clearly what happened?						
f) start with the most important information and then go on to the details?						
g) answer the 5 Ws and 'how'?						
h) use the *simple past*?						
4 WRITING A shopping survey: Did your partner ...						
i) answer all the questions?						
j) give a reason for each answer?						
k) write enough?						
5 WRITING A letter to a newspaper: Did your partr						
l) write their address, the date, and the name and address of the newspaper in the right place?						
m) start and end the letter correctly?						
n) explain their opinion clearly?						
o) use long forms (of verbs)?						
6 WRITING Opinions: Did your partner ...						
p) structure their text?						
q) write enough on the topic and give examples for the arguments?						
r) use linking words to connect longer sentences?						
s) sum up the arguments for and against and express their opinion?						

1 👥 What's the issue?

Look at the photos. Choose one that interests you and describe it to your partner. Say what you think of when you look at it.

2 What we care about 🎧

a) *Listen to eight young people talking about issues they care about. In a copy of the chart, match each photo to a speaker. There is no photo for two of the speakers.*

Speaker	Photo (A–F)	Key words and phrases
1		
2		
...		

b) *Listen again. For each speaker, add key words and phrases to your chart.*

c) 👥 *Compare your chart with a partner. Add more key words and phrases if you can.*

d) *Which issue do you care about most? Say why.*

– I care about poverty. Some kids have nothing and they live in really bad places.

– I care about facilities for young people. We need places where we can meet our friends and have fun.

– ...

QUIZ

How much do you care?

If you think something is unfair, do you care enough to get up and do something about it?
Take this quiz to find out.

1 You need a new T-shirt. Do you buy the one with the trendy label or the fair trade label?

(A) If the two T-shirts are the same price, I'd probably buy the fair trade T-shirt.

(B) I always choose fair trade products, and I tell my friends that they should too.

(C) The trendy label. It's really important to look good. Who cares about fair trade?

2 There's a new student at your school. You try to talk to him, but he doesn't speak your language very well. What do you do?

(A) I give up and wait until he's learned to speak my language.

(B) I ask him to play football or another game where language isn't important.

(C) I smile at him whenever I see him so he knows that I want to be friendly.

3 Do you leave your mobile phone on charge overnight?

(A) Sometimes. But I feel a bit guilty.

(B) Of course. That way my phone is always ready for me to use. That's all I care about.

(C) Never! Did you know that in the UK we waste £27 million a year this way?

4 Are you interested in the news?

(A) No – but I sometimes look at the TV pages in the newspaper, and the sports pages too.

(B) Not really, but sometimes I notice something interesting on the TV news when my parents are watching it.

(C) Yes, I get information from lots of places: news programmes, online news sites, blogs, …

5 You have three wishes. What do you wish for first?

(A) Good health for my family and friends.

(B) World peace.

(C) To be rich and good-looking.

6 Which statement do you agree with most?

(A) If you don't vote, you don't have the right to complain if you don't like something.

(B) The truth is: voting is a waste of time. The politicians don't listen anyway.

(C) Voting is important, but you also have to speak out and do something if you see a problem.

7 They want to close the youth club because the neighbours say there's too much noise. Your band will have nowhere to practise. What do you do?

(A) Email the local newspaper and radio station, make posters, create a petition, organize a march to the town hall, start an online campaign.

(B) Read the posters, sign the petition, join the facebook group, go on the march.

(C) Nothing. It's not likely that anyone will listen to a group of kids.

---

3 **How much do you care?**

a) *Do the quiz above. To work out your result, go to p. 102. Do you agree with your result?*

b) 👥 *Find out the results of the other people in your class. Were there any surprises?*

4 **Extra** **The story behind the picture**

Choose a person from one of the pictures on p. 46 and write 120 words about them. Say where the picture was taken and what the person is doing/ thinking/feeling/... Where was the person earlier in the day? Where will he/she be later?

▶ *SF Describing pictures (pp. 125–126)*

YOUR RIGHT TO BE HEARD

1 👥 **What's the right age?**

a) *Look at the chart below. At what age do you think you are allowed to do these things in Germany?*

	United States	Germany
get married	14–17 (if parents agree)*	…
get a driving licence	16–18 *	…
vote in an election	18	…
leave home	16 (if parents agree)	…
buy cigarettes	18	…
buy alcohol	21	…

* The rules are different in different states.

A: I think that in Germany you have to be 18/… before you can …
B: I think that you have to be older. / No, I think that you can vote/… when you're …

b) **Extra** *What about other countries that you know?*

c) *At what age should you be allowed to do these things? Discuss with your partner.*
– I think that 14/16/… is too young / too old / the right age to …
– I wouldn't want to wait until I was 18/…
– If they changed the age to 16/…, young people would be more/less/just as likely to get divorced/have accidents/alcohol problems …

2

COMMENTS   EMAIL   **PRINT**

WE ARE PEOPLE TOO! by Oliver Munslow (16) – 23 October 2010

> *Look at the title of the article and the photos. What do you think the article is about? Who do you think Oliver is talking to: adults or teenagers?*

END AGE DISCRIMINATION

To everybody out there that thinks young people are different, you're right! We're younger than adults. But that doesn't mean you don't need to listen to us or you don't have to respect us. We
5 have feelings and (this might surprise some of you) we are people too.
Did you know that here in Britain every citizen under 18 has important rights? For example, we all have the right to be listened to and taken
10 seriously, and we have the right to get together with our friends in public (as long as we respect the rights of other people and do not break the law).
But British children aren't taken seriously before they're 18. Too many adults think that my views 15 just don't count and that I don't deserve equal rights. Here are some everyday examples of discrimination against teenagers.
Nearly every day I see signs on shop doors that say 'Only 2 children at a time', 'No school bags', 20 or even 'No children unless they are with an adult'. Children must wait outside and watch adults going in and out of the shop in front of them. Then, when they go into the shop, they

Whenever I go to the cinema, I pay the same price as an adult because I am over 15. My sister is 19, but she pays less than me because she goes to university. So why can't you get a cheaper ticket if you're still at school? If I had a job, I would only get £3.64 an hour because of my age, compared to £4.92 an hour for 18 to 21-year-olds and £5.93 for workers over 22. So, 16-year-olds earn less than adults, but pay full price. That just doesn't make sense to me.

This country is a democracy. Every day MPs and town councillors make decisions that affect our lives. But, as a 16-year-old, although I can smoke, leave home, get married, apply for a job, fight in the army, and pay taxes to the government, I don't have the right to vote. Why should political parties care about the needs and wishes of young people when we can't vote for or against them?

We are old enough to breathe the air that has been polluted by the industries that you control. We are old enough to walk on the streets that are unsafe because of the drugs and crime problems that you haven't been able to solve. Surely we are old enough to help to improve things. Adults in this country should start to realize that we have important things to say and that we have the right to be heard.

must leave their bag outside. It doesn't matter if they have an expensive laptop, tennis racket or saxophone in the bag. It has to stay outside. I want to meet my friends outside the shops or the burger restaurant near where I live, but when I get there I have to leave immediately. Why? Because they are using that disgusting 'mosquito' device. Now this one really makes me angry!

The mosquito is a machine that makes a really annoying noise that only teenagers can hear. It hurts our ears, and shops use it to keep anti-social teenagers away. But it also keeps nice friendly teenagers away, people like me and my friends. In fact, teenage troublemakers are only a very small percentage of the youth population. But did anyone think about the huge majority that don't cause problems?

a) Are these statements true or false?

1 Oliver is writing about young people's rights.
2 He says that young people don't respect adults.
3 He thinks that adults don't listen to young people.

b) Why does Oliver feel that young people are discriminated against? Find at least three examples in the text.

c) Why do you think Oliver wrote this article?

▶ **Text File 5** *(pp. 117–121)*

3 Now you

a) 👥 *Discuss with a partner.*

– Are the things Oliver criticizes really age discrimination? Or are they sensible rules?
– Have you or anyone you know ever had the same kind of experience with adults as Oliver.

▶ *SF Having a discussion (p. 140)*

b) Write an email to Oliver.

– Say what you think of his article.
– Tell him what points you agree with / don't agree with.
– Describe what the situation is like for you and your friends in Germany.

P1   WORDS Have your say!

a) *Find words and phrases from the unit so far for these headings. Collect them in a network, mind map or chart.*

1 **Issues:** the environment, bus/train fares, …
2 **Sources of information:** TV news, blogs, …
3 **Ways to take action:** choose fair trade products, vote, …

b) 👥 *Compare your words and phrases with a partner.*

c) 👥 *Make appointments with three partners. Tell each partner:*

– what issues you care most about
– what sources of information you use most
– what kinds of action you prefer to take

P2   VIEWING The mosquito: An anti-teenager device 🎥

a) *Look at the texts from a TV report about the mosquito device and match them to the stills.*

> – '… a little device called the mosquito … only people between the ages of about thirteen and twenty-five can hear it …'
> – '… young adults were holding nightly drinking parties at Riverside Elementary until they installed the device … a year ago'
> – 'Most adults can't hear it …'

NB CROWD CLEARING DEVICE

NB CROWD CLEARING DEVICE

RIVERSIDE ELEMENTARY SCHOOL
ECOLE ELEMENTAIRE RIVERSIDE

NB CROWD CLEARING DEVICE

b) *Watch the film. Did you match the texts and stills correctly?*

c) *Watch again. Answer these questions.*

1 Where did the idea for the device come from?
   Ⓐ Canada   Ⓑ Great Britain   Ⓒ the US
2 The mosquito can be heard by …
   Ⓐ little kids, teenagers and dogs.
   Ⓑ teenagers and dogs.
   Ⓒ teenagers.
3 Which of these comments was not made by the teenagers in the report?
   Ⓐ 'It's disgusting.'
   Ⓑ 'It's just really annoying.'
   Ⓒ 'It's really bad for our ears.'
4 Why is the school using the mosquito?
   Ⓐ to stop teenagers bullying little kids
   Ⓑ to stop teenagers hanging around outside the school and drinking
   Ⓒ so that students leave school in time
5 How does one dad use the mosquito?
   Ⓐ to call his daughter on the phone
   Ⓑ to tell his daughter to come inside
   Ⓒ to wake his daughter up
6 How do some teenagers use the mosquito?
   Ⓐ as a secret ringtone their teachers can't hear
   Ⓑ to annoy other teenagers
   Ⓒ to train dogs

d) **Extra** *What's your opinion of the mosquito? Give reasons.*

I think it's a good/ bad/… idea because …
I (don't) think it would stop antisocial behaviour because …

P3   REVISION   Will the mosquito keep troublemakers away?

a) *Tom and Jill run a small shop. Tom wants to install a mosquito device outside. Jill is against the idea. Write down their arguments. Use **will** and **won't** in the main clauses. Be careful with* if-*clauses.*

Tom

1   mosquito – keep troublemakers away
     The mosquito will keep troublemakers away.
2   customers – feel safer – if fewer teens –
     hang around outside shop
3   if we – attract more customers – earn more

Jill

4   mosquito – not stop real troublemakers
5   mosquito – annoy all teenagers, not just
     troublemakers
6   if teenage customers – hear horrible noise
     – not shop here any more

b) 👥 *Act out a dialogue between Jill and Tom.*

c) **Extra** 👥 *A shop near your school wants to use the mosquito. What do you think about this?*
– I (don't) think they should use a mosquito because it will/won't …
– If they use a mosquito, I'll shop somewhere else …

▶ *GF 5: Talking about the future (p. 157) • GF 9: Conditional sentences (p. 163)*

P4   👥👥👥 SPEAKING   Role play: A discussion about video cameras at school

There are problems with smoking, vandalism, graffiti and bullying at school. The head teacher wants to install video cameras outside the school and in the corridors and classrooms. There is a meeting to discuss this question:

'Will video cameras make the school a cleaner and safer place?'

a) *Decide who will take the role of moderator. The rest of the class should make five groups.*

Moderator
Your job is to allow everyone to have their say (not to give your own opinion).
– *Go to p. 100.*
     Your role card has phrases you can use.
– *Read through them and practise them quietly while the others prepare their arguments.*

Other students
– *Go to p. 100.*
– *Each group chooses a role card and thinks of arguments (and examples to support them).*
– *Think about how to answer arguments from the other side.*
– *Make notes.*
– *Remember phrases you can use in a discussion.*

▶ *SF Having a discussion (p. 140)*

b) *Have the discussion. You could use the fishbowl method.*

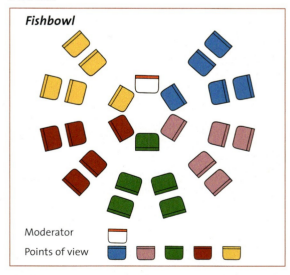

Fishbowl

Moderator
Points of view

c) *Which side had the better arguments? Have a class vote.*

d) **Extra** *Write a short text: Would video cameras make your school a cleaner and safer place? You can put your text in your DOSSIER.*

SPEAKING OUT

A class debate (Adapted from the novel *Speak* by Laurie Halse Anderson)

Speak is a novel about Melinda, who learns that it is important to speak out. In this text Melinda, the narrator of the story, describes a History class.

> *Some important new words are explained at the bottom of each page. You can also work out a lot of meanings yourself.*

▸ SF Using a dictionary (p. 128) • SF Reading literature (p. 137)

Mr. Neck storms into class like a bull. We slide into our seats[1]. I think for sure he's going to explode.

IMMIGRATION. He writes it on the board.
5 I'm pretty sure he spelled it right.

Mr. Neck: "My family has been in this country for over two hundred years. We built this place, fought in every war from the first one to the last one, paid taxes, and voted."

10 A cartoon bubble[2] forms over the heads of everyone in the class. ("WILL THIS BE ON THE TEST?")

Mr. Neck: "So tell me why my son can't get a job."

15 A few hands go up. Mr. Neck ignores them. It isn't a real question, it's one he asked so he could give the answer. I relax. This is like when my father complains about his boss. The best thing to do is to stay awake and look
20 sympathetic[3].

His son wanted to be a firefighter, but didn't get the job. Mr. Neck is sure that this is some kind of reverse[4] discrimination. He says we should close our borders so that real
25 Americans can get the jobs they deserve. I concentrate on trying to draw a pine tree.

Mr. Neck writes on the board again: "DEBATE: America should have closed her borders in 1900." That gets a reaction. I can
30 see kids counting on their fingers, trying to figure[5] when their grandparents or great-grandparents were born, when they came to America. When they figure out they would have been stuck[6] in a country that hated them,
35 or a place with no schools, or a place with no

future, their hands go up. They do not share Mr. Neck's opinion.

I don't know where my family came from. I don't know how long we've been in America. We've been in this school district since I was
40 in first grade; that must count for something. I start drawing an apple tree.

The arguments jump back and forth across the room. A few kids quickly figure out which side Mr. Neck is on, so they fight to throw out
45 the "foreigners". Anyone whose family immigrated in the last century has a story to tell about how hard their families have worked, what they do for the country, the taxes they pay. A member of the Archery[7] Club tries
50 to say that we are all foreigners and we should give the country back to the Native Americans, but she's buried[8] under disagreement. Mr. Neck enjoys the noise, until one kid challenges[9] him directly.
55

Brave kid: "Maybe your son didn't get that job because he's not good enough. Or he's lazy. Or the other guy was better than him, no matter what his skin color. I think the white people who have been here for two hundred
60 years are the ones pulling down the country. They don't know how to work – they've had it too easy."

---

[1] seat [siːt] *Sitz(platz)*   [2] bubble ['bʌbl] *Blase*   [3] sympathetic [ˌsɪmpə'θetɪk] *verständnisvoll, mitfühlend*
[4] reverse [rɪ'vɜːs] *umgekehrte(r, s), entgegengesetzte(r, s)*   [5] (to) figure (out) ['fɪgə] *herausfinden, herauskriegen*   [6] (to) be stuck [stʌk] *festsitzen*
[7] archery ['ɑːtʃəri] *Bogenschießen*   [8] (to) be buried ['berid] *begraben sein/werden*   [9] (to) challenge ['tʃælɪndʒ] *herausfordern*

The supporters of immigration clap and
65 cheer.

Mr. Neck: "You watch your mouth, mister.
You are talking about my son. I don't want to
hear any more from you. That's enough debate
– get your books out."

70 The Neck is back in control. Show time is
over. I try to draw a branch[1] coming out of a
tree for the 315th time. It looks terrible. I'm
concentrating on the drawing, so I don't notice
at first that David Petrakis my lab partner has
75 stood up. The class stops talking. I put my
pencil down.

Mr. Neck: "Mr. Petrakis, take your seat."

David Petrakis is never, ever in trouble. What
is he thinking? Has he finally gone crazy
80 under the pressure[2] of being smarter than
everyone?

David: "If the class is debating, then each
student has the right to say what's on his
mind[3]."

85 Mr. Neck: "I decide who talks in here."

David: "You opened a debate. You can't close
it just because it is not going your way."

Mr. Neck: "Watch me. Take your seat, Mr.
Petrakis."

90 David: "The Constitution does not
recognize[4] different classes of citizenship
based on how long you've lived here. I am a
citizen, with the same rights as your son, or
you. As a citizen, and as a student, I am
95 protesting the tone of this lesson as racist,
intolerant, and xenophobic[5]."

Mr. Neck: "Sit your butt in that chair,
Petrakis, and watch your mouth! I try to get a
debate going in here and you people turn it
100 into a race thing. Sit down or you're going to
the principal[6]."

David stares at Mr. Neck, looks at the flag for
a minute, then picks up his books and walks
out of the room. He says a million things
105 without saying a word. I make a note to study
David Petrakis. I have never heard a more
eloquent[7] silence.

▶ **Text File 6** (pp. 122–123)

Working with the text

1 The story
Finish these sentences about the story.
1 Mr. Neck starts a debate about …
2 He's upset because his son can't …
3 Mr. Neck believes …
4 He stops the debate when …
5 David Petrakis stands up and …
6 At the end of the story …

2 The characters
a) *What kind of person is Mr. Neck? How do you
know? Find examples in the text.*

b) *What does Melinda think of her classmate
David Petrakis and why?*

c) *What do Mr. Neck and David think about free
speech? Find examples in the text.*

3 VIEWING *Speak* 🎥
a) *Watch the film version of the classroom scene.
Describe it in your own words. What is different
from the book? What is the same?*

b) *Did the scene from the book help you to
understand the situation better? Explain.*

4 Extra 👥👥 Now you
*Think and make notes: Think of situations when it
could be important to speak out, e.g.*

> – a teacher blames the wrong student
> – somebody makes a racist comment
> – …

👥 *Pair: Tell your partner about your examples.
Then discuss this question:*

> Is it always easy to speak out when you think
> something is wrong?

👥👥 *Share: Report your ideas to another pair. Has
anyone experienced a situation like the ones
you've discussed. If so, tell the group about it.*

---

[1] branch [brɑːntʃ] *Zweig*   [2] pressure ['preʃə] *Druck*   [3] what's on his mind *was ihn beschäftigt; was ihm durch den Kopf geht*   [4] (to) recognize
['rekəgnaız] *anerkennen*   [5] xenophobic [ˌzenə'fəʊbɪk] *fremdenfeindlich*   [6] principal ['prɪnsəpl] *Schulleiter/in*   [7] eloquent ['eləkwənt] *beredt,
ausdrucksstark*

P1 WORDS Understanding new words (Suffixes)

Recognizing suffixes can help you to understand new words.

a) *Find the missing words. If you aren't sure, check your dictionary.*

1 -ness

happy	–	happiness
?	–	darkness
weak	–	?
polite	–	?
?	–	rudeness

2 -ity

real	–	?
?	–	stupidity
popular	–	?
?	–	responsibility

3 -ence

silent	–	?
different	–	?
?	–	intelligence

4 -er

| support | – | ? |
| foreign | – | ? |

5 -ment

announce	–	?
disagree	–	?
govern	–	?

6 -ion

discuss	–	?
react	–	?
?	–	decision
explode	–	?
immigrate	–	?
discriminate	–	?
concentrate	–	?

7 -ation

imagine	–	imagination
inform	–	information
?	–	organization
?	–	installation

b) *Use nouns from a) to complete the text.*
Oliver's article on youth rights criticizes the (1) ... (different) between what adults and teens earn. He sees this as an example of age (2) ... (discriminate). In general, he feels that many adults don't understand the (3) ... (real) of teenage life. But he hopes the (4) ... (govern) will start to take young people's issues more seriously. If they do, it will help to improve the (5) ... (popular) of politicians.

c) *Complete the text with nouns from these words.*

> discuss · immigrate · react · silent · weak

Mr Neck wanted to have a debate about ... (1) into the United States. But he ended the ... (2) after a student expressed an opinion he didn't like. Melinda was surprised by the ... (3) of David Petrakis, who told Mr Neck that free speech was a right under the constitution. She saw it as a sign of strength, not ... (4), when David walked out of the room in ... (5).

P2 WRITING Should young drivers be banned from driving at night? 🔊

a) *Some people want to ban under-25s from driving after 10 pm. Would you support this idea?*

b) *Listen to a radio programme on the topic. Take notes on the arguments. You can listen twice.*

for	against
lots of accidents at night	not fair to responsible drivers
...	...

c) 👥 *Collect more arguments for and against.*

d) *Imagine German politicians want to ban under-25s from driving after 10 pm. Write to your English friend and say what you think about the idea and why. Write at least 120 words.*

▶ SF From outline to written discussion (p. 148)

P3 **EVERYDAY ENGLISH** SPEAKING **Solving conflicts** 🎧

a) Which box below has phrases you can use to …
1 start a conversation
2 name a problem
3 disagree that there is a problem
4 apologize
5 accept an apology

A I'm sorry, I didn't mean to …
Sorry, I shouldn't have done … / said …
I'm sorry. I didn't know …

B Don't worry about it. / OK. No worries.

C I don't see what's wrong with …
Where's the problem?

D I don't like the way you …
What annoys me is …
The problem is …

E Can I have a word with you?
Excuse me, but …

c) 👥 *You're sharing a room with your partner.*
One of you has annoyed the other.
Discuss the problem. Look at p. 230 for ideas
about conflict situations.

b) Use phrases from a) to complete these
conversations at a youth hostel. Then listen and
check.

Fin Mia, … (1)
Mia Yes, of course.
Fin Er … Your perfume – it's very strong!
Mia Great, isn't it? It was from my boyfriend.
Fin Well, … (2) that it isn't great for me. Can
you stop using it, please?
Mia Sorry, but … (3) it. Are you crazy?
Fin I just have problems with perfume. It
hurts my eyes and my skin goes red.
And we share a room, so I can't sleep.
Mia Oh dear. Of course I'll stop using it.
… (4) it had that effect on you.
Fin … (5) And thanks.

Ali … (1) did you use my shampoo?
PJ Oh yeah. I forgot mine, so I used yours.
Ali OK, but … (2) that you've used it all.
PJ There's still some in the bottle, so … (3)
Ali Yeah, there's a bit in the bottle, but not
much. And … (4) didn't ask me first.
PJ But you weren't there. Anyway, … (5)
use so much. It was an accident.
Ali … (6) It does come out of the bottle very
quickly.
PJ Yes, it does. But I'll buy you some more
later, OK?

P4 **EVERYDAY ENGLISH** MEDIATION **Explaining rules**

Your family is visiting the US and wants to know about the alcohol rules there. You've found this article.
Write down the main points in German.

1 2 3 4 5 ▶

In the US, alcohol rules are decided by the individual states. Bars close at different times in
different cities, and some counties are 'dry', which means that you cannot buy alcohol there.
In some states, alcohol is only sold in special ABC (Alcohol and Beverage Control) stores.
You cannot drink alcohol in public. Taking a beer out of a bar onto the sidewalk is illegal in most
states. Walking down the street with a beer will definitely get you into trouble with the police.
Since 1984, it has been illegal in all US states for people under 21 to buy alcohol or to drink it in
public. Even grey-haired old ladies often have to show an official document (e. g. driving licence
or passport) with a photo and date of birth if they want to buy alcohol.
Many people in the US think the alcohol rules are unfair because young people are seen as
adults in most other areas of life.
18- to 20-year-olds can marry, have children, own cars, homes and guns, but they can't drink
a glass of wine in a restaurant, or even a glass of champagne at their own wedding.

▶ *SF Mediation (p. 149)*

1 WORDS Getting involved

Choose the right word to complete each sentence.

1 Last week, there was a meeting to prefer/protect/protest against plans to close our youth club.
2 The club leader made a conversation/speech/talk to the meeting.
3 Then we all had a chance to give/have/speak our say.
4 Quite a few people took part/place/turns in the discussion.
5 Some people thought we should advise/create/design a petition.
6 Others wanted to raise/rate/rise money to help the club.
7 I complained/signed/volunteered to organize a jumble sale.
8 After the meeting there was a protest journey/march/ride through the town centre.
9 I'm sure the politicians will listen to us. Because we'll soon be old enough to choose/elect/vote in elections!

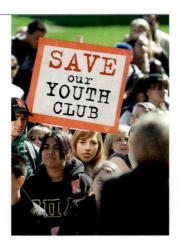

2 READING Which event? (Drawing conclusions)

a) Lily, 17, wants to get involved in helping animals. As a student she has very little money and spends most of it on her dog. Read about two events. Which of them is more suitable for her? When you read the texts, look for reasons why an event is suitable <u>and</u> why it may not be. Then choose an event for Lily.

RSPCA[1] Christmas Tree Decoration[2] Event Are you a dog owner who would like to help animals in need? Here's one way to give money to the RSPCA at Christmas time. Buy a decoration for our Christmas tree. We will put your dog's picture in the decoration and hang it from our tree in December. The decorations aren't cheap, but your money will help to pay for vets to look after homeless sick animals.	**RSPCA Volunteer Information Day** Volunteering with the RSPCA is a great way to meet people who share your love of animals. As a volunteer you'll have the opportunity to care for animals in need and make a real difference. Come to Volunteer Information Day and hear other volunteers talk about their experience of helping animals. Anyone between the ages of 16 and 70 can volunteer.

b) Read the information about two people, Ella and Adam. Then read about three events. Decide which event is most suitable for Ella and which is most suitable for Adam.

Ella works in a supermarket, but would love to be a gardener. Hobbies: action films, hiking

Adam is a biology student. He's very interested in global warming. Hobbies: singing, acting

Film and discussion	**Queen's Park project week**	**Westport Lake clean-up**
Earth 2100 is a documentary that explores how our world might look at the start of the next century if we do not take action immediately on climate change. The film, based on the latest research, also shows ways of creating a different future.	Act now to create a greener and more beautiful public space. *Friends of Green Park* spring project needs volunteers with green fingers to clean up after the long winter. A chance to practise your garden skills and get a few tips from the experts.	On World Environment Day this year we're planning to collect all the rubbish around Westport Lake. Come and help us … and bring your kids too. Remember: 'If children never experience nature, they'll never learn to love and protect it.'

[1] RSPCA *britischer Tierschutzverein*
[2] Christmas tree decoration *Christbaumschmuck*

▶ SF Drawing conclusions (p. 135)

 You could now do tasks 1 and 2 in the Practice test on pp. 59–60.

3 Are you going to work in the holidays? (*going to*-future)

a) Complete the dialogue. Use the going to-*future*.

Ava (1) … (you – work) in the holidays?
Are you going to …

Jon Yes. At least (2) … (I – look for) a job. What about you?

Ava Well, (3) … (Sam and I – work) in Mum's shop.

Jon That sounds really boring.

Ava Yeah, but (4) … (we – not – do) it for the whole holidays.
Just for a few weeks. And after that (5) … (we – spend) a
week with Dad in London.

Jon And (6) … (he – show) you all the sights?

Ava Well, maybe a few sights. But (7) … (he – not – spend) too
much time with us – I hope! We want to do some things
on our own. Anyway, what about you? (8) What kind of job … (you – look) for?

Jon Well, I'd like a job in a park or a garden. Or something similar. But one thing is sure.
(9) … (I – not – work) in a shop or anywhere inside. Not if I can be in the open air.

b) 👥 *Prepare a short dialogue about future plans and act it out.*
▶ GF 5: Talking about the future (p. 157)

4 WORDS Paraphrasing

If you can't think of the English word for something you want to say, you can paraphrase it.
Complete these examples. Match the sentence halves to paraphrase the words in the box.

Abgeordnete(r) • Moderator(in) • Partei • Untertitel • Wirtschaft • Ziel

1 It's an organization	a … producing and selling things.
2 They're words at the bottom of a screen	b … you in parliament.
3 It's a person who represents	c … really want to do.
4 It's somebody who leads	d … a discussion (on radio, TV, etc.)
5 It's something that you	e … that people can vote for in elections.
6 It's our system for	f … that help you to understand a film in a foreign language.

5 EVERYDAY ENGLISH Making suggestions

a) *You have a guest from abroad. You're busy today, so make suggestions about what your guest could*
do. Choose the correct phrase to complete each suggestion: A or B.

	A	B	
1	I suggest	You could	… spend the morning in the technology museum.
2	Why don't	Why not	… you check the opening times on the internet?
3	If I were you,	I suggest	… I'd take the underground into town.
4	Why don't	Why not	… ask at the station how much an all-day ticket costs?
5	If I were you,	I suggest	… that you have lunch in town.
6	You could	I'd recommend	… the Italian restaurant near the market.

b) *Use phrases from a) to make suggestions about what your guest could do after lunch.*

6   WORDS Politics

Find a similar way of expressing the ideas in each of the sentences below.
Replace the underlined words with words/phrases from the box.

> citizen · criticize · discriminates against ·
> elect a new government · illegal ·
> represent · responsibility · the majority

1 In our country, we <u>vote</u> every five years.
2 MPs <u>speak and act for</u> the people who elect them.
3 Every <u>man and woman in this country</u> has the right to say what they think.
4 It's the government's <u>job</u> to create opportunities for young people.
5 This law <u>isn't fair to</u> women.
6 <u>More than half of the people</u> want a change in the law.
7 Discrimination against minorities is <u>against the law</u>.
8 We all have the right to <u>say what we don't like about</u> the system.

7   READING (Working out the meaning of words)

a) *How can you work out the meaning of the green words in the box? Make a copy of the chart and write down the green words under the right headings. Sometimes there is more than one way to work out what a word means.*

I know a similar word in German	I know part of the word	The context makes the meaning clear
opposition	affordable	permitted
...	...	...

b) *Compare your results with a partner.*

> *Opposition is the same in German.*

> *The context helps too. The sentence is about people who criticize the government.*

c) *There are ten words in the article below that you haven't learned in this book. But you can probably understand most of them. Read the text. Say which red words you understood, and why.*

1 Smoking is not *permitted* inside.
2 We need *affordable* facilities for young people without much money.
3 The *opposition* attacked the government in parliament.
4 A *maximum* of four can play the game.
5 The farmer put up *fencing* to keep foxes out.
6 Parliament doesn't *sit* during the summer.
7 The South-East is the country's richest *region*.
8 We all hope for *lasting* peace.
9 It will be a *multi-national* event with *representatives* from 42 countries.
10 He's against everything. He's so *negative*.
11 I promised to be home early, but I didn't arrive back until after *midnight*.
12 *Integration* is important – nobody should feel that they don't belong.

NoWT plans cause angry protests

North West Transport (NoWT) has announced plans for a 10 % increase in bus and train fares. The cost of a monthly ticket will rise from £60 to £66. NoWT spokesperson Jean Simons said: 'It's a moderate increase and we hope it won't cause too much hardship. We're sorry, of course, but rising costs and inflation mean that we have to ask passengers to pay a bit more.' Sanjay Patel, who represents local students, takes a different view. 'This isn't acceptable. We're already paying more than we can afford. If the increase goes through, it will make things extremely difficult for a lot of people. We need lower fares, not an increase. NoWT is ripping us off again.'
There'll be a demonstration at the town hall this weekend. 'We call on everyone who is against the increase to support us.'

► *SF Working out the meaning of words (p. 134)*

1   READING Events

Five teenagers are looking for events that would be suitable for them. Read the teenagers' statements.
Then read the descriptions of the events (A–F) from a youth club notice board.
Decide which event would be best for each person. There are more events than people.

Jill: I live 15 miles from the next town and I'm too young to drive. I can now get home by bus on Saturday nights – thanks to our protests. But the bus is still too expensive. If they don't introduce affordable fares, I'll just have to stay at home and play table tennis with my kid brother.

Ben: I can't imagine living anywhere else. I love the fresh salt air and the little harbours with their colourful boats. Unfortunately lots of day tourists from big cities come here. And many of them make quite a mess with all the litter from their drinks and snacks.

Megan: I have lots of different rights. But I'm still 'too young' to choose the person who represents me in Parliament. Something has to be done to improve this situation.

Ethan: I'm really interested in politics but none of my friends are. And most young people don't show enough interest in what happens across the Channel. We need to be more open to ideas from our partner countries on the Continent.

Sally: For adults it's clear enough what the law allows. And it's the same for young kids. But if you're in between, it's almost impossible to know what is allowed and what isn't.

A Political Friday
This week's debate is about changing the law on the voting age. Fran Lloyd, Mayor of Norton, thinks that young people learn a lot between the ages of 16 and 18 and that 16 is too early to vote. Diana Gee, from Radio Kent, says 16-year-olds already know enough to vote. Expect a lively discussion.

B Pingothon
Help your local table-tennis club! We're organizing a 'Pingothon', a non-stop table-tennis match, in which each player plays for 5 minutes, before it's the next player's turn. We need players, people to sell snacks and drinks – and money, for a new table tennis table.

C Beach clean-up weekend
Once again local clubs are being asked to come to the beach (meet at North Bay) on Saturday or Sunday to help to tidy it up after the summer. Please take part. Wear gloves, bring plastic bags and give a couple of hours of your time for our most popular place.

D Bus trip to Europe's capital
Join us on a trip to the European Parliament in Brussels. We will have space for 50 people. The trip is supported by the EU and will cost only £15. We leave Dover on 7th July at 4 am (sorry!) and get back late the same day (about midnight). Passport needed! More info at www.kentineurope.org.uk

E Teen rules, OK?
Local citizens' advice bureau worker Diane Fry explains what young people can and can't do. Find out about your rights and responsibilities in many areas: voting, working, travelling at reduced fares, drinking, smoking, driving, passports, boyfriends, girfriends, etc., etc. **Sunday 10 am**

F March to Town Hall
Young people over 14 pay full fare on our local buses – a problem if you need the bus to get out at weekends. It's a £10 bus ride to and from the discos and clubs in Canterbury. Half fare would be £5. Join our protest march to the town hall. We want 'Fair fares for teens'! **Saturday, 2 pm**

2 MEDIATION An advertisement

*Du willst im Sommer in Großbritannien arbeiten
und hast die folgende Anzeige online gefunden.
Um deine Eltern von deinem Plan zu überzeugen,
mach dir Notizen auf Deutsch zu den folgenden
Punkten:*

1 *wo du wohnen und arbeiten wirst*
2 *was deine Hauptaufgabe sein wird*
3 *welche Voraussetzungen du unbedingt
  mitbringen solltest*
4 *was du verdienen wirst*
5 *welche Vergünstigungen sonst angeboten
  werden*

Torbay International Youth Camp is looking for …

➤ *Service team volunteers*

Your main job will be to
- organize daytime activities and evening
  entertainment for young people from all over
  the world

You will also be responsible for
- helping in the dining room during meals

Successful candidates must be
- between 17 and 20 years old
- able to communicate with 11 to 15-year-olds
- organized and energetic
- team players

It will be an advantage if you
- have experience of working with young
  people
- can speak at least one foreign language
- have a driving licence

We offer you
- free travel to Torbay (second class only)
- free accommodation (in a multi-national
  village)
- breakfast and two hot meals a day
- £25 pocket money per week
- a chance to meet and speak with people
  from different backgrounds

Interested? Apply online

---

3 MEDIATION Helping a visitor to Germany

*Your Scottish friend Maggie is staying with you and would like to find out about politics in Germany.
You find two interesting events in the newspaper. Maggie is out and you have to leave before she returns.
Leave a message for her. Describe each event briefly in English. Do not translate word for word.*

Mit Cartoons in die Politik einsteigen

Wir werden eine DVD zeigen, die die Programme
der im Deutschen Bundestag vertretenen
politischen Parteien erklärt. Die unterschiedlichen
Bereiche der Politik wie zum Beispiel Außenpolitik,
Innenpolitik, Gesundheit und Wirtschaft werden
mit Comicfiguren und lustigen Zeichnungen
illustriert. Der Film dauert ca. 45 Minuten und hat
englische Untertitel.

Was noch?
Anschließend werden wir diskutieren. Danach
gibt's Livemusik von Poll Position.

Wann und wo?
Freitag, 19.30, Jugendzentrum, Böllstraße 22

Live-Polit-Talk mit Studiogästen

Thema: Wohin, Europa?
Moderation: Tom Meyer
Gäste: EU-Abgeordnete aus Deutschland,
Großbritannien, Spanien und Litauen
Wann: Freitag 18.30–20.00
Wo: Fernsehzentrum Köln

Meyer wird jungen Europa-Abgeordneten Fragen
zur Zukunft Europas stellen. Insbesondere geht es
um die Einbeziehung junger Wählerinnen und
Wähler in politische Planungen.

Die Diskussion wird simultan ins Englische
übersetzt.

*Hi Maggie,
I've found two events you might
be interested in. You could go to
the youth club in Böllstraße,
where they're going to …*

4   READING Notices, short ads and signs

Read each short text. Then decide if the statements below are true or false.

Need a weekend job?
We're looking for a reliable and friendly student to help out with selling snacks in our sandwich bar on Saturdays and/or Sundays. You must be 16 or older and have a clean and tidy appearance. You will earn £8 an hour. For more information, come in and talk to the manager.

You're being watched
There are over 4 million CCTV cameras in Britain. They're watching you in the street, in shops, at railway stations, everywhere. To find out more, watch Panorama next Monday at 8.30 pm on **BBC 1**.

How well can you drive?
The RoSPA[1] Young Driver Assessment will tell you how good a driver you are. The assessment is for drivers aged between 17 and 24, and can be taken from six months after passing the driving test.

BRIDGETON TENNIS CLUB

Rules for Members

1   Tennis shoes must be worn on court.
2   Sports clothes must be worn during play.
3   A maximum of four people are allowed on each court.
4   People watching matches must stand outside the fencing.
5   Nets must be taken down at the end of play.
6   All litter[2] must be taken away.
7   Under-18s are not permitted to buy alcohol at the club bar.

Trip to the centre of power
Newton Youth Forum is organizing a special day trip to London, where our local MP Mike Worth will take us on a two-hour tour of the Houses of Parliament.
Tour starts: *May 5th, 8.45 am*
Departure from: *Newton Station*
Cost: *£5 per person (Forum members pay only £3)*
Return to Newton: *6.30 pm*
More information and booking:
www.newtonyouthforum.org.uk

1   At the tennis club, members can wear whatever they like.
2   The sandwich bar needs a cleaner.
3   If you want the job in the sandwich bar, you should go and see the manager.
4   The Newton Youth Forum trip to London starts at the Houses of Parliament.
5   The BBC TV programme is about CCTV cameras in public places in Britain.
6   RoSPA helps young people to pass their driving test.

7   There are litter bins at the tennis courts.
8   If you go on the trip to London, you will return to Newton the same day.
9   Only good drivers can do the RoSPA Young Driver Assessment.
10   The BBC programme about CCTV cameras is on in the evening.
11   Members of Newton Youth Forum have to pay £5 altogether for the trip to London.
12   You have to wait until you're 18 before you can buy alcohol at the tennis club bar.

---

[1] RoSPA *britische Gesellschaft zur Förderung der Straßensicherheit*   [2] litter *Abfall*

5 READING

Read the text and do the tasks.

Sunderland votes in UKYP election

Over 16,000 young people will be able to vote in the Sunderland region in this year's election to the UK Youth Parliament. Voting at 55 schools will take place over 7 days from 26th February. On 5th March, the names of the four winners will be announced.

UK Youth Parliament is an organization that allows young people between 11 and 18 to have their say. There are no parties, no government or opposition. The 600 Members of Youth Parliament (MYPs) elected across the UK meet to debate and to organize campaigns for change. An MYP can sit in the UK Youth Parliament and in regional youth parliaments.

This year 22 candidates are standing for election in the Sunderland area. The youngest, 11-year-old Will Black from West Windon Primary School, wants free recycling at all schools. 'At the moment, schools have to pay for the collection of all rubbish. We should have free collections for anything that can be recycled. Then schools would have a reason to recycle as much as possible.'

Barbara McKenzie, 16, from St Ambrose School for Girls, believes public transport for students should be cheaper. 'Young people need to be mobile, but they can't afford high fares while they're at school. We should only have to pay half of what adults pay.'

The oldest candidate in this year's election, 17-year-old Jack Smith, says that there aren't enough facilities for young people. 'There isn't a suitable place for music concerts in the area. The places we can use are too small, or they aren't available when we need them.' Jack, from Rosebrook Technology College, said: 'There's so much negative stuff about young people in the media, but many of us are working hard for lasting change.'

The UK Youth Parliament sits at different places each year. This year's main sitting, in July, will be held at the University of Ulster in Northern Ireland, where there will be three days to debate issues and plan campaigns. And during the year, there will probably be another chance to use the chamber of the House of Commons[1] for an afternoon. Last year, for the first time, MPs voted to allow the MYPs to hold a debate there.

1 True, false or not in the text?
   a) The article is about the results of the Youth Parliament elections.
   b) Adults vote in Youth Parliament elections.
   c) Members of Youth Parliament are called MYPs.
   d) Youth Parliament makes laws for under-18s.

2 How many people from Sunderland will be elected to the UK Youth parliament?
   A 4
   B 22
   C 55

3 MYPs can sit
   A only in the UK Youth Parliament.
   B in the national and regional youth parliaments.
   C only in a regional parliament.

4 Complete the sentences.
   a) Will Black wants ... because ...
   b) Barbara McKenzie believes ... because ...
   c) Jack Smith says that ... and that ...

5 'This year the main sitting of Youth Parliament will be in the House of Commons.'
   This statement is true/false because the text says ...

[1] House of Commons *Britisches Unterhaus*

How am I doing?

In the Practice test you did some typical exam (Abschlussprüfung) tasks. Check your answers on pp. 229–230 If you found some tasks difficult, the questions below will help you to find out what you need to practise.

1 How easy or hard was each task?

	easy	OK	quite hard	very hard
Task 1				
Task 2				
Task 3				
Task 4				
Task 5				

Reading

Tasks 1, 4 and 5 were reading tasks. The following questions will help you to think about how you did.

1 What was difficult about the reading tasks in general?

a) Some of the texts were quite long and/or complicated.

b) There were words and phrases that I just couldn't understand.

c) There was a lot of information in the texts. I sometimes couldn't find the exact answers.

d) The tasks weren't like the tasks that we usually do in class.

2 Problems with specific tasks:

Task 1

– I understood most of the texts but it was still hard to find the information that I needed to match people and events.

Task 4

– The mixture of text types (e. g. notices, ads, signs) made it hard to concentrate on the content.

– I wasn't always sure which text contained the information I needed to do the task.

Task 5

– The newspaper article was hard to read.

– The mixture of task types (e. g. true/false/ not in the text, multiple choice, etc.) made it more difficult to find answers.

3 How did you do the tasks?

a) I read each task carefully so that I knew what to look for in the texts.

b) I tried to understand the main ideas of each text first. That helped me to guess words and phrases that I wasn't sure about.

c) I scanned the texts when I was looking for a special piece of information.

e) If there was a task that I wasn't sure about, I left it out and came back to it later.

f) I checked my answers at the end and corrected any mistakes that I found.

▶ *SF Reading course (pp. 134–135)*

Mediation

Tasks 2 and 3 were mediation tasks. The following questions will help you to assess how you did. Ask your teacher for a copy of the assessment sheet and fill it in.

	Assessment sheet	☹	☺	☺				
	Name ...	1	2	3	4	5	Comments
2	a) It was easy for me to take notes on the English text in German.						
	b) In my notes, I concentrated on the most important information and didn't translate word for word.						
	c) I found information on all the important points (a–e).						
3	d) I found it easy to use German texts to write a message in English.						
	e) In my message, I only gave the most important information about the events (when, where, what). I didn't translate word for word.						
	f) I used short and simple sentences.						
	g) If I didn't know an important word in English, I tried to paraphrase it or to use a similar word or phrase.						

▶ *You will find more READING and MEDIATION tasks in the Exam File, pp. 90–97.*

English for jobs

Das Kapitel **English for jobs** bereitet dich auf Situationen in deinem zukünftigen Berufsalltag vor, in denen du Englisch brauchst.

Du verfolgst den beruflichen Werdegang von zwei englischen Jugendlichen von der Bewerbung über den damit verbundenen Schriftverkehr und das Vorstellungsgespräch bis hin zu verschiedenen Situationen am Arbeitsplatz.

Anhand realistischer Situationen wie z. B. dienstliche Telefonate, Kundengespräche oder Präsentationen von Produkten kannst du auf den folgenden Seiten wichtige Wörter und Wendungen für den englischsprachigen Arbeitsalltag auffrischen, ergänzen und anwenden.

EFJ 1 **1**   **Two personal statements** 🎧

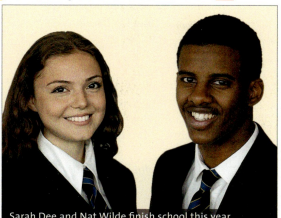

Sarah Dee and Nat Wilde finish school this year.

Which of these plus points do Nat and Sarah say they have? Listen and write them down in a copy of the chart. There is one more point than you need.

- can explain technology
- communicates well
- enjoys travelling
- speaks foreign languages
- has internet skills
- is a team worker
- is likeable
- is musical
- is organized
- is reliable
- likes helping others

Nat	Sarah
enjoys travelling	...

2   **Company websites**

a) *Read some job information that Sarah and Nat have found on the internet.*
Check the chart you made in 1 and decide which company they should apply to.

GHC opportunities

GHC is a private health care service[1] with 97 hospitals in the UK.
We are always looking for nurses who are able to travel around the country and stand in for colleagues who are ill or on holiday. A perfect job for those who like to help others. Send your CV with a letter of motivation[2] to:

WoW ELECTRONICS

Imagine working for a dynamic company with first-class training programmes to support you.
The UK's leading electronics store is taking on new sales assistants. You work well in a team? You like good service and contact with customers? You can explain how a camera or an MP3 player works? You're looking for a career where you can rise to the top?
Then send your CV to:

SAYGO CAREERS

Welcome to Saygo's careers website. With 15,000 employees in the UK and abroad, we're Britain's big player in the holiday industry. We offer opportunities in our UK offices and at our holiday destinations abroad. At Saygo we work to make our customers' dreams come true. If you'd like to join us, why not send in your CV? It could be the best career decision you make.

b) 👥 *Explain your decision to your partner.*

3   **A letter of motivation**

a) *Read about letters of motivation.*
▶ SF *Writing letters (p. 146)*

b) *Choose three key points from the list for a letter of motivation. Decide the best order.*
– information on my family background
– information on my qualifications and skills
– my reason for writing
– information on the history of the company
– thanks for reading the letter
– information on how much I'd like to earn

c) *You want to apply to a company from 2. Complete this letter of motivation.*

> …
> I am writing to you about the career opportunities that you mention on your company website. I would be very interested in working as …/in …
> I am 17 years old and will finish school in …

[1] health care service *Gesundheitsdienst*   [2] letter of motivation *Initiativbewerbung*

EFJ 2   **1**   **Accepting an invitation**

Sarah has been invited to an interview.

a) *Sarah would like to travel to the interview by car. She's also a vegetarian. Read the letter from WOW Electronics. Which of the points below will she need to ask about?*

> place of interview • interview dates • interview times • public transport • car parking facilities • whether there will be a meal • the kind of food the canteen offers

b) *Put the sentences from Sarah's email to Petra Pym in a suitable order.*

It will be interesting to meet other candidates during lunch.	Dear Ms Pym
I would like to travel to Brighton by car.	Yours sincerely Sarah Dee
Can you tell me if your canteen offers vegetarian food?	Please let me know when I should arrive at your office.
Thank you for your letter of 25th May.	Is there a car park near your office?
I would be available for an interview on Wednesday 16th June.	I look forward to meeting you.

c) 👥 *Compare your email with a partner.*

WOW ELECTRONICS

Ms Sarah Dee
12 Hallow Road
Redhill RH1 6DF

Dear Ms Dee

Thank you for your letter of motivation. We would like to invite you to an interview at our office in Brighton in the week 14th–18th June. Please let us know which date you would prefer.

Train and bus services to Brighton are excellent. If you wish, we can help with your travel arrangements.

We plan to interview ten candidates each day, and there will be an opportunity for group discussions during lunch in our canteen.

We look forward to hearing from you, if possible by email to the address below.

Yours sincerely

Petra Pym
pym@wow.co.uk

---

2   **Agreeing on details**

27th May

Dear Ms Dee

Thank you for your email of 26th May. I have noted that you will be available for an interview on Wed. 16th June. Would you prefer an interview at 9.30 am or 2.30 pm? If you choose the afternoon interview, please arrive in time for lunch at 12.15 pm.
I am afraid we do not have car parking spaces for candidates. It would probably be easier to come to Brighton by train or bus. If you decide to do this, we can book your tickets for you.
I am happy to say that our canteen offers vegetarian dishes too.
I look forward to meeting you.

Yours sincerely
Petra Pym

Read Petra Pym's email. Then complete Sarah's answer.

… Ms Pym

Thank you …
… at 2.30 pm and will make sure that I arrive …
I have decided … to Brighton by … I would be very happy if you could … as you offered in your mail.
I am very glad … vegetarian … Many thanks.
I … meeting you and the other candidates.

Yours …

▶ SF Writing letters (p. 146)

EFJ 3 **1** **Giving good answers**

a) How should Nat answer Ms Wood's questions?
Choose A or B.

Ms Wood__ Hello, nice to meet you, Nat.
My name is Polly Wood.

Nat__ (A) Hello Ms Wood. Nice to
meet you. (B) Hi, Polly!

Ms Wood__ Well, Nat. Thank you for your
interest in Saygo. Maybe you can tell
me why you'd like to work for us.

Nat__ (A) Because travelling is really cool.
(B) Well, I really enjoy travelling and
being in other countries.

Nat has been invited to an interview too.
It takes place today …

Ms Wood__ Maybe you can say something about your strengths. What are you good at?

Nat__ (A) Well, I'm really brilliant at languages. And I'm just so organized and reliable.
(B) Well, I speak two foreign languages quite well. And I'm very organized and reliable.

Ms Wood__ If you worked for Saygo abroad, you would have to spend a lot of time looking after
tourists with questions or problems.

Nat__ (A) I hope they won't have too many problems!
(B) Problems are there to be solved. I think I can do that.

Ms Wood__ Of course, there would also be quite a lot of desk work to do.

Nat__ (A) I realize that. I'm very happy to do office work. (B) No worries, Ms Wood!

b) 👥 *Compare your answers with a partner. Say why you chose one answer and not the other.*
Was it because of the content, the kind of language used, or both?

c) 👥 *Read the rest of the interview. Say why Nat's answers aren't very good. Think of better answers.*

Ms Wood__ Are you confident with using
a computer?

Nat__ Sure, I spend lots of time surfing
the internet.

Ms Wood__ OK, imagine everybody wants
something from you at the same
time. What do you do?

Nat__ I tell them to be patient. I'm not
a machine.

Ms Wood__ How soon would you be able to
start if we offered you a position?

Nat__ I don't know.

Ms Wood__ Why should we choose you?

Nat__ Why not?

Ms Wood__ Well, that's it. Thank you for
coming. We'll contact you soon.
Goodbye.

Nat__ See you.

▶ *SF Taking part in a job interview (p. 139)*

2 👥 **Now you: Role play**

Think of a job and the strengths that you need for it.

Partner A
– Start the interview.
– Find out about the candidate's strengths.
– Suggest a problem that might happen.
– Ask if B could start in May.
– Ask if B has any questions.
– Finish the interview.

Partner B
– React to the opening question.
– Say what your strengths are.
– Say how you would solve the problem.
– If you got the job, you could start in June.
– Ask a good question.
– Say goodbye.

EFJ 4   1   Leaving a message[1] 🎧

Sarah has started work at WOW. Right now, she's on the phone …

a) 👥 *Put Sarah's telephone conversation in the right order and write it down.*

Thank you, Tim. Bye.

01705 – 4912214

OK. That's great. Thanks.

Can I leave a message?

Hello, Tim. This is Sarah from WOW Electronics. Can you put me through[3] to Jane Parks, please?

Sure, I'll get a pen … OK, your message?

Yes, hold on[2], please. … I'm sorry, Sarah, but Jane isn't answering her phone.

Yes, of course. Can you give me your last name, Sarah?

CX Computers. Tim speaking.

And your phone number?

Could you ask her to phone me when she has a moment?

Dee. I'll spell it. D double E.

b) 👥 *Listen and check. Then practise the conversation. Use different names and phone numbers.*

2   More telephone phrases 🎧

a) *You will hear six short phone conversations. In which conversation do you hear the English phrases for these German ones?*

A   Am Apparat.

B   Kann ich etwas ausrichten?

C   Sie müssen sich verwählt haben.

D   Bleiben Sie am Apparat.

E   Ich gebe Ihre Nachricht weiter.

F   Ich verbinde.

b) 👥 *Listen again. Write down the phrases from a) in English. Compare with a partner.*

c) 👥 *Practise the phrases in short dialogues, like this:*

> Can you tell Mrs Parks that I'll call back later?

> Of course. I'll give her your message as soon as I see her.

3   👥 Now you: Guided dialogue

Prepare a dialogue and act it out.

Partner A: You get a call from a customer.

Eröffne das Gespräch.

Sage, dass du am Apparat bist. Frage, wie du helfen kannst.

Sage, dass Tim dafür zuständig ist. Biete an, B mit ihm zu verbinden.

Entschuldige dich: Tim antwortet nicht.

Wiederhole die Telefonnummer. Bitte B, ihren/seinen Nachnamen zu buchstabieren.

Partner B: You want to order something.

Stelle dich vor. Sage, mit wem du sprechen möchtest.

Sage, was du bestellen willst.

Sage, dass du am Apparat bleibst.

Frage, ob Tim dich zurückrufen kann. Nenne deine Telefonnummer.

Reagiere.

---

[1] (to) leave a message *eine Nachricht hinterlassen*   [2] (to) hold on *am Apparat bleiben*   [3] (to) put sb. through *jn. durchstellen*

EFJ 5 1 Speaking to a visitor 🎧

Nat is working at Saygo's office in Malaga. Last week he had a meeting there with Karin Lang, from Saygo's German office.

> Thanks for a successful meeting.

> The weather here has been like this for weeks.

> Bye, Karin.

> This is delicious!

> Where would you like to go for lunch?

> How was your trip?

> Was the flight OK?

> What about somewhere with ... food?

> It was nice to meet you.

> Can I call you a taxi?

> This is a nice building.

> Have you heard that joke about ...?

a) Look at the sentences above. When are they used during the meeting? Complete a copy of the chart.

Start of the meeting	Break for a meal	End of the meeting
Was the flight OK?	Where ...	...

b) 👥 Listen and check. Then compare your chart with a partner.

c) How can you react when somebody
– thanks you?
– apologizes to you?
– says something you agree with?
Find phrases in the box for each situation.

> Don't mention it. • Don't worry about it. • No problem. • Not at all.[1] • That's fine with me.[2] • That's OK. • That's true. • You're quite right. • You're welcome.

d) 👥 Listen again and check. Then compare your answers with a partner.

2 👥 Now you: Guided dialogue

Prepare a dialogue and act it out.

Partner A: You work for a German company.

Partner B: You're a guest from abroad.

Partner A	Partner B
Begrüße B. Frage, wie die Reise war.	Beschreibe deine Reise. Entschuldige dich, dass du zu spät kommst. Erkläre den Grund.
Reagiere auf die Entschuldigung.	Sage, dass das Wetter sehr angenehm ist.
Stimme zu. Sage, wie lange es schon gutes Wetter gibt.	Sage etwas Nettes über das Büro von A.
Erkläre, dass das Gebäude ganz neu ist. Sage, wann die Firma eingezogen ist.	Frage, was das für ein Gebäude links ist.
Antworte. Biete B etwas zu trinken an.	Bedanke dich.
Reagiere. Frage, wann B essen möchte.	Frage, ob 12.30 in Ordnung wäre?
Reagiere. Schlage vor, dass ihr mit der Arbeit beginnt.	Stimme zu.

---

[1] Not at all! *Nichts zu danken!*   [2] That's fine with me. *Von mir aus gern.*

EFJ 6   **1**   **Reacting to problems**

a) 👥 *Read the dialogue. What's wrong with the way Sarah speaks to the customer?*

Today Sarah is working in one of WOW's big stores. She has a customer with a problem. Unfortunately, she didn't sleep very well last night …

Sarah	What do you want?
Customer	I bought this mobile last week and it doesn't work very well.
Sarah	'Doesn't work very well.' What does that mean? Listen, mate. Just say exactly what's wrong with it.
Customer	Well, the keys[1] are hard to press and it doesn't take good photos.
Sarah	What do you expect if you buy a cheap phone?
Customer	Maybe you're right. Anyway, I'd like to change it. I don't mind paying more for a better phone.
Sarah	Wait there! I'll ask the manager.
Customer	Thank you. Could I ask you to be quick? I'm a bit late for a doctor's appointment.
Sarah	Well, why didn't you come here earlier? Honestly! Customers!

b) 👥 *Find better phrases for Sarah below. Then act out a politer dialogue.*

Starting a conversation
– Good morning/… How can I help you?
– Can I do anything for you, sir/madam?
Sounding friendly
– I see.
– Of course, sir/madam.
– That's no problem. I'll …
– Could I ask you to …

Reacting to problems
– What seems to be the problem?
– Could you be a bit more specific?
– I'll see what I can do.
– Of course, there are sometimes problems with less expensive models/older models/…
– I'm sorry, but …

2   👥   **Now you: Role play**

Partner B: Go to p. 98.
Partner A: Read the background information on the left. Then follow the instructions on the right. Be as polite and friendly as you can.

You're a sales assistant in an electronics store. The latest model of a popular TV has just arrived. Last week the older model was sold at a reduced price in a sale. Your company policy[2] is not to change goods that were sold in a sale. However, you know that your manager sometimes makes exceptions[3] if this helps to keep good customers. The manager is at a meeting today, so you can't speak to him till tomorrow.

A customer comes up to you.
– Start the conversation.
– Ask about the reason.
– Ask if the customer still has a receipt.
– React. Explain your company policy.
– Explain why you can't give an answer today.
– React.

---

[1] keys *(pl) Tasten*   [2] company policy *Unternehmenspolitik*   [3] exception *Ausnahme*

EFJ 7 **1**   **Deciding what to say** 🎧

Sarah has to present a new mobile to WOW sales assistants. She's discussing her list of points with a colleague. Is it too long?

SAMTO: New mobile
 1 How mobile phone technology works
 2 Earlier SAMTO models and history of product
 3 Country of production
 4 What the new SAMTO can do
 5 How to use the new SAMTO
 6 SAMTO uses 35 per cent less energy.
 7 Super ringtones!
 8 Price
 9 Details about guarantee[1]
10 Dangers of using mobile while driving a car

a) *Look at Sarah's list above. Then listen to Sarah's conversation with her colleague[2].*
Which points does she decide to drop from her list? Why? Do you agree with her?

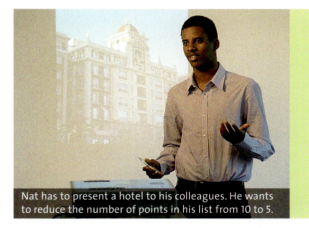

Nat has to present a hotel to his colleagues. He wants to reduce the number of points in his list from 10 to 5.

Beach City Hotel, Malaga
 1 Location: central, but busy street
 2 Extra: tennis club near hotel
 3 Rooms – clean, comfortable
 4 Hotel bar – happy hour until 7 pm
 5 Restaurant – good breakfast. Lunch/evening meal
    also offered
 6 Staff[3]
 7 New air conditioning next year
 8 Shuttle service[4] to airport
 9 Prices
10 Other hotels in Malaga

b) 👥 *Agree on 5 points to drop from Nat's list. Then listen to his presentation.*
Did he drop the same points as you?

2   **Structuring a presentation** 🎧

a) *Make a chart with headings for the different*
parts of a presentation: Introduction, Main part,
End. Match the points on the right to the correct
heading.

b) *Go to p. 140. Find phrases that you can use for*
each point in a). Add them to your chart.

c) *Listen to Nat's presentation again. Which*
phrases from your chart does he use?

• Go into detail about your main points.
• List the points you plan to make.
• Sum up your main ideas and say what your
  conclusion is.
• Thank your audience and offer to answer
  questions.
• Tell your audience what your main topic is.
• Use pictures to illustrate your main points.

3   **Now you: Presentation**
Prepare a short presentation. You could talk about a mobile phone or some
other appliance, a hotel or some other product or service.   ▶ SF Giving a presentation (p. 130)

---

[1] guarantee *Garantie*   [2] colleague *Kollege/Kollegin*   [3] staff *Personal*   [4] shuttle service *Zubringer(bus)*

EFJ 8   **1   Giving the figures** 🎧

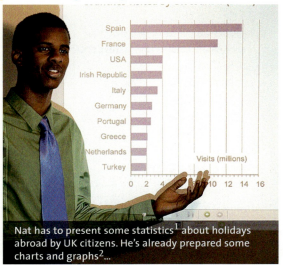

Nat has to present some statistics[1] about holidays abroad by UK citizens. He's already prepared some charts and graphs[2]...

> **Remember**
>
> When you talk about statistics you usually ...
>
> | describe | The chart here shows ...
> | explain | As you can see, there are ...
> | evaluate |[3] It's very clear that ...
>
> Sometimes you'll also want to ...
>
> | draw conclusions | This means ...

▶ SF Talking about charts (p. 131)

a) *Look at the two charts below and add missing figures to the text of Nat's presentation. What else could Nat say in his evaluation[4] and conclusion? Write down some ideas. Then listen and compare.*

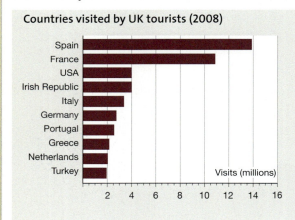

The chart here shows which countries people from the UK visited in 2008.
As you can see, there were just under 14 million visits to Spain and about 11 million visits to ... 4 million people went to ... Over 2 million travelled to Germany, ... And almost exactly 2 million went to ...
It's very clear that Spain and France are the most popular destinations[5] ...
This means we'll need to offer quite a lot of holidays in Spain and France ...

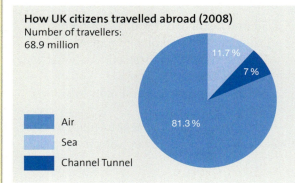

In the second chart we can see how ... 81 per cent of travellers went by ... Almost 12 per cent ... And 7 per cent used the ... The most popular kind of transport is ... This means ...

Source statistics: Office for National Statistics

b) 👥 *Look again at what Nat says in a). Write down the words he uses with numbers, e.g. **just under 14 million**. With a partner try and think of similar words and add them to your list.*

---

[1] statistics *(pl)* Statistiken   [2] graph *(Kurven-Diagramm)*   [3] (to) evaluate *bewerten*   [4] evaluation *Bewertung*   [5] destination *Reiseziel*

2   Talking about trends[1] 🎧

Look at the graphs and add missing figures to the text of Nat's presentation.
What could Nat say in his conclusion? Write down some ideas. Then listen and compare.

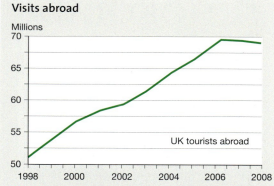

Visits abroad

The first graph shows how many people travelled abroad from the UK between 1998 and 2008.
As you can see, the numbers rose from about 35 million in ... to ... million in 2007, but fell to just under ... in 2008.

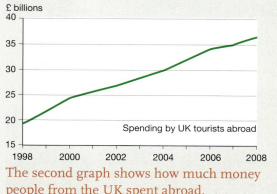

The second graph shows how much money people from the UK spent abroad.
Spending rose from about £35 billion[2] in 2007 to £38 billion in ... .
So it's clear that spending rose although the number of travellers fell.
It means that ...

Source statistics: Office for National Statistics

3   Now you: Presentation

👥 *Prepare a presentation of the statistics in these graphs and charts. Join up with another pair. Give your presentations. Discuss how they could be improved.*

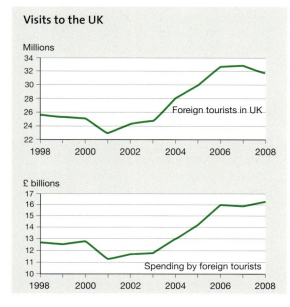

Source statistics: Office for National Statistics

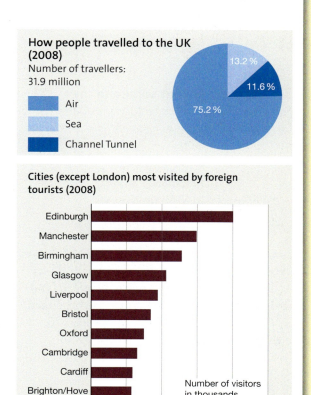

[1] trend *Trend*   [2] billion *Milliarde*

EFJ 9 **1** **Explaining a brochure**

Sarah's on holiday. She's visiting you! You know she loves chocolate, so you've decided to visit a famous chocolate factory with her ...

a) Read the brochure on the right. Make notes in English. Your notes should include four things that visitors to Schmidt-Schokolade can do, the opening hours and the cost of admission.

b) 👥 *Partner A: Use your notes from a) to talk about the factory tour.*
Partner B: Listen to your partner. Ask at least one question about the factory tour.

2 **Explaining what someone says** 🎧
You're with Sarah in the factory. She doesn't understand everything the guide says. Listen and answer her questions.

What was that about?

He's going to tell us ...

3 **Passing on questions**
Sarah wants you to ask the guide some questions. What do you say to him in German?
1 Is Schmidt chocolate available in England?
2 How many bars of chocolate are produced every day?
3 What percentage of production is for Christmas?
4 What's the most popular flavour?
5 Who invents the new flavours?
6 Does the firm make organic chocolate too?

▶ *SF Mediation (p. 149)*

SCHMIDT-SCHOKOLADE

Erleben Sie die Welt der Schokolade in unserer spannenden Ausstellung!

Öffnungszeiten: Mo–Fr 8.00 bis 18.30 Uhr, Sa 9.00 bis 18.00 Uhr.

Der Eintritt ist frei.

Woher kommt eigentlich der Kakao? Wie sieht ein Kakaobaum überhaupt aus? Wie gelangt die frische Joghurt-Füllung in die Tafel? Die unterhaltsame Ausstellung beantwortet viele Fragen rund um Schokolade und ist dabei eine Entdeckungsreise mit allen Sinnen: Sehend, hörend, riechend, schmeckend und fühlend erfahren neugierige Schokoladen-Liebhaber alles rund um die „Speise der Götter", den Kakao. Interaktiv und Schritt für Schritt wird der gesamte Prozess von der Kakaobohne bis hin zur fertigen Schokolade erklärt. Ein spannendes Quiz bietet Kindern und auch Erwachsenen viel Spaß – so lässt sich spielerisch die Welt der Schokolade entdecken!

Genießen Sie die ganze Vielfalt der Schokolade in unserem Schoko-Geschäft neben der Ausstellung. Probieren Sie unsere leckeren Schokoladen, bevor Sie sie kaufen, entdecken Sie neue Sorten und versorgen Sie sich mit leckerem Proviant für unterwegs. Außerdem gibt es in unserem Fabrikverkauf immer wieder günstige Angebote und ein umfangreiches, wechselndes Sortiment. Lassen Sie sich überraschen!

Nach Voranmeldung bieten wir auch Rundgänge durch unsere Fabrik an.

Inhalt

Im **Exam File** findest du ein breites Angebot an Prüfungsaufgaben. Damit kannst du
– das Trainingsangebot der *Getting ready for a test*-Seiten abrunden
– dich gezielt in verschiedenen Kompetenzen und wichtigen Aufgabenformaten testen
– dich selbstständig oder gemeinsam in der Klasse auf die Prüfung vorbereiten
– den „Ernstfall" der Abschlussprüfung üben.

Natürlich können hier nicht alle denkbaren Aufgabentypen geübt werden, aber du kannst davon ausgehen, dass dir die verschiedenen Übungen wichtige Hilfen für eine gelungene Prüfungsvorbereitung sind.

Weitere Hilfe bei der Prüfungsvorbereitung bieten die Tipps auf Seite 76 sowie der Prüfungswegweiser auf den Seiten 77–79.

▶ Wenn du eine *Listening*-Aufgabe zu Hause machen willst, geh zu www.englishg.de. Wähle die B-Ausgabe und gibt dort den Web-Code ein, der bei deiner Listening-Aufgabe steht.
▶ Die Lösungen zu allen **Exam File**-Aufgaben findest du unter www.englishg.de/examfile.

Kompetenz	Aufgaben	Seite	
SPEAKING	1 Talking about a photo 2 Talking about a cartoon 3 Discussing photos 4 Choosing presents for an English family 5 Deciding on a day trip to a theme park 6 Talking about holiday jobs 7 Role plays: Solving problems abroad	80	
WRITING	1 Guided writing: A questionnaire 2 Picture story: A parcel for Darkwood 3 The story behind the picture 4 A summer job 5 Text-based writing: A teen mag article 6 Text-based writing: A short story	83	
LISTENING	1 Report: Belinda's Britain 2 Announcements 3 Dialogue: Shopping 4 Dialogue: Practising for an interview 5 Personal statements: My future 6 Radio advertisement	87	
READING	1 A list of tips: What to do when you're down 2 A short biography: Jérôme Boateng, footballer 3 A short story: Money isn't everything 4 A holiday blog: One island, two countries	90	
MEDIATION	1 Signs (E>G) 2 A poster (E>G) 3 What's on TV this evening? (G>E) 4 A school brochure (E>G) 5 A flyer (E>G) 6 Passing on questions and answers (G>E>G)	95	

Dein Weg zum Prüfungserfolg

Eine Prüfung ist eine Gelegenheit zu zeigen, was du gelernt hast. Du brauchst keine Angst davor zu haben, denn alles, was in der Prüfung drankommt, kennst du schon aus dem Unterricht.

Während des Schuljahres

1 Bereite dich langfristig vor, nicht erst am Abend vor der Prüfung.
2 Überlege, welche Bereiche oder Themen du wiederholen solltest. Besprich das auch mit deinem Lehrer/deiner Lehrerin. Mach dir einen Plan, wie du deine Vorbereitung am besten einteilst.
3 Denk daran: Dein *Skills File* enthält viele nützliche Tipps und Hilfen.
4 Mach dich mit verschiedenen Prüfungsformaten vertraut. Hierzu gibt es im **Prüfungswegweiser** auf den Seiten 77 bis 79 hilfreiche Hinweise.

> Im **Prüfungswegweiser** findest du
> – eine Beschreibung typischer Prüfungsformate
> – Verweise auf Beispiele für die verschiedenen Formate
> – eine Übersicht typischer Arbeitsanweisungen
> – Tipps und Verweise auf das *Skills File*.

Am Abend vor der Prüfung

1 Entspanne dich. Du kannst lesen, dich in die Badewanne legen, Musik hören, fernsehen, ...
2 Geh zur gewohnten Zeit ins Bett.

Am Tag der Prüfung

1 Stehe rechtzeitig auf, damit du nicht hetzen musst.
2 Nimm dir Zeit für ein entspanntes Frühstück.
3 Lies etwas „zum Aufwärmen", aber schau nicht mehr in dein Schülerbuch.
4 Denk daran, du hast dich gut vorbereitet. Es gibt keinen Grund, nervös zu sein.

Während der Prüfung

1 Konzentriere dich auf den Test, lass dich nicht ablenken.
2 Lies dir die Aufgaben genau durch.

> Bevor du die Aufgaben bearbeitest, überlege genau, was du tun sollst. Lies die Aufgabenstellung langsam und gründlich und von Anfang bis Ende durch. Sollst du z. B. ganze Sätze schreiben oder dir nur Notizen machen? Du kannst besonders wichtige Dinge in der Aufgabenstellung unterstreichen und die Aufgabe, wenn nötig, für dich in einzelne Schritte unterteilen.

3 Löse zuerst die Aufgaben, die dir einfach scheinen. Wende dich erst danach den schwereren Aufgaben zu.
4 Aufgaben, die du bearbeitet hast, hakst du ab. So siehst du, wie du vorankommst, und behältst den Überblick.
5 Schau ab und zu auf die Uhr. Du solltest dir für den Schluss noch Zeit einplanen, um deine Antworten noch einmal durchzulesen und zu korrigieren.

Good luck!

VIEWING *Mr Bean – The Exam*
Watch the video. What tips would you give Mr Bean?

Prüfungswegweiser

Typische Aufgaben	Typische Arbeitsanweisungen
▶ *Beispiele im* Exam File	▶ Skills File

SPEAKING

Talking about photos, cartoons, etc. ▶ *S. 80, Aufgaben 1, 2, 3* Über Fotos, Cartoons usw. sprechen (allein oder in Partnerarbeit)	• *Talk about the photo/cartoon (to a partner).* • *Look at the photo/cartoon and describe what's happening /...* • *What is the message of the photo/cartoon?* • *Show your photo/cartoon to your partner and describe ...* • *Discuss ...* ▶ *SF Describing pictures (pp. 125–126)* ▶ *SF Describing cartoons (p. 126)*
Simulated situations　▶ *S. 81, Aufgaben 4, 5* Simulierte Situationen im Dialog bewältigen (z. B. Vorhaben, Auswahl, ... diskutieren oder erklären)	• *Choose ... and make a list. Then talk to your partner. Explain your choice. Finally, try to agree on ...* • *Look at the list/chart and think about/talk about ... Decide together on ...* ▶ *SF Having a discussion (p. 140)*
Guided dialogue　▶ *S. 82, Aufgabe 6* Einen gelenkten Dialog führen	• *Prepare a dialogue. Act it out.* • *Act out the conversation in English.* ▶ *SF Having a conversation (p. 139)*
Role play　▶ *S. 82, Aufgabe 7* Rollenspiel zu einer Situation, die auf einer Rollenkarte beschrieben wird	• *Look at the role card and act out your conversation.* • *Look at the picture/role card. Discuss the situation with your partner.* ▶ *SF Having a conversation (p. 139)*

In der mündlichen Prüfung kann es sein, dass zwei oder mehr Kandidat(inn)en gleichzeitig getestet werden. In diesem Fall können folgende Redemittel nützlich sein:

Einen Einstieg finden

– Would you like to begin?
– I'll start if you like.
– You first, please.
– Is it my turn or yours?

An den Partner/die Partnerin übergeben

– That's your special field.
– Maybe you can answer that question.
– Have you got any views on this?

Deinem Partner/Deiner Partnerin zustimmen/widersprechen

– I agree. / I think so too.
– You're quite right.
– I don't agree. / I don't think so.
– I don't think you're right there.

Wenn du deinen Partner nicht verstehst

– Could you say that again, please?
– Could you repeat that, please?
– I'm not sure if I understand what you mean.
– Can you explain what you mean, please?

Typische Aufgaben ▶ *Beispiele im* Exam File	**Typische Arbeitsanweisungen** Tipps ▶ **Skills File**

WRITING

Questionnaire/Form ▶ *S. 83, Aufgabe 1* Fragebogen/Formulare ausfüllen	• *Fill in the questionnaire/form.* • *Complete the survey.* • *Answer the questions …* Tipp Oft musst du keine ganzen Sätze schreiben. Achte genau auf die Arbeitsanweisung.
Story ▶ *S. 83, Aufgabe 2; S. 84, Aufgabe 3* Geschichten zu Bild- oder Textimpulsen schreiben	• *Look at the pictures. Then write a story of about … words.* • *Tell the story behind the picture. Use your imagination.* ▶ *SF Writing better sentences (p. 143)*
Email/Letter/Postcard/Letter of application ▶ *S. 84, Aufgabe 4; S. 85, Aufgabe 5c* E-Mails, Briefe, Bewerbungsschreiben usw. verfassen	• *Write an email/a letter/a postcard/a letter of application to …* • *Answer (Jack's) email/letter.* • *Write for more information.* ▶ *SF Writing letters (p. 146)*
Working with texts ▶ *S. 85, Aufgabe 5; S. 86, Aufgabe 6* Schreibaufgaben, die sich auf einen längeren Sach- oder Literaturtext beziehen.	• *First read the text. Then do the tasks below.* Tipp Hier helfen auch die Lesetechniken, die du gelernt hast. ▶ *SF READING COURSE (pp. 134–135)* ▶ *SF WRITING COURSE (pp. 143–144)*
Summary ▶ *S. 85, Aufgabe 5a; S. 86, Aufgabe 6* Texte (Literatur, Sachtext, …) oder einzelne Fakten zu einem Thema zusammenfassen	• *Sum up the story/article/main points …* • *Give a short summary of …* • *Write a summary of (100) words.* • *Say what happened (in the story/…).* ▶ *SF Summarizing texts (p. 142)*
Description/Creative writing ▶ *S. 85, Aufgabe 5b; S. 86, Aufgabe 6b:4* Beschreibung, Charakterisierung, kreatives Schreiben	• *What does the text say about …?* • *Describe …* • *Continue the story.* • *What happens next/when …?* Tipp Wenn du nach Ideen suchst, helfen dir die Brainstorming-Techniken, die du gelernt hast. ▶ *SF Brainstorming (p. 141)*
Article/Report ▶ *S. 85, Aufgabe 5d* Artikel/Bericht für ein Print- oder Onlinemagazin verfassen	• *Write an article for your school mag/…* • *Write a report on/about …* ▶ *SF Writing a report (p. 144)*
Giving your opinion ▶ *S. 86, Aufgaben 6b:2, 6b:3* Eigene Meinung zu einem Thema formulieren	• *What do you think about …? Give reasons for your opinion.* • *Write/Give your opinion.* • *What would you do or say if …?* • *Should/Would …?* ▶ *SF From outline to written discussion (p. 148)*

Typische Aufgaben	Typische Arbeitsanweisungen	Tipps
▶ *Beispiele im* **Exam File**		▶ **Skills File**

LISTENING

True/False ▶ *S. 87, Aufgabe 1* Entscheiden, ob Aussagen zum Hörtext richtig oder falsch sind	• *Decide if the statements are true or false (right or wrong).* • *Tick the correct answer.*	1 Du wirst **verschiedene Textsorten** (Dialoge, Bekanntmachungen …) und **verschiedene Akzente** hören.
Multiple choice ▶ *S. 87, Aufgabe 2* Aus mehreren Antworten die richtige auswählen	• *Choose/Write down the correct answer for each task.* • *Tick the right statement.*	2 Manchmal sollst du zeigen, dass du Details verstanden hast, z. B. einen Preis, Abfahrtszeiten o. Ä. Bei anderen Aufgaben geht es um die **Kernaussage**, z. B. ob
Missing information ▶ *S. 88, Aufgaben 3, 4; S. 89, Aufgabe 6* Lücken in Sätzen/Tabellen ergänzen	• *Complete the missing information.* • *Fill in the missing information.*	jemand mit seinen Eltern klar kommt oder sich optimistisch oder pessimistisch gibt.
Matching ▶ *S. 89, Aufgabe 5* Zuordnungsaufgaben	• *Choose the right statement.* • *Match the sentence parts.*	▶ *SF Listening (p. 132)*

READING

Matching ▶ *S. 90, Aufgabe 1b* Einen Text einem Bild oder einem anderen Text zuordnen	• *Match the tips to the photos.* • *Which statement/… goes with which picture/description/…*	1 In der Prüfung kann es **verschiedene Textsorten** geben: Listen, Poster, Blogs, Sachtexte, Kurzgeschichten …
Completing a chart ▶ *S. 91, Aufgabe 2b* Textinhalte tabellarisch wiedergeben	• *Complete the chart/table/grid/…* • *Fill in the chart/timeline/…*	2 Manchmal geht es um die **Hauptaussage** des Textes, manchmal um **Details**, und manchmal sollst du **Schluss-**
True/False ▶ *S. 93, Aufgabe 3b* Entscheiden, ob Aussagen zum Text richtig oder falsch sind	• *Are these statements true or false?* • *Tick the right answers and correct the wrong statements.*	**folgerungen** ziehen.
Multiple choice ▶ *S. 93, Aufgabe 3c; S. 94, Aufgabe 4b* Die richtige Antworten auswählen	• *Decide which answer is correct.* • *Tick the right/correct/best answer.* • *Mark the correct statement.*	3 Bei der Bewältigung unterschiedlicher Aufgaben helfen dir die verschiedenen **Lesetechniken**, die du gelernt hast.
Finish sentences ▶ *S. 93, Aufgaben 3d* Sätze über den Text vervollständigen	• *Complete/Finish these sentences (using information from the text).*	▶ *SF READING COURSE (pp. 134–135)*
Questions on the text ▶ *S. 93, Aufgabe 3e; S. 94, Aufgabe 4c* Fragen zum Textinhalt beantworten	• *Answer these questions.* • *Answer the questions in complete sentences.*	

MEDIATION

English > German ▶ *S. 95, Aufgaben 1, 2; S. 96, Aufgabe 4, S. 97, Aufgabe 5* Sprachmittlung Englisch >Deutsch	*Typische Arbeitsanweisungen* • *beschreiben die Situation (**Du bist mit deiner Familie in Urlaub in England** o. Ä.).* • *nennen häufig die Punkte, die du in der Zielsprache wiedergeben sollst.*	1 Hier kommen **mehrere Sprachkompetenzen** zum Einsatz – z. B. liest du einen Text, um dann Fakten mündlich oder schriftlich weiterzugeben.
German > English ▶ *S. 96, Aufgabe 3* Sprachmittlung Deutsch >Englisch		2 Nennt die Arbeitsanweisung nicht die Punkte, die du vermitteln sollst, gib nur die **Kerninformationen** weiter.
German > English > German ▶ *S. 97, Aufgabe 6* Sprachmittlung zwischen 2 Personen		▶ *SF Mediation (p. 149)*

SPEAKING

1 Talking about a photo

Talk about the photo. The questions below can help you.
– Why is the girl standing there?
– Where do you think she wants to go?
– What could she have in her bag and cases?
– If you could travel somewhere now, where would you go? What would you take with you?

2 Talking about a cartoon

Talk about the cartoon. The questions below can help you.
– What's happening.
– Why is the boss unhappy?
– What does the cartoon tell us about modern life?
– Do you agree with the message of this cartoon? Give reasons.

> build a house • communicate •
> communication • hammer • nail •
> send a message on twitter

3 Discussing photos

Work with a partner. Partner B: Go to p. 101.

a) Partner A: Show Partner B your photo and describe what you can see in it. Then Partner B will talk about his/her photo.
Discuss the different things that dogs can do for people. Say how you feel about dogs and why.

b) Partner A: Show Partner B your photo and describe what you can see in it. Then Partner B will talk about his/her photo.
Discuss different ways that people can spend their holidays. Say what kind of holiday you like best and why.

4   Choosing presents for an English family

You and your partner are going to stay with the Smith family in London for two weeks and you want to choose five typical German presents to take with you. You need presents for Mr and Mrs Smith and for each of their three children, Daniel (16), Laura (13) and Tim (7). Choose five of the things below and make a list. Then talk to your partner. Explain your choice. Finally, try to agree on one list.   *Our choice: 1. _____, 2.*

5   Deciding on a day trip to a theme park

You and your friend are in Ontario, Canada. You want to go on a day trip together to visit a Canadian theme park. Here is a programme with all the trips available today.

a) Look at the list and think about these questions:
– Which trip sounds really interesting to you? Why?
– Is there a trip you wouldn't like to go on? Why not?

b) Work with a partner. Talk about the different trips and theme parks. Decide together on the best day trip.

Trip	Theme park	What does the theme park offer?	What is included?	Price / person
1	Marineland (Niagara Falls)	Lots of sea animals. Exciting water shows with dolphins and sharks. Also many rides and roller coasters.	Bus ride, all entrance fees.	$89.00
2	Storyland (near Ottawa)	Fairy-tale trail. Mini-golf course. Small water park. Several playgrounds. Paddle boats. Daily shows.	Bus ride, entrance fee, lunch in café.	$39.95
3	African Lion Safari (near Hamilton)	More than 1,000 animals from all over the world in a wildlife park. 'Jungle Playground'.	Bus ride, entrance fee. Guided bus tour through park plus choice of guided boat tour or elephant ride in the park.	$65.99
4	Canada's Wonderland (near Toronto)	Over 200 attractions. 15 sensational roller coasters! Big water park. Live shows.	Bus ride, entrance fee, packed lunch.	$55.00

6   Talking about holiday jobs

Two friends, Joe and Lucy, meet in the street. They're talking about holiday jobs.
Prepare a dialogue with your partner. Act it out.

Partner A (Joe)

Begrüße Lucy und frage sie, wie es ihr geht.

Frage Lucy, was für einen Job sie macht.

Frage, ob das Zeitungsaustragen ein guter Ferienjob ist.

Antworte, dass du in einer Fabrik arbeitest.

Antworte, dass in der Fabrik Maschinen hergestellt werden, du aber nur am Computer sitzt.

Antworte ja, aber es fällt dir schwer, immer so früh aufzustehen.

Partner B (Lucy)

Grüße zurück und sage, dass es dir gut geht, und dass du gerade einen Ferienjob angefangen hast.

Erzähle, dass du Zeitungen austrägst.

Antworte, dass es bei gutem Wetter richtig Spaß macht, und frage Joe, ob er einen Ferienjob hat.

Frage, um was für eine Fabrik es sich handelt.

Frage, ob Joe diese Arbeit gefällt.

Sage, du wettest, Joe steht nicht so früh auf wie du.

7   Role plays: Solving problems abroad

Partner B: Go to p. 101.

a) *Partner A: Look at the role card and act out the conversation with your partner.*

You're in an internet café in a town abroad. You need a cheap hotel. You find one on the internet, but you aren't sure how far away it is or what kind of area it is in. You speak to the person at the next PC.
– Ask if he/she lives in this town.
– Give the name of the hotel you've found. Ask if your partner knows it.
– Give the address of the hotel. Ask how far it is from the café.
– Ask what kind of area it is in.
– Ask if your partner could suggest something else.
– React positively to this information. Ask for directions.
– React.

b) *Partner A: Look at the role card and act out the conversation with your partner.*

Your holiday in Spain is over. All European airports have been closed for a week for safety reasons. You can't fly back home. You are at a travel agent's. You want to find an alternative to flying.

– Explain why you can't fly.
– Say where you want to go and ask if you can buy a train ticket.
– You have to be home sooner. Ask about buses to Germany.
– Ask about your arrival time.
– Ask about the price.
– React and say if you want to buy the ticket.

WRITING

1 Guided writing: A questionnaire

A class from a school in the UK wants information about life in Germany. Answer the questions below.*
You must fill in each item. You may use your imagination. You needn't write complete sentences.

Hi from St. Mary's School! We would like your help with our European project. We're sorry we don't know much German, so we hope you can understand English. **What is life like in Germany?** Please fill in the questionnaire and return it to your teacher.	Country:		Town/City:	Age: ....
	Questions:			**Answers:**
	1. What do you have for breakfast?			
	2. What time do you have to be at school?			
	3. How long is a typical school day?			
	4. What do you have for lunch?			
	5. What after-school activities do you do?			
	6. How much homework do you get and when do you do it?			
	7. What do you have for your evening meal?			
	8. What do you do in the evening on school days?			
	9. Do you have to wear a school uniform?			
	10. Would you like to visit the UK? Why (not)?			

* Write in your exercise book or ask your teacher for a copy of the form.

2 Picture story: A Parcel for Darkwood

Look at the pictures. Then write a story (about 100 words). You can use the key words in your sentences. Use your imagination to explain what happened after Joe pressed the bell. What made him run away?

A Joe Lee – Whizz Parcel Service

B parcel for Dr Bones, The Old House, Darkwood

C long drive – big, old house – tall trees

D big door – bell

E hear noise – frightened

F end of day – back at Whizz – explain what happened

3   The story behind the picture

*Tell the story behind the picture.
Use your imagination. The
questions below can help you:*
- Who is the man?
- Who or what is he looking
  at?
- How does he feel?
- What is his life like?
- What will he do next?

4   A summer job

a) Read the job advertisement.

*b) You're interested in the job. Write an email to
ask for more information. Use the ideas below.
Before you write, decide the best order for the
different points:*
- where the school is
- how you can get there
- exact dates
- why you want to be in the soap
- where you can sleep
- three relevant facts about yourself
- how much you'll earn

*c) Imagine you got a part in the TV soap.
What happened on the first day of filming?
Write a report.*

> ### TV Europe: Summer jobs for students
>
> We are filming an episode for a new
> European TV soap. This summer we are
> filming in a German school while the
> students are on holiday. We are looking
> for reliable young people (14–19) with a
> good level of English. Would you like to
> be one of the students in the film (non-
> speaking role)?
>
> Write an email today to:
> j.gubbins@tv-europe.de

5   Text-based writing: A teen mag article

First read the text. Then do the tasks below.

———— SURVIVAL TRIP ————

Last summer four teachers and a national park ranger took a group of 20 students from Riverside High School in Launceston, the second largest city on the island of Tasmania, Australia, to Mt Cameron National Park.

They were away from 'civilization' (houses, shops, restaurants, roads, cinemas, etc.) for three days. The trip was to teach the students to look after themselves in a difficult situation. Each student was only allowed to take one bag with them for their sleeping bag, clothes and washing gear – but they had to make the bags themselves! Joseph Shrimpton, 17, told us he had made his bag from an old potato sack. The most difficult part was the strap[1], which he made by putting pieces of material together. It wasn't a very good bag and he was worried that the strap would break. Later, in the middle of the bush, the strap broke … Walking with the bag wasn't so easy after that!

On the first part of their journey from Launceston, the students went by normal coach.[2] However, on the second part, they travelled blindfold[3] in special minibuses for the bush, so that they couldn't see where they were going. When they were far enough into the national park, the buses stopped, the blindfolds were taken off, and the students were on their own!

They had to find out where they were and then, using their map-reading skills and finding the answers to questions the teachers had given them, they had to hike to where the park ranger had left basic equipment so that they could make 'tents' for the night. They hiked for three days, 20 kilometres per day, with two nights in the bush. They also had to discover where food had been hidden. There was food powder[4] (not very nice!) and a few cans of chilli con carne, which were for the student who had answered the most questions correctly during the hike each day. He or she was allowed to put the chilli con carne on the camp fire and eat it out of the can. Each of the others had to take turns at heating up their food powder with some water in the empty chilli con carne can, because they had no cooking things or plates with them. One evening the park ranger brought some insects which he cooked on the camp fire. Some students were brave (or hungry!) enough to eat them.

After three long days in the bush the buses were waiting to take the students back to Launceston. The teens were tired and dirty but most of them, at least, were very happy. They had survived! Carla McBeath said, 'Although it was hard, I learned to look after myself. But the insects were really awful!' ■

a) *Sum up the article. Say what happened before and during the trip.*

b) *What does the text say about food? Describe what the students ate and how they felt about it.*

c) *Choose task 1 or 2. Write about 120 words altogether.*
1 Write a letter to a friend about a hike you did.
2 Tasmania National Parks are looking for young people to help with survival camps in the summer. Write a letter of application to Phil Wilson, GPO Box 1751, HOBART, TAS 7001.

d) *Write an article for your school mag. Write about 120 words altogether. Choose topic 1 or 2.*
1 My most unusual holiday   2 My best class trip

---

[1] strap *Tragegurt*   [2] coach *Reisebus*   [3] blindfold *mit verbundenen Augen, mit Augenbinde*   [4] food powder *Lebensmittelpulver*

6   Text-based writing: A short story

a) *First read the text.*

Back home
Jody Miller from Chicago sat on the train, looking out of the window at the fine old trees whose leaves were just beginning to change
5 colour as fall approached. She was getting nearer by the minute to high school and the last year there before college. Her year in Germany was over. She was back home, in the Midwest. The college football season was
10 starting – Jody wondered if her cheerleader's costume would still fit her after all that German food – and it would soon be time for the baseball *World Series*. And then there was football's *Super Bowl* in the winter. But right
15 now she couldn't stop thinking about her time as an exchange student for a year at a *Realschule* in Freiburg, a lovely, warm, buzzing town in the south-west of Germany, full of students, sun, restaurants and cafés. As her
20 train approached the station and she realized it was time to get off, she thought about the wonderful trips she had made from Freiburg, up into the Black Forest for picnics, hiking and, in the long winter, cross-country skiing.
25   She got off the train and walked the last few minutes to her high school. She couldn't see any of her friends. She felt lonely. Where were they all? 'Come on,' she said to herself. 'The place isn't that bad. And you couldn't have
30 stayed in Germany. Well, maybe for one more year. But this is your home. This is where you'll get a job one day.'
    She couldn't stop thinking about Benny, a student at her school in Freiburg. He had
35 helped her with homework, explained all those difficult German words to her and been her

partner at the end-of-year school dance. She couldn't forget him, his blue eyes, his long blond hair, the way he spoke English, the way he looked at her. He would have been a reason   40
for staying in Germany forever. But what had he said to her at that dance, holding her in his arms? 'I'm sorry Jody. I already have a girlfriend. She's in California as an exchange student at the moment.' He already had   45
a girlfriend! Why did she think he was only interested in her? Why hadn't she asked? Why hadn't he told her earlier? Why? And what if she had stayed, would he have changed his mind? What if …? Stop it!   50
    She opened the door of the classroom and twenty happy faces were looking at her – her best friends Mel and Davina, Rosie, Helen and, in the corner, Dave. He had changed a lot in the time she had been away. Wow! There   55
was a banner across the classroom. 'Welcome back, Jody!' it said. Everybody was clapping. And then the teacher came in. She came over to Jody and hugged her. Then the clapping stopped and they all turned to the flag in the   60
corner of the room, as the well-known tune of the National Anthem sounded once more from the loudspeaker of this classroom in downtown Chicago. Jody smiled. She was back home, and it felt good!   65

b) *Now do these tasks.*
1 Sum up what we learn about Jody from the text. Give at least five facts. (Write about 50 words.)
2 Should Jody have stayed another year in Germany? Give reasons for your opinion based on the information in the text.
3 What do you think about exchange visits? Support your opinion with examples from the text. (Write about 120 words.)
4 Continue the story. Imagine Jody goes back to Freiburg in her next holiday. What happens? (Write about 150 words.)

LISTENING

1 Report: Belinda's Britain

Web-Code:
EG21-B6-087-1

a) First read the statements (1–8).

1 Belinda reports from the UK for viewers in the United States.
2 The topic of last week's report was about transport.
3 The British use public transport more than cars.
4 Travelling by train is more expensive than travelling by bus.
5 A lot of travelling within Britain is by air.
6 People in Britain often go short distances on foot.
7 Belinda prefers driving in London to driving in San Francisco.
8 If you park your car where it is not allowed, your car will be taken away.

b) Now listen to the report and decide if the statements (1–8) are true or false. Write your answers down.

c) Listen again and check your answers.

2 Announcements

Web-Code:
EG21-B6-087-2

You are going to hear four announcements.

a) First read the tasks (1–10).

Announcement 1

1 The non-stop train to York will leave today from platform
   A 3.   B 4.   C 5.
2 The non-stop train to York will be
   A 5 minutes late.
   B 10 minutes late.
   C 30 minutes late.
3 The train that stops in Peterborough will leave at
   A 5.53.   B 6.03.   C 6.30.

Announcement 2

4 You can buy a pair of Janglers jeans for
   A £10.   B £49.   C £59.
5 The café is on the
   A first floor.
   B second floor.
   C fifth floor.

Announcement 3

6 There are refreshment stations
   A every 2 kilometres.
   B every 5 kilometres.
   C every 42 kilometres.
7 The disco starts at
   A 5 pm.   B 8 pm.
   C 10 pm.
8 The marathon finishes at
   A Milson's Point.
   B Harbour Bridge.
   C Sydney Opera House.

Announcement 4

9 At 10.30 BBC1 will show
   A Jim in Germany.
   B Red Roses.
   C EastEnders.
10 You can watch the news on BBC1 at
   A 9.30 pm.   B 10 pm.   C 10.30 pm.

b) Now listen to the announcements. Write down the correct letter (a, b or c) for each task (1–10) while you are listening. Choose only one letter for each task.

c) Listen to the announcements again and check your answers.

3   Dialogue: Shopping

Web-Code:
EG21-B6-088-3

a) *First read the statements (1–10).*

1   Diana ordered ... tops from an online shop.
2   Only ... of the tops have arrived.
3   Diana has paid a total of ... for the tops.
4   The online shop's service number is ...
5   Prices at *Just Jeans* are reduced by ...
6   *HK Fashion* is ... *Just Jeans.*
7   Pete asks Diana to go ... with him.
8   Diana says the shops will be closed in ...
9   Pete wants to look at the ... in the VG Comp store.
10   Diana suggests that Pete tries the VG Comp ...

b) *Now listen to the dialogue. Write down the missing words to complete the statements (1–10) while you are listening.*

c) *Listen to the dialogue again and check your answers*

4   Dialogue: Practising for an interview

Web-Code:
EG21-B6-088-4

Dayamayee has a job interview at a call centre in Delhi tomorrow. In the dialogue she is practising with her friend Harita, who plays the interviewer.

Name	Dayamayee
Personal qualities	good at ... enjoys ...
Computer skills	can use ...
Attitude to modern technology	has got ...
Level of English	always got good ... speaks ... listens ...
Knowledge of Britain	has visited her ... reads ...
Work experience	part-time: ... weekend job: ...
Weaknesses	forgets ...

a) *Listen to the dialogue and complete the candidate profile for Dayamayee.*

b) *Listen to the dialogue again. Add any missing information.*

5   Personal statements: My future

a) First read statements A–F below.

b) Next listen to each speaker. Choose the right statement for each speaker.
While you listen, write the correct letter (A–F) next to the speaker's name.*
Be careful. There is one more statement than you need.

c) Listen again and check.

Statements

A I don't want my parents to plan my future for me.
B I don't know yet which career is right for me.
C I want to get advice from my parents before I decide what to do.
D My parents don't really understand how much I need a break.
E I plan to combine travelling with getting work experience.
F I don't see great job opportunities in my country.

Speaker	Statement
1 Pia	
2 Mikael	
3 Frans	
4 Marietta	
5 Sally	

* Copy the chart into your exercise book or ask your teacher for a copy.

6   Radio advertisement

a) Listen to the advertisement.
Complete the missing information.
1 The boy in the ad phones his ... because ...
2 BBB offers ... for ...
3 To book a room ...
4 In the second message, the boy ...
5 The ad wants to reach ... and promises ...

b) Listen again and check your answers.

1   A list of tips: What to do when you're down

a) *First read the text.*

Ten top tips when you're down

TIP 1   Talk to a friend. Good friends will want to help. So why not call one of your mates and tell them about your problem?

TIP 2   Talk to your parents. Listen to their advice. Try to understand them. Remember: they were young once too and had similar problems.

TIP 3   Sometimes it can help if you express your feelings in a creative way. Write a story or poem, draw or paint something or maybe write some music.

TIP 4   Physical activity can make you feel happier. Go swimming or running, or do some other sport. Be active.

TIP 5   Light makes us feel better. On a grey winter's day, try using a sun lamp. But nothing can beat real sunlight. So go out in the sunshine if you can.

TIP 6   The beauty of nature can make us feel more relaxed. Go for a walk outdoors and breathe in the fresh air.

TIP 7   Be kind to your body. Fill a bath and lie back in the hot, soapy water. Maybe try a massage or take up yoga.

TIP 8   A great therapy if you're feeling down is simply to laugh or smile. You could try watching a comedy on TV or reading a funny book.

TIP 9   Helping others can make you feel better about yourself. Why not volunteer to work with children or to help people who can't look after themselves?

TIP 10   Do something nice for yourself. Buy something that you really want – maybe the latest computer game or some trendy clothes.

b) *Now match each tip (1–10) to one of the pictures below (A–L).*
There are two more pictures than you need.

c) *Read the tips again. Choose three tips that you find helpful. Give reasons.*

READING

2   A short biography: Jérôme Boateng, footballer

a) *Read the text first. Then do the tasks below.*

Jérôme Boateng (born 3 September 1988 in
Berlin; height: 1.92 metres) is a German
footballer who plays for the English Premier
League team, Manchester City. Boateng is
5   a defender.

Boateng has both German and Ghanaian
nationality. His mother is German, his father
Ghanaian. His two half-brothers, Kevin-Prince
and George, are also footballers. Kevin-Prince
10   plays for Ghana's national team. Football is
a bit of a tradition in the Boateng family.
Jérôme's uncle also played for Ghana.

Boateng is a powerfully built sportsman who
can play any full-back position. His career
15   began in 1994 with the youth team of Tennis
Borussia Berlin. Then in July 2002, when he
was 13 years old, he joined Hertha BSC Berlin.
In January 2007, at only 18, he became
a Hertha first team member. He played his
20   first match against Hanover 96 in the 2006–07
Bundesliga season.

Boateng was offered a five-year contract with
Hertha, but decided against staying on with
the Berlin team. Instead, he moved to
25   Hamburg in August 2007 for a fee of € 1.1
million. There, he continued to develop his
game and became one of the key players in
Hamburg's defence. Other clubs were soon
interested in him, including Wolfsburg,
30   Arsenal and Manchester City. In June 2010, it
was announced that Boateng was moving to
Manchester – this time for a fee of over £ 10
million. The move was a big step in his career
and he felt very excited about it. 'I'm looking
35   forward to the challenge,' he said. Boateng's
contract with City runs for five years.

Boateng also has an impressive international
career. He played for the German U-16, U-17
and U-19 teams several times. He is also
40   a former German U-21 international player
and won the 2009 UEFA European Under-21
Football Championship with the German
team.

In October
2009, Boateng
played his first   45
match with the
(adult) German
national team
against Russia, but was sent off in the second   50
half after receiving two yellow cards[1]. This was
not typical of Boateng. People who have seen
him play describe him as calm and disciplined.
As he had always played with a minimum of
fouls, he himself was annoyed by his   55
behaviour on the field. But German national
coach, Joachim Löw, was sure that Boateng
would learn the right lessons from his
mistake.

In the summer of 2010, Boateng was   60
a member of the German team in the FIFA
World Cup in South Africa. In Germany's
match against Ghana, he played against his
own half-brother. This was the first time that
brothers played against each other in the   65
World Cup. Germany beat Ghana 1 – 0.

b) *Copy and complete the chart with the
information from the text.*

Name	Jérôme ...
Place/Date of birth Nationality	
Family (one detail about each member)	
Clubs (dates)	Tennis Borussia (1994 – ...)
International experience	

c) *What does the text tell us about Boateng's
character?*

d) *What was special about the 2010 World Cup?*

---

[1] two yellow cards   *(die) gelb-rote Karte*

3   A short story: Money isn't everything

a) First read the text.

Tim and Lisa had been going out together for six weeks now and it was time for Lisa to meet Tim's parents. She had been invited for tea at Tim's house on Sunday.

5   Lisa was very nervous. She had met Tim at the local youth club, but he lived on the other side of town. He only went to the same youth club because his grandma lived near there and he liked to visit her once a week between
10 leaving school and going to the youth club.

Tim's parents had a lot of money, not like Lisa's parents. Her mum was a single parent and worked at a supermarket. Her dad had disappeared, to New Zealand her mum
15 thought, when Lisa was only two. But Lisa wasn't unhappy. She had great fun with her mum and her younger brother. Money wasn't everything. And her home? Well, Lisa really didn't mind living in a caravan. Although,
20 when Tim asked her where she lived, she just said the name of the village outside the town where the youth club was.

'OK, this is our house,' said Tim, as they walked up to the front door.
25 'House?' said Lisa. 'It's a palace! I knew your parents were rich, but I never expected a huge place like this. Bye, Tim. I'm going home.' 'Lisa, please,' said Tim. 'Don't be so nervous. They're only my parents.'
30 He squeezed her hand. Lisa smiled. 'OK, I'll stay. But I'm not looking forward to this.'

They walked into the big, square hall. 'I'll introduce you to my parents,' Tim said.
35 'Mum! Dad!' he called. But nobody came. 'That's funny,' said Tim. 'I told Mum we were coming, so why aren't they here?' 'Are you sure they want to meet me?' Lisa asked.
40 Tim took Lisa's hand again. 'Of course they want to meet you! They can't wait. Come on. Let's go into the living room. I'm sure they'll be here in a few moments.'

Lisa followed Tim across the hall into the
45 living room. She looked around and saw beautiful furniture, expensive lamps, a plasma TV and a Danish stereo system. Modern paintings hung on the walls.

Lisa wanted to be polite. 'It's a very nice room,' she said to Tim.   50
'Do you really like it?' asked Tim.
Lisa didn't. 'It doesn't feel as if people live here,' she thought. 'It's so cold and impersonal.'

They waited for a few minutes, but there was   55
still no sign of Tim's parents.
'Maybe they're in the garden,' Tim said. 'I'll go and look.'
He went outside while Lisa stayed in the living room. After some minutes she heard the   60
sound of voices, loud and angry.
'Somebody's having an argument,' she thought. 'Maybe Tim and his parents are arguing about me.'
She walked out to the hall to be able to listen   65
better.

Standing in the hall, Lisa could hear that the voices were coming from upstairs. There were two people, a man and a woman.
'I don't understand you,' the man said. 'We've   70
got everything money can buy, but still you aren't happy.'
Then the woman: 'Money isn't everything. You're my husband, but you're never at home. We have a beautiful house, but you spend all   75
your time at the office. What kind of life is this?'

Lisa shivered. 'Tim's parents can't be very happy,' she thought.

80 'What do you mean?' the man asked. 'I'm at
home today. I'm not at the office. It's Sunday.'
    'Yes,' the woman answered. 'Sunday. A day
for the family, but we can't enjoy our house
together. No, we have to go downstairs and talk
85 to that girl Tim met at that awful youth club.'
    'Why don't you want to meet our son's
girlfriend?' the man asked. 'I don't see
a problem.'

'You don't see a problem?' the woman
shouted. 'That girl comes from the worst part   90
of town. Why your mother still lives there
I don't know. But I do know that I'd like
someone better for my son. ... No! Don't say
anything! Let's just go downstairs and be nice
to her, if we have to.'   95
    At that moment Tim came into the hall.
'What's the matter, Lisa?' he asked.

b) *Decide if these statements (1–5) are true, false or not in the text. Write your answers down.*
1   Lisa has often been invited to Tim's house.
2   Lisa and Tim have different family backgrounds.
3   Lisa's father works at a supermarket in New Zealand.
4   Lisa thinks you can be happy without a lot of money.
5   When Lisa met Tim, she told him that she lived in a caravan.

c) *Read the tasks (1–3) and decide which answer (A – D) is correct. Choose only one letter for each task.*
1   When Lisa sees Tim's house, she
    A is surprised at how small it is.
    B turns around and goes home.
    C feels more relaxed about meeting his parents.
    D feels more nervous about meeting his parents.
2   When Tim and Lisa enter the house,
    A Tim is surprised that his parents aren't there.
    B Tim's parents are there to welcome them.
    C only Tim's mum is there to welcome them.
    D Tim's parents are waiting in the living room.
3   When Lisa sees the living room in Tim's house, she
    A immediately likes it.
    B makes a polite comment about it.
    C tells Tim what she thinks about it.
    D wonders why nobody is there.

d) *Complete these sentences (1–4).*
1   Tim went into the garden because ...
2   Lisa went into the hall because ...
3   Lisa thinks Tim's parents can't be happy because ...
4   Tim's mother doesn't want to meet Lisa because ...

e) *Answer these questions (1–3). Use examples from the text to support your answers.*
1   Why do you think Lisa feels uncomfortable about meeting Tim's parents?
2   How does Tim try to make Lisa feel more relaxed?
3   Describe the relationship between Tim's parents.

f) *How do you think the story ends? Write 60–80 words.*

4   A holiday blog: One island, two countries

a) *First read the text.*

Hi. This is Wendy. Tim and I are just back from Ireland. Here are a few notes.

■ **Thursday 25th August:** Drove to Stranraer in Scotland and took the ferry. Flying is cheaper, but we wanted to use our car for the trip. Less than two hours at sea (ferry was really fast) and we were in Belfast, still in the UK. Northern Ireland is the part of Ireland that is still British.

■ **Friday 26th August:** The conflict between Catholics and Protestants in Northern Ireland killed so many people. But now – thankfully – it's over, and tourists go there to shop and enjoy the night life. Other attractions in Belfast (the capital): the shipyards where the *Titanic* was built (great!) and the wall paintings done by Protestants and Catholics in their areas of the city.

■ **Sunday 28th August:** Crossed the border into the Irish Republic today. We didn't need passports and, like in the UK, you drive on the left. But distances are in kilometres, not miles. And we had to change money – they use euros, not pounds. Dublin, the Republic's capital, is full of history – and full of people, with so many shops, cafés and pubs. Once, the Republic was quite poor. But joining the EU was good for Ireland. The economy grew and the Republic became the 'Celtic Tiger'. OK, so Ireland has had some economic problems recently. But I'm still writing on a laptop that was 'Made in Ireland' and there's a one in four chance that your computer was made there too.

■ **Tuesday 30th August:** But enough about industry. South-west of Dublin there's an absolute 'must' for tourists – the Rock of Cashel, a unique collection of medieval architecture and Celtic art. We loved walking around the historical buildings.

■ **Wednesday 31st August**: Another highlight was the Ring of Kerry, a 170 km narrow road around the Iveragh Peninsula. As we drove along, we stopped again and again to look at the mountains and the amazing views out to sea. At times we wished there were fewer other tourists. Later, there was a big Irish welcome at a great little bed and breakfast. We were sorry we couldn't stay longer.

b) *Now read the tasks (1–3) and decide which answer is correct:* A *,* B *or* C *.*

1 Wendy and Tim went to Northern Ireland by ferry because they
   A wanted to save time.
   B wanted to save money.
   C wanted to take their car with them.
2 Wendy says tourists in Northern Ireland
   A can get killed in the religious conflict.
   B can enjoy the shopping and nightlife.
   C can do wall painting in Belfast.
3 In the Irish Republic Wendy noticed that
   A cars drove on the right.
   B distances were in miles.
   C distances were in kilometres.

c) *Answer these questions (1–4).*
1 What does Wendy say about the Irish economy? (at least two things)
2 Which sight does Wendy describe as a 'must' for tourists? Why?
3 What is the Ring of Kerry? What did Wendy and Tim do there?
4 Name at least four things that Wendy liked about her holiday in Ireland.

MEDIATION

1   Signs

Du machst mit deiner Familie Urlaub in England. Deine Eltern verstehen nicht viel Englisch und wollen wissen, was diese Schilder bedeuten. Erkläre es ihnen kurz auf Deutsch.

CUSTOMER PARKING ONLY
All other cars will be removed at the owner's expense.

Swindon Post Office

Please take a number and wait for the next available counter.

Please give up this seat if a disabled person needs it.

CCTV cameras are in operation in this store. We ALWAYS prosecute thieves.

2   A poster

Du bist mit deiner Familie im Urlaub in Nova Scotia in Kanada. Dein kleiner Bruder fragt, was die auf dem Poster beschriebene Tour bietet. Erkläre ihm kurz auf Deutsch:
– was man auf der Tour alles sehen kann.
– wie man sich mit dem Skipper verständigen kann.
– wie lange die Tour dauert.
– wie es mit der Verpflegung an Bord aussieht.

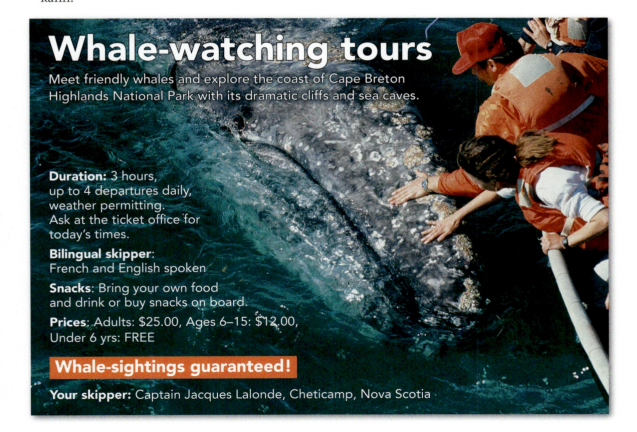

Whale-watching tours

Meet friendly whales and explore the coast of Cape Breton Highlands National Park with its dramatic cliffs and sea caves.

Duration: 3 hours, up to 4 departures daily, weather permitting. Ask at the ticket office for today's times.

Bilingual skipper: French and English spoken

Snacks: Bring your own food and drink or buy snacks on board.

Prices: Adults: $25.00, Ages 6–15: $12.00, Under 6 yrs: FREE

Whale-sightings guaranteed!

Your skipper: Captain Jacques Lalonde, Cheticamp, Nova Scotia

3 What's on TV this evening?

Your American guest has asked you to suggest some German TV programmes that she could watch this evening. Read this page from a TV magazine. Write her a message in English with the main information (one or two sentences for each programme). Do not translate word for word.

FERNSEHEN Tagestipps ab 17 Uhr	
19:40 RTL SOAP	**20:15** ARD KRIMI
Gute Zeiten schlechte Zeiten: **Will Pia keine lockere Beziehung?** Pia tut zwar furchtbar cool, wenn es um John geht, doch als dieser mit einem anderen Mädchen flirtet, wird sie eifersüchtig. John entgeht ihr Gefühlschaos nicht. Er stellt sie zur Rede.	**Tatort: „Tempelräuber"** Im heutigen Fall aus Münster muss Kommissar Thiel den Mord an einem Priester aufklären. Sein Partner Professor Boerne befindet sich diesmal in der ungewohnten Rolle des Zeugen.
20:15 Pro 7 SHOW	**21:15** RTL DOKUSOAP
Schlag den Raab Wer tritt heute im Wettkampf gegen Moderator Stefan Raab an? Den Kandidaten erwarten Spiele zu den Bereichen Sport, Quiz, Geschicklichkeit und noch vielen anderen. Dem Sieger winkt ein Gewinn von 1 Million Euro.	**Bauer sucht Frau** Bauer Heinrich gibt die Hoffnung nicht auf und sucht noch immer nach einer liebevollen Partnerin. Heute startet er einen neuen Versuch.

4 A school brochure

You would like to spend a school year in England. You have found this information on the internet.

✳ ✳ ✳ THE ROYAL BLUE COATS SCHOOL ✳ ✳ ✳

The Royal Blue Coats School, founded by Charles II in 1666, is a day school for boys and girls aged 12 to 18. It is situated in Hexham in the northeast of England in a quiet corner of the old town.

We offer 26 subjects and have strong music, art and drama departments. Students can also choose between many different extra-curricular activities and clubs.

✳ Sports: There are the traditional sports – rugby, cricket and hockey – and many others choices such as basketball, tennis and swimming (in our own swimming pool).

✳ Fees: £3,502 per term. (The school year, starting in September, has 3 terms.) Fees cover tuition[1] and books.

✳ Scholarships[2]: There are free places for a limited number of students. For information, contact the school secretary.

✳ School lunches: The charge is £167 per term in Years 7 to 9 and £180 per term in Years 10 to 13. Breakfast and snacks during mid-morning break are also available.

[1] tuition *Unterricht* [2] scholarship *Stipendium*

Berichte deinen Eltern in Stichworten auf Deutsch:
a was es für eine Schule ist.
b wo sich die Schule befindet.
c was zum regulären Unterricht und zu weiteren Angeboten gesagt wird.
d welche Sportarten angeboten werden.
e wie hoch das Schulgeld ist.
f wie die Kosten reduziert werden können.
g was über Verpflegung gesagt wird.

5 A flyer

Du hast mit deiner Familie eine Reise nach Arizona gewonnen. Deine Eltern verstehen diesen Flyer nicht. Erkläre auf Deutsch, was man bei einem Ausflug in den Canyon beachten sollte. Nenne drei Punkte.

Beautiful, but …

Every year thousands of visitors go to the Grand Canyon and look down to the Colorado River one mile below. The view is absolutely fantastic, and some people decide to hike down to the river. This can be quite difficult, as the paths into the canyon are steep – and then, when they get to the bottom, they have to climb back up the trail again. That's even tougher! It can take a very long time, especially in the summer when it can get really hot (40 degrees Celsius). The National Parks Service does NOT recommend doing the hike there and back in one day. Instead you can get a backcountry permit and spend the night on

a campsite. Or there are a limited number of beds available at the Phantom Ranch in the canyon.

The Grand Canyon is a beautiful place, but it can be dangerous too. Plan your trip well and be careful. Many people have gone down into the canyon and not come out again – at least, not alive …

6 Passing on questions and answers

During your stay in Arizona, you and your family talk to Susan Diefenbacker, a ranger at the Grand Canyon National Park. As your parents' English is not very good, you must help them.

Mutter Frag mal bitte, ob man heute in den Canyon hinabwandern kann.

You …

Susan I wouldn't recommend it in this heat. And it's really too late in the day now.

You …

Vater Schade. Ich würde gerne zum Fluss hinunter. Frag, wie es morgen wäre.

You …

Susan If you leave very early in the morning, it should be OK.

You …

Vater Toll! Gibt es sonst etwas, das wir beachten müssen?

You …

Susan Make sure you have suitable footwear – a good pair of strong shoes. It's a long and difficult walk.

You …

Mutter Und wie ist es, wenn wir auf dem Campingplatz im Canyon übernachten wollen? Muss man im Voraus reservieren?

You …

Susan Yes, but there are always a few backcountry permits available on the same day. Just come to the Visitors Center as soon as we open.

You …

Mutter Frag, wann das Center öffnet.

You …

Susan At 8 o'clock in the morning.

You …

Vater Gibt es etwas Besonderes, was wir auf die Wanderung mitnehmen sollten?

You …

Susan Lots of water! Four liters per person per day. Food and snacks – and plenty of time! Good luck to you all! Be safe and enjoy your visit!

You …

Mutter Bedanke dich bitte und sage ihr, dass wir hoffen, dass wir die Genehmigungen bekommen.

You …

Unit 1 Part **B**

P 4 👥 MEDIATION What's this film about? ▸ *p. 15*

You visit Partner A with your friend from England. You want to watch a film together.

a) *Read about the film* Die fetten Jahre sind vorbei.

Die Freunde Jan (Daniel Brühl) und Peter (Stipe Erceg) sind Mitte 20, leben zusammen in Berlin und finden, dass die Welt sehr ungerecht ist. Und wie protestieren sie dagegen? Sie brechen nachts in die Villen reicher Leute ein. Dort stehlen sie nichts, sondern stellen die Möbel auf den Kopf, hängen die Bilder um und hinterlassen Botschaften wie „Die fetten Jahre sind vorbei".

Die Probleme beginnen, als Jan und Peters Freundin Jule (Julia Jentsch) in die Villa eines wohlhabenden Managers (Burghart Klaußner) einbrechen. Jan und Jule, zwischen denen sich eine Liebesbeziehung entwickelt, werden auf frischer Tat ertappt. In ihrer Panik kidnappen sie den Manager. Gemeinsam mit Peter, der nichts von der Beziehung zwischen Jan und Jule weiß, halten sie ihre Geisel auf einer kleinen Berghütte gefangen – und aus Spaß wird krimineller Ernst.

b) *Partner A will talk about a different film. Listen carefully. Then explain in English what your film is about.*

c) *Your English friend can't decide which film to watch. You and Partner A have to choose. Listen to Partner A's opinion. Then say which film you think is better and why. Agree on a film.*

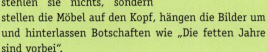

English for jobs

2 👥 Now you: Role play ▸ *p. 70*

Partner B: Read the background information on the left. Then follow the instructions on the right. Be as polite and friendly as you can.

Last week you bought a new TV at a reduced price in a sale. When you set up the TV at home, however, you realized that the screen was much too big for your living room. You decide to go back to the store and ask if you can change your new TV for a smaller one. You know that some stores don't change sale goods. However, you're a good customer there and you don't mind paying more if a smaller TV is more expensive.	– Your partner will start the conversation. – Say you would like to change your TV. – Give the reason. – Say yes. Explain about the sale. – Ask if A can make an exception[1]. Give a reason. – Ask when you can expect an answer. – Thank A and say when you'll return.

[1] exception *Ausnahme*

Unit 2 Part **B**

7 👥 You can make a difference ▶ *p. 36*

a) *Partner B: You and your partner have different tips under each heading in* Go Green. *Read your tips and make notes. Listen to your partner's tips. Then use your notes to tell him/her what you've read.*

Together, think of at least one more tip for each heading and write it down.

> My text says low-energy light bulbs save lots of electricity.

> Here it says newer fridges use much less energy.

GO Green!

Climate change is a problem for the whole world.
But don't just sit around and wait for governments to act.
Here are some simple things you can do to help to stop global warming:

Heat less water

Heating water uses more power in houses than anything else. So when you make tea or coffee, fill the kettle only as much as you need to.

Think trees

Every day forests are cut down to make new paper. But we need trees to reduce CO_2 in the atmosphere. Think about the paper you use. Is your printer paper 100% recycled?

Use low-energy products

If your parents have an old fridge, suggest they get a new one. New models use much less energy. They'll reduce your family power bills – and your carbon footprint.

Eat for the environment

Producing meat uses much more energy than growing grain, fruit or vegetables. Eating less meat helps to save energy. If you eat meat, choose chicken. Producing beef or lamb releases much more CO_2.

Don't waste energy

If you aren't using your computer, TV or stereo, turn them off completely. They all use energy which leads to more CO_2 in the atmosphere.

Reduce rubbish

Recycle paper, plastic and glass. Buy products without too much packaging. Rubbish that cannot be recycled is burned or taken to landfills and that costs energy.

Unit 1 Part **A**

4 👥 Role play ▶ *p. 9*

Partner B:

Listen to your partner's problem and try and give him/her some advice.
Then tell your partner about your problem:

You're worried about a friend. She has been missing school a lot and getting bad marks and she's not interested in hanging out with her friends any more. You think you saw her taking drugs at a party last Saturday. You think she's unhappy. You want to help her, but you don't know what to do.

Unit 3   Part A

P 4   👥👥👥   **SPEAKING Role play: A discussion about video cameras at school**   ▶ *p. 51*

Role cards

Moderator

You can use these phrases to …

▶ *start the discussion*

– Hello and thanks for coming.
– Each group has a special chair for the speaker. If anyone in the group wants to speak, swap places with the person sitting there.
– Our topic is … So, who would like to start?

▶ *ask questions*

– What's your opinion?
– Do you think/agree that …?
– What do you mean?
– Can you explain …?
– How? / Why?

▶ *end the discussion*

– I'll have to stop the discussion there.
– Thank you all for taking part.

Student 1   For   video cameras

– You would feel safer.
– Your cousin's school uses them and there is less bullying there now.
– You needn't worry about the cameras if you aren't doing anything wrong.
– Some people say the cameras shouldn't be in the toilets, but that's where the troublemakers hang out.

Parent   For   video cameras

– Kids who behave badly will be caught.
– The school will need less money for repairs, so there will be more money for other things (school trips, …).
– Teachers will need less time for controlling troublemakers, so they'll have more time for teaching and students will learn more.
– The school will be a nicer, cleaner place.
– …

Student 2   Against   video cameras

– Your friend's school has got video cameras. She says they make school feel like prison. Even if there are no microphones, you don't feel you can have a private conversation.
– You wouldn't feel comfortable with a camera watching everything you do.
– It would be better to have real people around the school to stop the troublemakers.
– Bullying will be harder to control because it will take place outside school.
– …

Teacher   Against   video cameras

– It's your job to make sure that students are well-behaved in class. You don't need a camera for that.
– You don't want to be watched all day.
– The money could be used for other things – computers, books, …
– If cameras are watching, students and teachers may be afraid to speak freely.
– …

Head teacher   For   video cameras

– You've seen a report about a school in London. The head teacher there says that the school is cleaner and safer because of video cameras. Students' marks are also better.
– Recent problems at school: 14 computers have been stolen, the toilets have been damaged and students have been bullied.
– There are students who smoke, spray graffiti and drop rubbish.
– It's expensive to buy new computers, clean graffiti and repair school buildings.
– …

Exam File

3 🏃 Discussing photos ▶ *p. 80*

a) *Partner B: Listen to Partner A talking about his/her photo. Then show Partner A your photo and describe what you can see in it.*
Discuss the different things that dogs can do for people. Say how you feel about dogs and why.

b) *Partner B: Listen to Partner A talking about his/her photo. Then show Partner A your photo and describe what you can see in it.*
Discuss different ways that people can spend their holidays. Say what kind of holiday you like best and why.

Exam File

7 Role plays: Solving problems abroad ▶ *p. 82*

a) *Partner B: Look at the role card and act out the conversation with your partner.*

You're in an internet café in your town. The person at the PC next to you asks you some questions.
– Say how long you've lived in the town.
– You don't know the hotel your partner asks about. Ask the name of the street.
– Say how far it is.
– Say that you don't like the area and explain why.
– Say that you can recommend a good, cheap hostel nearby. Describe what it's like.
– Offer to show Partner A the way to the hostel.

b) *Partner B: Look at the role card and act out the conversation with your partner.*

You work at a travel agent's in Spain.
All European airports have been closed for a week for safety reasons. You have a lot of customers looking for an alternative way home. Many of them are very stressed. Your next customer comes to your desk and describes his/her situation.
– You know all about the situation. Describe the reactions of some of your customers.
– All trains are fully booked out for several days. Say the earliest date your customer could travel.
– You can offer a bus seat for tomorrow. Give the departure time.
– Journeys to German cities take between 25 and 30 hours. Say when the bus will arrive.
– Say a ticket costs € 190.
– React.

QUIZ

How much do you care?

To work out your score, add up the points for each answer.

1: A = 2   B = 3   C = 1
2: A = 1   B = 3   C = 2
3: A = 2   B = 1   C = 3
4: A = 1   B = 2   C = 3
5: A = 2   B = 3   C = 1
6: A = 2   B = 1   C = 3
7: A = 3   B = 2   C = 1

17–21 points

Wow! No one cares more than you, do they? A fair world, human rights, peace –
all those things are really important to you. If you think something is unfair, you
speak out and you work hard to change things.
That's impressive! You have your own opinions and you want everyone to agree
with you. Hmm, just a minute! We're not saying you're bossy, but ... Our advice
to you: It's great that you care so much, but try not to be too direct – remember
that it's important to listen to what other people think. If you want to change
someone's opinion, it won't help if you shout: 'How stupid. You can't possibly
believe that!' You might be more successful if you say in a calm voice: 'That's an
interesting argument. I see what you mean, but ...' Try it!

12–16 points

You care a lot and you try to do as much as you can to make the world a better
place. Like most people, you know that you probably could do more. But
sometimes you think: 'The problems in the world are just too big and
I am too small. I can't change the world.'
Our advice to you: Remember the words of the American writer, Margaret Mead:
'A small group of thoughtful people can change the world. In fact it's the only
thing that ever has.' If you don't like something, it is important to speak out.
If you don't, no one will hear your opinions. You can make a difference!

7–11 points

You probably think you already know what your result says. You've heard it a
million times before: Young people are lazy ... they only think about themselves
... they're not interested ... they just don't care. But the truth is that you're just a
normal teenager!
You care about lots of things: sport, fashion, friends, family, music, going out,
having fun. Of course you want the world to be a better place, but you think no
one listens to your generation. Our advice to you: Remember it's your world too!
It's important to have your say when things happen that you don't like. Next time
you feel strongly about something, speak out and try to do something about it.
If you do, you will probably find life is more interesting than you thought.

Das Text File enthält zusätzliche Texte, z. B. Sachtexte, eine Kurzgeschichte, ein Kurzdrama, Liedtexte und Gedichte, in denen die Themen der Units wieder aufgegriffen werden.

Nicht alle in diesen Texten verwendeten Wörter und Wendungen sind dir schon begegnet – in manchen Texten sind dir vielleicht nur wenige Wörter unbekannt, andere enthalten mehr neuen Wortschatz. Aber du wirst die Texte sicherlich im Großen und Ganzen verstehen, auch ohne jedes einzelne Wort zu kennen.

Am Fuß der Seiten sind einige Wörter und Wendungen erklärt, die für das Verständnis wichtig sind, aber versuche zunächst, ohne diese Fußnoten zurechtzukommen. (Erinnere dich an die Worterschließungstechniken, die du im Lauf der letzten Jahre kennengelernt hast.

▶ *SF Working out the meaning of words (p. 134)*

TF 1   Making friends

start   profile   friends

ABOUT ME   Jay

Basic Info

Sex: Male[1]
Age: 16
Looking for: Friends, networking
Current[2] city: Wellington, New Zealand
Hometown: London, UK
School/Job: School/Yes
Status: In a relationship

Likes and Interests

Interests: Evolutionary biology, space travel[3], football, cricket
Music: Classical, jazz
Books: Everything except novels or poetry
Movies: SF[4], documentaries on science
Television: Football, SF series

1 2 3 4 5 ▶

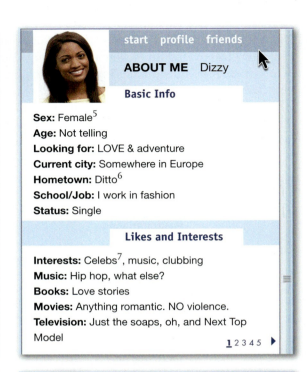

start   profile   friends

ABOUT ME   Dizzy

Basic Info

Sex: Female[5]
Age: Not telling
Looking for: LOVE & adventure
Current city: Somewhere in Europe
Hometown: Ditto[6]
School/Job: I work in fashion
Status: Single

Likes and Interests

Interests: Celebs[7], music, clubbing
Music: Hip hop, what else?
Books: Love stories
Movies: Anything romantic. NO violence.
Television: Just the soaps, oh, and Next Top Model

1 2 3 4 5 ▶

start   profile   friends

ABOUT ME   Cate

Basic Info

Sex: Female
Age: Look it up
Looking for: Friends
Current city: Sydney, NSW
Hometown: Melbourne, Victoria
School/Job: Actor. Oscar, Elf Queen.
Status: Married

Likes and Interests

Interests: Film, theatre, solar energy

start   profile   friends

ABOUT ME   Finn

Basic Info

Sex: Male
Age: 15
Looking For: Cool girls and guys
Current city: Hamburg, Germany
Hometown: Hamburg, Germany
School/Job: I go to school in Hamburg
Status: It's complicated

Likes and Interests

Interests: Sports (mainly[8] sailing), parties
Music: New German bands
Books: Not really
Movies: Action, action, action
Television: Sport

1   Confirm[9] or ignore[10]?

a) *If the people above asked to be your friend on a social networking site, which of them would you confirm as a friend? Which of them would you ignore? For what reasons?*

b) 👥 *Discuss your reasons for confirming or ignoring in a small group.*

c) 👥 *What information do the authors of these profiles <u>not</u> give about themselves? What you would say in <u>your</u> profile? What information would you leave out? Share your group's ideas with the class.*

---

[1] male [meɪl] *männlich*   [2] current ['kʌrənt] *gegenwärtige(r, s), derzeitige(r, s)*   [3] space travel *Raumfahrt*   [4] SF = science fiction [ˌsaɪəns 'fɪkʃn]
[5] female ['fiːmeɪl] *weiblich*   [6] ditto ['dɪtəu] *dito, ebenso*   [7] celebs [sə'lebz] *(kurz für* celebrities [sə'lebrətiz]*) Promis, Prominente*
[8] mainly *hauptsächlich, vorwiegend*   [9] (to) confirm [kən'fɜːm] *bestätigen*   [10] (to) ignore [ɪg'nɔː] *ignorieren*

2 Cate Blanchett wants to be my friend on Facebook (a short play by Alex Broun)

Characters

Barry	worker on a building site[1]
Morris	Barry's boss
Sarah	office worker on building site
Cate Blanchett	film star
Time	Morning. Working day.
Setting[2]	Building site office.

Barry sits at a desk working on a computer.
Morris enters.

Morris   Morning Barry.

Barry   Morris.

5 Morris   Are you going to start pouring that cement[3] this morning?

Barry   First thing. I'm just checking my Facebook.

Morris   Don't be too long.

10 Barry   I won't.

Morris looks through some folders[4].

Morris   Have you seen that bill from the cement company ?

Barry   In the folder.

15 *Morris continues to look.*

Barry   Do you know someone called *(reading)* Cate ... Blatchett?

Morris   Who?

Barry   Cate Blatchett?

20 Morris   Don't think so. Why?

Barry   She wants to be my friend on Facebook.

Morris stops looking in folder. Thinks. Beat[5].

Morris   How do you spell the last name?

25 Barry   B – l – a – n – c – h – e – t – t.

Morris thinks. Beat.

Morris   I think you'll find that's Blanchett.

Barry   Yeah.

Morris   (coming over to screen)

30   B – l – a – n – c – h – e – t – t. Blanchett.

Barry   Right. Do you know her then?

Beat.

Morris   No, I don't think so. *(He goes back to*

35   *folder.)* Are you sure that bill is in here?

Barry   Yeah. It says here she won an Oscar.

Morris   What for?

Barry   *The Aviator*. Best Supporting Actress.

Morris   Well that's clearly bullshit[6]. 40

Barry   You think so?

Morris   Of course. If you've won an Oscar, you don't talk about it on Facebook, do you? You let people work it out for themselves. 45

Barry   True.

Morris   It's probably someone who just wants to be famous. Just ignore her.

Barry   But then she'll know won't she?

Morris   No mate. That's the good thing about 50 Facebook. People don't know when you ignore them.

Barry   But she'll see I'm not in her friend list.

Morris   It'll be some time before she works 55 that out. How many friends has she got?

Barry   Three.

Morris   Maybe it won't be so long then. Are you sure that bill is in here? 60

Barry   Unless[7] Sarah has paid it already.

Morris   Is she here yet?

Barry   She's getting coffee.

Morris   Come and get me when she gets back. *(leaving)* And Baz, I really need 65 you to start pouring that cement.

Barry   I'm on my way.

---

[1] building site *Baustelle*   [2] setting ['setɪŋ] *Schauplatz, Handlungsrahmen*   [3] (to) pour cement [ˌpɔː sɪˈment] *Zement gießen*
[4] folder ['fəʊldə] *Mappe, Ordner*   [5] beat *kurze Pause*   [6] bullshit ['bʊlʃɪt] *(infml, vulgär) Bockmist, Schwachsinn*   [7] unless [ənˈles] *es sei denn*

Morris exits[1].

70 Barry — Confirm – ignore – confirm
– ignore.

Sarah enters with coffees.

Sarah — *(passing one to Barry)* Here you go.

Barry — Thanks.

Sarah — There's a woman at the front gate for

75 you.

Barry — Who?

Sarah — She says her name's Kate Blatchett.

Barry — Cate Blanchett?

Sarah — I'm pretty sure it was Blatchett.

80 Barry — What did she look like?

Sarah — Plain[2]. With a big hat. I'm not sure
why. There's no sun out there.

Barry — Could she be 'beautiful in certain[3]
lighting conditions[4]'?

85 Sarah — Maybe. Why?

Barry — *(pointing to computer)* That's what it
says here, under 'About Me'.
'Beautiful in certain lighting
conditions.'

90 Sarah — Is that her? Good picture.

Barry — She doesn't look like that?

Sarah — No way!

Barry — She wants to be my friend on
Facebook.

95 Sarah — Yeah? What did you say?

Barry — I haven't decided yet.

Sarah — What's she doing here?

Barry — I don't know.

Sarah — Maybe she's stalking[5] you.

100 Barry — Yeah, right. Morris wants to know
where that bill is for the cement.

Sarah — Under the folder.

Barry — Under? I said in.

Sarah — The paid ones are in. The unpaid
105 ones are under. I told him that years
ago.

Barry — Sorry. I didn't know. Hey, what do I
do about Cate Blatchett?

Sarah — Wasn't it Blanchett?

110 *Sarah exits. Barry looks at the screen again.*

Barry — Confirm – ignore – confirm –
ignore? *(Beat)* Ignore.

*Cate Blanchett enters, wearing dark glasses
and a large hat.*

Cate B. — Hi, I'm Cate Blanchett. 115

Barry — Not Blatchett?

Cate B. — No, Blanchett.

Barry — Nice to meet you. What are you
doing here?

Cate B. — I needed to speak to you. 120

Barry — Right. Any particular reason?

Cate B. — Many reasons.

Barry — Right. How did you find me?

Cate B. — I have people.

Barry — People? 125

Cate B. — Who do things for me.

Barry — What things?

Cate B. — Many and varied[6].

Barry — Great, but you're not actually allowed
on the site. 130

Cate B. — Of course. I'll be on my way soon.
But first, I'm wondering why you
haven't answered my friend request?

Barry — I have answered.

Cate B. — Confirm or ignore? 135

Barry — *(Beat)* Confirm.

Cate B. — Let me check.

Barry — *(blocking computer)* You can't.

Cate B. — Why not?

Barry — It's a work computer. No personal 140
surfing allowed.

Cate B. — *(looking at computer)* But I can see
your Facebook profile.

Barry — I was just checking it quickly before
the boss came in. But he's here now. 145

Cate B. — Is he?

Barry — Yes, he'll be back in a minute.

Beat.

Cate B. — So you definitely added me as a
friend? 150

Barry — Yep.

Beat.

Cate B. — *(suddenly)* You're lying[7]!

Barry — No I'm not.

Cate B. — Yes. You are! 155

Barry — All right. I am. I ignored your
request.

Cate B. — But why?

Barry — Does it matter[8] now?

Cate B. — Yes, it does. 160

Barry — I don't want to make it worse for you.

---

[1] (to) exit ['eksɪt] *abgehen, hinausgehen* [2] plain [pleɪn] *unscheinbar* [3] certain ['sɜːtn] *gewisse(r, s), bestimmte(r, s)* [4] lighting conditions
['laɪtɪŋ kən,dɪʃnz] *Lichtverhältnisse* [5] (to) stalk sb. [stɔːk] *jm. (belästigend) nachstellen* [6] varied ['veərɪd] *verschiedenartige(r, s)* [7] (to) lie
[laɪ] (-ing form lying) *lügen* [8] Does it matter? *Spielt das eine Rolle?*

Cate B.	Please Barry. If I understand why you ignored me, it will help me with the pain. And help me get more Confirms in the future.

Beat.

Barry	All right. *(Beat)* Are you sure you want to hear this?
Cate B.	Go on Barry. I can take it.
Barry	Well …
Cate B.	Say it Barry. Say it.
Barry	You're an actor.
Cate B.	So?
Barry	Well, it's not really a very honourable profession[1].
Cate B.	Isn't it?
Barry	No.

Beat.

Cate B.	I see. Why isn't acting an honourable profession?
Barry	Well, you're kind of famous.
Cate B.	Kind of? I'm …
Barry	But you don't really do anything. You're like one of those people.
Cate B.	Which people?
Barry	You know like Paris what's-her-name? Famous for being famous.
Cate B.	That's not true.

Beat.

Barry	Well actually it is.
Cate B.	But I won an Oscar.
Barry	Actually there's a few questions about that.
Cate B.	A Golden Globe.
Barry	Who hasn't?
Cate B.	I won the Volpi Cup at the Venice[2] Film Festival.
Barry	See, now you're just making that up[3].
Cate B.	I played Galadriel in *Lord of the Rings* 1, 2 and 3.
Barry	You shouldn't be telling people that.
Cate B.	*Return of the King* and *Two Towers* are two of the Top Ten moneymaking movies of all time.
Barry	That doesn't make them good.
Cate B.	Many people have congratulated me on my role as the Elf Queen.

Barry	Were any of them not members of your family?
Cate B.	You didn't like it?
Barry	You got the character wrong – really wrong.

Barry shakes his head sadly.

Cate B.	And your profession is honourable?
Barry	Now you're just being nasty[4]. And you know it.
Cate B.	Sorry.
Barry	That was cheap Cate. We build. Houses for people to live in, places of work, schools, hospitals. We make things that exist in the real world. While you create –
Cate B.	Fantasy?

Barry nods again sadly.

Cate B.	I entertain[5]. I give those little people, out there in the dark, an escape. From their hard daily lives.
Barry	At best, it gives them a few moments of pleasure[6]. At worse, it reminds them of their hard lives.

Beat.

Cate B.	I'm a mother. I've raised[7] three children.
Barry	There's something to be proud of.
Cate B.	Then will you accept my friend request?
Barry	I would if you'd put that in Facebook.
Cate B.	What does it say?
Barry	'Actor. Oscar, Elf Queen.'
Cate B.	I just forgot to put mother in.
Barry	You forgot being a mother? I'm not sure I really want to be friends with someone who puts being an 'actor' over being a 'mother'.
Cate B.	But I don't.
Barry	Cate …

Barry shakes his head again, sadly.

Cate B.	But I didn't write it. One of my people did.
Barry	Do you know what they say about bad builders?
Cate B.	No. What do they say?
Barry	Bad builders blame their tools.

Beat.

---

[1] an honourable profession [ˌɒnərəbl prəˈfeʃən] *ein ehrenwerter Beruf* [2] Venice [ˈvenɪs] *Venedig* [3] (to) make sth. up *sich etwas ausdenken* [4] nasty [ˈnɑːsti] *gemein* [5] (to) entertain [ˌentəˈteɪn] *unterhalten, zerstreuen* [6] pleasure [ˈpleʒə] *Vergnügen, Freude* [7] (to) raise children [reɪz] *Kinder großziehen, aufziehen*

Cate B.	You're not going to confirm me as a friend, are you?

Barry shakes his head.

260

Cate B.	Maybe if you got to know me a bit better.
Barry	I'm careful about who I accept as a friend.
Cate B.	You could come over for dinner? Andrew will cook.
265 Barry	I don't think it will work now.
Cate B.	Have you seen *Notes on a Scandal*? I can be pretty hot stuff.
Barry	You see, now that's just sad.

Beat.

270 Cate B.	*(dropping to her knees, begging[1])* Barry, please!
Morris	*(entering)* I still can't find … *(He sees Cate Blanchett kneeling in front of Barry.)*
275 Morris	Everything all right?
Barry	Good thanks Morris.

Beat.

Morris	Are you getting on to that cement?
Barry	I'm just on my way.
280 Sarah	*(entering)* Morris, the bill is under, not *(She also sees Cate Blanchett kneeling in front of Barry.)*

Beat.

Sarah	… in.

285 *Beat. Cate Blanchett stands.*

Barry	Morris. Sarah. This is Cate Blatchett.
Cate B.	Blanchett.
Morris	Nice to meet you.

Sarah gives a little wave.

290 Cate B.	Morris. Such a nice name. Strong. And Sarah. So … pretty.
Morris	As Barry knows, we have a rule about visitors on site.
Barry	I didn't invite her. *(Beat, looking at Cate Blanchett)* Well I didn't. *(to Morris)* She wants to know why I ignored her friend request on Facebook.
Morris	*(to Cate Blanchett)* Whatever the reason we've got a busy morning. So if you wouldn't mind …

295

300

Morris points at the door.

Cate B.	Of course. Well Barry, see you around. Online.
Barry	No you won't. Remember – 'ignore'. 305
Cate B.	Maybe you'll change your mind[2]. In a month or two?
Barry	Not likely.
Cate B.	A year? Five years?
Morris	*(moving Cate Blanchett towards the door)* We're really busy this morning. 310
Cate B.	*(to Morris)* Would you like to be my friend?
Morris	Sorry. I've got too many already.
Cate B.	*(to Sarah)* Sarah? 315
Sarah	*(shaking head)* Sorry.
Barry	*(to Cate Blanchett)* You're acting desperate[3] now.
Cate B.	Is that a big turn-off[4]?

Sarah, Barry and Morris nod their heads. 320

Cate B.	Right, well …
Morris	Straight down the path and back through the gate.
Cate B.	Morris, Sarah, Bazza.
Barry	It's Barry. 325
Cate B.	Of course. Goodbye.

Cate Blanchett exits.

Barry	I thought she'd never leave.
Sarah	Sad.
Barry	Very. 330

Morris looks at Barry.

Barry	What? I didn't invite her.

Morris moves to the folder.

Morris	Have a word with Neil at the gate. No visitors. And cement pouring – now. 335
Barry	I'm on it.
Morris	That'd be good.

Barry exits.

Morris	Facebook. More trouble than it's worth. *(to Sarah)* Now, where's that bill? 340

End play.

---

[1] (to) beg (-gg-) *bitten, betteln*   [2] (to) change one's mind [maɪnd] *seine Meinung ändern*   [3] desperate ['despərət] *verzweifelt*
[4] (to) be a turn-off ['tɜːn ˌɒf] *(infml) abstoßend wirken, abtörnend sein*

3 The plot

a) *Answer the questions on lines 1–157 of the play.*
Choose a, b or c. Give reasons for your choice.

1 At the start of the play Barry
   a) is checking his emails.
   b) is surfing the internet.
   c) is checking his Facebook.
2 Morris wants Barry
   a) to start pouring cement.
   b) to look for a bill.
   c) to look for information about Cate
   Blanchett.
3 Morris advises Barry
   a) to confirm Cate Blanchett as a friend.
   b) to find out more about her first.
   c) to ignore her.
4 Barry tells Morris that Cate Blanchett
   a) already knows him.
   b) hasn't got many people on her friend list.
   c) has got lots of people on her friend list.
5 Just before Cate arrives, Barry decides to
   a) confirm her friend request.
   b) ignore her friend request.
   c) think a little longer about what to do.
6 When Cate asks Barry if he has confirmed
   or ignored her, Barry
   a) tells the truth immediately.
   b) first tells a lie, then tells the truth.
   c) first tells the truth, then tells a lie

b) 👥 *Look at lines 157–214. What is the main*
question that Cate and Barry are discussing?
Who uses the following arguments?
– Honourable people don't become actors.
– Cate is very famous.
– Cate has won important awards.
– Cate has played in films that have made lots
  of money.
– Cate wasn't very good in the role of Elf
  Queen.
What can you say now about Barry's attitude to
Cate?

c) *Look at the rest of the discussion between Cate*
and Barry in lines 214–274. Answer the following
questions.
1 Why do Cate and Barry think that their jobs
  are useful?
2 How does Barry react when Cate says that
  she's a mother?
3 Why do you think Barry says 'You see, now
  that's just sad.' (l. 272)

d) *Look at lines 279–344. Why does Barry say to*
Cate: 'You're acting desperate now.'?
What do Sarah and Morris think of Cate?

e) *Write a short magazine advertisement for the*
play. Explain enough about the plot to get people
interested, but don't give too much away.

4 Friends online and friends for real

a) 👥👥 *Is Barry's attitude to Cate fair? Is the plot*
realistic? Why (not)? Discuss in small groups.
– I think Barry is friendly/unfriendly/cruel …
– He was right/wrong to ignore her because …
– I found the whole play realistic/unrealistic
  because …
– …

b) 👥 *Imagine a famous star sent you a friend*
request. What reasons might you have for
confirming or ignoring it? Makes notes and
compare your ideas with a partner.

c) 👥👥 *How many of your online friends are*
friends in real life too?
Is there a difference when you only know
someone online? Discuss.
– None[1]/Some/Most of my online friends are
  friends in real life too.
– The difference between my real and online
  friends is …
– It makes/doesn't make a difference if you've
  met someone in real life.
– You behave the same/differently to someone
  you haven't met in real life.
– …

---

[1] none [nʌn] *keine(r, s)*

TF 2   My love is like ...

1   Love songs and poems

a) *Have you noticed that most songs and poems seem to be about love? What's your favourite love song or poem at the moment? What do its lyrics say about love?*

b) *Read the songs and poems. Which aspects of love from the list below are they about?*
– losing your lover
– having a laugh about love
– asking someone to be your lover
– saying how wonderful your lover is
– talking about someone else's love affair
– ...

Bye bye love

Chorus
  Bye bye love
  Bye bye happiness
  Hello loneliness
  I think I'm gonna cry
  Bye bye love
  Bye bye sweet caress[1]
  Hello emptiness
  I feel like I could die
  Bye bye my love, goodbye

There goes my baby
With someone new
She sure looks happy
I sure am blue[2]
She was my baby
Till he stepped in[3]
Goodbye to romance
That might have been[4]
Chorus
I'm through with romance
I'm through with love
I'm through with counting
The stars above
And here's the reason
That I'm so free
My loving baby
Is through with me
Chorus

Felice Bryant (1925–2003) Boudleaux Bryant (1920–1987)

Love is all around

I feel it in my fingers, I feel it in my toes.
Well love is all around me, and so the feeling grows.
It's written on the wind, it's everywhere I go.
So if you really love me, come on and let it show.
You know I love you, I always will.
My mind's made up[5] by the way that I feel.
There's no beginning, there'll be no end
'Cause on my love you can depend[6].
I see your face before me as I lay on my bed.
I kinda get to thinking of all the things you said.
You gave your promise to me and I gave mine to you.
I need someone beside[7] me in everything I do.

Reg Presley (born 1943)

Celia Celia

When I am sad and weary[8]
When I think all hope has gone
When I walk along High Holborn[9]
I think of you with nothing on

Adrian Mitchell (1932–2008)

One parting[10]

Why did he write to her
'I can't live with you'?
And why did she write to him
'I can't live without you'?
For[11] he went west, she went east
And they both lived.

Carl Sandburg (1878–1967)

Goodbye

He breathed in air, he breathed out light.
Charlie Parker[12] was my delight[13].

Adrian Mitchell (1932–2008)

---

[1] caress [kə'res] *Zärtlichkeit, Liebkosung*   [2] blue *(infml) deprimiert, down*   [3] (to) step in *ins Spiel kommen*   [4] ... that might have been ..., *die hätte sein können*   [5] my mind's made up *ich habe mich entschieden*   [6] (to) depend on sth. [dɪ'pend] *sich auf etwas verlassen*   [7] beside [bɪ'saɪd] *neben*   [8] weary ['wɪəri] *erschöpft*   [9] High Holborn [ˌhaɪ 'həʊbən] *(Straße in London)*   [10] parting *Abschied*   [11] for *denn*   [12] Charlie Parker *amerik. Jazzmusiker (Altsaxophon) und Komponist (1920–1955)*   [13] delight [dɪ'laɪt] *Entzücken*

2 Taking a closer look 🎧

In their poems and songs, writers use special techniques to express feelings. Read the *Study Skills* box and then answer the questions below.

a) *Write down the rhyme schemes of the two songs. What effect do the rhymes have?*

b) *Listen to* Bye bye love *and describe its rhythm (fast, slow, peaceful, jumpy, …). How does it make the listener feel?*

c) *Read the poems again and find repetitions. What effect do the repetitions have?*

3 What do you think?

Which is the best love song/poem – the one you chose in 1a or one of the songs or poems on p. 110? Give reasons. (the music, the rhythm, the words, the message, …)
I think … is the best because …
It makes me feel happy/sad/calm/…
… (want to) dance/laugh/sing along/…
The music/words/rhythm … is/are beautiful/sad/thoughtful/…
The message is interesting/good/… because …

STUDY SKILLS | **Poem and song techniques (1)**

Rhyme[1]: *Rhymes create a pattern[2] you can hear. When this pattern continues through a poem or song, it gives them a rhyme scheme[3], which you can write down like this: AABBCC – ABAB – … Rhymes are a good way to structure a poem or song and to make it sound good.*

Rhythm[4]: *The variation[5] of stress on the words and syllables gives a song or poem its* rhythm. *The rhythm of a poem/song creates a feeling or mood[6]. For example, a slow rhythm can make it sound thoughtful or relaxed feeling. A fast rhythm can make it sound exciting or happy.*

Repetition[7]: *If a sound, a word or a phrase is repeated, this shows us that the idea is important. It can also hold the poem together.*

▶ *SF Reading literature (pp. 137–138)*

---

[1] rhyme [raɪm] *Reim*   [2] pattern ['pætn] *Muster*   [3] rhyme scheme [skiːm] *Reimschema*   [4] rhythm ['rɪðəm] *Rhythmus, Takt*
[5] variation [ˌveəri'eɪʃn] *Veränderung, Variation*
[6] mood [muːd] *Stimmung*   [7] repetition [ˌrepə'tɪʃn] *Wiederholung*

4   Pictures in the mind 🎧

a) Read or listen to the poem on the right and draw or describe in writing the picture that it creates in your mind.

b) 👥 Explain your picture to your partner.

STUDY SKILLS	**Poem and song techniques (2)**

*Images[9]: Poets[10] paint pictures with words and show us a new way of seeing things. Sometimes these images are immediately clear, sometimes it takes time to understand them. In a metaphor[11] a poet talks about something as if it is something else, e.g. **The garden was a sea of flowers**, or as if it can do something it cannot, e.g. **Time flies**. In a simile[12], a poet creates an image by comparing one thing to another, e.g. **a face as white as snow**, or **She fights like a tiger**.*

▶ *SF Reading literature (pp. 137–138)*

c) Look at the following images from the poem 'A red, red rose'.
Decide whether they are metaphors or similes.
– my Love's like a red, red rose …
– my Love's like the melody …
– While the sands o' life shall run
– And rocks melt wi' the sun

d) Choose one image from the poem and explain what it means and how it works. The language below might help.

> *My Love's like a red, red rose … is a metaphor/simile.*
> It compares … to …
> It says that … is like …
> It says that … but you can't really …
> It means that …
> It gives you the picture of …

A red, red rose

O, my Love's like a red, red rose,
That's newly sprung[1] in June.
O, my Love's like the melody
That's sweetly played in tune[2].
As fair art thou[3], my bonnie lass[4],
So deep in love am I;
And I will love thee[5] still, my dear,
Till a' the seas go dry.
Till a' the seas go dry, my dear,
And rocks melt wi' the sun:
I will love thee still, my dear,
While the sands o' life shall run[6]:
And fare thee well[7], my only love!
And fare thee well, a while!
And I will come again, my love,
Tho' it were ten thousand mile[8]!

Robert Burns (1759–1796)

5   Now you

Choose a) or b) or c).
a) Find your favourite
word – image – rhyme – idea
from the poems. Use them to write your own poem. (It doesn't have to rhyme!)

b) Write your own four-line poem. Start each line like the Robert Burns poem on this page:
My love is like …

c) Learn your favourite English poem or song and recite[13] it to the class.

---

[1] (to) spring, sprang, sprung [sprɪŋ, spræŋ, sprʌŋ] *(aus dem Boden) schießen*   [2] (to) play a melody in tune [tjuːn] *eine Melodie richtig spielen*
[3] art thou [ɑːt 'ðaʊ] *(veraltet) bist du*   [4] bonnie lass [ˌbɒni 'læs] *hübsches Mädchen*   [5] thee [ðiː] *(veraltet) dich; dir*   [6] while the sands o' life shall run *etwa: während die Zeit vergeht*   [7] fare thee well *(veraltet) lebe wohl*   [8] tho' it were ten thousand mile *und wenn es tausend Meilen wären*   [9] image ['ɪmɪdʒ] *Bild*   [10] poet ['pəʊɪt] *Dichter/in*   [11] metaphor ['metəfə] *Metapher*   [12] simile ['sɪməli] *Vergleich*
[13] (to) recite [rɪ'saɪt] *vortragen, aufsagen*

TF 3 Viewing: The Meatrix

1 The Matrix

Read the summary of the plot of The Matrix. *Make notes under the headings in the box.*

Characters ·
Pills ·
Dream world ·
Real world

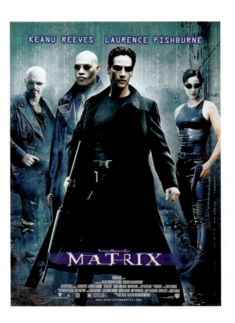

Neo has a feeling that somehow something isn't right in the world. Morpheus offers Neo two pills. With the red pill he will find out the truth. With the blue pill his life will continue as before. Neo takes the red pill and he realizes that he is living in a dream world called the Matrix. The Matrix was created by intelligent machines to control humans because they need them to provide energy. The humans think that their lives are continuing as normal, but this is an illusion. In the real world they are just batteries for the machines.

2 The Meatrix

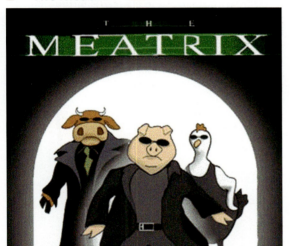

a) Compare the Meatrix *poster with the* Matrix *poster. What might* The Meatrix *be about?*

b) 👥 *Partner A: Watch the cartoon, but cover your ears so that you can't hear the sound.¹ Partner B: Listen, but don't look at the screen. When the cartoon ends discuss these questions: Who are the two main characters? Where is the story set at first? Where is it set later?*

c) 👥 *Which of these statements are wrong? Correct them.*
1 At first Leo, the pig, thinks he is living on a family farm.
2 Leo tells Moopheus about the Meatrix.
3 Leo doesn't want to find out the truth about the Meatrix.
4 Leo realizes he's living on a factory farm.
5 Moopheus describes what is bad about factory farming.
6 Leo doesn't want to help stop the Meatrix.

d) Watch the film again (with pictures and sound) and check your answers. What is the Meatrix?

3 The message

a) What is the main message of the cartoon?

b) How does The Meatrix *use* The Matrix *to get this message across²? (Think about the titles, the plots and the characters of both films.)*

c) What do you think of the cartoon?

---

¹ (to) cover one's ears *sich die Ohren zuhalten*   ² (to) get a message across *eine Botschaft rüberbringen*

TF 4
Uniting Europe

1 AIRBUS – a European dream?

Over the last 40 years, Airbus, a truly[1] European company, has become one of the world's two largest aircraft[2] producers.

It all started with a group of European aircraft companies in 1969. These companies – from France, Germany, Spain and the United Kingdom – had enough good ideas, but still did not build many planes. On their own, they were too small to compete with a huge American producer like Boeing. So they came together and founded Airbus.

Would it be possible for companies from four different countries to work together successfully? Roger Béteille, one of Airbus's founding fathers, was worried that national interests would make it difficult. But in the end all the partners agreed, firstly, to produce different parts at sites[3] in each country and, secondly, to use just one assembly line[4] and test flight centre in Toulouse, France.

This meant that Airbus had to develop[5] a transport system to move large aircraft parts from all over Europe to Toulouse, by road and sea

The A380 can carry up to 525 passengers.

and also with huge cargo[6] planes called Belugas. Today, 15 sites in France, Germany, Spain and the UK produce parts which are then transported to the Airbus assembly lines – there are three today – in Toulouse and Hamburg and in Tianjin in Northern China.

Starting with the A300 in the 1970s, Airbus has always produced aircraft that use little fuel and are quiet and cheap to run[7]. Today the company produces a range[8] of eco-efficient planes with seats[9] for between 107 and 525 passengers.

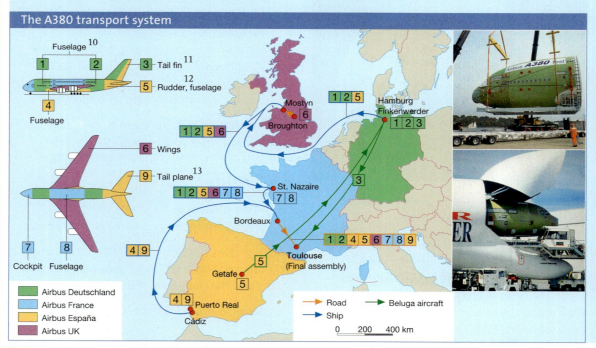

The A380 transport system

Fuselage[10]

1 2 3 - Tail fin[11]

5 - Rudder, fuselage[12]

4

Fuselage

6 - Wings

9 - Tail plane[13]

7 Cockpit 8 Fuselage

1 2 5 — Hamburg Finkenwerder
1 2 3

1 2 5 6 — Mostyn / Broughton

1 2 5 6 7 8 — St. Nazaire
7 8

3

Bordeaux

1 2 4 5 6 7 8 9 — Toulouse (Final assembly)

4 9 — Getafe
5
5

4 9 Puerto Real / Cádiz

Airbus Deutschland
Airbus France
Airbus España
Airbus UK

Road → Beluga aircraft
Ship

0   200   400 km

---

[1] truly ['tru:li] *wahrhaft* [2] aircraft ['eəkrɑ:ft] *Flugzeug* [3] site *Standort* [4] assembly line [ə'sembli laɪn] *Montagestraße* [5] (to) develop [dɪ'veləp] entwickeln; aufbauen [6] cargo plane ['kɑ:gəʊ pleɪn] *Frachtflugzeug* [7] (to) run *betreiben* [8] range [reɪndʒ] *Sortiment, Reihe* [9] seat [si:t] *Sitz(platz)* [10] fuselage ['fju:zəlɑ:ʒ] *Flugzeugrumpf* [11] tail fin ['teɪlfɪn] *Heckruder* [12] rudder ['rʌdə] *Seitenruder* [13] tail plane ['teɪlpleɪn] *Leitwerk*

So is Airbus a perfect model of European cooperation? When things are going well, it seems so. But there are problems too. For example, the fact that production sites in different countries used different computer software was one reason behind big delays[1] in delivering[2] the A380 to the company's customers. These delays have caused a fall in profits[3], so that since 2007 production sites have been sold off and thousands of jobs lost. When Airbus has to decide where to cut jobs, it is then that national governments disagree, and national interests begin to play at least as big a role as the idea of European cooperation.

Sam – Apprentice

'I joined Airbus as an apprentice after secondary school. I took part in an intercultural awareness[4] programme, working with British, French and German apprentices. It was a most enjoyable experience, from which I learned a lot and made a number of great friends from all three countries. I feel very lucky to have this apprenticeship. I would like to continue along the Airbus career path as far as I can, and later look for a chance to work in another country.'

a) *Read about Airbus and then answer these questions.*

1 What are the advantages for European countries of building planes together?
2 When is it more difficult to put the idea of European cooperation into practice[5]?
3 Why does Sam enjoy being an apprentice at Airbus?

b) *Look at the map on p. 114 and with the help of the skills and language boxes say:*
– what kind of map it is.
– what is produced in each country and how it gets to Toulouse.

c) *Do you agree or disagree with the following?* It would be a better idea if Airbus planes were all made in one place.

Make notes on your reasons and use them to discuss the question in class. You could think about:

European cooperation • transport problems • the environment • jobs in your country • competition with American companies • ...

GEOGRAPHY SKILLS **Talking about maps**

When you talk about maps,
– look at the title and the key[6] and make sure you understand what the map is about.
– start with a general statement about the map, then talk about the details.

Activate your English

– This is a physical[7]/political/thematic map.
– The map shows ...
– (Broughton) is situated[8] in/near/...
– ... is about ... km away from ...
– ... is between ... and ...
– The wings/... are produced/made/... in ...
– They are transported/flown from ... to ...
– They are transported by road/ship/air/cargo plane/...
– The aircraft parts are put together in ...

2 Young people and the European Union

On p. 115, Sam talks about how cooperation across borders in the European Union (EU) was an advantage for him.

a) *What does the EU mean to you personally? Think about the question for a minute and write down your answers. Then collect all the answers in class.*

b) *Read the skills box on the right. Then describe the chart below. Say:*
– *what the chart is about.*
– *what kind of chart it is.*
– *what the source and date are.*
– *what you have learned from the chart.*

GEOGRAPHY SKILLS | **Interpreting charts**

– Charts and graphs[1] contain statistics[2] on a specific topic. The topic and the source and date of the statistics are usually given at the top or bottom.
– The statistics can refer to a situation at a specific time or to changes over a longer period[3].
– The statistics can be presented in different forms: bar chart, pie chart or line graph.
– Be sure you know what the numbers in a chart are: ordinary[4] numbers, percentages, etc.

▶ *SF Talking about charts (p. 131)*

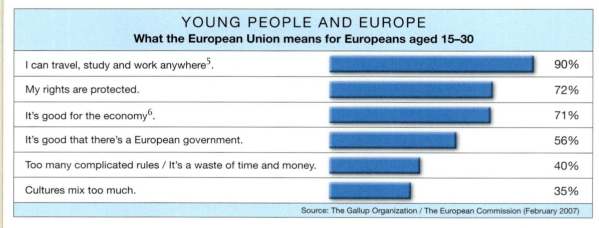

YOUNG PEOPLE AND EUROPE
What the European Union means for Europeans aged 15–30

I can travel, study and work anywhere[5].	90%
My rights are protected.	72%
It's good for the economy[6].	71%
It's good that there's a European government.	56%
Too many complicated rules / It's a waste of time and money.	40%
Cultures mix too much.	35%

Source: The Gallup Organization / The European Commission (February 2007)

---

c) *Make a survey for your class:*
– *Copy the statements from the chart.*
– *Decide which statements express how you feel about Europe. Put a tick (✓) beside them.*
– *Collect all results and make a class bar chart.*
– *Compare your class results with the chart above.*

Activate your English
– This group's results are similar to/different from …
– The most important issue for us/them is …
– I find their results very interesting/strange/ hard to believe/…

---

[1] graph [græf], [grɑːf] *Diagramm, Graph*   [2] statistics [stəˈtɪstɪks] *(pl) Statistik(en)*   [3] period [ˈpɪəriəd] *Zeitspanne, Zeitraum*   [4] ordinary [ˈɔːdnri]
normal, gewöhnlich   [5] anywhere *hier: überall*   [6] economy [ɪˈkɒnəmi] *Wirtschaft*

TF 5 **If only Papa hadn't danced** (by Patricia McCormick)

Before you read

Look at the picture. Think about where the people are, who they could be, what their relationship is and what will happen next. Make some notes. Then discuss your ideas in a group.

Now read the story. Some important new words are explained at the bottom of the page.

But who could blame him? When the results of the presidential election were tacked up on the polling station[1] doors, a lot of people danced and sang in the streets – none[2] of
5 them more joyfully than Papa. Finally the Old Man had lost. The Old Man, who'd ruled[3] the country since Papa was a baby, had been beaten fair and square. The man who robbed[4] from the poor to make himself rich was
10 finished.

But not everyone in the village danced that night. The rich men, the ones made fat by the Old Man, stood in the shadows and watched.

The next day, when Papa and his friends
15 gathered around the radio, they heard that the election results had been a mistake. There would have to be a recount[5]. Papa spat in the dust and said it was a lie. A week passed, then another – while the Old Man stayed in his
20 grand house in the capital. While his men were supposedly[6] counting the ballots[7] again. Papa and his friends grumbled among themselves, but not loud enough for anyone else to hear.
25 Then one night we awoke to the hot breath[8] of fire. The corn patch[9] just outside our hut was ablaze[10]. We jumped from our beds and

ran to the field to beat down the flames with branches[11]. But it was no good. Our entire crop[12] was gone.
30

At dawn Papa sought out[13] the police. They came to our home, looked at our field with eyes of stone and told us to empty the house of all we owned.

'Take what you can,' one of the policemen 35 said. 'They will be back tonight. This time they will torch[14] your house.'

'They?' I asked Papa when the policemen had left. 'Who are they?'

Papa sighed and shook his head. 'Our 40 neighbours and tribesmen,' he said. 'People we have known our whole lives. People whose bellies[15] have been filled by the Old Man.'

Mama clucked her tongue at Papa. 'Everyone saw you celebrating,' she said. 'They know you 45 voted against the Old Man and now we will pay for it.' She looked out and saw the smouldering[16] remains[17] of our neighbours' fields. The crops of those who'd danced with Papa were in ashes. The others were as lush 50 and green as they'd been the day before.

And so we packed our things – the few we had, the fewer we could carry – into a few

---

[1] polling station ['pəʊlɪŋ steɪʃn] *Wahllokal* [2] none [nʌn] *keine(r, s)* [3] (to) rule *beherrschen; herrschen* [4] (to) rob (-bb-) [rɒb] *rauben* [5] recount ['riːkaʊnt] *Nachzählung* [6] supposedly [sə'pəʊzɪdli] *angeblich* [7] ballot ['bælət] *Stimme, Stimmzettel* [8] breath [breθ] *Atem* [9] patch [pætʃ] *(kleines) Feld, Beet* [10] ablaze [ə'bleɪz] *in Flammen* [11] branch [brɑːntʃ] *Zweig* [12] crop [krɒp] *Ernte* [13] (to) seek sb. out, sought, sought [siːk, sɔːt] *an jn. herantreten* [14] (to) torch [tɔːtʃ] *anzünden* [15] belly *Bauch* [16] smouldering ['sməʊldərɪŋ] *schwelend* [17] remains [rɪ'meɪnz] *Überreste*

bundles and an old cardboard suitcase. I put
55 my bundle on my head, took one last look at
our home, then turned to face our future.

'Where will we go?' I asked Papa.

'We will walk until we find a friendly place
where we can stay,' he said. 'When it is safe,
60 when the recount is finished, when the
rightful president takes office[1], then we will
return home.'

As we came to the centre of the village, we
met up with other families like ours. The
65 fathers hung their heads, the mothers looked
only at the dirt beneath their feet and the
children tugged[2] listlessly at their parents'
hands. 'Why?' they asked. 'Why must we leave
home?' The parents did not dare[3] to answer
70 – in case[4] 'they' were listening.

The world beyond the village was new and
strange – a vast plain[5] of parched[6] grass and
shimmering heat. We walked by night,
through bushes alive with the sounds of
75 frenzied insects, and slept by day under the
scanty shade of the acacia tree. We walked and
walked and walked.

At last we came upon a settlement. From a
distance it bloomed up from the earth like a
80 flower. We saw, shimmering on the horizon,
what we thought was our safe place, the place
where we would rest[7] until we could go home.
But as we drew near[8], we saw that the village
looked just like ours. One house was nothing
85 but a smouldering heap[9], the one next door
untouched.

And so we walked on and on, each village
the same.

We gathered news as we walked. 'The Old
90 Man is still in power,' said people who joined
our dusty procession. 'He won't give up
without a fight,' they added.

I asked Papa about the man who had won
the election. 'He won't give up without a fight
95 either,' Papa told me. The next day on the
radio we heard that he had fled the country.

That night, there was just one tiny strip[10] of
dried meat left[11]. Mama cut it three ways and

handed each of us a piece. Papa shook his
head. 100

'Give mine to the child,' he said. 'I'm a
tough old bird. I can make do.'

The next morning, when we awoke, we
found corn to eat. Corn and biscuits and a bit
of fruit. But Papa wouldn't touch a thing. He 105
turned away and whispered to Mama, 'I was a
fool to hope for change. And now I am a thief.
Now I'm no better than the Old Man.'

In the afternoon we came upon a great river.
Wide and sluggish[12], it looked as hot and 110
steamy as we were. I knew from my studies
that we had come to the edge[13] of our country.
On the other side of the river was a free
country, a land of cities and farms, a nation
where the people had voted for a president 115
who had spent years in jail fighting for justice.

Mama knelt[14] in the shallows and splashed
water on her face. But as I knelt down next to
her, I saw that she was trying to cover her
tears. 120

'*This* is our homeland,' she said. 'No one
wants us over there.' She gestured to the
tawny hills across the river.

It was then that I saw the long metal fence
which uncoiled, like a snake, all along the 125
riverbank[15] on the other side. The fence was
tall and crowned with rings of wire[16]: wire
with teeth that could slice[17] the clothes from
your back, the skin from your bones. In the
distance I saw a man in an orange jumpsuit 130
patching[18] a hole at the bottom of the fence – a
spot where some lucky person must have
slipped through the night before. His tools
were at his feet, a pistol in his belt[19].

Papa came over and said I was needed. 135
There was a sign, he said, that he needed me
to read. He brought me to a spot where
someone had hand-painted a warning: *Beware
of*[20] *crocodiles.*

That night, we hid in the bushes until the 140
sky was black. We would wade across at
midnight, when the man in the orange
jumpsuit had gone home and when the

---

[1] (to) take office *sein Amt antreten*   [2] (to) tug (-gg-) [tʌg] *ziehen*   [3] (to) dare *(es) wagen, sich trauen*   [4] in case *für den Fall, dass*   [5] plain [pleɪn] *Ebene*   [6] parched [pɑːtʃt] *ausgetrocknet, verdorrt*   [7] (to) rest *ausruhen*   [8] (to) draw near, drew, drawn *näherkommen*   [9] heap [hiːp] *Haufen*   [10] a tiny strip ['taɪni] *ein winziger Streifen*   [11] (to) be left *übrig sein*   [12] sluggish ['slʌgɪʃ] *träge*   [13] edge [edʒ] *Rand, Kante*   [14] (to) kneel, knelt, knelt [niːl, nelt] *(sich hin)knien*   [15] riverbank *Flussufer*   [16] wire ['waɪə] *Draht*   [17] (to) slice [slaɪs] *schneiden*   [18] (to) patch [pætʃ] *flicken*   [19] belt [belt] *Gürtel*   [20] beware of ... [bɪ'weə] *Vorsicht vor ...*

crocodiles, we hoped, would be sound asleep.

145 When it was time to go, I walked straight towards the river, knowing my nerve would fail if I faltered[1] for even a moment. But Papa stopped me at the water's edge.

'Wait here,' he said. And then he scooped
150 Mama up into his arms and waded silently into the darkness.

It seemed a lifetime until he returned. He didn't say a word, just lifted me up onto his shoulders and strode into the water. Every
155 stick[2] I saw was a crocodile. Under every rock, every ripple[3] in the water, was a pair of ferocious jaws[4]. When we reached the other side, I leapt from his shoulders and kissed the sand.

160 Once more Papa stepped into the river – this time to fetch our suitcase. Surely our luck wouldn't hold again ... I watched his back disappear into the dark and thought how much I loved that broad back; how it
165 shouldered all our woes[5], and now all our hopes. Finally Papa emerged[6] from the darkness with all our worldly possessions[7] balanced on his head.

Then we got down on our hands and knees
170 and crawled along the base of the fence, like scorpions looking for a place to dig[8]. But the sand was unyielding and the fence invincible[9]. Everywhere our fingers scrabbled for[10] a weakness, someone – the man in the orange
175 jumpsuit, most likely – had mended[11] it with links of chain[12] held tight with wire.

The sky overhead had begun to brighten and the horizon was edged with pink. Soon it would be light[13] and we'd be trapped between
180 the waking crocodiles and the man with the gun in his belt.

We came to a spot in the fence where a thorn bush grew on the other side. Papa said we would have to dig here: no time to keep
185 looking. Perhaps the roots[14] of the bush had loosened the sand, he said. If not, at least we could hide behind the bush, if only for a while.

And so all three of us dug – Mama in the middle and Papa and I on either side – our
190 hands clawing furiously at the earth. I'd only made a few inches of progress[15] when the sky turned red. It would be dawn in less than an hour. I redoubled my effort[16], working the outer edge of the bush where the soil[17] was a
195 bit looser. Soon I'd dug a hole barely big enough for a man's foot. I lifted my head to call out to Papa to come and see my work – and saw the man in the orange jumpsuit striding towards us.

200 Mama wailed[18] piteously, then plucked at her hem where she'd hidden the tiny bit of money we had. She knelt in the sand, her arms outstretched, our few coins in her upturned palms[19].

205 But the man shook his head. He placed his hand on the belt that held his gun.

'Take me,' Papa begged him. 'Spare[20] the woman and the girl.'

Again the man shook his head. Then he
210 reached into his pocket and took out a giant cutting tool. With one mighty snap he severed[21] the links where the fence had been patched. He yanked[22] on the fence so hard it cried out in protest, and peeled it back as if it
215 were made of cloth.

'Hurry,' he said. 'Once the light comes, I will have to go back to patrolling.'

We didn't fully comprehend[23] what he was saying, but we didn't wait.

220 'You go first,' Papa said to me. 'I want you to be the first in our family to taste[24] freedom.'

I scrambled through the fence, stood next to the man in the orange jumpsuit and looked back at our homeland as the sun began to turn
225 its fields to gold.

'You will miss it for a long time,' the man said to me. 'I still do.'

I stared up at him.

'Yes,' he said. 'I outran[25] the Old Man long
230 ago.'

Mama crawled through and kissed the man's

---

[1] (to) falter ['fɔːltə] *zögern, zaudern*   [2] stick *Stock*   [3] ripple ['rɪpl] *Kräuseln, kleine Welle*   [4] ferocious jaws [fə,rəʊʃəs 'dʒɔːz] *furchteinflößende Kiefer*   [5] woes (pl) [wəʊz] *Sorgen*   [6] (to) emerge from [i'mɜːdʒ] *auftauchen aus, hervortreten aus*   [7] possessions (pl) [pə'zeʃnz] *Besitz(tümer), Habe*   [8] (to) dig, dug, dug [dɪg, dʌg] *graben*   [9] invincible [ɪn'vɪnsəbl] *unbesiegbar*   [10] Everywhere our fingers scrabbled for ... *Überall, wo unsere Finger nach ... suchten/ wühlten*   [11] (to) mend *reparieren*   [12] chain [tʃeɪn] *Kette*   [13] light *hell*   [14] root [ruːt] *Wurzel*   [15] progress ['prəʊgres] *Fortschritt(e)*   [16] effort ['efət] *Bemühungen*   [17] soil [sɔɪl] *Erde*   [18] (to) wail [weɪl] *jammern, heulen*   [19] palm [pɑːm] *Handfläche*   [20] (to) spare [speə] *verschonen*   [21] (to) sever ['sevə] *durchtrennen*   [22] (to) yank [jæŋk] *reißen, ziehen*   [23] (to) comprehend [,kɒmprɪ'hend] *verstehen*   [24] (to) taste [teɪst] *schmecken, kosten*   [25] (to) outrun sb. *jm. davonlaufen*

boots. He simply helped her to her feet.

'Quickly now,' he said, once Papa had made it through. 'Walk, as fast as you can, until you 235 see a house with white flowers out front. Go round to the back and tell them Robert sent you. They will feed you and hide you until night. Then they will send you to the next safe house, which will send you to the next, and the 240 next – until finally you are in the city and can be swallowed up[1] by all the people there.'

'How do we know we can trust these people?' Mama asked.

'They are our countrymen,' he said. 'You will 245 find many of us here. Now go!'

We did as he instructed, and found the house with the white flowers just as the morning sun broke through the clouds. A woman there brought us inside, gave us water and meat and led us to mats where we could 250 rest. It had been so long since I'd slept on anything other than bare, open ground that I fell asleep at once.

I awoke sometime later and saw that Papa's mat was empty. I stood and wandered outside. 255 The sun was setting, so all I could see was his silhouette against the deepening sky. He raised his arms to the heavens and started to hum[2]. And then I saw Papa dance.

Working with the text

1 Your impressions[3]

Think back to your discussion on the picture on p. 117. How close were your ideas to what happened in the story?

2 The plot

Use the key words in the boxes to write down the plot of If only Papa hadn't danced.
The narrator's[4] father dances when he hears that the Old Man has lost the election. ...

▶ SF Reading literature (pp. 137–138)

> **STUDY SKILLS** Reading fiction[6] (1)
>
> **Setting[7] and plot**
> The **setting** of a story is the place and time it happens: the Australian outback in the 1950s, Africa today, a fantasy world in the future …
> The **plot** is the action and events that take place in a story. These events often happen because one event causes another. Stories also often use flashbacks[8] in their plots.

narrator's father · dance · Old Man · lose election ▶	Old Man · rule country · long time ▶	next day · recount · one night · family's fields · burn ▶	police · tell family · house will burn · next night
same thing · happen · everyone · vote against Old Man ▶	so · family · pack up their things · leave home ▶	family · walk across country · night · sleep · day ▶	one afternoon · come to · wide river · edge of their country
other side · a free country · but also · metal fence ▶	crocodiles · in river · but family decide · cross river at night ▶	father · carry wife/daughter/ possessions across ▶	then · family try to · dig hole under fence · before light
but · man in orange jumpsuit · repair fence · pistol ▶	family think · man · arrest[5] them · but · man · cut fence ▶	he · also from their country · send them · safe house ▶	that evening · narrator · see father · dance again

---

[1] swallow up [ˌswɒləʊ_'ʌp] *verschlingen*   [2] (to) hum (-mm-) [hʌm] *summen*   [3] impression [ɪm'preʃn] *Eindruck*   [4] narrator [nə'reɪtə] *Erzähler/in*
[5] (to) arrest [ə'rest] *verhaften*   [6] fiction ['fɪkʃn] *Erzählliteratur, Belletristik*   [7] setting ['setɪŋ] *Schauplatz, Handlungsrahmen*
[8] flashback ['flæʃbæk] *Rückblende*

3 The characters

a) Make a network with the characters' names:
Old Man, Narrator, Papa, Mama, Man in jumpsuit.
Add notes to show the links between them (e.g.
father of, same homeland as, ...).

b) Choose a character from your network. Find
parts of the text that tell you what kind of person
he/she is. Collect information like this:

Name	Characterization	Source
Papa	Papa spat in the dust and said it was a lie. ...	lines 17–18

c) 👥 What conclusions can you draw from your
chart? Say how you see the character you chose.

d) Use your chart to write a characterization.

4 The atmosphere

a) Without checking the text, finish this sentence:
The atmosphere in the story is ...

b) Read the box on the right. Then find examples
of how the writer creates atmosphere. Collect
them in a chart like this:

How	Example	Source
image	the hot breath of fire.	lines 25–26
adjective	smouldering ...	...

c) 👥 Compare and explain your charts.
– 'Hot breath' makes you feel the fire is alive.
– 'Smouldering remains' gives you the feeling
  the family has lost everything.
– ...
Would you change your sentence from a)? Why?

5 What do you think?

a) Which adjective(s) best describe(s) the story?

> boring • depressing • exciting • interesting •
> moving[6] • sentimental • unbelievable • ...

b) The country in the story has elections, but it is
a dictatorship[7], not a democracy. Find examples of
how a dictatorship affects people's behaviour.

STUDY SKILLS Reading fiction (2)

Characterization[1]
Writers can use words like *cruel, honest,
prejudiced, sentimental,* etc. to tell us about
the characters in a story.
Writers can also say indirectly what kind of
person a character is, e.g. when they tell us
what the character does, thinks or feels.
For example:

> *The purse was full of money. Enough to pay her
> bills. She picked it up and walked on.
> 'But it belongs to someone else,' a voice inside
> her whispered.
> She stopped and turned slowly towards the
> police station. She knew she had to hand it in*[2].

In these lines, the writer shows us that the
character is an honest person.

▶ *SF Reading literature (pp. 137–138)*

STUDY SKILLS Reading fiction (3)

Atmosphere
The **atmosphere** is the feeling that a writer
creates in a story. It can be exciting, scary,
romantic, sad, etc.
To create atmosphere, a writer can work
with
– images[3] (e.g. metaphors[4] or similes[5])
– adjectives (e.g. *smouldering* remains,
  parched grass)
– details of the plot (e.g. 'The parents did
  not dare to answer – in case 'they' were
  listening.')

▶ *SF Reading literature (pp. 137–138)*

6 Different points of view

*Write either lines 141–160 through the eyes of the
father of the family or lines 189–205 through the
eyes of the man in the orange jumpsuit.*

▶ *SF Reading literature (pp. 137–138)*

You can put your text in your DOSSIER.

---

[1] characterization [ˌkærəktəraɪˈzeɪʃn] *Charakterisierung* [2] (to) hand sth. in *etwas abgeben, einreichen* [3] image [ˈɪmɪdʒ] *Bild* [4] metaphor
[ˈmetəfə] *Metapher* [5] simile [ˈsɪməli] *Vergleich* [6] moving *bewegend* [7] dictatorship [ˌdɪkˈteɪtəʃɪp] *Diktatur*

TF 6 Two presidents

1 The US president

a) Name the current president of the USA. Is there a picture of this president on the right?

b) 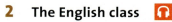 *Write down the names of the presidents on the right and of other US presidents you know. What else do you know about them?*

c) *What do you know about the job of the US president? Make notes and share your information in class.*

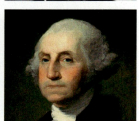

2 The English class 🎧

a) Listen. Where is the class taking place? What happens?

b) Copy the chart on the right. Then listen again and fill as many examples in the chart as you can.

c) *Compare your chart with a partner and make corrections.*

What does the US president do?	
Head of the government	Head of state
– The president runs ...	...

3 The president's busy life

Read the president's schedule. Find more examples of his roles as head of the government and head of state and add them to your chart.

THE WHITE HOUSE Office of the Press Secretary[1]

The President's schedule for next week

- On Monday, the President will celebrate Father's Day. At an event in Washington, he will discuss the important role of fathers in building healthy families.

- On Tuesday, the President will discuss the political situation in the Middle East with the National Security Advisor and military advisors. Later the President will have lunch with the King of Norway. In the evening, the President will receive the women's national soccer team.

- On Wednesday, the President will meet senators[2] from both parties to discuss new laws on energy and climate. In the afternoon the President will travel to Michigan, where he will present the awards to the winners of this year's Young Scientist competition.

- On Thursday, the President will meet the Cabinet to discuss education reform. In the evening, the President will speak to the nation on television to announce new plans for dealing with[3] the economic crisis.

- On Friday, the President will travel to Banff, Canada, where he will take part in the G8 Summit[4]. In the afternoon, the President will meet the British Prime Minister to discuss political and economic cooperation between the United States and the United Kingdom. In the evening, the President will have a working dinner with G8 leaders.

[1] press secretary ['pres ˌsekrətri] *Pressesprecher/in* [2] senator ['senətə] *Senator/in* [3] (to) deal with, dealt, dealt [diːl, delt] *fertigwerden mit, umgehen mit* [4] summit ['sʌmɪt] *Gipfel, Gipfeltreffen*

4 The president of the Federal Republic of Germany

a) Name the current German president. Collect other facts you know about him/her.
Is there a picture of the current president below? Can you name any of the people in the pictures?

b) Think about the statements below. Decide if they are true or false. Correct the wrong statements.
👥 *Discuss your answers with a partner and change them if necessary.* 👥 *Then compare your answers*
in a group and share what you think with the whole class.

1 The German president is the head of state.
2 He/She is the head of the government.
3 He/She signs legislation[1] before it can become law.
4 He/She often vetoes legislation.
5 He/She chooses ministers for the cabinet.
6 He/She give speeches on important days in the life of the country, like the Day of German Unity.
7 He/She lives in a palace in Berlin.
8 He/She represents Germany at political summits like the G8.
9 He/She makes Germany's foreign policy[2].
10 He/She is elected by the people.

c) Explain how the role of the German president is similar to and different from the role of the US president. Which other important person in German politics plays a similar role to the US president?

5 Talking about German politics

a) Find more information about the role of the German president <u>or</u> about another role in German political life, e.g. the chancellor[3], the premiers[4] of the German states (Bavaria, Hamburg, etc.), the speaker of the German parliament, a member of parliament, the leader of a political party, etc.

b) Prepare a short talk to explain the political role you chose to an American student.
The language on the right might be helpful.
👥 *Give your talk in a small group.*
Comment on the other talks in your group.

Activate your English

– ... has a(n) executive[5]/political/ representational[6] role.
– One of the duties[7] of the ... is to ...
– The ... is elected by parliament/the people/...
– ... is the head of state/head of the government.
– ... signs legislation into law.
– ... chooses ministers for the cabinet.
– ... is in charge of[8] foreign/economic/... policy.
– ... runs the debates in parliament.
– ... makes speeches on ...
– ... meets foreign heads of government/state.
– ... runs the government in the state of ...

---

[1] legislation [ˌledʒɪs'leɪʃn] *Gesetze; Gesetzgebung* [2] foreign policy ['pɒləsi] *Außenpolitik* [3] chancellor ['tʃɑːnsələ] *Bundeskanzler/in*
[4] premier ['premiə] *Ministerpräsident/in* [5] executive [ɪg'zekjətɪv] *Exekutiv-* [6] representational [ˌreprɪzen'teɪʃnl] *repräsentativ*
[7] duty ['djuːti] *Pflicht* [8] (to) be in charge of sth. *für etwas zuständig sein, für etwas die Verantwortung tragen*

Skills File – Inhalt

Das **Skills File** dieses Bandes fasst alle Arbeits- und Lerntechniken zusammen, die du in den Bänden 1 bis 6 kennengelernt hast.

Die Themen, die in Band 6 neu sind, sind mit **NEW** gekennzeichnet:
– **NEW   Describing Cartoons**, Seite 126
– **NEW   Reading literature**, Seite 137.

Die Hinweise im Skills File helfen dir bei der Arbeit mit Hör- und Lesetexten, beim Sprechen, beim Schreiben von eigenen Texten, bei der Sprachmittlung und beim Lernen von Methoden.

STUDY AND LANGUAGE SKILLS

SF Learning words

Worauf solltest du beim Lernen und Wiederholen von Vokabeln achten?

– Lerne immer 7–10 Vokabeln auf einmal.
– Lerne neue und wiederhole alte Vokabeln regelmäßig – am besten jeden Tag
  5–10 Minuten.
– Lerne mit jemandem zusammen. Fragt euch gegenseitig ab.
– Schreib die neuen Wörter immer auch auf und überprüfe die Schreibweise
  mithilfe des *Dictionary* oder *Vocabulary*.

Wie kannst du Wörter besser behalten?

Wörter kannst du besser behalten, wenn du sie in Wortgruppen sammelst und
ordnest:
– **Gegensatzpaare** sammeln, z. B. **(to) allow ◄► (to) ban**; **divorced ◄► married**;
  single room ◄► double room
– Wörter mit **gleicher oder ähnlicher Bedeutung** sammeln, z. B.
  big – huge – large; **(to) scream – (to) shout**
– Wörter in **Wortfamilien** sammeln, z. B. **(to) produce, producer, product,**
  production, …; (to) drive, driver, driving licence, driving instructor, …
– Wörter in **Wortnetzen** (*networks*) sammeln und ordnen.

SF Describing pictures

Wie kann ich Bilder beschreiben?

– Um zu sagen, wo genau etwas
  abgebildet ist, benutze:
  at the top/bottom · in the
  foreground/background ·
  in the middle · on the left/right
– Diese Präpositionen sind auch
  hilfreich:
  behind · between · in front of · next
  to · under
– Um zu beschreiben, was die Personen
  auf dem Bild tun, benutze das **present**
  progressive.
  Someone is riding a horse.

Wie kann ich beschreiben, was die Personen fühlen?

Oft sollst du dich in eine Person auf einem Foto hineinversetzen und beschreiben,
was sie fühlt oder denkt. Schau dir das Foto genau an und nimm dir Zeit, dir die
Situation vorzustellen. Beim Formulieren helfen dir *phrases* wie:
Maybe the woman/man in the photo feels … /is thinking about … ·
I think he/she feels/wants to/…

Manchmal sollst du dir vorstellen, was die Person getan hat, bevor das Foto
gemacht wurde. Achte auf Details im Foto (Hat die Person einen Gegenstand in
der Hand? Wie sieht sie aus? Was tut sie?) und überlege dir, wie es zu der im Foto
gezeigten Situation gekommen sein könnte (Warum ist die Person traurig,
fröhlich etc.?). Verwende die **past tenses**:

Maybe he found out that … • Perhaps he was looking for a place to relax/…

Wenn du beschreiben sollst, was wohl als Nächstes geschehen wird bzw. was die
Person danach tun wird, verwendest du die **future tenses**:

He looks as if he's going to cry/… • Maybe he'll decide to …

SF **NEW Describing cartoons**   ▶ *Unit 2, Part B (p. 36)*

Cartoons sind humorvolle Zeichnungen, die häufig ein aktuelles Thema
aufgreifen.

Wie beschreibe ich einen Cartoon?

Bei der Beschreibung eines Cartoons gehst du
zunächst vor wie bei der Beschreibung von Fotos
oder anderen Zeichnungen.

1. Beschreibe die Personen oder Dinge: Was tun
   sie gerade? Wo befinden sie sich? usw.
   **The cartoon shows … • In the foreground/
   background/… there is/are …**

2. Achte darauf, ob der Cartoon eine
   Bildunterschrift (*caption*), Sprechblasen oder
   Gedankenblasen (*speech bubbles, thought
   bubbles*) hat.
   In the caption it says that …

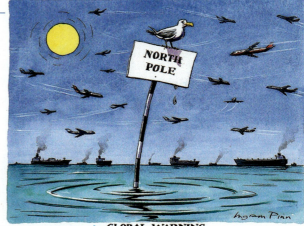

▶ **GLOBAL WARNING**

Wie analysiere ich die Aussage eines Cartoons?

1. Sag, worum es in dem Cartoon geht, welches Thema er behandelt:
   The cartoon is about …

2. Wenn du analysierst, welche Botschaft (*message*) der Cartoon-Zeichner
   vermitteln möchte, solltest du alle Elemente des Cartoons noch einmal
   zusammen betrachten: die Zeichnung sowie die Bildunterschrift und Sprech-
   oder Gedankenblasen. Achte darauf, ob die Personen oder Dinge positiv oder
   negativ dargestellt werden. Bedenke, dass ein Cartoon auch ernste Themen
   humorvoll darstellt und oft stark übertreibt!
   I think the cartoon shows us that … • The artist wants to say that …

Manchmal sollst du Stellung zur Botschaft des Cartoons nehmen und deine
eigene Meinung sagen:
**I like/don't like the cartoon because … • I think the artist is right/wrong
because …**

SF Check yourself

How am I doing?

Damit du weißt, wie gut du die Kompetenzbereiche (**Listening**, **Speaking**, **Reading**, **Writing**, **Mediation**) beherrschst und wo du noch Schwächen hast, solltest du dich immer wieder selbst überprüfen. Das kannst du auf unterschiedlichen Wegen tun. Eine Reihe von Tipps kennst du vermutlich schon. Du kannst dich auch nach jedem *Getting ready for a test* mithilfe der *How am I doing*-Seiten selbst überprüfen. Dabei gehst du wie folgt vor:

1. Du bearbeitest die Aufgaben und überprüfst deine Ergebnisse.

2. Dann schaust du dir die Bereiche, in denen du Fehler gemacht hast, noch einmal an. Die Verweise zeigen dir, auf welchen Seiten im Schülerbuch du Tipps oder Übungen zu diesen Bereichen findest.

3. Nun solltest du gezielt diese Bereiche üben. Dies kannst du z.B. mithilfe des *Exam File* oder des *Workbook* tun. Frag auch deinen Lehrer oder deine Lehrerin, wo du noch weitere Übungen finden kannst.

Die Arbeit mit einer persönlichen Fehlerliste

Führe eine Liste der Fehler, die du oft machst, und nutze sie beim Schreiben von Texten als persönliche Checkliste. Hefte diese Liste in deinem Englischordner ab oder lege dir dafür ein extra Heft an (z.B. in DIN-A5).
Das Heft kannst du z.B. nach folgenden Schwerpunkten unterteilen:

1. Drittel: *Words*   2. Drittel: *Grammar*   3. Drittel: *Spelling*

Dann untersuchst du deine Klassenarbeiten und andere schriftliche Arbeiten auf deine Fehlerquellen hin. Dein/e Englischlehrer/in zeigt durch Abkürzungen am Rand, was für eine Art Fehler du gemacht hast.

WORDS

Wrong	Correct	REMEMBER
He goes to school with the bus.	He goes to school by bus.	mit dem Bus fahren – go by bus
We've got a strong teacher.	We've got a strict teacher.	Nicht verwechseln! streng – strict / strong – stark
I climbed on a tree.	I climbed a tree.	auf einen Baum klettern – climb a tree

> **Tipp**
>
> • Ergänze das Heft jedes Mal, wenn du eine Klassenarbeit oder einen Text von deinem Lehrer/deiner Lehrerin zurückbekommen hast.
> • Überprüfe, ob du bestimmte Fehler immer wieder machst. Wenn ja, such dafür Übungen in deinem Englischbuch, deinem *Workbook*, deinem *e-Workbook* oder frag deinen Lehrer/deine Lehrerin nach Übungen.
> • Schau dir vor jeder Klassenarbeit die Fehler an, die du oft machst.
> • Mach dir mithilfe des Grammatikteils die Regeln, die dir besonders schwerfallen, noch einmal bewusst.

SF Using a dictionary

Wie benutze ich ein zweisprachiges Wörterbuch?

Du verstehst einen Text nicht, weil er zu viele Wörter enthält, die dir unbekannt sind, und die Worterschließungstechniken (▶ *SF Working out the meaning of words, p. 134*) helfen dir nicht weiter? Du sollst einen Text auf Englisch schreiben und dir fehlt das eine oder andere Wort, um deine Ideen auszudrücken? Du willst z.B. sagen, die Handlung in *Twilight* dreht sich um die schwierige Beziehung zwischen Bella und Edward, aber du kennst das englische Wort für „drehen" nicht? In jedem Fall hilft dir ein zweisprachiges Wörterbuch.

- Die **Leitwörter** oben auf der Seite helfen dir, schneller zu finden, was du suchst. Auf der linken Seite steht das erste Stichwort, auf der rechten Seite das letzte Stichwort der Doppelseite.

- „**drehen**" ist das **Stichwort**. Alle Stichwörter sind alphabetisch geordnet: **d** vor **e**, **da** vor **de** und **dre** vor **dri** usw.

- Die **kursiv gedruckten** Hinweise helfen dir, die für deinen Text passende Bedeutung zu finden.

- Die **Ziffern** 1, 2 usw. zeigen, dass ein Stichwort mehrere ganz verschiedene Bedeutungen hat.

- **Beispielsätze** und **Redewendungen** sind dem Stichwort zugeordnet. In den Beispielsätzen und Redewendungen ersetzt eine **Tilde** (~) das Stichwort.

- Im englisch-deutschen Teil der meisten Wörterbücher findest du außerdem Hinweise auf **unregelmäßige Verbformen**, auf die **Steigerungsformen der Adjektive** und Ähnliches.

- Die **Lautschrift** gibt Auskunft darüber, wie das Wort ausgesprochen und betont wird.

Wie benutze ich ein einsprachiges Wörterbuch?

Wenn du englische Texte liest oder selbst einen englischen Text schreibst, kannst du auch ein einsprachiges englisches Wörterbuch zu Hilfe nehmen. Hier findest du mehr über ein englisches Wort heraus als in einem zweisprachigen Wörterbuch:

- Das einsprachige Wörterbuch erklärt die **Bedeutung** eines englischen Wortes **auf Englisch**. Manche Wörter haben mehrere Bedeutungen. Lies alle Einträge und Beispielsätze genau und vergleiche sie mit deinem englischen Text, um die richtige Bedeutung herauszufinden.

- Das Wörterbuch hilft dir auch, die passenden Verben, Präpositionen, Nomen, ... zu „deinem" Wort zu finden und die richtigen Wendungen zu verwenden.

Dr.

Dr. (*Abk. für* **Doktor**) Dr., Doctor
Drache dragon
Drachen *Papierdrachen* kite; *Fluggerät* hang glider

Drehbuch screenplay, script
drehen 1 *Verb mit Obj* turn; *Film* shoot*; *Zigarette* roll 2: **sich ~** turn; *schnell* spin*; **sich ~ um** *übertragen* be* about
Drehkreuz turnstile; **Drehorgel** barrel organ [ˈɔːgən]; **Drehort** location; **Drehstuhl** swivel chair; **Drehtür** revolving door
Drehung turn; *um eine Achse* rotation
Drehzahl (number of) revolutions *Pl od.* revs *Pl*
Drehzahlmesser rev counter
drei three
Drei three; *Note etwa* C; **ich habe eine ~ geschrieben** I got a C
dreidimensional 1 *Adj* three-dimensional 2 *Adv:* **etwas ~ darstellen** depict sth. three-dimensionally; **Dreieck** triangle [ˈtraɪæŋgl]; **dreieckig** triangular [traɪˈæŋgjʊlə]

Tipp

Nimm nicht einfach die erste Übersetzung, die dir angeboten wird! Lies den Wörterbucheintrag, bis du die richtige Übersetzung gefunden hast.

---

deadly [ˈdedli] *adj*
1 *able or likely to kill people* {= lethal}: This is no longer a deadly disease.
deadly to The HSN virus is deadly to chickens.
a deadly weapon The new generation of biological weapons is more deadly than ever.
2 (*only before noun*) {= complete}:
deadly silence There was deadly silence after his speech.
a deadly secret Don't tell anyone – this is a deadly secret.
in deadly earnest *completely serious*: Don't you laugh – I am in deadly earnest!
3 (*informal*) *very boring*: Many TV programmes are pretty deadly!
4 *always able to achieve something*: The new Chelsea striker is said to be a deadly

SF Research

Wo kann ich Informationen finden?

Wenn du nach Informationen suchst, solltest du immer **mehrere Quellen** verwenden. Du kannst im Internet, in einem Lexikon, Atlas, Wörterbuch, Schulbuch oder in anderen Quellen suchen. Auch CDs und DVDs sind mögliche Quellen. Benutze auch einige englische Quellen, das kann dir beim Ausformulieren deines englischen Textes helfen.

– Internet/Lexikon: alle Wissensgebiete, wichtige Personen und Ereignisse
– Atlas: geografische und politische Übersichten, Städte, Flüsse
– Wörterbücher: Rechtschreibung und Bedeutung von Wörtern
– Schulbücher: verschiedene Wissensgebiete
– Zeitungen/Zeitschriften: aktuelle Informationen zu allen Themenbereichen

Wie kann ich das Internet zur Recherche nutzen?

Eine wichtige Informationsquelle ist das Internet. Aber manchmal findest du dort so viele Informationen, dass du schnell den Überblick verlierst. Diese Tipps sollen dir helfen, nicht im *World Wide Web* verloren zu gehen.

– Fertige eine Liste mit Schlüsselwörtern (**key words**) zu deinem Thema an, z. B.
  carbon calculator, carbon footprint, …
– Probiere, mit welchem Schlüsselwort oder welcher Kombination von Schlüsselwörtern du die besten Ergebnisse erzielst:
  „carbon calculator", …
– Wenn du dir zunächst einen Überblick verschaffen willst, kannst du auch ein Nachschlagewerk im Internet anklicken wie z. B.:
  www.infoplease.com   www.en.wikipedia.org
  Manchmal gibt es dort auch Links, die dir weiterhelfen können.
– Suchmaschinen (wie z. B. *Google*, *Altavista* oder *Yahoo*) helfen dir, Websites zu deinem Thema zu finden. Verwende eine Suchmaschine und gib deine Schlüsselwörter in das Suchfenster ein.
– Wenn die angezeigten Websites dir nicht helfen oder du zu viele Websites angezeigt bekommst, versuch es noch einmal, indem du deine Schlüsselwörter präzisierst.

mit **allen** Wörtern	carbon calculator footprint	10 Ergebnisse
mit der **genauen Wortgruppe**	carbon calculator	
mit **irgendeinem** der Wörter		
ohne die Wörter		

> **Tipp**
> • Verwende immer mehrere Internet-Quellen, um sicherzugehen, dass die Informationen stimmen.
> • Suche Antworten auf die **5 Ws** (**who, what, where, when, why**).
> • Bei englischen Quellen brauchst du nicht alles zu verstehen. Konzentriere dich auf das Wesentliche.
> • Schreib die Quellen nicht wortwörtlich ab, sondern mach dir Notizen in deinen eigenen Worten ▸ *Reading course S. 134–135.*

SF Giving a presentation

Wie mache ich eine gute Präsentation?

Vorbereitung
- Schreib die wichtigsten Gedanken in Stichworten auf, z. B. auf nummerierte Karteikarten oder in einer Mindmap.
- Übe deine Präsentation zu Hause vor einem Spiegel. Sprich laut, deutlich und langsam und mach Pausen an geeigneten Stellen.

Folien oder Poster
- Folien (für Overhead-Projektoren oder Computerpräsentationen) oder Poster sind gut, um
  - zu zeigen, wie dein Vortrag aufgebaut ist
  - Tabellen, Diagramme usw. für alle lesbar zu präsentieren
  - die wichtigsten Punkte zusammenzufassen.
- Schreib groß und für alle gut lesbar.

Durchführung
- Bevor du beginnst, sortiere deine Vortragskarten.
- Häng das Poster auf oder leg deine Folie auf den ausgeschalteten Projektor oder bereite den Beamer vor.
- Warte, bis es ruhig ist. Schau die Zuhörenden an.
- Erkläre zu Anfang, worüber du sprechen wirst.
- Lies nicht von deinen Karten ab, sondern sprich frei.

> My presentation is about ...
> First, I'd like to talk about ...
> Second, ...

> This picture/photo/ ... shows ...

Schluss
- Beende deine Präsentation mit einem abschließenden Satz.
- Frag die Zuhörenden, ob sie Fragen haben. Bedanke dich fürs Zuhören.

> That's the end of my presentation. Have you got any questions?

Ausführlichere sprachliche Hilfen für Präsentationen findest du unter:
▶ *SF Giving a presentation – useful phrases (p. 140)*

SF Using visual materials with a presentation

Wofür sind visuelle Materialien gut?

Deine Zuhörer/innen können sich viel mehr merken, wenn du nicht nur sprichst, sondern ihnen auch etwas zum Anschauen bietest (Visualisierungen). Das können z. B. Fotos, Cartoons, Landkarten, Zeitleisten, Diagramme, Poster oder Filmausschnitte sein.

Was muss ich bei visuellen Materialien beachten?

Vorbereitung
- Das Gerüst deines Vortrags sollte stehen, bevor du anfängst, dir darüber Gedanken zu machen, welche Visualisierungen gut passen könnten.
- Diagramme und Tabellen sind gut, um Zahlen zu verdeutlichen; Zeitleisten sind gut, um eine Entwicklung zu zeigen; Fotos und Cartoons sind gut, wenn man seinen Vortrag auflockern will.

Durchführung
- Bezieh deine visuellen Materialien in deinen Vortrag ein, um etwas zu veranschaulichen, aber lies nicht einfach von der Folie etc. ab.

Tipp

Denke daran, dass Schriften und Bilder so groß sein sollten, dass alle im Klassenraum sie gut lesen und sehen können.

SF Talking about charts

Welche Informationen kann ich Diagrammen (*charts*) entnehmen?

Diagramme stellen statistische Vergleiche zwischen mindestens zwei Dingen dar. Es werden entweder absolute Zahlen oder Prozentsätze miteinander verglichen.

Welche unterschiedlichen Formen von Diagrammen gibt es?

– **Bar charts (Säulendiagramme)** beschreiben häufig die Anzahl oder Größe von zwei oder mehr Dingen.
– **Pie charts (Kreis-/Tortendiagramme)** geben einen schnellen Überblick über die prozentuale Verteilung.
– **Charts (Tabellen)** ermöglichen den Vergleich unterschiedlicher Daten anhand von Zahlen und Prozentsätzen.
– **Line graphs (Kurvendiagramme)** stellen den Zusammenhang zwischen zwei zu vergleichenden Größen dar.

Wie kann ich beschreiben, was die Diagramme darstellen?

Um ein Diagramm zu beschreiben, solltest du folgende Fragen beantworten:
– **What is the chart/table/graph about?**
   The bar/pie chart is about … • The line graph deals with … • It is taken from …
– **What does the chart/table/graph compare or show?**
   The chart/table/graph compares the size/number of … • It shows the different … • The pie chart is divided into … slices that show …
– **What does the chart tell you? What information does it give you?**
   … has the largest/second largest • … is twice/three times/… as big as … • There are more than/nearly twice as many … as there are … • A huge majority/small minority/ … • … per cent of …

Wenn vorhanden, solltest du Aussagen über den Zeitraum der Statistik ergänzen:
   The chart is about the years …

> ### Tipp
>
> Benutze das **simple past**, wenn du dich auf einen Zeitpunkt in der Vergangenheit beziehst: **Over 14 million tourists from the UK visited Spain in 2008.**
>
> Benutze das **simple present**, wenn du deine Schlussfolgerungen wiedergibst:
> **Spain is one of the most popular countries with tourists from the UK.**
>
> Benutze das **present perfect**, wenn du dich auf einen Zeitraum beziehst, der von der Vergangenheit bis heute reicht:
> **How many people have visited Spain since 2008?**

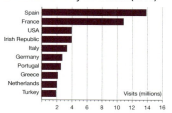

Countries visited by UK tourists (2008)

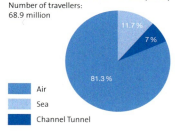

How UK citizens travelled abroad (2008)
Number of travellers: 68.9 million

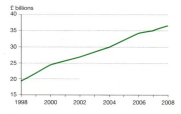

Spending by UK tourists abroad

LISTENING AND READING SKILLS

SF Listening

Was muss ich beim *Listening* beachten?

Vor dem Hören:
- Überlege, worum es in dem Hörtext gehen wird. Frag dich, was du schon über das Thema weißt.
- Lies die Aufgaben gut durch, damit du weißt, worauf du achten sollst:
  - auf die **Hauptgedanken** oder die **Kernaussage** des Textes, z. B. wenn du sagen sollst, um welches Thema es geht, oder welche Meinung der Sprecher zu dem Thema hat.
  - auf bestimmte **Details**, z. B. wenn du Namen, Uhrzeiten, Jahreszahlen heraushören sollst.
- Bereite dich darauf vor, Notizen zu machen. Leg z. B. eine Tabelle oder Liste an.

Beim Hören:
- Keine Panik! Du musst nicht alles verstehen. Konzentriere dich auf das Wesentliche. Oft werden wichtige Informationen auch wiederholt.

- Achte auf Geräusche und unterschiedliche Stimmen. Was ein Sprecher/eine Sprecherin besonders betont, das ist wichtig!

- Wenn du gezielt nach Informationen suchst, denk an die Aufgabe und lass dich von anderen Einzelheiten nicht ablenken. Aufgepasst: die Informationen, die du suchst, kommen vielleicht in einer anderen Reihenfolge vor, als du sie erwartest.

- Manche Signalwörter machen es dir leichter, den Hörtext zu verstehen:
  - Aufzählung: **and**, **another**, **too**
  - Gegensatz: **although**, **but**
  - Grund, Folge: **because, so**, **so that**
  - Vergleich: **larger/older/... than**, **more**, **most**
  - Reihenfolge: **before**, **after**, **then**, **next**, **later**, **when**, **at last**, **at the same time**

- Mache kurze Notizen, z. B. Anfangsbuchstaben, Symbole oder Stichworte.

Nach dem Hören:
- Vervollständige deine Notizen sofort.
- Konzentriere dich beim zweiten Hören auf das, was du beim ersten Mal nicht gut verstanden hast.

Worauf sollte ich bei automatischen Telefonansagen achten?

Wenn du eine telefonische Auskunft einholen willst, hörst du manchmal eine automatische Telefonansage.
- Keine Panik! Du kannst eine automatische Telefonansage mehrmals hören.
- Achte besonders auf Zahlen! Meist wirst du aufgefordert, bestimmte Tasten auf deinem Telefon zu drücken, um die gewünschte Information zu erhalten. Oft werden diese Zahlen wiederholt.
- Überlege dir vorher, welche Informationen du suchst und auf welche Schlüsselwörter du dafür achten solltest. Schreib sie auf.
- Höre besonders genau zu, wenn deine Schlüsselwörter genannt werden, und mach dir Notizen zu ihnen.

SF   Taking notes

Worum geht es beim Notizenmachen?

Wenn du beim Lesen oder Zuhören Notizen machst, kannst du dich später besser an das Gehörte oder Gelesene erinnern. Das ist nützlich, wenn du etwas vortragen, nacherzählen oder einen Bericht schreiben sollst.

Wie mache ich Notizen?

In Texten oder Gesprächen gibt es immer wichtige und unwichtige Wörter. Die wichtigen Wörter werden Schlüsselwörter (**key words**) genannt, und nur diese solltest du notieren. Meist sind das Substantive und Verben, manchmal auch Adjektive oder Zahlen.

Hmm, da hab ich wohl ein paar Symbole zu viel benutzt ...

> **Tipp**
>
> • Verwende Ziffern (z. B. **7** statt „seven").
> • Verwende Symbole und Abkürzungen, z. B. ✔ (für „ja") und **+** (für „und") oder **US** für „United States", **E.** für „Edward".
>   Du kannst auch eigene Symbole erfinden.
> • Verwende **not** oder ⤬ statt „doesn't" oder „don't".

SF   Marking up a text

Wann sollte ich einen Text markieren?

Du hast einen Text mit vielen Fakten vor dir liegen und sollst später über bestimmte Dinge berichten. Dann wird es dir helfen, die für die Aufgabenstellung wichtigen Informationen im Text zu markieren.

Wie gehe ich am besten vor?

Lies den Text und markiere nur die für dein Thema wichtigen Informationen. Nicht jeder Satz enthält für deine Aufgabe wichtige Wörter, und oft reicht es aus, nur ein oder zwei Wörter in einem Satz zu markieren.

– Du kannst wichtige Wörter einkreisen.

– Du kannst sie unterstreichen.

– Du kannst sie mit einem Textmarker hervorheben.

ABER:

Markiere nur auf Fotokopien von Texten oder in Büchern, die dir gehören, oder verwende eine Folie und einen wasserlöslichen Folienstift.

Sydney Opera House
The Sydney Opera House is one of the most famous buildings in the world. It houses the large Concert Hall (2,678 seats), the Opera Theatre (1,507 seats), other smaller theatres and a place for open-air events.

Sydney Opera House
The Sydney Opera House is one of the most famous buildings in the world. It houses the large Concert Hall (2,678 seats), the Opera Theatre (1,507 seats), other smaller theatres and a place for open-air events.

Sydney Opera House
The Sydney Opera House is one of the most famous buildings in the world. It houses the large Concert Hall (2,678 seats), the Opera Theatre (1,507 seats), other smaller theatres and a place for open-air events.

READING COURSE

Working out the meaning of words

Das Nachschlagen unbekannter Wörter im Wörterbuch kostet Zeit und nimmt auf Dauer den Spaß am Lesen. Oft geht es auch ohne Wörterbuch!

Hmm, *guarantee* sieht so aus wie „Garantie" oder?

Was hilft dir, unbekannte Wörter zu verstehen?

1. **Bilder** zeigen oft die Dinge, die du im Text nicht verstehst. Wenn es Bilder zum Text gibt, dann schau sie dir vor dem Lesen genau an.

2. Oft hilft dir der **Textzusammenhang**, z.B. *When we reached the station, Judy went to the ticket machine to buy our tickets.*

3. Manche englischen Wörter werden **ähnlich wie im Deutschen** geschrieben oder ausgesprochen, z.B. excellent, millionaire, nation, reality.

4. Manchmal stecken in unbekannten Wörtern **bekannte Teile**, z.B. friendliness, helpless, understandable, gardener, tea bag, waiting room.

Super! Das ist es!

Skimming and scanning

Skimming: Lesen, um sich einen Überblick zu verschaffen

Beim **Skimming** überfliegst du einen Text schnell, um dir einen ersten **Überblick** zu verschaffen, worum es geht. Du willst herausfinden, ob ein Text, den du im Internet oder in einem Buch gefunden hast, überhaupt nützliche Informationen zu deinem Thema (z.B. für ein Referat) enthält. Achte beim Skimming auf:
– die **Überschrift**
– die **Zwischenüberschriften** und **hervorgehobene** Wörter oder Sätze
– die **Bilder** und **Bildunterschriften**
– den **ersten** und **letzten Satz** jedes Absatzes
– **Grafiken**, **Statistiken** und die **Quelle** des Textes.

Scanning: Lesen, um nach bestimmten Informationen zu suchen

Beim **Scanning** suchst du in einem Text nach **bestimmten Informationen**, die z.B. für ein Referat wichtig sind. Dazu brauchst du nicht den gesamten Text zu lesen, sondern du suchst nach Schlüsselwörtern (**key words**) und liest nur dort genauer, wo du sie findest. Geh dabei so vor:

Schritt 1: Denk an das Schlüsselwort, nach dem du suchst, oder schreib es auf.

Schritt 2: Geh mit den Augen und dem Finger schnell durch den Text, in breiten Schlingen wie bei einem „S" oder „Z" oder von oben nach unten wie bei einem „U". Dabei hast du das Schriftbild oder das Bild des Wortes, nach dem du suchst, vor Augen. Das gesuchte Wort wird dir sofort „ins Auge springen". Lies nur dort weiter, um Näheres zu erfahren.

Schritt 3: Wenn das Schlüsselwort, nach dem du suchst, im Text nicht vorkommt, überleg dir, welche anderen Wörter mit den benötigten Informationen zu tun haben, und such nach diesen.

Finding the main ideas of a text

Wenn du Texte wie Zeitungsartikel, Berichte oder Kommentare richtig verstehen willst, ist es gut, wenn du ihre Hauptaussagen erkennst und nachvollziehst, wie sie zusammenhängen. Dabei hilft dir ein Blick auf die Struktur dieser Texte.

Wie finde ich die Hauptaussagen eines Textes?

1. Jeder Text dreht sich um ein Thema oder hat eine Hauptaussage. Diese findest du oft im ersten Absatz. Lies ihn deshalb besonders gründlich durch.

2. Die Hauptaussage wird in der Regel durch weitere Aussagen bzw. Gedanken unterstützt. Du findest sie oft im ersten oder letzten Satz der nachfolgenden Absätze.

3. Diese weiteren Aussagen bzw. Gedanken werden meist durch Beispiele und Begründungen ergänzt.

We are people too!

By Oliver Munslow (16) – 23 August 2010

To everybody out there that thinks young people are different, you're right! We're younger than adults. But that doesn't mean you don't need to listen to us or you don't have to respect us. We have feelings and (this might surprise some of you) we are people too.

Did you know that here in Britain every citizen under 18 has important rights? For example, we all have the right to be listened to and taken seriously, and we have the right to get together with our friends in public (as long as we respect the rights of other people and do not break the law).

But British children aren't taken seriously until they're 18. Too many adults think that our views just don't count and that we don't deserve equal rights. Here are some examples of discrimination against teenagers from my everyday life (in fact, most of these things happened to me this week).

Every day I see signs on shop doors that say '2 children at a time', or 'no school bags', or even 'no children unless they are with an adult'. (…)

> **Tipp**
>
> Die folgenden Wörter oder Wendungen werden oft im Zusammenhang mit Begründungen oder Beispielen verwendet:
>
> **and so • because • e.g. / for example • etc. • for lots of reasons • this shows that • that's why • …**

Drawing conclusions

Wenn du Fragen zu einem Text beantworten sollst oder bei einer Recherche Informationen zu einer bestimmten Frage suchst, kann es sein, dass du an mehreren Stellen schauen musst oder dass die Antwort nicht 1:1 im Text steht.

Wie funktioniert schlussfolgerndes Lesen?

1. Die einfachste Form des schlussfolgernden Lesens besteht darin, die Informationen aus verschiedenen Textstellen zusammenzuführen. Bei dem Text *The Carbon Diaries* 2015 (S. 34–35) sollst du sagen, wie Laura, Kim und ihre Mutter zu *carbon rationing* stehen. Dazu musst du dir mehrere Stellen ansehen.

2. Manchmal steht die Antwort auf eine Frage nicht direkt im Text. Dann musst du sie dir erschließen. Du fragst dich z. B., ob Laura Brown und ihre Familie durch die Ausnahmesituation mehr gemeinsam unternehmen. Dafür musst du Aussagen im Text finden, die etwas mit der Frage zu tun haben:

   Lines 84–89: *Dad spends all night on his laptop, Mum is always lost on a bus somewhere and Kim just lives in her room – an evil ball of silence. (…)*

   Conclusion: *The family don't spend more time together because of carbon rationing. In fact, they spend less time together.*

SF Reading English texts

Was unterscheidet Sachtexte und literarische Texte?

Wenn du einen Text liest, solltest du dir klar machen, ob er sich mit der Wirklichkeit auseinandersetzt, also ein Sachtext (*non-fictional text*) ist, oder ob er von einer erdachten Welt handelt, also ein literarischer Text (*fictional text*) ist.

Sachtexte (oder nicht-fiktionale Texte) sind z. B. Berichte in Zeitungen, wissenschaftliche Artikel, Kommentare sowie Gebrauchsanleitungen und Broschürentexte. Hier informiert der Autor oder die Autorin über ein Thema der realen Welt oder nimmt Stellung dazu.

Literarische (oder fiktionale) Texte sind z. B. Kurzgeschichten und Romane. Der Autor oder die Autorin wählt Figuren (*characters*) aus und erzählt von ihren Gefühlen und Handlungen, von deren Motiven und Hintergründen. Oft verwendet der Autor für seine Geschichte eine anschauliche Sprache (z. B. ausschmückende Adjektive, Vergleiche).

Was ist das Besondere beim Lesen von längeren literarischen Texten auf Englisch?

Geschichten zu lesen macht Spaß! Wenn du eine Geschichte (*story*) oder einen Roman (*novel*) liest, tauchst du in eine andere Welt ein. Dabei ist es nicht so wichtig, dass du beim Lesen jedes Wort verstehst. Lass dich einfach von der Handlung durch die Geschichte tragen.

Hier sind ein paar Tipps, die es dir erleichtern, längere literarische Texte auf Englisch zu lesen.

Vor dem Lesen:
1. Lies die **Einführung** und die **Überschrift(en)** und sieh dir die **Bilder** zum Text an. Sie geben dir erste Informationen über das, was dich erwartet. Stell dir vor, worum es in der Geschichte gehen könnte.

2. Bei Lektüren oder Romanen gibt es hinten auf dem Buchumschlag meist einen kurzen **Klappentext** mit einer Zusammenfassung der Handlung – natürlich ohne, dass das Ende verraten wird.

Während des Lesens:
1. Tauche ein in die Geschichte. Lies zügig! Kümmere dich nicht um einzelne Wörter, die du nicht kennst oder nicht verstehst. Lies einfach weiter. Das Wichtigste ist, dass du im Großen und Ganzen die Handlung verstehst. Wenn du merkst, dass du der Handlung nicht mehr folgen kannst, weil du zu viele Wörter nicht verstehst, dann nutze alle dir bekannten Techniken, um die Bedeutung zu erschließen:
   – Sieh dir noch einmal die Bilder an.
   – Beachte den Textzusammenhang.
   – Kennst du ähnliche englische oder deutsche Wörter?
   – Vielleicht kennst du Teile der unbekannten Wörter?
   ▶ *SF Working out the meaning of words, p. 134*

2. Wenn das alles nicht hilft, dann schlage das unbekannte Wort im Wörterbuch nach. ▶ *SF Using a dictionary, p. 128*

▶ ▶ ▶

> **Tipp**
>
> Beim Lesen von englischen Lektüren oder Büchern kann dir eine Lesetagebuch (**reading log**), wie du es sicher aus dem Deutschunterricht kennst, das Verstehen und Behalten erleichtern.

3. Um der Handlung besser folgen zu können, kann es helfen, wenn du nicht die ganze Geschichte hintereinander liest. Hör ab und zu auf zu lesen und denk darüber nach, was du bis dahin gelesen hast. Erzähl jemandem, was bisher geschah und was du noch nicht verstanden hast. Oft klären sich manche Fragen im Gespräch. Dann lies weiter.

SF NEW   Reading literature   ▶ *TF 2, TF 5 (pp. 110–112, pp. 117–121)*

Was ist das Besondere an literarischen Texten?

Literarische Texte sind oft in einer besonderen Form oder Sprache verfasst. Sie zeigen eine Welt oder Umgebung, die der Autor oder die Autorin erdacht hat. Im Englischen nennt man diese Texte auch *fiction*, weil sie von einer erfundenen (englisch: *fictional*) Welt handeln – im Gegensatz zu *non-fiction*, die sich mit der wirklichen Welt auseinandersetzt.

Alles, was du bereits über das Lesen von Texten im Allgemeinen gelernt hast (▶ *SF Reading course, pp. 134–135; SF Reading English texts, pp. 144–145*), wird dir auch beim Lesen von Literatur helfen.

Literarische Gattungen und ihre Merkmale

Grundsätzlich unterscheidet man drei Arten von literarischen Texten: Gedichte (*poetry*), Erzähltexte (*fiction: stories, novels, etc.*) und Dramen (*plays*).

Du kannst Literatur natürlich einfach zum Vergnügen lesen, zum Beispiel, weil dir die Geschichte, ein bestimmtes Thema oder die dargestellten Personen interessant erscheinen. Zum besseren Verständnis ist es aber hilfreich, wenn du etwas über formale, stilistische oder technische Besonderheiten des Textes weißt. Überlege dir, warum der Autor oder die Autorin gerade diese Mittel einsetzt und welches Gefühl bei dir dadurch während des Lesens entsteht.

Das sind die Besonderheiten der drei Arten von literarischen Texten:

Erzähltexte (z. B. Kurzgeschichten, Romane) bestehen aus einem fortlaufenden Text, der manchmal durch Kapitel untergliedert ist. Um die Figuren (*characters*) der Geschichte herum wird eine Handlung (*plot*) entwickelt, die in einen bestimmten Handlungsrahmen eingebettet ist: ein bestimmter Ort, eine Zeitspanne und ein näher beschriebener Schauplatz (*setting*).

Die Charakterisierung der Figuren kann direkt erfolgen, indem sie mit bestimmten Adjektiven (*cruel, sentimental, …*) beschrieben werden (*direct characterization*). Bei der indirekten Charakterisierung (*indirect characterization*) wird beschrieben, was die Figuren sagen, tun oder fühlen.

Durch besondere sprachliche Mittel (s. Gedichte, S. 138) schafft der Autor eine bestimmte Atmosphäre (*atmosphere*). Diese kann z. B. bedrohlich oder humorvoll sein. Die Ereignisse werden von dem Erzähler (*narrator*) der Geschichte aus einer bestimmten Erzählperspektive (*point of view*) beschrieben: Der Ich-Erzähler (*first-person narrator*) nimmt am Geschehen Teil und erzählt aus der Ich-Perspektive, was ihm (und anderen) widerfährt, während der Er-Erzähler (*third-person narrator*) außerhalb des Geschehens steht.

▶ ▶ ▶

> A few hands go up. Mr. Neck ignores them. It isn't a real question, it's one he asked so he could give the answer. I relax. This is like when my father complains about his boss. The best thing to do is to stay awake and look sympathetic.
> [...]
>
> (aus dem Roman *Speak*, S. 52)

Ich-Erzähler
(*first-person narrator*)

> Standing in the hall, Lisa could hear that the voices were coming from upstairs. There were two people, a man and a woman. 'I don't understand you,' the man said. 'We've got everything money can buy, but still you aren't happy.'
> [...]
> Lisa shivered. 'Tim's parents can't be very happy,' she thought.
>
> (aus der Kurzgeschichte *Money isn't everything*, S. 92)

Er-Erzähler
(*third-person narrator*)

Gedichte bestehen meist aus gebundener Sprache, d.h. aus Verszeilen (*verses*) und Strophen (*stanzas*). Die Sprache von Gedichten unterscheidet sich von der Alltagssprache oft durch die Verwendung von Reimen (*rhyme*), Rhythmus (*rhythm*) und Wiederholungen (*repetition*) sowie einer bildhaften Sprache (Bilder: *images*), z.B. Vergleiche (*similes*) und Metaphern (*metaphors*).

Dramen bestehen in der Regel aus Monologen und Dialogen in direkter Rede. Meist geben Bühnenanweisungen (*stage directions*) Handlungsanweisungen für die Darsteller, sie sind aber auch ein wichtiger Hinweis für den Leser, um sich den Schauplatz (*setting*) vorstellen oder die Aussagen der Figuren besser interpretieren zu können.

> **A red, red rose**
> O, my Love's like a red, red rose,
> That's newly sprung in June.
> O, my Love's like the melody
> That's sweetly played in tune.
> [...]
>
> (aus dem Gedicht *A red, red rose*, S. 113)

Über literarische Texte sprechen und schreiben

Wenn du über literarische Texte sprechen oder schreiben sollst, sind folgende Formulierungen hilfreich:

Setting and plot
The story/novel/play is about …
The story/novel/play is set in …
The text tells the story of …
The action takes place during/in …

Point of view
The story is told from the main character's/… point of view.
… is the narrator of the story.

Characters and characterization
The main character(s) is/are …
He/She seems to be a strong/weak/brave/… person.

Poems
The poem describes/imagines …
The lines of the poem (don't) rhyme.
The poem has a slow/lively/… rhythm.
In line(s) … you can find a simile/metaphor/…

Language
The language in the text creates an exciting/a thrilling/… atmosphere.
I think … is a metaphor/an image for …
The word/phrase … is repeated in line …

Your reaction
The text made me feel happy/sad/angry/…
I liked it/didn't like it when …
I found the ending/story/characters interesting/funny/…

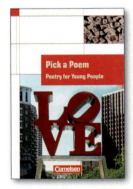

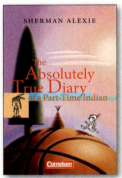

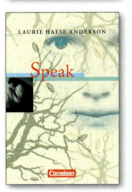

SPEAKING AND WRITING SKILLS

SPEAKING COURSE

Having a conversation

Ein Gespräch beginnen

Es gibt immer mehrere Möglichkeiten:
– **wenn du etwas erfragen willst** (*z. B. den Weg oder die Uhrzeit*)
   Excuse me, do you know … • Excuse me, can you tell me …
– **wenn du jemanden begrüßen möchtest oder kennenlernst**
   Hi. • Hello. • Good morning/evening.
   Oft kann man das Gespräch dann mit einer allgemeinen Bemerkung
   weiterführen: **Great day today! • That's a great …**
– **wenn du jemanden wiedertriffst**
   Hi, how are you doing? • Hi, …, how are things? • Hi, … Good to see/meet you.

Fantastic concert, isn't it?

Ein Gespräch führen

Für den weiteren Verlauf des Gesprächs sind diese Wendungen nützlich:
– **sich vorstellen: By the way, my name's … • I'm … • Nice to meet you.**
– **Smalltalk machen: Have you … before? • Have you ever …? •
   Where are you from? • Do you like …? • What about you?**
– **um Hilfe bitten und anderen helfen: Do you know where …? •
   Can you tell me …? • Sure, no problem • Why don't you …?**
– **sich verabschieden: See you tomorrow/next week. • Bye!**

Und wenn du etwas nicht verstanden hast, kannst du immer nachfragen:
Sorry, I didn't get that. • Sorry, could you say that again, please?

> **Tipp**
>
> Oft hört man zur Begrü-
> ßung auch **How are you?**
> Es wird nicht erwartet, dass
> du darauf eine ausführliche
> Antwort gibst. Am besten
> sagst du einfach **Fine,
> thanks. How about you?**

Taking part in a job interview

Sich vorbereiten

Auf ein Vorstellungsgespräch musst du dich unbedingt vorbereiten. Du solltest
Fragen zu den folgenden Bereichen beantworten können:
– deine Eigenschaften (**personal qualities**), Stärken (**strengths**) und Schwächen
   (**weaknesses**)
– deine Interessen (**interests**) und Arbeitserfahrungen (**work experience**)
– was dich an dem Jobangebot reizt (**why you're interested in the job**).

Überleg dir auch eigene Fragen, z. B. zu deinem Tätigkeitsbereich (**What kind of
work would I have to do?**) oder Tätigkeitsbeginn (**When would I have to start?**).

Am I dressed suitably for the job interview?

Well, …

Im Vorstellungsgespräch

Im Vorstellungsgespräch ist es wichtig, dass du freundlich bist und dich als
positiver und interessierter Mensch präsentierst.
– **bei der Begrüßung: Hello, nice to meet you. • Good morning.**
– **warum du dich bewirbst: I'm really interested in … • I'm good at …, so I think …**
– **wenn es um deine Joberfahrungen geht: I really enjoyed working with …**
– **bei der Verabschiedung: Goodbye and thank you very much.**

> **Tipp**
>
> • Hör gut zu, wenn du
>   etwas gefragt wirst.
> • Sprich nicht zu viel, aber
>   auch nicht zu wenig.
> • Sprich nicht zu schnell.

Having a discussion

Seine Meinung zum Ausdruck bringen und erklären

1. **Expressing an opinion:** In einer Diskussion ist es gut, wenn du möglichst klar und deutlich sagst, was du zu einer bestimmten Frage denkst:
   I think ... • In my opinion, ...

2. **Giving reasons and examples:** Genauso wichtig ist es, dass du Beispiele und Argumente nennst, die deine Meinung unterstützen – schließlich willst du deine Gesprächspartner von deinem Standpunkt überzeugen!
   because ... • First ... / Second ... / And finally... • For example ... • Let me explain ... • That's why ...

Auf andere in einer Diskussion reagieren

1. **Asking for clarification:** Manchmal ist es notwendig nachzuhaken, weil man ein Argument nicht verstanden hat:
   Could you say that again? • Sorry, but I don't understand what you mean.

2. **Agreeing with someone:** Wenn du die Meinung eines anderen unterstützen willst, kannst du das so zum Ausdruck bringen:
   I agree (with you/...) • That's a good point. • You're right.

3. **Disagreeing with someone:** Oft widerspricht man nicht direkt, sondern leitet seine Reaktion mit **Sorry, ...** oder **I don't think ...** ein. Zeig immer Respekt für die Meinung des oder der anderen.
   I don't think you can say ... • I see what you mean, but ... •
   Sorry, but that's not right. • Sorry, I don't agree with you. • Yes, but ...

Giving a presentation – useful phrases

Einleitung

Nenne zu Beginn deines Vortrags dein Thema und gib einen kurzen Überblick darüber, worum es in deinem Vortrag geht:
The topic of my talk today is ... • I'm going to divide this talk into four sections. •
First, I'll give you some general facts about ... • Next I'll look at ... • Finally I'll ...

Während der Präsentation

Mach deutlich, wenn du einen neuen Abschnitt in deinem Vortrag beginnst.
Now please have a look at ... • On the next slide ... • Now I'd like to draw your attention to ... • As you can see in ...

Schluss

Fasse am Ende deines Vortrags die wichtigsten Punkte zusammen. Frag deine Zuhörer, ob sie etwas nachfragen oder kommentieren möchten.
To sum up my talk I ... • Please feel free to ask questions or comment on anything I've said.
Ausführlichere Hinweise zur Vorbereitung und Durchführung einer Präsentation findest du unter: ▶ *SF Giving a presentation (p. 130)*

SF Paraphrasing

Worum geht es beim *Paraphrasing*?

Paraphrasing bedeutet, etwas mit anderen Worten zu erklären. Das ist hilfreich, wenn dir ein bestimmtes Wort nicht einfällt oder wenn dein Gegenüber dich nicht verstanden hat (siehe auch ► *SF Mediation, p. 149*).

Wie gehe ich beim *Paraphrasing* vor?

- Man kann mit einem Wort umschreiben, das dieselbe Bedeutung hat:
  to train is the same as to practise
  Oder man sagt das Gegenteil: **alive is the opposite of dead**
- Manchmal braucht man mehrere Wörter, z. B. wenn man etwas beschreibt oder erklärt. Dabei benutzt man ein allgemeines Wort (**general word**) und nennt weitere Eigenschaften.
  A racing car is a very fast car.
- Oder du umschreibst das Wort mit **... is/are like ...**
  A chef is like a cook, he or she is the main cook in a restaurant.
- Du kannst auch einen Relativsatz (**relative clause**) verwenden:
  A garage is a place where cars are checked and repaired.
  A nurse is a person who looks after people who are ill, usually in a hospital.

SF Brainstorming

Wofür ist Brainstorming gut?

Bei vielen Aufgaben ist es nützlich, wenn du im ersten Schritt möglichst viele Ideen zum Thema sammelst. Dabei hilft dir das **Brainstorming**.

Wie gehe ich beim Brainstorming vor?

Schritt 1:
Schreib alle Ideen so auf, wie sie dir einfallen. Es ist zunächst völlig egal, ob sie gut sind oder nicht. Du kannst die Ideen durcheinander auf einen Zettel schreiben oder schon etwas geordnet, z. B. für jede eine neue Zeile.

Schritt 2:
Lies alle deine Ideen durch und wähle die besten aus. Dann sortiere sie und fasse sie sinnvoll zusammen. Dabei kannst du folgende **Techniken** anwenden:
1. Leg eine **Mindmap** an. Schreib das Thema in die Mitte eines Blattes Papier. Überlege, welche Oberbegriffe zu deiner Sammlung von Ideen passen. Verwende unterschiedliche Farben. Ergänze jede Idee, die zu einem Oberbegriff passt, auf einem Nebenast. Nimm dafür nur wichtige Schlüsselwörter. Du kannst statt Wörtern auch Symbole verwenden und Bilder ergänzen.
2. **The 5 Ws**: Schreib die **5 W-Fragen Who? What? Where? When? Why?** in eine Tabelle. Die Ideen, die dir zu jeder Frage kommen, kannst du darunter schreiben.

SF Summarizing texts

Wenn du einen Text zusammenfasst, gibst du die wichtigten Informationen oder Ereignisse in kürzerer Form wieder. Eine schriftliche Zusammenfassung nennt man im Englischen **summary**.

Wie gehe ich beim *summarizing* vor?

1. Lies den Text mindestens einmal genau durch, damit du verstehst, worum es geht. Mach dir noch keine Notizen.

2. Lies den Text erneut, Satz für Satz, durch. Am besten arbeitest du mit einer Kopie, damit du Passagen im Text markieren kannst. Markiere die Textstellen, die dir Antworten auf die 5 Ws geben.
Wenn du keine Kopie hast, mache dir in Stichpunkten Notizen zu den **5 Ws**:
Who?   Who is the text about?
What?   What happens?/What does he/she do?
Where?   Where does it happen?
When?   When does it happen?
Why?   Why does it happen? / Why does he/she do this?

3. Schreibe eine Zusammenfassung des Texts in deinen eigenen Worten. Bei fiktionalen Texten musst du **simple present** verwenden (auch wenn du eine Geschichte zusammenfasst, die in der Vergangenheit spielt).
In der **Einleitung** erklärst du in ein oder zwei Sätzen, worum es in dem Text geht:
The story is about ... • **The text describes ...** • **The article shows ...** • **In the story we get to know ...**
Im **Hauptteil** gibst du die wichtigsten Ereignisse (z.B. einer Geschichte) oder die Hauptpunkte eines Textes (z.B. eines Zeitungsartikels) wieder. Bringe die Informationen in eine logische Reihenfolge. Verwende dafür deine Notizen zu den **5 Ws**. Schreibe den Text nicht einfach ab, sondern benutze deine eigenen Worte.
Überprüfe deinen Entwurf noch einmal. Enthält dein Text wirklich die wichtigsten Gedanken oder Ereignisse aus dem Original? Achte auch auf sprachliche Fehler und darauf, dass deine Sätze durch **linking words** verbunden sind, wie z.B.
and • **that's why** • **but** • **because** • **...**

4. Bei einer schriftlichen Zusammenfassung (*summary*) musst du den korrigierten Entwurf zum Schluss in eine Reinschrift bringen.

WRITING COURSE

Writing better sentences

Linking words

Eine Geschichte klingt interessanter, wenn du die Sätze mit **linking words** miteinander verbindest. Dabei gibt es mehrere Möglichkeiten:
– **Time phrases** wie **at 7 o'clock**, **every morning**, **a few minutes later**, **then**, **next**
– **Konjunktionen** wie **although**, **because**, **but**, **so ... that**, **that**, **when**, **while**
– **Relativpronomen** wie **that** und **who**

Adjektive und Adverbien

– Mit Adjektiven kannst du Personen, Orte oder Erlebnisse genauer und interessanter beschreiben. Vergleiche: **The man looked into the room.**
   ▶ **The young man looked into the empty room.**
– Mit Adverbien kannst du beschreiben, **wie** jemand etwas macht:
   The young man looked nervously into the empty room.

Using paragraphs

Structuring a text

Bei guten Texten lassen sich drei Hauptabschnitte erkennen:
– eine **Einleitung**, die in das Thema einführt
– ein **Hauptteil**, der meist aus mehreren Absätzen besteht
– ein **Schluss**, der den Text mit einer Zusammenfassung oder etwas Persönlichem zu einem interessanten Ende bringt.

Topic sentences

Am Anfang eines Absatzes sind kurze, einleitende Sätze (**topic sentences**) gut, weil sie den Lesern sofort sagen, worum es geht, z. B.
1. Orte: **My trip to ... was fantastic.** • **... is famous for ...** • **... is a great place.**
2. Personen: **... is great/funny/interesting/clever ...**
3. Aktivitäten: **... is great fun.** • **Lots of people ... every day.**

Wie kann ich meine Absätze interessant gestalten?

– Beginne mit einem interessanten Einstiegssatz:
   You'll never guess what happened to me today! • **Did I tell you that ...?**
– Fange für jeden neuen Aspekt einen neuen Absatz an.
– Beende deinen Text mit einer Zusammenfassung oder etwas Persönlichem.

Writing a report – structuring information

Worauf kommt es bei einem Bericht an?

– Gib dem Leser **eine schnelle Orientierung**, was passiert ist.
– Beginne mit **wichtigen Informationen** und gib erst dann Detailinformationen.
– Ein Bericht gibt immer Antworten auf die **5 Ws**:
  Who? What? When? Where? Why? und manchmal auch auf **How?**
– Verwende das **simple past**.

Correcting your text

Ein Text ist noch nicht „fertig", wenn du ihn zu Ende geschrieben hast. Du solltest ihn immer mehr als einmal durchlesen:
– einmal, um zu sehen, ob er vollständig und gut verständlich ist
– noch einmal, um ihn auf Fehler zu überprüfen, z.B. Rechtschreibfehler (*spelling mistakes*) oder Grammatikfehler (*Grammar mistakes*).

Spelling mistakes

Lies deinen Text langsam, Wort für Wort, Buchstabe für Buchstabe. Wenn du unsicher bist, hilft dir ein Wörterbuch. Beachte folgende Regeln:

> **Tipp**
>
> • Manche Wörter haben Buchstaben, die man nicht spricht, aber schreibt, z.B. **knife**, **climb**.
> • Manchmal ändert sich die Schreibweise, wenn ein Wort eine Endung erhält,
>   z.B. **take → taking, terrible → terribly, lucky → luckily,**
>   **try → tries** (**aber** stay → stays), **run → running, drop → dropped**.
> • Beim Plural tritt manchmal noch ein **-e** zum **-s**, z.B. **church → churches**.

Grammar mistakes

Diese Tipps helfen dir, typische Fehler zu vermeiden:

> **Tipp**
>
> • Im **simple present** wird in der 3. Person Singular **-s** angehängt: **she knows**.
> • **Unregelmäßige Verben:** Manche Verben bilden die Formen des *simple past* und des Partizip Perfekt (*past participle*) unregelmäßig. Die unregelmäßigen Formen musst du lernen. Die Liste steht auf S. 224–225.
>   **go – went – gone; buy – bought – bought**
> • **Verneinung bei Vollverben:** Im *simple present* mit *don't/doesn't*, im *simple past* mit *didn't*, z.B. **He doesn't speak French, he didn't learn it at school.**
> • **Satzstellung:** Im Englischen gilt immer (auch im Nebensatz):
>   a) subject – verb – object (S-V-O)   **... when I saw my brother.**
>   **... als ich meinen Bruder sah.**
>   b) Orts- vor Zeitangabe **I bought a nice book in town yesterday.**
>   **Ich habe gestern in der Stadt ein schönes Buch gekauft.**

SF Writing a CV

Was ist ein CV?

„CV" bedeutet „Lebenslauf". Ein Lebenslauf ist eine Zusammenfassung deiner bisherigen Ausbildung, deiner Fähigkeiten und deiner Interessen. Du brauchst einen Lebenslauf, wenn du dich um eine berufliche Anstellung bewirbst. Amerikaner benutzen statt *CV* das Wort *résumé*.

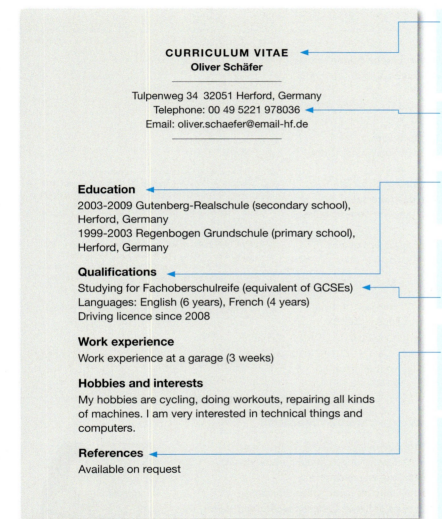

Geburtsdatum und -ort werden in einem britischen CV **oft nicht** genannt. In der Regel fügst du auch **kein Foto** von dir bei.

Gib bei deiner Telefonnummer auch die **internationale Vorwahl** mit an.

Fettgedruckte Überschriften und eine **klare Gliederung** erleichtern das Lesen.

GCSEs gibt es nur in Großbritannien, in den USA entspricht das dem **US high school diploma**.

An dieser Stelle kann auch eine **konkrete Person** als **Referenz** genannt werden. Selbstverständlich musst du ihn oder sie vorher fragen!

Du kannst auch den Abschnitt **Personal statement** hinzufügen, in dem du deine persönlichen Stärken hervorhebst, z.B.
I am a hard-working, reliable student and I like working in a team. I am looking forward to getting more experience in the work place.

> **Tipp**
>
> Bevor du deinen Lebenslauf losschickst, geh folgende Checkliste durch:
> - Habe ich weißes A4-Papier benutzt? Ist das Blatt sauber und ordentlich?
> - Habe ich den Lebenslauf mit einem Computer geschrieben?
> - Ist die Seite klar gegliedert und gut lesbar?
> - Habe ich alle zentralen Bereiche abgedeckt: meine Erfahrungen, meine Interessen, meine Fähigeiten und persönlichen Eigenschaften?
> - Habe ich auch wirklich keine sprachlichen Fehler in meinem Schreiben?

SF Writing letters

Beim Schreiben von Briefen und E-Mails musst du unterschiedliche Regeln beachten, je nachdem, ob du einen förmlichen Brief (*formal letter*) an unbekannte Personen, Behörden, Zeitschriften usw. schreibst oder einen persönlichen, informellen Brief (*informal letter*) an Freunde oder Verwandte.

Worauf kommt es bei förmlichen Briefen an? (*Formal letters*)

1. Schreibe deine Adresse (ohne Namen) und das Datum in die rechte obere Ecke. Verwende keine typisch deutschen Buchstaben wie z.B. ß, ä, ö oder ü.
2. Die Anschrift steht links.
3. Die Anrede lautet *Dear Sir or Madam*. Wenn du den Namen des Adressaten kennst, beginne deinen Brief mit *Dear Mr/Mrs/Ms ...*
4. Verwende Langformen. (*I am, I would like* statt *I'm, I'd like* etc.)
5. Nenne zu Beginn den Grund deines Briefes.
6. Bedanke dich bei Bitten und Anfragen im Voraus. (*I look forward to hearing from you. Thank you.*)
7. Beende den Brief mit *Yours faithfully*, wenn du den Adressaten nicht kennst. Hast du den Adressaten am Anfang des Briefes mit Namen angeredet, dann schreibe *Yours sincerely*.
8. Unterschreibe den Brief und tippe zusätzlich deinen Namen.

> **Tipp**
>
> Beachte, was du zum Schreiben von Texten gelernt hast:
> - Vor dem Schreiben: Ideen sammeln, dann sortieren.
> - Während des Schreibens: Sätze verbinden und ausbauen; strukturieren.
> - Nach dem Schreiben: Überprüfe deinen Brief inhaltlich und sprachlich. ▶ *SF Writing course, pp. 143–144*

Example for a letter of application

1. Schillerstr. 17
37067 Goettingen
Germany

4 May 2011

2. Jane Hall
Meadows Home Farm Shop
Harston
Cambridge CB22 4BE
Great Britain

3. Dear Ms Hall

4.

5. I am writing to you about the advertisement in the Cambridge Weekly News of 21st April. I would love (4) to work for you at Meadows Home Farm this summer.

I am 16 years old and I have a good level of English but would like to improve my speaking skills. I am hard-working, friendly and a fast learner. At home I look after two horses, so farm work is not new to me. I have also worked in a sports shop so I have experience in serving people and working in a team. My hobbies are horse riding, playing volleyball and hiking. Please find my CV enclosed with this letter.

Thank you for your time. I look forward to hearing (6) from you.

7. Yours sincerely

Tamara Wille

8. Tamara Wille

Was muss ich bei einem Bewerbungsschreiben beachten?

Eine schriftliche Bewerbung besteht aus einem Lebenslauf (▶ *SF Writing a CV, p. 145*) und einem Anschreiben. Bei einem Bewerbungsschreiben musst du alle Regeln für das Schreiben von förmlichen Briefen beachten.
Wenn du dich auf eine ausgeschriebene Stelle bewirbst, solltest du dich in deinem Anschreiben auf die Stellenanzeige beziehen (*letter of application*). Wenn du bei einer Firma anfragst, ob sie eine Praktikums- oder Arbeitsstelle haben, begründest du in deinem Anschreiben, warum du dich für diese Firma interessierst (*letter of motivation*).
In beiden Fällen solltest du hervorheben, warum gerade du für ein Praktikum oder die ausgeschriebene Stelle genau die richtige Person bist!

▶▶▶

Letter of application

– Sage, auf welche Stellenanzeige du dich beziehst.
  I am writing about your advertisement in …
– Nenne deine Stärken. Gehe dabei besonders auf die Qualifikationen und Interessen ein, die in der Stellenanzeige genannt werden. Zeige auch, dass du dich über das Unternehmen informiert hast.
  I have studied English for six years and my level is quite high.
  I am a friendly, … person and I enjoy working in a team/serving customers …
  As you can see on my CV, I have done work experience in …
– Danke dem Adressaten für seine Aufmerksamkeit und sage, dass du dich auf eine Antwort freust.
  Thank you very much for your time. I look forward to hearing from you.

Letter of motivation

– Sage, woher du das Unternehmen kennst und warum du dich an es wendest. Nenne den Zeitpunkt, ab dem du eine Stelle oder ein Praktikum antreten könntest.
  I learned about your company through internet research/at our school's career information day/…
  I am writing to apply for a summer job/a part-time job/…
  I am 16 years old and I will finish school in …
– Nenne deine Stärken, Interessen und Qualifikationen, die für das Unternehmen interessant sein könnten. Zeige, dass du dich über das Unternehmen informiert hast.
  I have good computer skills/… • I am good at …
  I am very interested in … • I like working in a team/serving customers/…
  On your website I learned that your company …
– Danke dem Adressaten für seine Aufmerksamkeit und kündige an, dass du dich wieder melden wirst.
  Thank you very much for your time. I will contact you in two weeks to see if you need more information.

Was ist wichtig bei einem Leserbrief an eine Zeitung oder Zeitschrift?

– Wenn du auf einen Zeitschriftenartikel reagieren und einen Leserbrief (*letter to a newspaper/magazine* oder *letter to the editor*) schreiben sollst, beginne deinen Brief mit
  Dear Sir or Madam / Dear Editor
  (oder mit dem Namen des Autors des Artikels).

Was ist bei persönlichen Briefen anders? (*Informal letters*)

Hier sind die Regeln nicht ganz so streng. Aber beachte Folgendes:
– Schreibe deine Adresse (ohne Namen) und das Datum in die rechte obere Ecke.
– Verwende keine typisch deutschen Buchstaben wie z. B. ß, ä, ö, oder ü.
– Du benötigst keine Anschrift.
– Du kannst deinen Brief mit *Dear/Hello/Hi* … beginnen.
– Nenne zu Beginn den Grund deines Briefes, stelle auch Fragen.
– Beende den Brief mit einem freundlichen Gruß/Ausblick/…
– Schließe deinen Brief mit *Yours/Best wishes/Love/…* ab.

SF From outline to written discussion

Worum geht es bei einem *outline*?

Oft sollst du zu strittigen Fragen wie z.B. **Should driving on Sundays be banned?** schriftlich Stellung nehmen und deine Position überzeugend darlegen. Dabei sollst du zeigen, dass du dich intensiv mit dem Thema auseinandergesetzt und Pro und Kontra abgewogen hast. Dafür ist es hilfreich, wenn du erst Argumente sammelst und sie dann **vor** dem Schreiben des Textes gliederst. Diese Gliederung nennt man *outline*. Es erleichtert dir das anschließende Schreiben.

Wie gehe ich bei einem *outline* vor?

1. Collecting ideas
Hierbei kannst du unterschiedliche Techniken nutzen. Dabei ist es sinnvoll, wenn du neben den Argumenten auch konkrete Beispiele notierst, die deine Aussage verdeutlichen.

▶ *SF Brainstorming (p. 141)*

2. Outlining
Mit Hilfe des *outline* strukturierst du die Ideen, die du zuvor gesammelt hast. Überleg dir, welche Meinung du zu der gestellten Frage hast. Führ im *outline* erst die Argumente auf, die gegen deine Meinung sprechen. Stell erst danach die Argumente und Beispiele vor, die deine Meinung stützen.
Da eine Erörterung aus vier Teilen besteht, ordne deine Ideen stichwortartig nach dem Schema rechts.

> 1 Introduction
>
> 2 First point of view: Arguments and examples
>
> 3 Second point of view: Arguments and examples
>
> 4 Conclusion

Wie mache ich aus dem *outline* eine Erörterung?

1. Introduction
In der Einleitung stellst du das Thema vor und beschreibst, worum es geht. Dabei kannst du von einer persönlichen Erfahrung oder einem allgemein bekannten Problem ausgehen.
Lots of people think … • It is generally believed that … • I once … •
You often hear people say that • …, so the question is: should … or not?

2. Present the first point of view
Zunächst führst du die Argumente an, die gegen deine Überzeugung sprechen.
First …; Second …; • Another argument for/against … is … •
For example, … • It might also be argued that … • Finally … • So … • That's why …

3. Present the second point of view
Präsentiere dann die Argumente, die deine Meinung stützen. Wichtig ist, dass du eine Überleitung schreibst und deine Argumente mit Beispielen (z.B. aus deiner eigenen Erfahrung) anreicherst.
However, lots of people feel … • Other people disagree. They think that … •
It's also important to remember … • It is only partly true that …

4. Conclusion
Am Schluss wägst du das Für und Wider noch einmal ab und sagst deine Meinung. Nenn keine neuen Argumente mehr.
To sum up, I would say that … • After looking at both sides, I think …

MEDIATION SKILLS

SF Mediation

Wann muss ich zwischen zwei Sprachen vermitteln?

Manchmal musst du zwischen zwei Sprachen vermitteln. Das nennt man *mediation*.

1. Du gibst englische Informationen auf Deutsch weiter:
   Du fährst z.B. mit deiner Familie in die USA und deine Eltern oder Geschwister wollen wissen, was jemand in einem Café gesagt hat oder was an einer Informationstafel steht.

2. Du gibst deutsche Informationen auf Englisch weiter:
   Vielleicht ist bei dir zu Hause eine Austauschschülerin aus den USA oder Dänemark zu Gast, die kein Deutsch spricht und Hilfe braucht.

3. In schriftlichen Prüfungen musst du manchmal in einem englischen Text gezielt nach Informationen suchen und diese auf Deutsch wiedergeben. Oder du sollst Informationen aus einem deutschen Text auf Englisch wiedergeben.

Entschuldigung, kannst du mir vielleicht helfen? Mein Englisch ist nicht so gut.

Worauf muss ich bei *mediation* achten?

– Übersetze nicht alles wörtlich.
– Gib nur das Wesentliche weiter. Oft gibt dir die Fragestellung Hinweise, worauf es ankommt.
– Verwende kurze und einfache Sätze.
– Wenn du ein Wort nicht kennst, umschreibe es oder ersetze es durch ein anderes Wort.

You can go by train from Sydney to Perth. Trains go twice a week. The next train leaves Sydney on Saturday at 3 in the afternoon and arrives in Perth on Tuesday at 9 in the morning.

Was kann ich tun, wenn ich ein wichtiges Wort nicht kenne?

Vielleicht findest du es manchmal schwer, mündliche Aussagen oder schriftliche Textvorlagen in die andere Sprache zu übertragen, z.B. weil:
– dein Wortschatz nicht ausreicht
– dir bekannte Wörter „im Stress" nicht einfallen
– spezielle Fachbegriffe auftauchen.

Wir können mit dem Zug fahren, das dauert von Samstagnachmittag bis Dienstag früh.

Manche Wörter kannst du umschreiben, z.B. mithilfe von Relativsätzen wie:
It's somebody/a person who ...
It's something that you use to ...
It's an animal that ...
It's a place where ...

▶ *SF Paraphrasing, p. 141*

Was hältst du davon, wenn wir einen Hubschrauberrundflug machen würden? Frag doch mal, wo man so was machen kann?

Excuse me, we'd like to do a tour around Uluru with ... something that you can fly with.

A helicopter ...

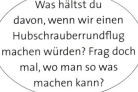

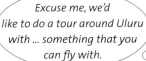

Grammar File – Inhalt

Im **Grammar File** (S. 150–169) werden wesentliche grammatische Themen aus den Klassen 5 bis 9 noch einmal zusammengefasst.

> In der **linken Spalte** stehen Beispielsätze und Übersichten.

> In der **rechten Spalte** stehen Erklärungen und Hinweise.

Indirect speech (reporting verb: simple past)

Kate said that she loved basketball. She told me she was training hard for their next match.

◄ Steht das **einleitende Verb im *simple past*** (*she said, told me, answered* usw.), werden die Zeitformen der direkten Rede meist um eine Zeitstufe in die Vergangenheit „zurückverschoben" (*backshift of tenses*).

He said his name was Alex.
Er sagte, dass er Alex heißt.

❗ Im Englischen steht vor der indirekten Rede **kein Komma** und das Wort *that* wird oft weggelassen.

Veränderungen der Zeitformen bei einleitendem Verb im *simple past*

	Direct speech	Indirect speech
present ► past	'I don't like football.' 'I'm training hard.'	She **said** she didn't like football. She **added** that she was training hard.
past ► past perfect	'We played very well last week.'	She **said** they had played very well last week.
can ► could	'I can get you a ticket for our next match.'	She **told** me she could get me a ticket for their next match.

Additional information

The present perfect progressive

I've **been writing** e-mails all day.
Ich **schreibe** (schon) den ganzen Tag E-Mails.

„Additional information"-Abschnitte enthalten Grammatik, die du nicht unbedingt selbst zu verwenden brauchst. Du solltest aber verstehen, was dort erklärt wird, damit du keine Schwierigkeiten mit Texten hast, in denen diese Grammatik vorkommt.

GF 1 Word order   Wortstellung

1.1   S – V – O

S – V – O

Subject – Verb – Object				
	Subject	**Verb**	**Object**	
1	Rob	likes	ice cream.	
	The Clarks	have bought	a house	in Bath.
2	Ella	didn't like	the film.	
	Ava	can't speak	German	very well.
3	Can Jamie	speak	German?	
	Did you	like	the film?	

Die wichtigste Wortstellungsregel ist
Subject – **V**erb – **O**bject
(Subjekt – Prädikat – Objekt).
Sie gilt in bejahten und verneinten
Aussagesätzen (1, 2) und in Fragen (3).

▶ *Fragebildung: 2 (p. 153)*

---

1 We're going to have **a big party**.
Wir werden **eine große Party** veranstalten.

2 We **often** have fish on Fridays.
Wir essen **freitags oft** Fisch.

3 Yesterday **we** celebrated Grandpa's birthday.
Gestern feierten **wir** Opas Geburtstag.
When I arrived, **the film** had already begun.
Als ich ankam, hatte **der Film** schon begonnen.

4 He'll go out with you if you ask **him**.
..., wenn du **ihn** fragst.
Elisabeth told me   that she loves **Jeremy**.
..., dass sie **Jeremy** liebt.

! Beachte die Unterschiede zum Deutschen:

1 Die Teile des Prädikats (*are going to have*) dürfen nicht durch das Objekt (*a big party*) getrennt werden.

2 Prädikat und Objekt (*have fish*) dürfen nicht durch Adverbien (*often*) oder Zeitangaben (*on Fridays*) getrennt werden.

3 Die Wortstellung ist auch dann S – V – ..., wenn der Satz mit einer Zeitangabe (*yesterday*) oder einem Nebensatz (*When I arrived*) beginnt.

4 Die Wortstellung S – V – O gilt auch in Nebensätzen (*if you ask him; that she loves Jeremy*).

1.2   Adverbs and phrases of place and time

Adverbien und Orts- und Zeitangaben

1 Luckily she was able to stop the car.
At first we couldn't see anything.

2 We don't often get up before 10 on Sundays.
I usually make breakfast for everybody.
We had never been to Spain before.

3 Try to speak clearly, then you'll do well.
The guide answered the questions politely.
They went outside and played in the garden.
We're flying to Spain tomorrow.

We were in Italy last summer.

Wir waren letzten Sommer in Italien.

Every Friday evening we do the shopping.
Sometimes you can see foxes from my window.
In Britain, school usually starts at 8.45 or 9.00.

1 **Satzadverbien** wie *perhaps, maybe, suddenly, luckily, finally, of course, at first* beziehen sich auf den ganzen Satz. Sie stehen in der Regel am Satzanfang.

2 **Adverbien der unbestimmten Zeit oder Häufigkeit** wie *already, always, ever, just, never, often, sometimes, usually* stehen gewöhnlich vor dem Vollverb.

3 Nach dem Vollverb (+ Objekt) stehen gewöhnlich
 – **Adverbien der Art und Weise** (*clearly, politely, well*)
 – **Ortsangaben** (*outside, in Bristol, on the roof*)
 – **Zeitangaben** (*tomorrow, a year ago, in 2008*).

! Wenn ein Satz mit einer Orts- <u>und</u> einer Zeitangabe endet, dann gilt die Regel **Ort vor Zeit** – wie im Alphabet: **O vor Z**.

◀ Manchmal stehen Adverbien, Ortsangaben und Zeitangaben auch an anderen Stellen im Satz.

GF 2 **Making questions** Fragebildung

Word order in questions (except in subject questions)

1 Are you from Scotland?
   Do you like pizza?
   Have you got a pet?
2 Where are you from?
   What is your favourite food?
   Why did they move to Wales?

Auxiliary	Subject	Main verb	
Can	you	drive a moped?	
Is	Jake	washing the dishes?	
Have	you	seen 'Twilight' yet?	
Will	they	arrive on time?	
Do	you	like pizza?	Magst du …?
Does	she	live in Bristol?	Wohnt sie …?
Did	they	move to Wales?	
Don't	they	live here any more?	

Question word	Auxiliary	Subject	Main verb
When	can	you	come to Bath?
What	have	they	bought?
Where	will	you	stay?
How	do	you	know?
Why	does	Ella	want to move?
Who	did	you	meet in London?

2.2 Word order in subject questions

Question word (= Subject)	Verb	
Who	can drive	a moped?
Who	likes	ice cream?
What	makes	you laugh?
Whose sister	moved	to Bristol?
Which bus	goes	to Bath?

Statement	Subject question	Object question
Liz likes Jake.	Who likes Jake?	Who does Liz like?
Liz mag Jake.	Wer mag Jake?	Wen mag Liz?
Noise causes headaches.	What causes headaches?	What does noise cause?

Wortstellung in Fragen
(außer in Fragen nach dem Subjekt)

1 **Entscheidungsfragen *(Yes/No questions)*** können nur mit „Ja" oder „Nein" beantwortet werden.

2 **Fragen mit Fragewörtern *(Questions with questions words)*** erfragen weitere Informationen („Wer?" „Was?" „Wann?" „Wo?" „Warum?" „Wie?").

◄ **Entscheidungsfragen** beginnen immer mit einem **Hilfsverb *(auxiliary verb)*:**
Can …? Is …? Have …? Will …? …

Die Wortstellung ist also:
Auxiliary – S – V – …

In *simple present*- und *simple past*-Fragen braucht man eine Form des Hilfsverbs *do*:
Do …? Does …? Did …?
Die deutschen Entsprechungen haben meist kein Hilfsverb.

◄ Auch in **Fragen**, die mit einem **Fragewort** beginnen, steht ein **Hilfsverb** vor dem Subjekt:
When can …? What have …? Where will …? …

Die Wortstellung ist also:
Question word – Auxiliary – S – V – …

Wie die Entscheidungsfragen erfordern auch Fragewort-Fragen im *simple present* und im *simple past* eine Form des Hilfsverbs *do*:
How do …? Why does …? Who did …?

Wortstellung in Fragen nach dem Subjekt

◄ Fragen nach dem Subjekt sind **„Wer oder was?"**-Fragen. In solchen Fragen tritt das Fragewort an die Stelle des Subjekts. Vergleiche:

Jenny *likes ice cream.*   *Jenny mag Eis.*
Who *likes ice cream?*   *Wer mag Eis?*

! Mit *who, what, whose …* und *which …* kann man nach dem Subjekt oder nach dem Objekt fragen. Fragen nach dem Subjekt werden **ohne *do/does/did*** gebildet.

GF 3   Talking about the present   Über die Gegenwart sprechen

Du möchtest ausdrücken,

– dass etwas **regelmäßig** geschieht   →   Hanna **gets up** at 7 o'clock every morning.
  ▸ *The simple present: GF 3.1*   Hanna steht jeden Morgen um 7 Uhr auf.

– dass etwas **gerade jetzt** geschieht   →   It's 7 o'clock. Hanna **is getting up**.
  ▸ *The present progressive: GF 3.2*   Es ist 7 Uhr. Hanna steht (gerade) auf.

3.1   The simple present

Dave Wilson **usually** gets the bus to school.
On Mondays his mother takes him in the car.
He **never** cycles to school because it's too far.

Dave and his family live in Manchester.
He plays hockey and collects models of old cars.
His dad works for a building company.

Das **simple present** wird verwendet,

◀ um über Handlungen und Ereignisse zu sprechen, die **wiederholt, regelmäßig, immer** oder **nie** geschehen (oft mit Zeitangaben wie *always, never, usually, sometimes, often, every week, on Mondays* usw.).

◀ um über **Dauerzustände**, **Hobbys** und **Berufe** zu sprechen.

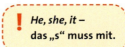

! **He, she, it – das „s" muss mit.**

Verneinte Sätze	I don't cycle to school.	Dave doesn't walk to school.
Fragen	Do you go to school by bus? **Where** do the Wilsons live?	Does your mother take you in the car? **When** does Dave's mother take him in the car?

3.2   The present progressive

What's Dave doing? –
Just now he's cleaning his bike.

Dave (on the phone)   I can't talk right now, Jack.
I'm cleaning my bike.

This week Dave's grandma is staying at the Wilsons' because Dave's mum is ill.

Das **present progressive** wird verwendet,

◀ um über Handlungen und Ereignisse zu sprechen, die **jetzt gerade im Gange** sind (oft mit Angaben wie *at the moment, now, just*).

! Die Handlung, um die es geht, kann für einen Augenblick unterbrochen sein, z. B. durch ein Telefonat. Wichtig ist, dass sie noch nicht abgeschlossen ist.

◀ um über **vorübergehende Zustände** zu sprechen (begrenzter Zeitraum: *this week*).

Verneinte Sätze	The Wilsons aren't working.	Dave isn't watching TV.
Fragen	Are you watching TV? **What** are you doing?	Is Dave cleaning his bike? **Who** is Dave talking to?

Dave's dad works for a building company.
Look, he's working at his desk at the moment.

GF 4   Talking about the past   Über die Vergangenheit sprechen

Du möchtest ausdrücken,

– dass etwas in der Vergangenheit **geschah**; das Geschehen ist **abgeschlossen** und **vorbei** ▸ *The simple past: GF 4.1*	→ Emma **left** school in 2007. Emma ging im Jahr 2007 von der Schule ab.
– dass etwas in der Vergangenheit **gerade im Gange (noch nicht abgeschlossen) war** ▸ *The past progressive: GF 4.2*	→ We **were leaving** the building when we heard the explosion. Wir waren gerade dabei, das Gebäude zu verlassen, …
– dass etwas **vor etwas anderem** in der Vergangenheit stattgefunden hatte ▸ *The past perfect: GF 4.3*	→ Connor **had** already **left** when we arrived. Connor war schon gegangen, als wir ankamen.
– dass etwas **irgendwann** geschehen ist, oft mit **Auswirkungen auf die Gegenwart**	→ Jane **has left** her purse at home, so she can't pay for her bus ticket. Jane hat ihre Geldbörse zu Hause gelassen, …
– dass ein Zustand **in der Vergangenheit begonnen** hat und **noch andauert** ▸ *The present perfect: GF 4.4*	→ We**'ve had** our dog for three years now – since 2008. Wir haben unseren Hund jetzt seit drei Jahren …

4.1   The simple past

Last Friday Katie's family flew to Spain.
Letzten Freitag ist Katies Familie nach Spanien geflogen / flog Katies Familie nach Spanien.
Two years ago the Websters moved to Bath.
Vor zwei Jahren sind die Websters nach Bath gezogen.

Wenn man über Vergangenes berichtet, benutzt man überwiegend das *simple past*. Man beschreibt damit Handlungen, Ereignisse und Zustände, die zu einer bestimmten Zeit in der Vergangenheit *(yesterday, last Friday, two years ago, in 2003, between 2005 and 2008, …)* stattfanden.

! Im Deutschen wird in diesen Fällen oft das Perfekt verwendet, im Englischen jedoch nicht.

Verneinte Sätze	They didn't fly to France.	Katie didn't want to go at first.
Fragen	Did you go on holiday last year? **Where** did you go?	Did Katie like it? **When** did the Websters move to Bath?

4.2   The past progressive

What were you doing yesterday at 3.30? –
I was waiting for my sister at the school doors.
She was still talking to our Maths teacher.

Angela was just crossing the road when she saw her boyfriend.
Angela war gerade dabei, die Straße zu überqueren, …

Das *past progressive* wird verwendet,

◄ um über Handlungen und Ereignisse zu sprechen, die zu einer bestimmten Zeit in der Vergangenheit noch im Gange, also noch nicht abgeschlossen waren.

◄ wenn man beschreiben will, was gerade vor sich ging *(she was just crossing the road)*, als etwas anderes passierte *(she saw her boyfriend)*.

Verneinte Sätze	You weren't listening.	It wasn't snowing when we left the house.
Fragen	Were you watching TV? **What** were they doing?	Was she crossing the road when it happened? **What** was she doing?

▶ ▶ ▶

4.3

The past perfect

When Emma arrived home, her parents **had** already **eaten**.
Als Emma zu Hause eintraf, hatten ihre Eltern bereits gegessen.

Wenn man sagen will, dass etwas noch <u>vor etwas anderem</u> in der Vergangenheit stattgefunden hatte, dann benutzt man das **past perfect**.

Verneinte Sätze	They **hadn't gone** to bed.	Emma **hadn't eaten** anything all day.
Fragen	**Had** you **seen** that film before? **What had** they **done**?	**Had** Emma **eaten** when she came home? **Where had** she **been** all day?

4.4

The present perfect

Will Smith is great. I've **seen** most of his films.
Luke **has already done** his Maths homework, but he **hasn't started** his French **yet**.
Have you **ever been** to Paris?
– No, I **haven't**. But I've **always wanted** to go.

Mel **has lost** her mobile. Her dad is very angry.

We've **had** our new car **since April**. Wir **haben** unser neues Auto <u>seit April</u>.	We've **had** our new car **for three months**. Wir **haben** unser neues Auto <u>seit drei Monaten</u>.
since + **Zeitpunkt**	*for* + **Zeitraum**

! Das **present perfect** hat mit der **Vergangenheit** <u>und</u> **mit der Gegenwart** zu tun. Es wird verwendet,

◄ wenn man sagen will, **dass** jemand etwas getan hat oder **dass** etwas geschehen ist. Dabei ist nicht wichtig, wann es geschehen ist – ein genauer Zeitpunkt wird nicht genannt. Das *present perfect* steht oft mit Adverbien der <u>unbestimmten</u> Zeit wie *already, just, never, ever, not ... yet*.
Oft hat die Handlung Auswirkungen auf die Gegenwart (Mels Vater ist wütend, weil sie ihr Handy verloren hat).

◄ für **Zustände**, die in der Vergangenheit begonnen haben und jetzt noch andauern (oft mit *since* bzw. *for*).

! Im Deutschen steht in diesen Fällen meist das Präsens, im Englischen **muss** das *present perfect* stehen.

Verneinte Sätze	I **haven't been** to Paris yet.	Luke **hasn't done** his French homework.
Fragen	**Have** you **been** to Paris? **What have** you **done**?	**Has** Mel **found** her mobile yet? **Which** of these films **have** you **seen** already?

Additional information

4.5

The present perfect progressive

I've **been writing** e-mails all day.
Ich **schreibe** (schon) den ganzen Tag E-Mails.

We've **been learning** French for four years.
Wir **lernen** seit vier Jahren Französisch.

Auch das **present perfect progressive** hat mit der Vergangenheit <u>und</u> mit der Gegenwart zu tun. Es wird verwendet für **Vorgänge** und **Handlungen**, die in der Vergangenheit begonnen haben und jetzt noch andauern (oft mit *since* bzw. *for*).

! Auch hier steht im Deutschen meist das Präsens – aber im Englischen das *present perfect progressive*.

GF 5 Talking about the future   Über die Zukunft sprechen

Du möchtest ausdrücken,

– dass etwas für die Zukunft **geplant** ist ▸ *The going to-future: GF 5.1*	→	I'm **going to watch** the new Bond film tonight. Ich sehe mir heute Abend den neuen Bond-Film an.

– wie etwas in der Zukunft **sein wird**
  (**Vorhersagen, Vermutungen**)
  ▸ *The will-future: GF 5.2*
	→	It **will be** warm and sunny in Spain. I'm sure
		you'**ll like** it there.
		Es wird warm und sonnig sein in Spanien. Ich bin
		sicher, dass es dir dort gefallen wird.

– dass etwas für die Zukunft **fest verabredet** ist
  (es steht schon im Kalender)
  ▸ *The present progressive: GF 5.3*
	→	We'**re having** a party on Saturday. Would you
		like to come?
		Wir geben nächsten Samstag eine Party. ...

5.1 The *going to*-future

My boyfriend says he'**s going to be** an engineer.
Mein Freund sagt, er will Ingenieur werden.

Look at those clouds. There'**s going to be** a
storm.
... Es wird ein Gewitter geben.

Das **Futur mit *going to*** wird verwendet,

◂ wenn man über **Vorhaben, Pläne, Absichten** für die
Zukunft sprechen will.

◂ um auszudrücken, dass etwas **wahrscheinlich gleich
geschehen wird** – es gibt bereits deutliche **Anzeichen**
dafür (*hier*: die Wolken am Himmel).

5.2 The *will*-future

It **will be** cold and windy, and we **will get** some
rain in the afternoon.
I'**ll be** 15 next October.

I expect Ella **will be** late again as usual.
Ich nehme an, Ella kommt wie üblich wieder zu spät.

Just a moment. I'**ll open** the door for you.
Moment. Ich mache Ihnen die Tür auf.
I **won't tell** anyone what's happened. I promise.
Ich sage niemandem, was passiert ist. ...

Das **Futur mit *will*** wird verwendet,

◂ um **Vorhersagen** über die Zukunft zu äußern.
Oft geht es dabei um Dinge, die man nicht beeinflussen
kann, z. B. das Wetter.

◂ um eine **Vermutung** auszudrücken (oft eingeleitet mit
I think, I'm sure, I expect, maybe).

◂ wenn man sich **spontan** – also ohne es im Voraus
geplant zu haben – zu etwas **entschließt**. Oft geht es
dabei um **Hilfsangebote** oder **Versprechen**.

5.3 The present progressive (future meaning)

We'**re driving** to Scotland next Friday to visit
my grandparents.
I'**m meeting** a friend in town tonight.

Das *present progressive* wird verwendet, wenn etwas **für
die Zukunft fest geplant** oder **fest verabredet** ist
(manchmal spricht man vom *diary future*). Durch eine
Zeitangabe wie *tonight* oder aus dem Zusammenhang
muss klar sein, dass es um etwas Zukünftiges geht.

Additional information

5.4 The simple present (future meaning)

The next train to Bath **goes** in ten minutes.
The next drawing class **starts** on 2 September.

Das *simple present* wird verwendet, wenn ein **zukünftiges
Geschehen** durch einen **Fahrplan**, ein **Programm** oder
Ähnliches festgelegt ist (manchmal spricht man vom
timetable future). Verben wie *arrive, leave, go, open, close,
start, stop* werden häufig so verwendet.

GF 6 The simple form and the progressive form
Die einfache Form und die Verlaufsform

6.1 **Simple and progressive form in contrast**   Einfache Form und Verlaufsform im Vergleich

	Simple form	Progressive form
Present tense	sing(s)	am/are/is singing
Present perfect	have/has sung	have/has been singing
Past tense	sang	was/were singing
Past perfect	had sung	had been singing
***will*-future**	will sing	will be singing

Anders als im Deutschen gibt es im Englischen eine **einfache Form** *(simple form)* und eine **Verlaufsform** *(progressive form)* des Verbs.

The simple form

1a Olivia plays tennis every Saturday.
(regelmäßig, jeden Samstag)
2a Mr Bale works in an office in the city centre.
(immer, jeden Tag)
3a Ella left home at 7.15.
(die Handlung ist beendet)

◄ Die *simple form* wird verwendet

 – für regelmäßig oder wiederholt stattfindende Handlungen (**1a**)
 – für Dauerzustände (wenn etwas immer so ist) (**2a**)

 – für abgeschlossene Handlungen (**3a**).

The progressive form

1b Olivia is playing tennis right now.
(sie ist gerade dabei, das Spiel ist im Gange)
2b This week Mr Bale is working at home.
(nur diese Woche, denn sein Büro wird renoviert)
3b Ella was leaving the house when she heard the explosion.
(als sie die Explosion hörte, war sie dabei zu gehen)

◄ Die *progressive form* wird verwendet

 – für Handlungen, die gerade im Verlauf sind (**1b**)

 – für vorübergehene Zustände (wenn etwas nur vorübergehend der Fall ist) (**2b**)
 – für Handlungen, die zu einem bestimmten Zeitpunkt noch nicht abgeschlossen sind (**3b**).

He was washing the dishes when he heard a funny noise.
Er war gerade beim Abwaschen, ...

! Im Deutschen gibt es keine Verlaufsform. Aber manchmal sagt und hört man Sätze wie „Ich bin gerade dabei, meine Hausaufgaben zu machen" oder „Er war (gerade) beim Abwaschen", um zum Ausdruck zu bringen, dass etwas im Gange und noch nicht abgeschlossen ist bzw. war.

! Beachte:
Nur **Tätigkeitsverben** *(activity verbs)* wie *do, drink, go, sit, write* können in der *progressive form* verwendet werden.
► *Tätigkeits- und Zustandsverben: 6.2–6.3 (p.159)*

6.2 Activity verbs

(in a shop window)   This shop repairs bikes!
(on the phone)   Jack is repairing his bike.
                        Can he call you back?

It gets dark very early here in winter.
At 6 o'clock it was already getting dark.

Tätigkeitsverben

Tätigkeitsverben bezeichnen **Tätigkeiten** *(do, go, read, repair, …)* oder **Vorgänge** *(become, get, rain, …)*. Sie beschreiben also, was jemand **tut** oder was **geschieht**. Tätigkeitsverben können sowohl in der *simple form* als auch in der *progressive form* verwendet werden.

6.3 State verbs

Zustandsverben

Zustandsverben *(state verbs)* bezeichnen **Zustände**. Sie werden in der Regel **nur in der *simple form*** verwendet.

Zu den **Zustandsverben** gehören

The price doesn't include breakfast.
Emily seems really happy at her new school.
Jake's uncle owns a nice house in the country.

– Verben, die **Eigenschaften**, **Besitz** oder **Zugehörigkeit** ausdrücken: *be, include, look* („aussehen"), *seem, sound, mean* („bedeuten"), *need, own, belong, …*

Do you believe their story?
I don't know the answer to question 5.
Anna didn't understand what Julie meant.

– Verben des **Meinens** und des **Wissens**: *believe, know, mean* („meinen"), *remember, suppose, understand, …*

Lucy doesn't like people who talk a lot.
I don't mind waiting for you here.
We prefer brown bread to white. It's healthier.

– Verben des **Mögens** und **Wollens**: *like, love, hate, mind, prefer, want, …*

GF 7 **The passive** Das Passiv

7.1 **Active and passive**

Active und Passiv

Active: **Alexander Fleming** discovered penicillin in 1928.
Alexander Fleming entdeckte 1928 das Penicillin.

Passive: **Penicillin** was discovered in 1928.
Penicillin wurde 1928 entdeckt.

Active: The manager asked **Mel** to help out.
Passive: **Mel** was asked to help out.
Mel wurde gebeten auszuhelfen.

Active: The manager paid **her** £6 an hour.
Passive: **She** was paid £6 an hour.
Ihr wurden £6 die Stunde bezahlt. /
Sie erhielt £6 die Stunde.

◀ Beide Sätze beschreiben denselben Sachverhalt, betrachten ihn aber aus unterschiedlichen Blickwinkeln:

– Der **Aktivsatz** handelt von Fleming und informiert uns über eine Entdeckung, die er 1928 machte.

– Der **Passivsatz** handelt von Penicillin und informiert uns über den Zeitpunkt seiner Entdeckung.

◀ Das Passiv lässt sich im Englischen von allen Verben bilden, die im Aktivsatz ein Objekt haben.

7.2 **Use**

Gebrauch

1 A new sports centre has been opened in Paddington. ... ist eröffnet worden ...
2 The first goal was scored in the seventh minute. ... wurde erzielt ...
3 Breakfast is served from 7 to 10.30 am. ... wird serviert ...
4 The two bank robbers have been sentenced to ten years. ... sind verurteilt worden ...

This picture was painted by **a 12-year old girl**.
... wurde von einem 12-jährigen Mädchen gemalt.

Part of this building was destroyed by **fire**.
... wurde durch ein Feuer zerstört.

In **Passivsätzen** steht nicht, wer die Handlung ausführt. Oft ist das unwichtig oder nicht bekannt (Sätze 1 und 2), manchmal ist es auch offensichtlich und daher nicht erwähnenswert (Sätze 3 und 4).

Das Passiv findet man oft in Nachrichten, in Zeitungsartikeln (z.B. über Unfälle, Sportereignisse, Verbrechen), in offiziellen Texten, in technischen Beschreibungen und auf Schildern.

! Wenn in Passivsätzen „Täter" oder „Verursacher" doch genannt werden sollen, dann verwendet man die Präposition **by ...** („von", „durch").

7.3 **Form**

Form

Das Passiv bildet man mit einer **Form von be** und der 3. Form des Verbs (Partizip Perfekt, *past participle*).

Simple present	I am often invited to parties.	... werde oft eingeladen
Simple past	The bridge was built in the 1950s.	... wurde gebaut
Present perfect	All the sandwiches have been eaten.	... sind gegessen worden
***will*-future**	Our new CD will be released next week.	... wird veröffentlicht werden
Modals	Mobile phones must be turned off now.	... müssen ausgeschaltet werden
	Concert tickets can be bought online.	... können gekauft werden

GF 8 Modals and their substitutes
Modale Hilfsverben und ihre Ersatzverben

8.1 **Substitutes**   Ersatzverben

1 I'd love to be able to speak Spanish.
   Ich würde liebend gern Spanisch sprechen können.
2 Being able to speak Spanish must be great.
   Spanisch sprechen zu können muss toll sein.
3 We weren't allowed to use a dictionary.
   Wir durften kein Wörterbuch benutzen.

Modale Hilfsverben *(can, may, must, …)* können **nicht alle Zeitformen** bilden. Daher gibt es zu bestimmten modalen Hilfsverben **Ersatzverben**, von denen man
– den Infinitiv (1),
– die *-ing*-Form (2)
– und alle Zeitformen (3, *simple past*) bilden kann.

„können": *can – (to) be able to*

My little brother can / is able to swim.

Tim could / was able to read when he was four.
I could smell fire, but I couldn't see any smoke.

Jacob hasn't been able to finish his essay.

I'm taking driving lessons, so next year I'll be able to drive.

present:	*can* und *am/is/are able to*
past:	*could* und *was/were able to* *could* steht vor allem in verneinten Sätzen und Fragen sowie mit Verben der Wahrnehmung *(smell, see, hear, …).*
present perfect:	*have/has been able to*
will-future:	*will/won't be able to*

„dürfen": *can, may – (to) be allowed to*

Can / May I have a sleepover on Friday, Mum?
We aren't allowed to stay up late in the week.

Under-12s couldn't / weren't allowed to see the film without an adult.

I've always been allowed to have pets.

Will you be allowed to go to the party on Friday?

Jeans must not be worn at this school.
At my school we're not allowed to wear jeans.

present:	*can, may* und *am/is/are allowed to*
past:	*could* und *was/were allowed to*
present perfect:	*have/has been allowed to*
will-future:	*will/won't be allowed to*

! Für ausdrückliche **Verbote** wird *must not (mustn't)* oder *be not allowed to* verwendet.

„müssen": *must – (to) have to*

Teacher You must work harder, Noah.
His teacher says Noah has to work harder.
I needn't get up at 6 tomorrow. / I don't have to get up at 6 tomorrow.

I had to rewrite my essay.
We didn't have to wait long.

Lauren has had to go to the dentist's.

You will have to go to the dentist's too if you eat so many sweets.

present:	*must* und *have/has to* (*have/has to* ist häufiger als *must*) **!** **Verneinung:** *needn't* oder *don't/doesn't have to*
past:	*had to* **!** **Verneinung:** *didn't have to*
present perfect:	*have/has had to*
will-future:	*will/won't have to*

▶ ▶ ▶

8.2 **Modals – what do they express?**   Modale Hilfsverben – was drücken sie aus?

Fähigkeit

I can speak French and a little German.	Ich **kann** Französisch und ein bisschen Deutsch.
My sister could read when she was only four.	Meine Schwester **konnte** lesen, als sie erst vier war.

Bitte / Aufforderung

Can I borrow this CD?	**Kann** ich diese CD ausleihen?
Can you be quiet, please?	**Kannst** du bitte leise sein?
Could you show me how to start the DVD?	**Könntest** du mir zeigen, wie man die DVD startet?
Would you help me to wash the dishes?	**Würdest** du mir helfen abzuwaschen?

Erlaubnis / Verbot

You can use my ruler.	Du **kannst** mein Lineal benutzen.
May I use your phone, please?	**Darf** ich mal dein Telefon benutzen, bitte?
You can't take photos in the museum.	Du **darfst** im Museum **nicht** fotografieren.
In 1968, children could leave school at 15.	… **konnten/durften** Kinder mit 15 die Schule verlassen.
But they couldn't vote till they were 21.	Aber sie **konnten/durften** erst mit 21 wählen.
You mustn't tell Mel about the concert. It's a surprise.	Du **darfst** Mel **nichts** von dem Konzert erzählen. …

Vorschlag / Ratschlag

Can/Can't we go on a bike trip?	**Können** wir **(nicht)** eine Radtour machen?
You could talk to your teacher.	Du **könntest (doch)** mit deiner Lehrerin sprechen.
You should tell her the truth.	Du **solltest** ihr die Wahrheit sagen.

Angebot

Can/May I help you with your bags?	**Kann/Darf** ich Ihnen mit Ihren Taschen helfen?
Would you like to stay for dinner?	**Möchtest** du **(nicht)** zum Essen bleiben?

Notwendigkeit, Verpflichtung

You've got a cold. You must stay at home.	Du hast eine Erkältung. Du **musst** zuhause bleiben.
You needn't tell Mel about the concert. She already knows.	Du **brauchst** Mel **nicht** von dem Konzert zu erzählen. …
Bicycles should be left outside.	Fahrräder **sollten** draußen abgestellt werden.

Möglichkeit, Wahrscheinlichkeit

That must be Luke.	Das **muss** Luke sein.
– No, it can't be Luke. Luke is in Spain.	– Nein, das **kann nicht** Luke sein. Luke ist in Spanien.
Where's Dad? – He could be at Grandma's.	… – Er **könnte** bei Oma sein.
Sarah may still be at her friend's.	Sarah ist **vielleicht** noch bei ihrer Freundin.
John might come today if he's in town.	John kommt **vielleicht** heute vorbei, …
Kathy should be here by now.	Kathy **sollte** jetzt (eigentlich) hier sein.
There's someone at the door. It will be Janet.	Es ist jemand an der Tür. Das **wird** Janet sein.

GF 9   Conditional sentences   Bedingungssätze

9.1

Type 1 and type 2

If you run, you'll catch the bus.
Wenn du rennst, kriegst du den Bus noch.

If you miss the bus, you can take / should take / must take a taxi.
Wenn du den Bus verpasst, kannst/sollst/musst du ein Taxi nehmen.

If you ran, you would catch the bus.
Wenn du rennen würdest, würdest du den Bus noch kriegen.

If you caught the bus, you could be home in time for dinner.
Wenn du den Bus kriegen würdest, könntest du rechtzeitig zum Abendessen daheim sein.

Typ 1 und Typ 2

◀ **Typ 1 („Was <u>ist</u>, wenn …"-Sätze)**
Diese Bedingungssätze beziehen sich auf die **Gegenwart** oder die **Zukunft**.
Sie drücken aus, was unter bestimmten Bedingungen **geschieht** oder **geschehen kann/soll** usw.

if-Satz (Bedingung)	Hauptsatz (Folge)
If you run,	*you'll catch the bus.*
If you miss the bus,	*you can take a taxi.*
simple present	***– will-future*** ***– can/should/must* + Infinitiv**

◀ **Typ 2 („Was <u>wäre</u>, wenn …"-Sätze)**
Diese Bedingungssätze beziehen sich auch auf die **Gegenwart** oder die **Zukunft**.
Sie drücken aus, was unter bestimmten Bedingungen **geschehen würde** oder **könnte**.

if-Satz (Bedingung)	Hauptsatz (Folge)
If you ran,	*you would catch/could catch/ might catch the bus.*
simple past	***would/could/might* + Infinitiv**

Additional information

9.2

Type 3

If you had run, you would have caught the bus.
Wenn du gerannt wärst, hättest du den Bus noch gekriegt.

If you had caught the bus, you could have had dinner with us.
Wenn du den Bus gekriegt hättest, hättest du mit uns Abendbrot essen können.

Typ 3

◀ **Typ 3 („Was <u>wäre gewesen</u>, wenn …"-Sätze)**
Diese Bedingungssätze beziehen sich auf die **Vergangenheit**.
Sie drücken aus, was unter bestimmten Bedingungen **geschehen wäre** oder **hätte geschehen können**.
Der Sprecher stellt sich nur vor, was geschehen wäre, aber in Wirklichkeit nicht geschehen ist:
Wenn du gerannt wärst, hättest du den Bus erwischt – aber da du nicht gerannt bist …

if-Satz (Bedingung)	Hauptsatz (Folge)
If you had run,	*you would have caught/ could have caught the bus.*
past perfect	***would/could* + *have* + Partizip Perfekt**

GF 10 **Relative clauses**   Relativsätze

10.1   **Use**

1 Isn't that **the boy** who/that stole your mobile?
... der Junge, der dein Handy gestohlen hat?

2 That's **the shop** that/which sells cheap CDs.
... der Laden, der billige CDs verkauft.

Gebrauch

Relativsätze beziehen sich auf ein **Nomen**.
Sie bestimmen dieses Nomen genauer: Erst durch den
Relativsatz weiß man, wer oder was genau gemeint ist.

Relativsätze werden mit den Relativpronomen
who oder **that** für **Personen (1)** und
that oder **which** für **Dinge (2)** eingeleitet.

10.2   **Contact clauses**

1 There's **the boy** who I invited to my party.
or There's **the boy** I invited to my party.
... der Junge, den ich ... eingeladen habe.

2 These are **the photos** that Dad took.
or These are **the photos** Dad took.
... die Fotos, die Dad gemacht hat.

3 Jake is **the boy** who invited us to the party.
... der Junge, der uns ... eingeladen hat.

4 This is **the photo** that won first prize.
... das Foto, das den ersten Preis gewonnen hat.

Relativsätze ohne Relativpronomen

Wenn das Relativpronomen **Objekt des Relativsatzes** ist,
wird es oft **weggelassen (1, 2)**.
Relativsätze ohne Relativpronomen werden
contact clauses genannt.

! Wenn – wie in **3** und **4** – das **Relativpronomen direkt vor
dem Verb** steht, dann ist es **Subjekt** und darf <u>nicht</u>
weggelassen werden.

That's the hotel that was recommended in the guidebook.

And that's the hotel we stayed in.

GF 11 Indirect speech   Die indirekte Rede

11.1   Statements   Aussagesätze

> I love basketball.
> I'm training hard for our next match.

Direct speech	Kate says, 'I **love** basketball. **I'm training** hard for our next match.'	◀ In der **direkten Rede** wird **wörtlich** wiedergegeben, was jemand sagt oder gesagt hat. Direkte Rede steht in Anführungszeichen (deutsch: „...“; englisch: '...').
Indirect speech (reporting verb: simple present)	Kate says that she loves basketball. She says she's training hard for their next match.	◀ In der **indirekten Rede** (*indirect* oder *reported speech*) wird **berichtet**, was jemand sagt oder gesagt hat. Die indirekte Rede wird mit Verben wie *say, tell sb., add, answer, explain, think* eingeleitet
Indirect speech (reporting verb: simple past)	Kate said that she loved basketball. She told me she was training hard for their next match.	◀ Steht das **einleitende Verb im *simple past*** (*she said, told me, answered* usw.), werden die Zeitformen der direkten Rede meist um eine Zeitstufe in die Vergangenheit „zurückverschoben“ (*backshift of tenses*).

He said his name was Alex.
Er sagte, dass er Alex heißt.

! Im Englischen steht vor der indirekten Rede **kein Komma** und das Wort *that* wird oft weggelassen.

Veränderungen der Zeitformen bei einleitendem Verb im *simple past*

	Direct speech	Indirect speech
present ▶ past	'I don't like football.' 'I'm training hard.'	She **said** she didn't like football. She **added** that she was training hard.
past ▶ past perfect	'We played very well last week.'	She **said** they had played very well last week.
can ▶ could	'I can get you a ticket for our next match.'	She **told** me she could get me a ticket for their next match.
***will*-future** ▶ ***would* + infinitive**	'It'll be fun.'	She **said** it would be fun.
***going to*-future** ▶ ***was/were going to* + infinitive**	'We're going to have a party after the match.'	She **said** they were going to have a party after the match.
present perfect ▶ **past perfect**	'I've never been so excited.'	She **added** that she had never been so excited.

- Verben im *past perfect* bleiben unverändert, da man sie nicht weiter „zurückverschieben“ kann.
- In der Umgangssprache bleiben *past*-Formen der direkten Rede oft unverändert, werden also nicht ins *past perfect* „zurückverschoben“:
  Kate   We played very well last week. ▶ Kate said they played very well last week.

▶▶▶

11.2 Questions

Direct question (yes/no question)	'Do you train every day, Kate?'
Indirect question	Alex asked Kate if/whether she trained every day.
Direct question (with question word)	'When did you join the team?'
Indirect question	Alex wanted to know when Kate had joined the team. ..., wann Kate sich der Mannschaft angeschlossen hat.

Fragen

Auch bei Fragen in der indirekten Rede werden die Zeitformen in die Vergangenheit „zurückverschoben", wenn das einleitende Verb im *simple past* steht.

◄ Handelt es sich bei der direkten Frage um eine **Frage ohne Fragewort** *(yes/no question)*, dann wird die indirekte Frage mit **if** oder **whether** („ob") eingeleitet.

◄ Wenn die direkte **Frage mit einem Fragewort** beginnt *(why, how, what, when, where* usw.), dann wird das Fragewort in der indirekten Frage beibehalten.

11.3 Advice, requests, commands

Ratschläge, Bitten, Aufforderungen

Kate advised Alex not to miss their next match.
Kate riet Alex, ihr nächstes Spiel nicht zu verpassen.

Alex asked Kate to get him some tickets.
Alex bat Kate, ihm Eintrittskarten zu besorgen.

◄ **Ratschläge** können mit *advise sb. to do sth.* (bzw. *advise sb. not to do sth.*) wiedergegeben werden.

◄ **Bitten** werden meist mit *ask sb. to do sth.* (bzw. *ask sb. not to do sth.*) wiedergegeben.

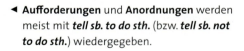

◄ **Aufforderungen** und **Anordnungen** werden meist mit *tell sb. to do sth.* (bzw. *tell sb. not to do sth.*) wiedergegeben.

GF 12 Adjectives: comparison   Adjektive: Steigerung

12.1 Forms

	Komparativ (Comparative)	Superlativ (Superlative)
clean	cleaner	cleanest
big	bigger	biggest
happy	happier	happiest
useful	more useful	most useful
famous	more famous	most famous
expensive	more expensive	most expensive
difficult	more difficult	most difficult
good	better	best
bad	worse	worst
much/many	more	most
(a) little	less	least

Formen

Steigerungsformen werden verwendet, um Personen oder Dinge miteinander zu vergleichen.

◄ **Steigerung** mit *-er/-est*:
 – **einsilbige** Adjektive
 – **zweisilbige** Adjektive, die auf **-y** enden

◄ **Steigerung** mit *more/most*:
 – die meisten **zweisilbigen** Adjektive, die <u>nicht</u> auf **-y** enden
 – Adjektive mit **mehr als zwei Silben**

◄ **unregelmäßige Steigerung**:
 – *good, bad*
 – *much/many, (a) little*

Additional information

She's cleverer / more clever than her sister.
Sie ist cleverer als ihre Schwester.

That's the stupidest / most stupid thing
I've ever heard.
Das ist das Dümmste, was ich je gehört habe.

Manche zweisilbigen Adjektive können mit *-er/-est* oder mit *more/most* gesteigert werden; Beispiele:
clever, simple, stupid.
Wenn du dir nicht sicher bist, musst du die Steigerungsformen in einem Wörterbuch nachschlagen.

12.2 The adjective in comparisons

Das Adjektiv in Vergleichen

Lucy, 15 | John, 14 | Ella, 14

Ella is **as old as** John.

She's **not as old as** Lucy.

Lucy is **old**er **than** her.
(*nicht*: ... older than ~~she~~)

Lucy is **the old**est.

◄ *as ... as*   „so ... wie"

◄ *not as ... as*   „nicht so ... wie"

◄ **Komparativ + *than***:
 older than   „älter als"
 more expensive than   „teurer ... als"

◄ *the* + **Superlativ**:
 the oldest   „der/die älteste, am ältesten"

Grammatical terms (Grammatische Fachbegriffe)

active ['æktɪv]	Aktiv	Beckham **scored** the final goal.
activity verb [æk'tɪvəti vɜːb]	Tätigkeitsverb	do, go, make, read, repair
adjective ['ædʒɪktɪv]	Adjektiv	good, red, new, boring
adverb ['ædvɜːb]	Adverb	always, badly, here, really, today
adverb of frequency ['friːkwənsi]	Häufigkeitsadverb	always, often, never
adverb of indefinite time [ɪnˌdefɪnət 'taɪm]	Adverb der unbestimmten Zeit	already, ever, just, never
adverb of manner ['mænə]	Adverb der Art und Weise	badly, happily, quietly, well
advice (no pl) [əd'vaɪs]	Rat, Ratschlag	You should see a doctor.
article ['ɑːtɪkl]	Artikel	the, a/an
auxiliary [ɔːg'zɪliəri]	Hilfsverb	be, have, do; will, can, must
backshift of tenses ['bækʃɪft]	Verschiebung der Zeitformen *(bei der indirekten Rede)*	*'I'm sorry.'* ► Sam said he **was** sorry.
command [kə'mɑːnd]	Befehl, Aufforderungssatz	Open your books. Don't talk.
comparison [kəm'pærɪsn]	Steigerung	old – older – oldest
conditional sentence [kənˌdɪʃənl 'sentəns]	Bedingungssatz	I'd call him if I knew his number.
conjunction [kən'dʒʌŋkʃn]	Konjunktion	and, or, but; because, before
contact clause ['kɒntækt klɔːz]	Relativsatz ohne Relativpronomen	She's the girl **I love**.
countable noun ['kaʊntəbl]	zählbares Nomen	girl – girls, pound – pounds
definite article ['defɪnət]	bestimmter Artikel	the
direct speech [ˌdaɪrekt 'spiːtʃ]	direkte Rede, wörtliche Rede	**'I'm sorry.'**
future ['fjuːtʃə]	Zukunft, Futur	
gerund ['dʒerənd]	Gerundium	I like **dancing**. **Dancing** is fun.
going to-future	Futur mit *going to*	**I'm going to watch** TV tonight.
if-clause ['ɪf klɔːz]	*if*-Satz, Nebensatz mit *if*	**If I see Jack**, I'll tell him.
imperative [ɪm'perətɪv]	Imperativ (Befehlsform)	Open your books. Don't talk.
indirect speech [ˌɪndərekt 'spiːtʃ]	indirekte Rede	Sam said **(that) he was sorry**.
infinitive [ɪn'fɪnətɪv]	Infinitiv (Grundform des Verbs)	(to) open, (to) see, (to) read
irregular verb [ɪˌregjələ 'vɜːb]	unregelmäßiges Verb	(to) go – went – gone
main clause	Hauptsatz	**I like Scruffy** because I like dogs.
modal, modal auxiliary [ˌməʊdl_ɔːg'zɪliəri]	modales Hilfsverb, Modalverb	can, could, may, must
negative statement [ˌnegətɪv 'steɪtmənt]	verneinter Aussagesatz	I don't like bananas.
noun [naʊn]	Nomen, Substantiv	Sophie, girl, brother, time
object ['ɒbdʒɪkt]	Objekt	My sister is writing **a letter**.
object form ['ɒbdʒɪkt fɔːm]	Objektform (der Personalpronomen)	me, you, him, her, it, us, them
object question ['ɒbdʒɪkt ˌkwestʃən]	Frage nach dem Objekt	Who does Jake love?
participle ['pɑːtɪsɪpl]	Partizip	planning, taking; planned, taken
participle clause [ˌpɑːtɪsɪpl 'klɔːz]	Partizipialsatz	I saw a boy **playing in the street**.
passive ['pæsɪv]	Passiv	The goal **was scored** by Beckham.
past [pɑːst]	Vergangenheit	
past participle [ˌpɑːst 'pɑːtɪsɪpl]	Partizip Perfekt	cleaned, planned, gone, taken
past perfect [ˌpɑːst 'pɜːfɪkt]	Plusquamperfekt, Vorvergangenheit	He cried – he **had hurt** his knee.
past progressive [ˌpɑːst prə'gresɪv]	Verlaufsform der Vergangenheit	At 7.30 I **was having** dinner.
personal pronoun [ˌpɜːsənl 'prəʊnaʊn]	Personalpronomen (persönliches Fürwort)	I, you, he, she, it, we, they; me, you, him, her, it, us, them
plural ['plʊərəl]	Plural, Mehrzahl	
positive statement [ˌpɒzətɪv 'steɪtmənt]	bejahter Aussagesatz	I like oranges.
possessive determiner [pəˌzesɪv dɪ'tɜːmɪnə]	Possessivbegleiter (besitzanzeigender Begleiter)	my, your, his, her, its, our, their
possessive form [pəˌzesɪv fɔːm]	s-Genitiv	Jo's brother; my sister's room
possessive pronoun [pəˌzesɪv 'prəʊnaʊn]	Possessivpronomen	mine, yours, his, hers, ours, theirs

preposition [ˌprepəˈzɪʃn]	Präposition	*after, at, in, next to, under*
present [ˈpreznt]	Gegenwart	
present participle [ˌpreznt ˈpɑːtɪsɪpl]	Partizip Präsens	*cleaning, planning, going, taking*
present perfect [ˌpreznt ˈpɜːfɪkt]	*present perfect*	We**'ve made** a cake for you.
present perfect progressive [ˌpreznt ˌpɜːfɪkt prəˈɡresɪv]	Verlaufsform des *present perfect*	We**'ve been waiting** for an hour.
present progressive [ˌpreznt prəˈɡresɪv]	Verlaufsform der Gegenwart	The Hansons **are having** lunch.
progressive form [prəˈɡresɪv fɔːm]	Verlaufsform	
pronoun [ˈprəʊnaʊn]	Pronomen, Fürwort	
quantifier [ˈkwɒntɪfaɪə]	Mengenangabe	*some, a lot of, many, much*
question tag [ˈkwestʃən tæɡ]	Frageanhängsel	This place is great, **isn't it?**
question word [ˈkwestʃən wɜːd]	Fragewort	*what?, when?, where?, how?*
reflexive pronoun [rɪˌfleksɪv ˈprəʊnaʊn]	Reflexivpronomen	*myself, yourself, themselves*
regular verb [ˌreɡjələ ˈvɜːb]	regelmäßiges Verb	(to) help – helped – helped
relative clause [ˌrelətɪv ˈklɔːz]	Relativsatz	There's the girl **who helped me.**
relative pronoun [ˌrelətɪv ˈprəʊnaʊn]	Relativpronomen	*who, that, which, whose*
reported speech [rɪˌpɔːtɪd ˈspiːtʃ]	indirekte Rede	Sam said **(that) he was sorry.**
request [rɪˈkwest]	Bitte	Can you help me with this?
short answer [ˌʃɔːt ˈɑːnsə]	Kurzantwort	Yes, I am. / No, I don't.
simple form [ˈsɪmpl fɔːm]	einfache Form	
simple past [ˌsɪmpl ˈpɑːst]	einfache Form der Vergangenheit	Jo **wrote** two letters yesterday.
simple present [ˌsɪmpl ˈpreznt]	einfache Form der Gegenwart	I always **go** to school by bike.
singular [ˈsɪŋɡjələ]	Singular, Einzahl	
state verb [ˈsteɪt vɜːb]	Zustandsverb	*be, know, like, sound, want*
statement [ˈsteɪtmənt]	Aussagesatz	
subject [ˈsʌbdʒɪkt]	Subjekt	**My sister** is writing a letter.
subject form [ˈsʌbdʒɪkt fɔːm]	Subjektform (der Personalpronomen)	*I, you, he, she, it, we, they*
subject question [ˈsʌbdʒɪkt ˌkwestʃən]	Frage nach dem Subjekt	Who loves Jake?
subordinate clause [səˌbɔːdɪnət ˈklɔːz]	Nebensatz	I like Scruffy **because I like dogs.**
substitute [ˈsʌbstɪtjuːt]	Ersatzverb (eines modalen Hilfverbs)	*be able to, be allowed to, have to*
tense [tens]	Zeitform	
uncountable noun [ʌnˈkaʊntəbl]	nicht zählbares Nomen	*bread, milk, money, news, work*
verb [vɜːb]	Verb	*hear, open, help, go*
***will*-future**	Futur mit *will*	I think it **will be** cold tonight.
word order [ˈwɜːd ˌɔːdə]	Wortstellung	
yes/no question	Entscheidungsfrage	Are you 13? Do you like comics?

Das **Vocabulary** (S. 170–182) enthält alle neuen Wörter und Wendungen aus Band 6, die du lernen musst. Sie stehen in der Reihenfolge, in der sie in den Units vorkommen.

Das **Dictionary** (S. 183–221) enthält den Wortschatz der Bände 1 bis 6 in alphabetischer Reihenfolge. Dort kannst du nachschlagen, was ein Wort bedeutet, wie man es ausspricht oder wie es genau geschrieben wird.

So ist das Vocabulary aufgebaut:

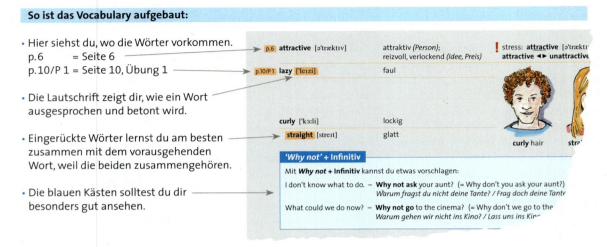

- Hier siehst du, wo die Wörter vorkommen.
  p. 6 = Seite 6
  p. 10/P 1 = Seite 10, Übung 1

- Die Lautschrift zeigt dir, wie ein Wort ausgesprochen und betont wird.

- Eingerückte Wörter lernst du am besten zusammen mit dem vorausgehenden Wort, weil die beiden zusammengehören.

- Die blauen Kästen solltest du dir besonders gut ansehen.

p.6 **attractive** [əˈtræktɪv]	attraktiv (Person); reizvoll, verlockend (Idee, Preis)	**!** stress: **attractive** [əˈtræktɪ] **attractive ◄► unattractive**
p.10/P1 **lazy** [ˈleɪzi]	faul	
curly [ˈkɜːli]	lockig	
straight [streɪt]	glatt	

curly hair   str

'Why not' + Infinitiv

Mit **Why not** + Infinitiv kannst du etwas vorschlagen:

I don't know what to do. – **Why not ask** your aunt? (= Why don't you ask your aunt?)
Warum fragst du nicht deine Tante? / Frag doch deine Tante

What could we do now? – **Why not go** to the cinema? (= Why don't we go to the
Warum gehen wir nicht ins Kino? / Lass uns ins Kino

Tipps zum Wörterlernen findest du im Skills File auf Seite 125.

Abkürzungen:

n	= *noun*		*v*	= *verb*
adj	= *adjective*		*adv*	= *adverb*
prep	= *preposition*		*conj*	= *conjunction*
pl	= *plural*		*no pl*	= *no plural*
p.	= *page*		*pp.*	= *pages*
sb.	= *somebody*		*sth.*	= *something*
jn.	= *jemanden*		*jm.*	= *jemandem*
AE	= *American English*		*BE*	= *British English*
infml	= *informal* (umgangssprachlich, informell)			

Symbole:

! Hier stehen Hinweise auf Besonderheiten, bei denen man leicht Fehler machen kann.

◄► ist das „Gegenteil"-Zeichen:
attractive ◄► unattractive

~ Die **Tilde** in den Beispielsätzen steht für das neue Wort. Beispiel:
(to) **notice** – Lilly was at the party too, but I didn't **~** her.

Unit 1: Love life!

p.6			
charming [ˈtʃɑːmɪŋ]	charmant		She's quite ~. It's impossible not to like her.
arrogant [ˈærəgənt]	arrogant, überheblich	**!**	stress: **arrogant** [ˈærəgənt] *French:* arrogant, e
loyal (to sb.**)** [ˈlɔɪəl]	loyal (gegenüber jm.)	**!**	a ~ friend = a good, reliable friend stress: **loyal** [ˈlɔɪəl] *French:* loyal, e
confidence [ˈkɒnfɪdəns]	Selbstvertrauen, Selbstsicherheit; Zuversicht		She never seems nervous – she's so full of ~. It will be a difficult match, but we're full of ~. adjective: **confident** – noun: **confidence**
attractive [əˈtræktɪv]	attraktiv (Person); reizvoll, verlockend (Idee, Preis)	**!**	stress: **attractive** [əˈtræktɪv] **attractive ◄► unattractive**
appearance [əˈpɪərəns]	Aussehen, (äußere) Erscheinung		He dresses terribly. He just doesn't care about his ~. *French:* l'apparence (f)

(to) **notice** [ˈnəʊtɪs]	bemerken, merken	Lilly was at the party too, but I didn't ~ her. When she wanted to pay, she ~**d** that she had lost her purse.

curly hair   **straight hair**

curly [ˈkɜːli]	lockig	
straight [streɪt]	glatt	

sense of humour [ˌsens_əv ˈhjuːmə]	(Sinn für) Humor	❗ German: English: • Sie hat **(viel) Humor**. She's got **a great sense of humour**. • Er hat **keinen Humor**. He's got **no sense of humour**. ❗ stress: **hu**mour [ˈhjuːmə]

peanut [ˈpiːnʌt]	Erdnuss	a couple of **peanuts**
unlike [ˌʌnˈlaɪk]	anders als; im Gegensatz zu	John is very arrogant, ~ his younger brother, who is really charming.
p.7 **lovable** [ˈlʌvəbl]	liebenswert	
thin [θɪn]	dünn	❗ German: **dünn** ◄► **dick** English: **1. thin** ◄► **fat** (people, animals) **2. thin** ◄► **thick** (books, ice, soup, …)
in a friendly/strange/different **way**	auf freundliche/seltsame/andere Art und Weise	He looked at her **in a strange** ~ and suddenly she felt very scared. When you paraphrase something you try to say it **in a different** ~.

Relationships: going out, asking sb. out

(to) **go out**	Olivia and Jacob would like to **go out**. Ella and Grace **went out** for a pizza last Friday.	**1.** ausgehen, weggehen, sich verabreden
	Noah and Ava **have been going out (together)** for over a year now. There's Aidan. He used to **go out** with my sister.	**2.** miteinander gehen, zusammen sein
(to) **ask sb. out**	Why don't you **ask him out** if you fancy him? Guess what! Colin **asked me out** for a pizza!	jn. einladen, zusammen auszugehen

chat-up line (infml)	Anmachspruch	I can never think of a good ~-~ **line** when I meet someone I fancy.
(to) **chat** sb. **up (-tt-)** (infml)	jn. anquatschen, anbaggern	If you fancy the team captain, why don't you ~ him **up**?

PART A   Real-life relationships

p.8 **real-life**	im wirklichen Leben, aus dem wirklichen Leben	I like reading magazines with ~-~ stories.
not (…) either [ˈaɪðə, ˈiːðə]	auch nicht; auch kein	I'm not going to the party. – I'm **not** going ~. Jane can't speak French, and Sophie ca**n't** ~. Can you lend me £5? – Sorry, I have**n't** got any money ~.

perhaps [pə'hæps]	vielleicht	maybe
situation [ˌsɪtʃu'eɪʃn]	Situation, Lage	❗ stress: **situation** [ˌsɪtʃu'eɪʃn] *French:* la situation
mean [miːn]	gemein	He took the little boys' ball away. That was really ~.
p.9 (to) **break up (with** sb.**)** [ˌbreɪk_'ʌp]**, broke** [brəʊk]**, broken** ['brəʊkən]	sich trennen (von jm.)	Why did you ~ ~ **with** your boyfriend?
(to) **mess things up** *(infml)*	alles durcheinanderbringen, alles vermasseln	
(to) **last** [lɑːst]	halten *(fortdauern, von Bestand sein)*	I don't think his relationship with Tina will ~. I wouldn't buy cheap shoes. They won't ~ very long.
whether ['weðə]	ob	I don't know ~ I can come to your party or not. ❗ German **ob** = 1. **if**; 2. **whether** **whether** ist etwas förmlicher als **if**
(to) **flirt** [flɜːt]	flirten	
Why not tell her ...?	Warum erzählst/sagst du ihr nicht ...?	

> ### 'Why not' + Infinitiv
>
> Mit **Why not** + **Infinitiv** kannst du etwas vorschlagen:
>
> I don't know what to do. — **Why not ask** your aunt? (= Why don't you ask your aunt?)
> *Warum fragst du nicht deine Tante? / Frag doch deine Tante.*
>
> What could we do now? — **Why not go** to the cinema? (= Why don't we go to the cinema?)
> *Warum gehen wir nicht ins Kino? / Lass uns ins Kino gehen.*

p.10/P 1 **lip** [lɪp]	Lippe	**lips**
lazy ['leɪzi]	faul	**lazy ◄► hard-working**
(to) **mention** sth. **(to** sb.**)** ['menʃn]	etwas erwähnen (jm. gegenüber)	My friends will help you if you ~ my name. He missed the meeting because nobody ~**ed** it **to** him. *French:* mentionner
p.11/P 3 (to) **keep** sth. **going**	etwas in Gang halten, etwas aufrechterhalten	(to) **keep** a conversation / a relationship / a party / a fire **going**
I didn't catch your name. [kætʃ]	Ich habe deinen Namen nicht verstanden.	I **didn't** ~ your name. / I **didn't** ~ what you said. Could you repeat it, please?
around here	hier in/aus der Gegend	Do you live **around** ~? / Are you from **around** ~?

PART B On-screen relationships

p.12 **romantic** [rəʊ'mæntɪk]	romantisch; Liebes-	*French:* romantique
in fact [ɪn 'fækt]	tatsächlich; in Wirklichkeit; um genau zu sein	It might look difficult, but **in** ~ it's quite easy. Yes, I know her. **In** ~, we were in the same class.
(to) **dump** sb. [dʌmp] *(infml)*	mit jm. Schluss machen	She ~**ed** her boyfriend but now she'd like to have him back.
the film/novel **is set in** ...	der Film/Roman spielt in ...	The film **is** ~ **in** 16th century London.

(to) **direct** a film/play [dəˈrekt]	bei einem Film/Theaterstück Regie führen	The film **was ~ed** by Sofia Coppola.
director [dəˈrektə]	Regisseur/in	Sofia Coppola was the **~**.
the film **stars** ... [stɑːz]	der Film hat ... in der Hauptrolle / in den Hauptrollen	The film **~** Johnny Depp and Keira Knightley.
law [lɔː]	Jura, Rechtswissenschaften	❗ **law** = **1.** Gesetz; **2.** Jura, Rechtswissenschaften
racism [ˈreɪsɪzəm]	Rassismus	*French:* le racisme
fantasy [ˈfæntəsi]	Fantasy(film, -roman)	
(to) **be based on** [beɪst]	basieren auf	The play **is ~ on** a book by Wolfram Hänel.
unfortunately [ʌnˈfɔːtʃənətli]	leider, unglücklicherweise	I wanted to go skiing but **~** there was no snow. **unfortunately** ◄► **fortunately** (glücklicherweise)
vampire [ˈvæmpaɪə]	Vampir/in	❗ stress and pronunciation: **vampire** [ˈvæmpaɪə] *French:* le/la vampire
pregnant [ˈpregnənt]	schwanger	❗ She's **six months pregnant**. = ... **im** sechsten Monat schwanger.
control (of/over) [kənˈtrəʊl]	Kontrolle (über)	Keep calm and don't lose **~**. (= ... verlier nicht die Beherrschung.)
(to) **bite** [baɪt], **bit** [bɪt], **bitten** [ˈbɪtn]	beißen	In the last episode, he is **bitten** by a vampire and dies.
special effects *(pl)* [ˌspeʃl̩ˈɪfekts]	Spezialeffekte	
effect [ɪˈfekt]	(Aus-)Wirkung, Effekt	The dry weather had a bad **~** on all the plants. *French:* l'effet *(m)*
review [rɪˈvjuː]	*(Buch-, Film-)*Kritik, Besprechung, Rezension	
(to) **review** [rɪˈvjuː]	besprechen, rezensieren *(Buch, Film)*	
reviewer [rɪˈvjuːə]	Rezensent/in, Kritiker/in	
p.13 **4 out of** 5	4 von 5	19 **~ of** 28 students in our form are girls.
religion [rɪˈlɪdʒn]	Religion	❗ stress: **religion** [rɪˈlɪdʒn] *French:* la religion

Religions

Person	Adjective	Building	Other 'religion words':
Christian [ˈkrɪstʃən]	**Christian**	**church, cathedral**	**religious** [rɪˈlɪdʒəs] *religiös; gläubig*
Catholic [ˈkæθlɪk]	**Catholic**		**service** [ˈsɜːvɪs] *Gottesdienst*
Protestant [ˈprɒtɪstənt]	**Protestant**		**mass** [mæs] *Messe*
Hindu [ˈhɪnduː]	**Hindu**	**temple** [ˈtempl] *Tempel*	**priest** [priːst] *Priester*
Jew [dʒuː]	**Jewish**	**synagogue** [ˈsɪnəgɒg] *Synagoge*	**minister** [ˈmɪnɪstə] *Pfarrer/in, Pastor/in*
Muslim [ˈmʊzlɪm]	**Muslim**	**mosque** [mɒsk] *Moschee*	**nun** [nʌn] *Nonne*

intelligent [ɪnˈtelɪdʒənt]	intelligent, klug	**!**	stress: **intelligent** [ɪnˈtelɪdʒənt] *French:* intelligent, e
patient [ˈpeɪʃnt]	geduldig		The train is late so we'll have to be ~. **patient** ◄► **impatient** (ungeduldig) *French:* patient, e – impatient, e
kind [kaɪnd]	freundlich, nett		It was very ~ of you to offer to help, thanks.
p.14/P 1 **brilliant** [ˈbrɪliənt]	großartig, glänzend, hervorragend	**!**	super, great, fantastic stress: **brilliant** [ˈbrɪliənt] *French:* brillant, e
historical [hɪˈstɒrɪkl]	historisch, alt		The city's ~ cathedral was built in the 13th century. *French:* historique
sentimental [ˌsentɪˈmentl]	sentimental		Do you cry when you watch a ~ film? *French:* sentimental, e
(to) recommend sth. **(to** sb.**)** [ˌrekəˈmend]	(jm.) etwas empfehlen	**!**	We want to go to the cinema. Can you ~ a good film? *No infinitive after* **recommend***:* I'd **recommend** travelling by bus. Ich würde **empfehlen**, mit dem Bus zu reisen.
p.14/P 2 **award** [əˈwɔːd]	Auszeichnung, Preis		The Oscar is the most famous film ~.
p.15/P 3 **creative** [kriˈeɪtɪv]	kreativ, schöpferisch	**!**	stress and pronunciation: **creative** [kriˈeɪtɪv] *French:* créatif, créative
bet [bet]	Wette		verb: **(to) bet** – noun: **bet**
if so	wenn ja; wenn dem so ist		Have you got her phone number? And if ~, could you mail it to me?
politics [ˈpɒlətɪks]	Politik		*French:* la politique
environment [ɪnˈvaɪrənmənt]	Umwelt; Umgebung		*French:* l'environnement *(m)*

Unit 2: The world we live in

p.28 **heating** [ˈhiːtɪŋ]	Heizung	It was really cold in our classroom today. The ~ wasn't working.
heat [hiːt]	Hitze, Wärme	It's so hot in here. I can't sleep in this ~. **heat** ◄► **cold**
(to) heat [hiːt]	heizen, erhitzen	We use oil to ~ our flat in winter.
double glazing [ˌdʌbl ˈgleɪzɪŋ]	(Fenster mit) Doppelverglasung	
kettle [ˈketl]	(Wasser-)Kessel, Wasserkocher	
console [ˈkɒnsəʊl]	Konsole, Steuerpult	
insulation [ˌɪnsjuˈleɪʃn]	Isolierung, Wärmedämmung	
microwave [ˈmaɪkrəweɪv]	Mikrowelle	
remote control [rɪˌməʊt kənˈtrəʊl] *(infml auch:* **remote***)*	Fernbedienung; Fernsteuerung	
whiteboard [ˈwaɪtbɔːd]	Weißwandtafel, Whiteboard	
gadget [ˈgædʒɪt]	(kleines) Gerät, Apparat; technische Spielerei	

electric kettle

microwave

remote control

games console

interactive whiteboard

p.29	**carbon footprint** [ˌkɑːbən ˈfʊtprɪnt]	„CO₂-Fußabdruck", CO₂-Bilanz	
	carbon [ˈkɑːbən]	Kohlenstoff; *(oft auch kurz für:)* Kohlendioxid	
	carbon dioxide (CO₂) [daɪˈɒksaɪd], [ˌsiː_əʊ ˈtuː]	Kohlendioxid (CO₂)	❗ stress: d**ioxide** [daɪˈɒksaɪd]
	scientist [ˈsaɪəntɪst]	(Natur-)Wissenschaftler/in	*French:* le/la scientifique
	(to) release [rɪˈliːs]	freilassen *(Gefangene)*; freisetzen, ablassen *(Gas)*	After 25 years the murderer was ~**d** from prison. How much CO₂ do cars ~?
	amount (of) [əˈmaʊnt]	Menge, Betrag	You can add a small ~ **of** salt to the soup. £300! I wouldn't pay that ~ for a pair of jeans.
	cause [kɔːz]	Ursache, Verursacher/in; Grund	Doctors still don't know the ~ of the disease. verb: **(to) cause** – noun: **cause** *French:* la cause
	global warming [ˌgləʊbl ˈwɔːmɪŋ]	Erwärmung der Erdatmosphäre, globaler Temperaturanstieg	
	(to) allow sb. **to do** sth. [əˈlaʊ]	jm. erlauben, etwas zu tun; jm. ermöglichen, etwas zu tun	My parents don't ~ me to travel abroad. The internet ~**s** you to keep in touch with family and friends.
	conditions *(pl)* [kənˈdɪʃnz]	Bedingungen, Verhältnisse	**living ~** („Lebensbedingungen"), **weather ~** („Wetterverhältnisse, -bedingungen")
	(to) communicate (with) [kəˈmjuːnɪkeɪt]	kommunizieren (mit), sich verständigen (mit)	Teenagers sometimes find it difficult to ~ **with** their parents. *French:* communiquer
	emission [iˈmɪʃn]	Emission, (Schadstoff-)Ausstoß	❗ stress: **emission** [iˈmɪʃn] *French:* l'émission *(f)*

emissions

	tonne [tʌn]	Tonne *(Gewichtseinheit)*	1000 kilos ❗ pronunciation: **tonne** [tʌn]
	(to) be made up (of)	zusammengesetzt sein (aus); bestehen (aus)	This pie chart **is ~ up of** five sections.
	appliance [əˈplaɪəns]	Gerät *(meist elektrisch)*	Most homes have ~**s** like dishwashers and washing machines.
	target [ˈtɑːgɪt]	Ziel; Zielscheibe	What's your personal ~ for the coming year? Houses with open windows are easy ~**s** for thieves.
	climate [ˈklaɪmət]	Klima	❗ pronunciation: **climate** [ˈklaɪmət] *French:* le climat
	gas [gæs]	Gas	❗ **gas** = 1. Gas; **2.** *(AE)* Benzin *French:* le gaz („Gas")

PART A Changing the future

pp.30/31 **invention** [ɪnˈvenʃn]   Erfindung

what the future **may** bring   was die Zukunft bringen mag

Möglich? Wahrscheinlich? Sicherlich? – *may, might, could, should, must*

	may might could should must			
My parents		be at home now.	*Meine Eltern*	sind jetzt **vielleicht** zu Hause. **könnten** jetzt **vielleicht** zu Hause sein. **könnten** jetzt zu Hause sein. **sollten/müssten eigentlich** jetzt zu Hause sein. **müssen** jetzt zu Hause sein.

mobility [məʊˈbɪləti]	Mobilität, Beweglichkeit	*French:* la mobilité
power [ˈpaʊə]	Kraft, Energie, Strom	
(to) **lead (to** sth.) [liːd], **led, led** [led]	(zu etwas) führen	Like most people, I just want to ~ a normal life. Listening to very loud music can ~ **to** hearing problems.
revolution [ˌrevəˈluːʃn]	Revolution	❗ stress: **revolution** [ˌrevəˈluːʃn] *French:* la révolution
coal [kəʊl]	Kohle	
battery [ˈbætri, ˈbætəri]	Batterie	
(to) **be able to afford** sth. [əˈfɔːd]	sich etwas leisten können	Our car is very old, but we **can't** ~ a new one.
second [ˈsekənd]	Sekunde	There are 60 ~**s** in a minute.
fossil fuel [ˌfɒsl ˈfjuːəl]	fossiler Brennstoff	Coal, oil and gas are ~ ~**s**.
solar [ˈsəʊlə]	Solar-, Sonnen-	❗ stress: **solar** [ˈsəʊlə] *French:* solaire
pollution [pəˈluːʃn]	(Umwelt-)Verschmutzung	*French:* la pollution

Verbs and nouns

(to) **act**
  action [ˈækʃn]
	handeln, sich verhalten
	Tat, Handlung; Handeln
			(to) **invent** [ɪnˈvent]
			  invention
				erfinden
				Erfindung

(to) **communicate** **communication** [kəˌmjuːnɪˈkeɪʃn]	kommunizieren Kommunikation, Verständigung		(to) **pollute** [pəˈluːt] **pollution**	verschmutzen, verunreinigen Verschmutzung

(to) **discuss** sth. [dɪˈskʌs]
 	
  discussion
	etwas besprechen,
	über etwas diskutieren
	Diskussion
			(to) **react (to)**
			  reaction (to) [riˈækʃn]
				reagieren (auf)
				Reaktion (auf)

keyboard [ˈkiːbɔːd]	Tastatur	a **keyboard** a **keyboard**
brain [breɪn]	Gehirn	
choice [tʃɔɪs]	Wahl, Auswahl	verb: (to) **choose** – noun: **choice** *French:* le choix
experiment [ɪkˈsperɪmənt]	Experiment	❗ stress: **experiment** [ɪkˈsperɪmənt]

Tipps zum Wörterlernen → S.125 · Dictionary (English – German) → S.183–221

p.32/P1	**household** [ˈhaʊshəʊld]	Haushalt; Haushalts-	I often do ~ jobs like cleaning, cooking and washing the dishes.
	antibiotic [ˌæntibaɪˈɒtɪk]	Antibiotikum	*French:* l'antibiotique *(m)*
	discovery [dɪˈskʌvəri]	Entdeckung	verb: (to) **discover** – noun: **discovery** *French:* la découverte
	infectious [ɪnˈfekʃəs]	ansteckend	*French:* infectieux, infectieuse
	medicine [ˈmedsn, ˈmedɪsn]	Medizin, Arznei	**!** stress: **medicine** [ˈmedsn, ˈmedɪsn] *French:* le médicament
	penicillin [ˌpenɪˈsɪlɪn]	Penizillin	**Penicillin** is used to fight infectious diseases. **!** stress: **penicillin** [ˌpenɪˈsɪlɪn]
	(to) **test**	testen, prüfen	I'd like to ~ the printer before I decide to buy it.
p.32/P2	**then**	damals	I was five when the photo was taken – I didn't even go to school ~.
p.32/P3	**bone** [bəʊn]	Knochen	
	X-ray [ˈeks reɪ]	Röntgenstrahl; Röntgenbild	
	thanks to penicillin	dank Penizillin; wegen Penizillin	The party was a great success ~ **to** John, who organized everything.
p.33/P4	(to) **realize** [ˈriːəlaɪz]	sich *(einer Sache)* bewusst sein/ werden; verwirklichen, realisieren	I didn't ~ you were French. I suddenly ~**d** that I'd left my books at home. With the help of government money we were able to ~ the project.
p.33/P5	**application** [ˌæplɪˈkeɪʃn] *(kurz auch:* **app***)*	Anwendung, Anwendungs- programm, -software	It's a useful little ~ that you can download from the internet.

PART B   Saving the planet

Now only £15

p.34	(to) **reduce** [rɪˈdjuːs]	verringern, vermindern, reduzieren	Look, they've ~**d** the price from £25 to £15. *French:* réduire
	(to) **take** sb. **through** sth.	etwas mit jm. (genau) durchgehen	If you need help with the software, I can ~ you **through** the instructions.
	heavy [ˈhevi]	schwer *(von Gewicht)*; heftig, stark	**!** heavy = 1. schwer – a **heavy** suitcase 2. heftig, stark – **heavy** storms, **heavy** traffic, a **heavy** smoker
	stereo [ˈsteriəʊ]	Stereo; Stereoanlage	
	on and on	immer weiter	We walked ~ **and** ~ until finally we saw the village before us.
	(to) **be a no-no** [ˈnəʊ nəʊ] *(infml)*	tabu sein, nicht in Frage kommen	Religious discrimination **is a** big ~-~.
	one by one	einer nach dem anderen	She opened her presents ~ **by** ~.
	gone [gɒn]	weg, fort	I went back to get my purse, but it was ~.
	(to) **pretend** [prɪˈtend]	so tun, als ob	Lilly ~**ed** to be asleep when her mum entered the bedroom. *French:* prétendre
	(to) **swipe** a card [swaɪp]	eine Karte durchziehen	We had to ~ a card at the door to get into our hotel room.

coat [kəʊt]	Mantel	 **coats**
responsible [rɪ'spɒnsəbl]	verantwortlich; verantwortungsbewusst	The team captain is ~ for organizing matches. We need a reliable and ~ person to look after the house while we're away. *French:* responsable
p.35 (to) **break down** [ˌbreɪk 'daʊn]	zusammenbrechen; (Gerät) ausfallen, eine Panne haben	He **broke** ~ when he heard the bad news. On our way to Italy our car **broke** ~ so we had to spend two days in a hotel in Würzburg.
the machine **kept** breaking down	das Gerät fiel immer wieder aus	Why do you ~ asking the same question?

(to) keep

1. keep	behalten	Can I **keep** your pen or do you want it back?
2. keep	aufbewahren	Butter should be **kept** in the fridge.
3. keep sth. warm/fresh ...	etwas warm/frisch ... halten	Good insulation **keeps** your house warm.
4. keep in touch	in Verbindung bleiben; Kontakt halten	Nice meeting you. Let's **keep in touch**.
5. keep (on) doing sth.	etwas weiter tun; etwas immer wieder tun	We **kept (on) walking** till we got to a small village. My little brother **keeps asking** silly questions.

freezing ['fri:zɪŋ]	eisig; eiskalt	It's ~ (cold) outside. There's even ice on the windows.
(to) **rip** sb. **off** (-pp-) [ˌrɪp 'ɒf] (infml)	jn. übers Ohr hauen, jn. abzocken	I wouldn't shop there. It's much too expensive and they'll ~ you **off** if they can.
evil ['i:vl]	böse (bösartig, feindselig), übel, schlimm	an ~ monster; an ~ smell
24/7 (twenty-four seven)	rund um die Uhr, sieben Tage die Woche	= twenty-four hours, seven days a week
meter ['mi:tə]	(Gas-, Strom-)Zähler	 a **gas meter**
(to) **melt** [melt]	schmelzen	The sun came out, and the snow began to ~. The sun ~**ed** the ice on the windows.
power cut ['paʊə kʌt]	Stromabschaltung, Stromausfall	
it **gives me the creeps** [kri:ps]	es ist mir unheimlich; es ist mir nicht geheuer	Let's get out of this place. It **gives me the** ~. That man **gives me the** ~. He looks so scary.
p.36 (to) **make a difference**	etwas bewirken, bewegen	Help to save the planet! Get involved! You can **make a** ~!
low [ləʊ]	niedrig	**low** ◀▶ **high**
light bulb ['laɪt bʌlb]	Glühbirne	**light bulbs**
charger ['tʃɑ:dʒə]	Ladegerät	
(to) **breathe (in/out)** [bri:ð]	(ein-/aus)atmen	You should ~ **in** through your nose and **out** through your mouth.

agriculture [ˈægrɪkʌltʃə]	Landwirtschaft	*French:* l'agriculture *(f)*
chemical *(n; adj)* [ˈkemɪkl]	Chemikalie; chemisch	❗ stress: <u>**chemical**</u> [ˈkemɪkl]
organic [ɔːˈgænɪk]	organisch, biologisch; Bio-	**organic** vegetables/eggs/meat/food production
packaging [ˈpækɪdʒɪŋ]	Verpackung	
bill [bɪl]	Rechnung	piece of paper telling you what you have to pay ❗ *(in a restaurant)* Could we have the **bill**, please? (= Bitte zahlen. / Die Rechnung, bitte.) ❗ You **pay the bill**, but you **pay for** a meal.
complete [kəmˈpliːt]	vollständig, komplett	adjective: **complete** (vollständig, komplett) – adverb: **completely** (völlig) *French:* complet, complète *(adj)* – complètement *(adv)*
(to) **cut** sth. **down**	etwas zurückschneiden; *(Baum)* fällen	
p.37/P 2 **on the one hand … on the other hand**	einerseits … andererseits	**On the one ~**, technology makes life easier for us. **On the other ~**, our appliances use a lot of energy.

Unit 3: Have your say!

p.46 **Have your say!**	*etwa:* Übe dein Mitspracherecht aus! / Rede mit!	Adults shouldn't decide everything. Young people should **have their ~** too.
issue [ˈɪʃuː]	Thema, (Streit-)Frage	Global warming is one of the big **~s** of our time.

(to) care

Which issues do you **care about** most?	Welche Themen liegen dir besonders am Herzen? / Welche Themen sind dir am wichtigsten?
I **care about** health … and the environment.	Gesundheit ist mir wichtig … und die Umwelt.
Do you **care** enough to stand up and have your say?	Ist es dir wichtig genug, dass du aufstehst und deine Meinung sagst?
A lot of people just **don't care**.	Vielen Menschen ist es einfach egal.
Who cares about fashion? I don't!	Wen interessiert schon Mode? Mich nicht!

poverty [ˈpɒvəti]	Armut	adjective: **poor** [pɔː, pʊə] – noun: **poverty** [ˈpɒvəti] *French:* la pauvreté
facilities *(pl)* [fəˈsɪlətiz]	Einrichtungen, Anlagen	We need more sports **~** for kids in this area.
p.47 **trade** [treɪd]	Handel	the activity of buying and selling
on charge [tʃɑːdʒ]	am Ladegerät; am Netz *(zum Aufladen)*	
(to) **charge** [tʃɑːdʒ]	(auf)laden *(Batterie, Handy)*	
wish [wɪʃ]	Wunsch	
(to) **wish for** sth. [wɪʃ]	sich etwas wünschen	I never get what I **~ for** on my birthday!
(to) **complain (to** sb. **about** sth.**)** [kəmˈpleɪn]	sich beschweren, sich beklagen (bei jm. über etwas)	If the food isn't hot enough, you should **~ to** the waiter. *French:* se plaindre
truth [truːθ]	Wahrheit	(to) **tell the truth** ◄► (to) **tell lies** [laɪz] *die Wahrheit sagen* ◄► *lügen* Don't **tell lies**. Be honest and **tell the truth**.

politician [ˌpɒləˈtɪʃn]	Politiker/in	**!** stress: <u>**pol**</u>itics ['pɒlətɪks] (Politik) pol**i**tical [pəˈlɪtɪkl] (politisch) politi<u>**ci**</u>an [ˌpɒləˈtɪʃn] (Politiker/in) *French:* le politicien, la politicienne

---

Politics

Politicians usually belong to political **parties**.	**party** ['pɑːti] Partei
In a **democracy**, the **citizens** elect **members of parliament (MPs)**.	**democracy** [dɪˈmɒkrəsi] Demokratie **citizen** ['sɪtɪzn] Staatsbürger/in **member of parliament** Parlaments- mitglied, Abgeordnete/r
After living in the UK for five years, foreigners can apply for British **citizenship**.	**citizenship** ['sɪtɪzənʃɪp] Staatsbürgerschaft
In the UK, the **prime minister (PM)** is the head of the government. Governments need the support of a majority of MPs.	**prime minister** [ˌpraɪm ˈmɪnɪstə] Premier- minister/in, Ministerpräsident/in
The head of a city government or **town council** is called 'mayor'. The mayor and the **town councillors** usually work in the **town hall**.	**town council** ['kaʊnsl] Stadtrat (Gremium) **town councillor** ['kaʊnsələ] Stadtrat/-rätin **town hall** ['hɔːl] Rathaus
Germany has a written **constitution** containing its basic laws. The UK has no written constitution.	**constitution** [ˌkɒnstɪˈtjuːʃn] Verfassung

---

(to) **speak out** [ˌspiːk_ˈaʊt]	seine Meinung (offen) sagen	If nobody **speaks ~**, people won't realize that there's a problem.
petition [pəˈtɪʃn]	Unterschriftensammlung, Petition	*French:* la pétition
campaign [kæmˈpeɪn]	Kampagne, (Werbe-)Feldzug	**!** spelling: cam**paign** *French:* la campagne
(to) **sign** [saɪn]	unterschreiben, unterzeichnen	*French:* signer

Time to speak out. Come and have your say! Sign the petition and join our online campaign! March to the town hall: Friday, May 14, 2 pm

likely ['laɪkli]	wahrscheinlich	Everyone is angry, so it's ~ that lots of people will join the protests.
(to) **be likely to be/do** sth.	wahrscheinlich etwas sein/tun	It**'s ~ to be** sunny in the afternoon. We**'re ~ to finish** the project in time.
p.102 **bossy** ['bɒsi]	rechthaberisch, herrisch	
thoughtful ['θɔːtfl]	nachdenklich; aufmerksam, rücksichtsvoll	You're looking ~. Is there a problem? He brought me some flowers. – How very ~.

PART A Your right to be heard

p.48 (to) **take** sb./sth. **seriously**	jn./etwas ernst nehmen	My older sister doesn't ~ me **seriously**.
public ['pʌblɪk]	Öffentlichkeit	**!** in public – in <u>der</u> Öffentlichkeit
(to) **deserve** [dɪˈzɜːv]	verdienen *(zu Recht bekommen)*	We've worked very hard, so I think we ~ a break.

Tipps zum Wörterlernen → S.125 · Dictionary (English – German) → S.183–221

equal ['i:kwəl]	gleich *(Rechte, Bezahlung usw.)*	Do women and men always have ~ rights? Divide £ 1 into five ~ parts. – Easy. 20 p.
two at a time	zwei auf einmal *(zur selben Zeit)*	❗ **one at a time** = **einzeln**: Please come in separately, **one at a time**.
unless [ən'les]	es sei denn; wenn ... nicht	You'll get into trouble with your parents ~ you work harder. (= ... if you don't work harder)
p.49 **It doesn't matter.**	Es spielt keine Rolle. / Es macht nichts (aus).	Sorry, I forgot the potatoes. – **It doesn't ~**. We can have rice instead.
disgusting [dɪs'gʌstɪŋ]	widerlich, ekelhaft	The food was ~. I felt sick after eating it.
mosquito [mə'ski:təʊ]	Moskito, Stechmücke	
device [dɪ'vaɪs]	Vorrichtung, Gerät	My bike has a little ~ that counts the miles I've cycled.
annoying [ə'nɔɪɪŋ]	lästig, unangenehm	I find it really ~ when people smoke near me.
(to) **annoy** sb. [ə'nɔɪ]	jn. ärgern, stören	Other people's headphones often ~ me.
(to) **make sense**	sinnvoll sein, einen Sinn ergeben	That doesn't **make** ~ to me. (= Das leuchtet mir nicht ein.)
(to) **affect** [ə'fekt]	sich auswirken auf, betreffen	How will climate change ~ us in the future?
army ['ɑ:mi]	Armee, Heer	❗ stress: **army** ['ɑ:mi] *French:* l'armée *(f)*
tax [tæks]	*(die)* Steuer	The ~ on petrol is about 70 % of the price.

surely

Mit **surely** will man den Leser oder Hörer zur Zustimmung bewegen.	**Surely** we are old enough to make our own decisions. *Wir sind **doch wohl** alt genug, für uns selbst zu entscheiden.* (Ich bin davon überzeugt, und ich möchte, dass man mir zustimmt.)
	Surely we should ask her first. *Wir sollten sie **doch wohl** erst fragen.*
In verneinten Sätzen bringt **surely** zum Ausdruck, dass man überrascht ist oder dass man etwas kaum glauben kann. (Oft stehen solche Sätze mit Fragezeichen.)	**Surely** that's **not** snow, in the middle of June!? *Das ist **doch sicher nicht** Schnee, mitten im Juni!? / Das ist **doch nicht wirklich** Schnee, mitten im Juni!?*
	You do**n't** believe that, **surely**? *Das glaubst du **doch wohl nicht wirklich**, oder?*

(to) **improve** [ɪm'pru:v]	(sich) verbessern	(to) become or make better
(to) **criticize (for)** ['krɪtɪsaɪz]	kritisieren (wegen)	The report ~**d** schools **for** giving too much homework. ❗ stress: **criticize** ['krɪtɪsaɪz] *French:* critiquer
sensible ['sensəbl]	vernünftig	What a silly idea! Try and be more ~. ❗ *Nicht verwechseln:* **sensible** ['sensəbl] = vernünftig **sensitive** ['sensətɪv] = sensibel
p.50/P1 **fare** [feə]	Fahrpreis	
(to) **take action** ['ækʃn]	handeln; etwas unternehmen	We can't just do nothing. We'll have to ~ **action**.
p.50/P2 (to) **hold** [həʊld], **held, held** [held]	abhalten, veranstalten	(to) **hold** a competition/ concert/meeting/...
p.51/P4 **corridor** ['kɒrɪdɔ:]	Gang, Korridor	a school **corridor**

moderator ['mɒdəreɪtə]	Vermittler/in, Moderator/in	❗ **presenter** = Moderator/in *(von Fernsehshow, Nachrichten)*
		moderator = Vermittler/in *(z.B. in Konflikten, Diskussionen)*
(to) **feel comfortable** ['kʌmftəbl]	sich wohl fühlen	I don't **feel ~** in big crowds.
		John doesn't **feel ~** talking to girls.

PART B Speaking out

p.54/P 1	**suffix** ['sʌfɪks]	Nachsilbe, Suffix	-able, -ness, -ment, -ity are **~es**.
	(to) **immigrate (to)** ['ɪmɪgreɪt]	einwandern, immigrieren (in)	(to) come to a country to live there *French:* immigrer
	immigration (to) [ˌɪmɪ'greɪʃn]	Einwanderung, Immigration (in, nach)	*French:* l'immigration *(f)*
	(to) **concentrate (on)** ['kɒnsntreɪt]	sich konzentrieren (auf)	Be quiet, please. I can't **~ on** my homework. ❗ German: Ich kann **mich** nicht **konzentrieren** ... English: I can't **concentrate** ... *French:* se concentrer
	concentration [ˌkɒnsn'treɪʃn]	Konzentration	*French:* la concentration
	free speech [ˌfriː 'spiːtʃ]	Redefreiheit	In a democracy, **free ~** is a basic right.
p.55/P 3	**conflict** ['kɒnflɪkt]	Konflikt	❗ stress: **conflict** ['kɒnflɪkt] *French:* le conflit
	(to) **accept** [ək'sept]	annehmen, akzeptieren	Most shops in Britain **~** credit cards. *French:* accepter
	apology [ə'pɒlədʒi]	Entschuldigung *(Bitte um Verzeihung)*	verb: (to) **apologize** – noun: **apology** (to) offer/accept an **apology**
	No worries. ['wʌriz] *(infml)*	Kein Problem! / Ist schon in Ordnung!	Sorry, I'm late. – No **~**, we still have lots of time.
	I didn't mean to ...	Ich wollte nicht ...; Es war nicht meine Absicht, zu ...	I'm sorry, **I didn't ~ to** be rude. **I didn't ~ to** hurt you. Can you forgive me?

Oh I'm sorry, I didn't mean to interrupt you.

No worries. We were just going to stop for lunch.

'I shouldn't have done ...' – *should + have + past participle*

Mit **should/shouldn't + have + past participle** kannst du sagen, was jemand in einer bestimmten Situation hätte tun sollen bzw. hätte nicht tun sollen:

Oh look, the floor is all wet. You **should have closed** the window.   ... Du **hättest** das Fenster **schließen sollen**.

I'm sorry, I **shouldn't have said** that.   ... ich **hätte** das **nicht sagen sollen**.

Can I have a word with you?   Kann ich mal kurz mit dir reden?

Das **Dictionary** (S. 183–221) enthält den Wortschatz der Bände 1 bis 6 von *English G 21*.
Wenn du wissen möchtest, was ein Wort bedeutet, wie man es ausspricht oder wie es genau geschrieben wird, kannst du hier nachschlagen.

Im **Dictionary** werden folgende **Abkürzungen und Symbole** verwendet:

jm. = jemandem	sb. = somebody	*pl* = *plural*	*AE* = *American English*
jn. = jemanden	sth. = something	*no pl* = *no plural*	*infml* = *informal*

°   Mit diesem Kringel sind Wörter markiert, die nicht zum Lernwortschatz gehören.
▶   Der Pfeil verweist auf Kästchen im **Vocabulary** (S. 170–182), in denen du weitere Informationen zu diesem Wort findest.

Die **Fundstellenangaben** zeigen, wo ein Wort zum ersten Mal vorkommt.
Die Ziffern in Klammern bezeichnen Seitenzahlen:

I, II, III usw.	=	Band 1, 2, 3 usw.
VI 1 (13)	=	Band 6, Unit 1, Seite 13
VI 1 (13/173)	=	Band 6, Unit 1, Seite 173 (im Vocabulary, zu Seite 13)

Tipps zur Arbeit mit einem Wörterbuch findest du im Skills File auf Seite 128.

> **Tipp**
>
> Auf der **Audio-CD im Work-book** findest du sowohl dieses englisch-deutsche Wörterverzeichnis als auch ein deutsch-englisches Wörterverzeichnis mit dem Lernwortschatz der Bände 1–6.

A

a [ə]
1. ein, eine I
2. once/twice a week einmal/zweimal pro Woche III
a bit ein bisschen, etwas II • **a few** ein paar, einige II • **a little** ein bisschen, ein wenig IV • **a lot (of)** eine Menge, viel, viele II
He likes her a lot. Er mag sie sehr. I

able ['eɪbl]**: be able to do sth.** etwas tun können; fähig sein / in der Lage sein, etwas zu tun III
be able to afford sth. sich etwas leisten können VI 2 (30)

Aboriginal [ˌæbə'rɪdʒənl] Aborigine-(die Ureinwohner/innen Australiens betreffend) V

Aborigine [ˌæbə'rɪdʒəni] *Ureinwohner/in Australiens* V

about [ə'baʊt]
1. über I
2. ungefähr II
ask about sth. nach etwas fragen I • **be about to do sth.** im Begriff sein, etwas zu tun; kurz davor sein, etwas zu tun V • **do sth. about sth.** etwas unternehmen (gegen etwas) V • **This is about Mr Green.** Es geht um Mr Green. I
How about ...? Wie wär's mit ...? III • **What about ...? 1.** Was ist mit ...? / Und ...? I; **2.** Wie wär's mit ...? I
What are you talking about? Wovon redest du? I • **°What are the pages about?** Wovon handeln die

Seiten? • **What was the best thing about ...?** Was war das Beste an ...? II • **°Say what you like about ...** Sag, was du an ... magst

above [ə'bʌv]
1. oben III
2. über, oberhalb (von) III

°abridged [ə'brɪdʒd] gekürzt *(Buch)*

abroad [ə'brɔːd] im Ausland II
go abroad ins Ausland gehen/fahren II

accent ['æksənt] Akzent II

accept [ək'sept] annehmen, akzeptieren VI 3 (55)

accident ['æksɪdənt] Unfall II

ache [eɪk] wehtun IV

acid ['æsɪd] Säure IV

across [ə'krɒs]
1. (quer) über III
2. hinüber, herüber III

act [ækt]
1. handeln, sich verhalten IV
2. aufführen, spielen I
°Act out ... Spiele/Spielt ... vor.

action ['ækʃn] Tat, Handlung; Handeln VI 2 (31/176) • **take action** handeln; etwas unternehmen VI 3 (50)

action film ['ækʃn fɪlm] Actionfilm VI 1 (14)

active ['æktɪv] aktiv, tätig IV

activity [æk'tɪvəti] Aktivität, Tätigkeit I

actor ['æktə] Schauspieler/in II

actually ['æktʃuəli]
1. eigentlich; in Wirklichkeit III
2. nebenbei bemerkt; übrigens IV

ad [æd], *BE auch:* **advert** ['ædvɜːt]
(kurz für: **advertisement**) Anzeige,

Inserat; *(im Fernsehen)* Werbespot V

°adapt [ə'dæpt] adaptieren, anpassen; bearbeiten

°adapted [ə'dæptɪd] adaptiert; bearbeitet

add (to) [æd] hinzufügen, ergänzen, addieren (zu) I • **°add up** addieren, zusammenzählen

address [ə'dres] Adresse V

adjective ['ædʒɪktɪv] Adjektiv I

admission [əd'mɪʃn] Eintritt, Eintrittspreis IV

adult ['ædʌlt] Erwachsene(r) III

advantage (over) [əd'vɑːntɪdʒ] Vorteil (gegenüber) IV

adventure [əd'ventʃə] Abenteuer IV

adverb ['ædvɜːb] Adverb I

advertise ['ædvətaɪz] Werbung machen (für); inserieren V

advertisement [əd'vɜːtɪsmənt]
(infml: **ad** [æd]*, BE auch:* **advert** ['ædvɜːt]*)* Anzeige, Inserat; *(im Fernsehen)* Werbespot V

advertiser ['ædvətaɪzə] Inserent/in; Werbekunde/-kundin V

advice *(no pl)* [əd'vaɪs] Rat, Ratschlag, Ratschläge V • **take someone's advice** auf jemandes Rat hören V

advise sb. [əd'vaɪz] jn. beraten V
advise sb. to do sth. jm. raten, etwas zu tun V

adviser [əd'vaɪzə] Berater/in V

affect [ə'fekt] sich auswirken auf, betreffen VI 3 (49)

afford [ə'fɔːd]**: be able to afford sth.** sich etwas leisten können VI 2 (30)

afraid [ə'freɪd]
1. be afraid (of) Angst haben (vor) I
2. I'm afraid leider II
African-American [ˌæfrɪkən_ə'merɪkən] afro-amerikanisch IV
after ['ɑːftə] nach *(zeitlich)* I
after that danach I
after ['ɑːftə] nachdem II
afternoon [ˌɑːftə'nuːn] Nachmittag I • **in the afternoon** nachmittags, am Nachmittag I • **on Friday afternoon** freitagnachmittags, am Freitagnachmittag I
again [ə'gen] wieder; noch einmal I **once again** noch einmal III
against [ə'genst] gegen I
age [eɪdʒ] Alter III; Zeitalter VI 2 (30)
for ages ewig, eine Ewigkeit IV
kids my age Kinder/Jugendliche in meinem Alter V • **under age** minderjährig V
ago [ə'gəʊ]: **a minute ago** vor einer Minute I
agree (on) [ə'griː] sich einigen (auf) I • **agree with sb./sth.** jm./etwas zustimmen; mit jm./etwas übereinstimmen II
agriculture ['ægrɪkʌltʃə] Landwirtschaft VI 2 (36)
air [eə] Luft III
air conditioning *(no pl)* ['eə kən,dɪʃnɪŋ] Klimatisierung, Klimaanlage V
airport ['eəpɔːt] Flughafen III
album ['ælbəm] Album III
alcohol ['ælkəhɒl] Alkohol V
alive [ə'laɪv] am Leben, lebendig IV
all [ɔːl] alle; alles I • **2 all** 2 beide (2:2 unentschieden) III • **all around the castle** ganz um die Burg herum II • **all day** den ganzen Tag (lang) I • **all over the world** auf der ganzen Welt III
all right [ɔːl 'raɪt] gut, in Ordnung II • **it's all right with her** es ist ihr recht; sie ist einverstanden V • **all the time** die ganze Zeit I • **all we have to do now …** alles, was wir jetzt (noch) tun müssen, … II
from all around Wales aus ganz Wales II • **from all over England/the UK** aus ganz England/aus dem gesamten Vereinigten Königreich III • **This is all wrong.** Das ist ganz falsch. I
all-day ticket [ˌɔːl deɪ 'tɪkɪt] Tagesfahrkarte III
allow sb. to do sth. [ə'laʊ] jm. erlauben, etwas zu tun; jm. ermöglichen, etwas zu tun VI 2 (29) • **be allowed** erlaubt sein IV • **be allowed to do sth.** etwas tun dürfen III

°**allowance** [ə'laʊəns] Freibetrag; erlaubte Menge
almost ['ɔːlməʊst] fast, beinahe II
alone [ə'ləʊn] allein I • **leave sb. alone** jn. in Ruhe lassen IV
along [ə'lɒŋ]: **along the road** entlang der Straße / die Straße entlang II • **along with sb./sth.** (zusammen) mit jm./etwas V • °**sing along** mitsingen
alphabet ['ælfəbet] Alphabet I
°**alphabetical** [ˌælfə'betɪkl] alphabetisch
already [ɔːl'redi] schon, bereits II
also ['ɔːlsəʊ] auch II
although [ɔːl'ðəʊ] obwohl III
altogether [ˌɔːltə'geðə] insgesamt, alles in allem V
always ['ɔːlweɪz] immer I
am [ˌeɪ_'em]: **7 am** 7 Uhr morgens/vormittags I
amazing [ə'meɪzɪŋ] erstaunlich, unglaublich II
ambitious [æm'bɪʃəs] ehrgeizig V
ambulance ['æmbjələns] Krankenwagen II
American football [əˌmerɪkən 'fʊtbɔːl] Football I
amnesty ['æmnəsti] Amnestie, Begnadigung IV
amount (of) [ə'maʊnt] Menge, Betrag VI 2 (29)
an [ən] ein, eine I *siehe* **a**
analysis [ə'næləsɪs], *pl* **analyses** [ə'næləsiːz] Analyse, Auswertung IV
ancestor ['ænsestə] Vorfahre/Vorfahrin V
anchor ['æŋkə] Anker IV
anchorman/anchorwoman ['æŋkəmæn, 'æŋkəwʊmən] *(AE auch kurz:* **anchor***)* Moderator/in *(von Nachrichtensendungen)* IV
and [ənd, ænd] und I • **and so on (etc.** [et'setərə]**)** und so weiter (usw.) IV • **on and on** immer weiter VI 2 (34)
angel ['eɪndʒl] Engel II
angry (about sth./with sb.) ['æŋgri] wütend, böse (über etwas/auf jn.) II
animal ['ænɪml] Tier II
anniversary [ˌænɪ'vɜːsəri] Jahrestag IV • **anniversary of sb.'s death** js. Todestag IV
announce [ə'naʊns] ankündigen, bekanntgeben III
announcement [ə'naʊnsmənt] Durchsage, Ansage; Ankündigung, Bekanntgabe III
annoy sb. [ə'nɔɪ] jn. ärgern, stören VI 3 (49/181)

annoying [ə'nɔɪɪŋ] lästig, unangenehm VI 3 (49)
anorak ['ænəræk] Anorak, Windjacke III
another [ə'nʌðə] ein(e) andere(r, s); noch ein(e) I • **another 45 p** weitere 45 Pence, noch 45 Pence II • **one another** einander, sich (gegenseitig) III
answer ['ɑːnsə] antworten; beantworten I
answer (to) ['ɑːnsə] Antwort (auf) I
anti- ['ænti] anti- V • **anti-social** asozial; antisozial VI 3 (49)
antibiotic [ˌæntibaɪ'ɒtɪk] Antibiotikum VI 2 (32)
any ['eni] jede(r, s) beliebige; irgendein(e) IV • **any …?** (irgend) welche …? I • **(at) any time** jederzeit V • **not (…) any** kein, keine I **not (…) any more** nicht mehr II
anybody ['enibɒdi] (irgend)jemand II; jede(r) IV • **not (…) anybody** niemand II
anyone ['eniwʌn] IV *siehe* **anybody**
anything ['eniθɪŋ] (irgend)etwas II; alles IV • **not (…) anything** nichts II
anyway ['eniweɪ]
1. sowieso I
2. trotzdem II
3. Anyway, … Aber egal, … / Wie dem auch sei, … V
anywhere ['eniweə] irgendwo(hin) II • **not (…) anywhere** nirgendwo(hin) II
apart [ə'pɑːt] auseinander, getrennt IV
apartment [ə'pɑːtmənt] *(AE)* Wohnung IV
apologize (to sb. for sth.) [ə'pɒlədʒaɪz] sich (bei jm. für etwas) entschuldigen V
apology [ə'pɒlədʒi] Entschuldigung *(Bitte um Verzeihung)* VI 3 (55)
appear [ə'pɪə] erscheinen, auftauchen III
appearance [ə'pɪərəns] Aussehen, (äußere) Erscheinung VI 1 (6)
appetite ['æpɪtaɪt] Appetit III
apple ['æpl] Apfel I
appliance [ə'plaɪəns] Gerät *(meist elektrisch)* VI 2 (29)
application [ˌæplɪ'keɪʃn]
1. Bewerbung V • **letter of application** Bewerbungsschreiben V
2. *(kurz auch:* **app***)* Anwendung, Anwendungsprogramm, -software VI 2 (33)
apply (for sth.) [ə'plaɪ] sich bewerben (um/für etwas); etwas beantragen IV

appointment [ə'pɔɪntmənt] Termin, Verabredung I

appreciate [ə'priːʃieɪt] schätzen, zu schätzen wissen IV

apprentice [ə'prentɪs] Auszubildende(r), Lehrling V

apprenticeship [ə'prentɪʃɪp] Lehre, Ausbildung V

April ['eɪprəl] April I

architect ['ɑːkɪtekt] Architekt/in V

archive ['ɑːkaɪv] Archiv IV

are [ɑː] bist; sind; seid I • **How are you?** Wie geht es dir/Ihnen/euch? II • **The pencils are 35p.** Die Bleistifte kosten 35 Pence. I • **You're joking, aren't you?** Du machst Witze, nicht wahr? / Das ist nicht dein Ernst, oder? II

area ['eəriə]
1. Bereich; Gebiet, Gegend III
2. Fläche V

argue ['ɑːgjuː]
1. sich streiten, sich zanken I
°**2.** argumentieren

argument ['ɑːgjumənt]
1. Argument, Begründung III
2. Streit III

arm [ɑːm] Arm I

armchair ['ɑːmtʃeə] Sessel I

army ['ɑːmi] Armee, Heer VI 3 (49)

around [ə'raʊnd] in ... umher, durch; um ... (herum) III • **all around the castle** ganz um die Burg herum II • **around here** hier in/aus der Gegend VI 1 (11) • **around six** um sechs Uhr herum, gegen sechs III • **around the lake** um den See (herum) III • **around the town** in der Stadt umher, durch die Stadt III • **from all around Wales** aus ganz Wales II • **look around** sich umsehen III • **walk/run/jump around** herumgehen/-rennen/-springen, umhergehen/-rennen/-springen III

arrival (arr) [ə'raɪvl] Ankunft III

arrive [ə'raɪv] ankommen, eintreffen II

arrogant ['ærəgənt] arrogant, überheblich VI 1 (6)

art [ɑːt] Kunst I

article ['ɑːtɪkl] (Zeitungs-)Artikel I

artificial [ˌɑːtɪ'fɪʃl] künstlich, Kunst- III

artist ['ɑːtɪst] Künstler/in III

artistic [ɑː'tɪstɪk] künstlerisch V

as (conj) [əz, æz] als, während II • **as you can see** wie du sehen kannst II • **as if** als ob IV • **as long as** solange, sofern IV • **as soon as** sobald, sowie II

as (prep) [əz, æz] als II • **as a child** als Kind II

as ... as [əz, æz] so ... wie II • **as big/exciting as** so groß/aufregend wie II • **just as ... as** genauso ... wie V

ask [ɑːsk] fragen I • **ask about sth.** nach etwas fragen I • **ask questions** Fragen stellen I • **ask sb. for sth.** jn. um etwas bitten II • **ask sb. out** jn. einladen, zusammen auszugehen VI 1 (7/171) • **ask sb. to do sth.** jn. darum bitten, etwas zu tun V • **ask sb. the way** jn. nach dem Weg fragen II
▶ S.171 Relationships: asking sb. out

asleep [ə'sliːp]: **be asleep** schlafen I

Assembly [ə'sembli] Versammlung *(morgendliche Schulversammlung, oft mit Andacht)* III

assess [ə'ses] einschätzen, beurteilen V

assessment [ə'sesmənt] Einschätzung, Beurteilung V

assistant [ə'sɪstənt] Assistent/in V

at [ət, æt]: **at 7 Hamilton Street** in der Hamiltonstraße 7 I • **at 8.45** um 8.45 I • **at 16** mit 16, im Alter von 16 Jahren II • **at any time** jederzeit V • **at break** in der Pause *(zwischen Schulstunden)* II • **at first** zuerst, am Anfang IV • **at home** daheim, zu Hause I • **at last** endlich, schließlich I • **at least** zumindest, wenigstens I • **at night** nachts, in der Nacht I • **at school** in der Schule I • **at someone's place** bei jemandem zu Hause I • **at that table** an dem Tisch (dort) / an den Tisch (dort) I • **at the back (of the room)** hinten, im hinteren Teil (des Zimmers) II • **at the bottom (of)** unten, am unteren Ende (von) II • **at the chemist's/hairdresser's** beim Apotheker/Friseur III • **at the end (of)** am Ende (von) I • **at the moment** im Moment, gerade II • **at the Shaws' house** im Haus der Shaws/ bei den Shaws zu Hause I • **at the station** am Bahnhof I • **at the top (of)** oben, am oberen Ende, an der Spitze (von) I • **at the weekend** am Wochenende I • **at work** bei der Arbeit / am Arbeitsplatz I • **one at a time** einzeln VI 3 (48/181) • **two at a time** zwei auf einmal *(zur selben Zeit)* VI 3 (48)

ate [et, eɪt] *siehe* eat

athletics [æθ'letɪks] Leichtathletik III

Atlantic: the Atlantic (Ocean) [ət,læntɪk_'əʊʃn] der Atlantische Ozean, der Atlantik IV

atmosphere ['ætməsfɪə] Atmosphäre III

attach (to) [ə'tætʃ] anhängen, anheften (an) *(an Brief, Mail)* V

attack [ə'tæk] angreifen III

attack [ə'tæk] Angriff III

attention [ə'tenʃn] Aufmerksamkeit V • **draw sb.'s attention to sth.** jn. auf etwas aufmerksam machen; jemandes Aufmerksamkeit auf etwas lenken V

attitude (to, towards) ['ætɪtjuːd] Haltung (gegenüber), Einstellung (zu) IV

attract [ə'trækt] anziehen, anlocken V

attraction [ə'trækʃn] Attraktion, Anziehungspunkt II

attractive [ə'træktɪv] attraktiv *(Person)*; reizvoll, verlockend *(Idee, Preis)* VI 1 (6)

audience ['ɔːdiəns] Publikum; Zuschauer/innen, Zuhörer/innen II

August ['ɔːgəst] August I

aunt [ɑːnt] Tante I • **auntie** ['ɑːnti] Tante II

Aussie ['ɒzi] *(infml)* Australier/in; australisch V

auto ['ɔːtəʊ] *(AE)* Auto, PKW IV

autumn ['ɔːtəm] Herbst I

available [ə'veɪləbl] verfügbar, erreichbar; vorrätig V

avenue ['ævənjuː] Allee IV

average ['ævərɪdʒ] Durchschnitt; durchschnittlich IV

award [ə'wɔːd] Auszeichnung, Preis VI 1 (14)

away [ə'weɪ] weg, fort I

awesome ['ɔːsəm] *(AE, infml)* klasse, großartig IV

awful ['ɔːfl] furchtbar, schrecklich II

B

baby ['beɪbi] Baby I • **have a baby** ein Baby/Kind bekommen II

back [bæk]
1. Rücken; Rückseite V
2. at the back (of) hinten, im hinteren Teil (von) II

back (to) [bæk] zurück (nach) I

back door [ˌbæk 'dɔː] Hintertür II

background ['bækgraʊnd] Hintergrund II • **background file** *etwa:* Hintergrundinformation(en) II

°**back inside cover** [ˌbæk_ˌɪnsaɪd 'kʌvə] hintere Umschlaginnenseite

bacon ['beɪkən] Schinkenspeck III
bad [bæd] schlecht, schlimm I
be bad at sth. schlecht in etwas sein; etwas schlecht können III
bad timing schlechtes Timing III
badly ['bædli]: **do badly** schlecht abschneiden (in Prüfung) V
badminton ['bædmɪntən] Badminton, Federball I • **badminton racket** ['rækɪt] Badmintonschläger III
bag [bæg] Tasche, Beutel, Tüte I
bagel ['beɪgl] Bagel (ringförmiges Brötchen) IV
baggy ['bægi] weit (geschnitten) (Hose) V
bagpipes (pl) ['bægpaɪps] Dudelsack III
ball [bɔːl]
1. Ball I
2. Ball (Tanzveranstaltung) IV
ballet ['bæleɪ] Ballett V
ban (-nn-) [bæn] sperren; ein (Aufenthalts-)Verbot erteilen V
ban sb. from sth. jn. von etwas ausschließen V
banana [bə'nɑːnə] Banane I
band [bænd] Band, (Musik-)Gruppe I
bank [bæŋk] Bank, Sparkasse I
bank clerk ['bæŋk klɑːk] Bankangestellte(r) V
bank robber ['bæŋk ˌrɒbə] Bankräuber/in I
bar [bɑː] Bar II
barbecue ['bɑːbɪkjuː] Grillfest, Grillparty V
bar chart ['bɑː tʃɑːt] Balkendiagramm V
baseball ['beɪsbɔːl] Baseball I
baseball cap ['beɪsbɔːl kæp] Baseballmütze II
based [beɪst]: **be based on** basieren auf VI 1 (12)
basic ['beɪsɪk] grundlegend; Grund-, Haupt- V
basket ['bɑːskɪt] Korb I • **a basket of apples** ein Korb Äpfel I
basketball ['bɑːskɪtbɔːl] Basketball I
°**bastard** ['bɑːstəd] (infml, abwertend) Mistkerl, Schweinehund I
bat [bæt]: **table tennis bat** Tischtennisschläger III
bath [bɑːθ] Bad, Badewanne II
have a bath baden, ein Bad nehmen II
bathroom ['bɑːθruːm] Badezimmer I
battery ['bætri, 'bætəri] Batterie VI 2 (30)
bay [beɪ] Bucht III

be [biː], **was/were, been** sein I
be a farmer, a teacher, ... Bauer, Lehrer/in, ... sein/werden IV • **be a no-no** (infml) tabu sein, nicht in Frage kommen VI 2 (34)
beach [biːtʃ] Strand II • **on the beach** am Strand II
bean [biːn] Bohne IV
bear [beə] Bär II
beard [bɪəd] Bart II
beat [biːt], **beat, beaten** schlagen; besiegen III
beaten ['biːtn] siehe **beat**
beautiful ['bjuːtɪfl] schön I
beauty ['bjuːti] Schönheit III
became [bɪ'keɪm] siehe **become**
because [bɪ'kɒz] weil I
because of [bɪ'kɒz ˌəv] wegen V
become [bɪ'kʌm], **became, become** werden II
bed [bed] Bett I • **Bed and Breakfast (B&B)** [ˌbed ˌən 'brekfəst] Frühstückspension I • **go to bed** ins Bett gehen I
bedroom ['bedruːm] Schlafzimmer I
bedspread ['bedspred] Tagesdecke III
beef [biːf] Rindfleisch III
been [biːn] siehe **be**
°**beer** [bɪə] Bier I
before [bɪ'fɔː] vor (zeitlich) I
before [bɪ'fɔː] bevor II
before [bɪ'fɔː] (vorher) schon mal II
the night/week/... before in der Nacht/Woche/... zuvor III
began [bɪ'gæn] siehe **begin**
begin (-nn-) [bɪ'gɪn], **began, begun** beginnen, anfangen (mit) III
beginning [bɪ'gɪnɪŋ] Beginn, Anfang; Einleitung II
begun [bɪ'gʌn] siehe **begin**
behave [bɪ'heɪv] sich verhalten, sich benehmen V • **Behave yourself.** Benimm dich (anständig)! V
behaviour [bɪ'heɪvjə] Verhalten, Benehmen V
behind [bɪ'haɪnd] hinter II • **stay behind** zurückbleiben, daheimbleiben IV
belief [bɪ'liːf] Glaube, Überzeugung V
believable [bɪ'liːvəbl] glaubhaft IV
believe (in) [bɪ'liːv] glauben (an) IV
bell [bel] Klingel, Glocke I
belong (to) [bɪ'lɒŋ] gehören (zu) II
below [bɪ'ləʊ]
1. unten III
2. unter, unterhalb (von) III
bench [bentʃ] (Sitz-)Bank IV
°**bend** [bend], **bent, bent** [bent] (ver)biegen

°**bent** [bent] siehe **bend**
besides [bɪ'saɪdz] außerdem IV
best [best] am besten II • **the best ...** der/die/das beste ...; die besten I • **like sth. best** etwas am liebsten mögen III • **What was the best thing about ...?** Was war das Beste an ...? II • **Best wishes** etwa: Alles Gute / Mit besten Grüßen (als Briefschluss) IV
bestseller [ˌbest'selə, 'best,selə] Bestseller, Verkaufsschlager VI 1 (12)
bet [bet] Wette VI 1 (15)
bet (-tt-) [bet], **bet, bet** wetten IV
You bet! (infml) Aber klar! / Und ob! IV
better ['betə] besser I • **like sth. better** etwas lieber mögen II
between [bɪ'twiːn] zwischen II
°**beverage** ['bevərɪdʒ] Getränk I
Bible ['baɪbl]: **the Bible** die Bibel V
big [bɪg] groß I
big wheel [ˌbɪg 'wiːl] Riesenrad III
bike [baɪk] Fahrrad I • **ride a bike** Rad fahren I
bilingual [ˌbaɪ'lɪŋgwəl] zweisprachig IV
bill [bɪl]
1. (BE) Rechnung VI 2 (36)
2. (AE) (Geld-)Schein, Banknote V
bin [bɪn] Mülltonne II
biography [baɪ'ɒgrəfi] Biografie III
biology [baɪ'ɒlədʒi] Biologie I
bird [bɜːd] Vogel I
birth [bɜːθ] Geburt V • **date of birth** Geburtsdatum V • **place of birth** Geburtsort V
birthday ['bɜːθdeɪ] Geburtstag I
for his birthday zu seinem Geburtstag III • **Happy birthday.** Herzlichen Glückwunsch zum Geburtstag. I • **My birthday is in May.** Ich habe im Mai Geburtstag. I • **My birthday is on 13th June.** Ich habe am 13. Juni Geburtstag. I **When's your birthday?** Wann hast du Geburtstag? I
biscuit ['bɪskɪt] Keks, Plätzchen I
bit [bɪt]: **a bit** ein bisschen, etwas II
bit [bɪt] siehe **bite**
bite [baɪt], **bit, bitten** beißen VI 1 (12)
bitten ['bɪtn] siehe **bite**
black [blæk] schwarz I
black bear ['blæk beə] Schwarzbär III
blame sb. (for) [bleɪm] jm. die Schuld geben (an); jm. Vorwürfe machen (wegen) III
blanket ['blæŋkɪt] Decke (zum Zudecken) III
bleep [bliːp] piepsen II

bleep [bliːp] Piepton II
blew [bluː] *siehe* **blow**
blind [blaɪnd] blind V
block [blɒk] (Häuser-, Wohn-)Block IV
block [blɒk] blockieren, (ver)sperren IV
blog [blɒg] *digitales Tagebuch* IV
blond *(bei Frauen oft: **blonde**)* [blɒnd] blond, hell IV; V
blood [blʌd] Blut III
bloody ['blʌdi] blutig V
blouse [blaʊz] Bluse II
blow [bləʊ], **blew, blown** wehen, blasen III
blown [bləʊn] *siehe* **blow**
blue [bluː] blau I
board [bɔːd]
1. (Wand-)Tafel I • **on the board** an der/die Tafel I
2. on board an Bord V
boat [bəʊt] Boot, Schiff I
body ['bɒdi] Körper I
bodyguard ['bɒdigaːd] Leibwächter/in, Leibwache IV
bold print [ˌbəʊld 'prɪnt] Fettdruck III
bone [bəʊn] Knochen VI 2 (32)
book [bʊk] Buch I
book [bʊk] buchen, reservieren V
booklet ['bʊklət] Broschüre II
bookshelf ['bʊkʃelf], *pl* **bookshelves** ['-ʃelvz] Bücherregal V
boot [buːt] Stiefel I; V
boot camp ['buːt kæmp] Erziehungslager *(für junge Straftäter/-täterinnen)* I
border ['bɔːdə] Grenze IV
bored [bɔːd]: **be/feel bored** gelangweilt sein, sich langweilen IV **get bored** sich langweilen IV
boring ['bɔːrɪŋ] langweilig I
born [bɔːn]: **be born** geboren sein/werden II
borough ['bʌrə, AE: 'bɜːrəʊ] (Stadt-)Bezirk IV
borrow sth. ['bɒrəʊ] etwas (aus)leihen, sich etwas borgen V
boss [bɒs] Chef/in, Boss III
bossy ['bɒsi] rechthaberisch, herrisch VI 3 (102)
both [bəʊθ] beide I
bottle ['bɒtl] Flasche I • **a bottle of milk** eine Flasche Milch I
bottom ['bɒtəm] unteres Ende II **at the bottom (of)** unten, am unteren Ende (von) II
bought [bɔːt] *siehe* **buy**
boulevard ['buːləvaːd] Boulevard IV
bowl [bəʊl] Schüssel I • **a bowl of cornflakes** eine Schale Cornflakes I

box [bɒks] Kasten, Kästchen, Kiste I
boy [bɔɪ] Junge I
boyfriend ['bɔɪfrend] (fester) Freund IV
°bracket ['brækɪt] Klammer *(in Texten)*
brain [breɪn] Gehirn VI 2 (30)
brainstorm ['breɪnstɔːm] brainstormen *(so viele Ideen wie möglich sammeln)* III
brave [breɪv] mutig IV
bread *(no pl)* [bred] Brot I
break [breɪk] Pause I • **at break** in der Pause *(zwischen Schulstunden)* II • **take a break** eine Pause machen IV
break [breɪk], **broke, broken** (zer-)brechen; kaputt gehen IV • **break down** zusammenbrechen; *(Gerät)* ausfallen, eine Panne haben VI 2 (35) • **break up (with sb.)** sich trennen (von jm.) VI 1 (9)
breakable ['breɪkəbl] zerbrechlich IV
breakfast ['brekfəst] Frühstück I **have breakfast** frühstücken I
breathe (in/out) [briːð] (ein-/aus-) atmen VI 2 (36)
°bride [braɪd] Braut
bridge [brɪdʒ] Brücke I
bridle path ['braɪdl paːθ] Reitweg III
bright [braɪt] hell, leuchtend II
brilliant ['brɪliənt] großartig, glänzend, hervorragend VI 1 (14)
bring [brɪŋ], **brought, brought** (mit-, her)bringen I
British ['brɪtɪʃ] britisch; Brite, Britin II
°brochure ['brəʊʃə] Prospekt, Broschüre
broke [brəʊk] *siehe* **break**
broken ['brəʊkən] gebrochen; zerbrochen, kaputt II *siehe* **break**
brother ['brʌðə] Bruder I
brought [brɔːt] *siehe* **bring**
brown [braʊn] braun I
budgie ['bʌdʒi] Wellensittich I
build [bɪld], **built, built** bauen II
builder ['bɪldə] Bauarbeiter/in V
building ['bɪldɪŋ] Gebäude II
built [bɪlt] *siehe* **build**
bulletin board ['bʊlətɪn bɔːd] *(AE)* Anschlagtafel, „schwarzes Brett" IV
bully ['bʊli] einschüchtern, tyrannisieren II
bully ['bʊli] (Schul-)Tyrann III
bunk (bed) [bʌŋk] Etagenbett, Koje II

burn [bɜːn] brennen; verbrennen IV **burn sth. down** etwas niederbrennen IV
bus [bʌs] Bus I
bush [bʊʃ] Busch, Strauch V • **the bush** der Busch *(unkultiviertes, „wildes" Land in Australien, Afrika)* V
business ['bɪznəs] Unternehmen; Geschäft(e) IV • **do business with** Handel treiben mit; Geschäfte machen mit V • **Mind your own business.** Das geht dich nichts an! / Kümmere dich um deine eigenen Angelegenheiten! II • **start a business** ein Unternehmen gründen V
businesswoman/-man ['bɪznəswʊmən, -mæn] Geschäftsfrau/Geschäftsmann IV
bus pass ['bʌs paːs] Monatskarte *(für den Bus)* III
bus stop ['bʌs stɒp] Bushaltestelle III
busy ['bɪzi] belebt, verkehrsreich; hektisch III; beschäftigt IV
but [bət, bʌt] aber I
butter ['bʌtə] Butter IV
button ['bʌtn] Knopf III
buy [baɪ], **bought, bought** kaufen I
°buzz [bʌz] *hier:* den Summer/die Glocke betätigen
by [baɪ]
1. von I
2. an; (nahe) bei II
by car/bike/... mit dem Auto/Rad/... II • **by ten o'clock** bis (spätestens) zehn Uhr III • **by two degrees / ten per cent** um zwei Grad / zehn Prozent V
by the way [ˌbaɪ ðə 'weɪ] übrigens; nebenbei (bemerkt) III
go by vergehen, vorübergehen *(Zeit)* V • **one by one** einer nach dem anderen VI 2 (34)
Bye. [baɪ] Tschüs! I

C

cab [kæb] Taxi IV
cabin ['kæbɪn] Hütte III
cable ['keɪbl] Kabel *(auch kurz für Kabelfernsehen)* IV
café ['kæfeɪ] *(kleines)* Restaurant, Imbissstube, Café I
cage [keɪdʒ] Käfig I
cake [keɪk] Kuchen, Torte I
°calculate ['kælkjuleɪt] berechnen, ermitteln
°calculator ['kælkjuleɪtə] Taschenrechner

calendar ['kælɪndə] Kalender I

call [kɔ:l] rufen; anrufen; nennen I
call sb. names jn. mit Schimpfwörtern hänseln, jm. Schimpfwörter nachrufen III

call [kɔ:l] Anruf, Telefongespräch I
make a call ein Telefongespräch
führen II

called [kɔ:ld]: **be called** heißen,
genannt werden III

calm [kɑ:m] ruhig, still V

calm down [ˌkɑ:m 'daʊn] sich
beruhigen II

calorie ['kæləri] Kalorie IV

came [keɪm] *siehe* **come**

camel ['kæml] Kamel II

camera ['kæmərə] Kamera, Foto-
apparat I

camp [kæmp] Camp, (Ferien-)Lager
IV

camp [kæmp] zelten III

campaign [kæm'peɪn] Kampagne,
(Werbe-)Feldzug VI 3 (47)

camping gear ['kæmpɪŋ gɪə] Campingausrüstung, Campingsachen
IV

can [kən, kæn]
1. können I
2. dürfen II
Can I help you? Kann ich Ihnen
helfen? / Was kann ich für Sie tun?
(im Geschäft) I

can [kæn] Dose, Büchse V

canal [kə'næl] Kanal III

cancer ['kænsə] Krebs *(Krankheit)* V

candidate ['kændɪdət] Kandidat/in,
Bewerber/in V

candle ['kændl] Kerze V

canned [kænd] Dosen-; ... in Dosen
V

canoe [kə'nu:] paddeln, Kanu
fahren III

canoe [kə'nu:] Kanu, Paddelboot III

canyon ['kænjən] Cañon IV

cap [kæp] Mütze, Kappe II

capital ['kæpɪtl] Hauptstadt III

capital letter [ˌkæpɪtl 'letə] Groß-
buchstabe III

captain ['kæptɪn] Kapitän/in V

caption ['kæpʃn] Bildunterschrift III

car [kɑ:] Auto I • **car park** Parkplatz III

caravan ['kærəvæn] Wohnwagen II

carbon ['kɑ:bən] Kohlenstoff; *(oft
auch kurz für:)* Kohlendioxid
VI 2 (29)

carbon dioxide (CO₂) [ˌkɑ:bən
daɪ'ɒksaɪd], [ˌsi:ˌəʊ 'tu:] Kohlendioxid (CO₂) VI 2 (29)

carbon footprint [ˌkɑ:bən 'fʊtprɪnt]
„CO₂-Fußabdruck", CO₂-Bilanz
VI 2 (29)

card [kɑ:d] (Spiel-, Post-)Karte I

cardboard ['kɑ:dbɔ:d] Pappe V

care about sth. [keə] etwas wichtig
nehmen IV; VI 3 (46/179) • **I don't
care.** Es/Das ist mir egal. IV;
VI 3 (46/179) • **I didn't care.** Es war
mir egal. IV • **Who cares?** Wen interessiert das (schon)? VI 3 (46/179)
▶ S.179 (to) care

career [kə'rɪə] Karriere III

careful ['keəfl]
1. vorsichtig II
2. sorgfältig II

caretaker ['keəteɪkə] Hausmeister/
Hausmeisterin II

car park ['kɑ: pɑ:k] Parkplatz III

carriage ['kærɪdʒ] Eisenbahnwagen,
Waggon V

carrot ['kærət] Möhre, Karotte I

carry ['kæri] tragen V

cartoon [kɑ:'tu:n] Cartoon (Zeichen-
trickfilm; Bilderwitz) II

case [keɪs] Fall II

cash [kæʃ] Bargeld V • **pay cash**
bar bezahlen V

castle ['kɑ:sl] Burg, Schloss II

cat [kæt] Katze I

catch [kætʃ], **caught, caught**
fangen; erwischen II • **I didn't
catch your name.** Ich habe deinen
Namen nicht verstanden. VI 1 (11)

cathedral [kə'θi:drəl] Kathedrale,
Dom III
▶ S.173 Religions

Catholic ['kæθlɪk] Katholik/in;
katholisch VI 1 (13/173)
▶ S.173 Religions

caught [kɔ:t] *siehe* **catch**

cause [kɔ:z] verursachen V

cause [kɔ:z] Ursache, Verursacher/
Verursacherin; Grund VI 2 (29)

CD [ˌsi:'di:] CD I • **CD player** CD-
Spieler I

ceilidh ['keɪli] *Musik- und Tanzveranstaltung, vor allem in Schottland
und Irland* III

celebrate ['selɪbreɪt] feiern V

cell [sel] Zelle V

cellphone ['selfəʊn] *(AE)* Handy,
Mobiltelefon V

Celsius (C) ['selsiəs] Celsius III

cent (c) [sent] Cent I

centimetre (cm) ['sentɪmi:tə] Zenti-
meter III

central ['sentrəl] Zentral-, Mittel- III

centre ['sentə] Zentrum, Mitte I

century ['sentʃəri] Jahrhundert II

certificate [sə'tɪfɪkət] Bescheini-
gung, Zertifikat V

°**chain** [tʃeɪn] Kette V

chair [tʃeə] Stuhl I

°**champagne** [ʃæm'peɪn] Cham-
pagner

champion ['tʃæmpiən] Meister/in,
Champion I

championship ['tʃæmpiənʃɪp] Meis-
terschaft III

chance [tʃɑ:ns] Chance, Möglichkeit, Aussicht II

change [tʃeɪndʒ]
1. (sich) ändern; (sich) verändern IV
2. wechseln IV
3. umsteigen IV
4. sich umziehen IV
change channels umschalten
(Fernsehen) IV

change [tʃeɪndʒ]
1. (Ver-)Änderung; Wechsel IV
2. Wechselgeld I; Kleingeld IV

channel ['tʃænl] Kanal, Sender II

character ['kærəktə]
1. Charakter, Persönlichkeit IV
2. Person, Figur *(in Roman, Film)* IV

charge [tʃɑ:dʒ] (auf)laden *(Batterie,
Handy)* VI 3 (47/179)

charge [tʃɑ:dʒ]: **on charge** am Ladegerät; am Netz *(zum Aufladen)*
VI 3 (47)

charger ['tʃɑ:dʒə] Ladegerät VI 2 (36)

charity ['tʃærəti] Wohlfahrtsorgani-
sation II

charming ['tʃɑ:mɪŋ] charmant
VI 1 (6)

chart [tʃɑ:t] Tabelle, Diagramm,
Schaubild V

°**charts (pl)** [tʃɑ:ts] Hitliste, Charts

chat (-tt-) [tʃæt] chatten, plaudern
II • **chat sb. up** *(infml)* jn. anquat-
schen, anbaggern VI 1 (7/171)

chat [tʃæt] Chat, Unterhaltung II

chat room ['tʃæt ru:m] Chatroom III

chat-up line ['tʃæt ˌʌp laɪn] *(infml)*
Anmachspruch VI 1 (7)

cheap [tʃi:p] billig, preiswert II

check [tʃek] (über)prüfen, kontrollieren I

check in [ˌtʃek 'ɪn] einchecken
(Hotel, Flughafen) V

check out [ˌtʃek 'aʊt] auschecken
(aus Hotel) V

checkpoint ['tʃekpɔɪnt] Kontroll-
punkt I; Grenzübergang V

cheek [tʃi:k] Wange IV

cheeky ['tʃi:ki] frech, dreist V

cheer [tʃɪə] jubeln, Beifall klatschen
II

cheerleader ['tʃɪəli:də] Cheerleader
*(Stimmungsanheizer/in bei Sport-
ereignissen)* IV

cheese [tʃi:z] Käse I

chef [ʃef] Koch, Köchin *(Berufsbe-
zeichnung)* V

chemical ['kemɪkl] Chemikalie; chemisch VI 2 (36)

chemist ['kemɪst] Drogerie, Apotheke II • **at the chemist's** beim Apotheker III

chemistry ['kemɪstri] Chemie V

cheque (for) [tʃek] Scheck (über) V

chicken ['tʃɪkɪn] Huhn; (Brat-)Hähnchen I

child [tʃaɪld], *pl* **children** ['tʃɪldrən] Kind I

childcare ['tʃaɪldkeə] Kinderbetreuung V

childcare assistant ['tʃaɪldkeər_ə,sɪstənt] Kinderpfleger/in; Erzieher/in V

childproof ['tʃaɪldpruːf] kindersicher *(Flasche, Verschluss)* V

chips (pl) [tʃɪps]
1. *(BE)* Pommes frites I
2. *(AE)* (Kartoffel-)Chips IV

chocolate ['tʃɒklət] Schokolade I

choice [tʃɔɪs] Wahl, Auswahl VI 2 (30)

choir ['kwaɪə] Chor I

choose [tʃuːz], **chose, chosen** (sich) aussuchen, (aus)wählen I

chore [tʃɔː] (Haus-)Arbeit; *(lästige)* Pflicht V

chorus ['kɔːrəs] Refrain III

chose [tʃəʊz] *siehe* **choose**

chosen ['tʃəʊzn] *siehe* **choose**

Christian ['krɪstʃən] Christ/in V; christlich VI 1 (13/173)
  ▶ S.173 Religions

church [tʃɜːtʃ] Kirche I
  ▶ S.173 Religions

cigarette [ˌsɪgəˈret] Zigarette IV

cinema ['sɪnəmə] Kino II • **go to the cinema** ins Kino gehen II

circle ['sɜːkl] Kreis IV

circus ['sɜːkəs]
1. Zirkus III
2. (runder) Platz *(in der Stadt)* III

citizen ['sɪtɪzn] Staatsbürger/in VI 3 (47/180)
  ▶ S.180 Politics

citizenship ['sɪtɪzənʃɪp] Staatsbürgerschaft VI 3 (47/180)
  ▶ S.180 Politics

city ['sɪti] Stadt, Großstadt I

city centre [ˌsɪti 'sentə] Stadtzentrum, Innenstadt I

civil ['sɪvl]: **civil rights** *(pl)* Bürgerrechte IV • **civil war** Bürgerkrieg IV

clap (-pp-) [klæp] (Beifall) klatschen IV

clarification [ˌklærəfɪˈkeɪʃn] Klarstellung, Klärung V

class [klɑːs]
1. (Schul-)Klasse I

2. Unterricht; Kurs IV

°**class rep** *(kurz für:* **class representative)** Kurs-, Klassensprecher/in

class teacher Klassenlehrer/in I

classical ['klæsɪkl] klassisch III

classmate ['klɑːsmeɪt] Klassenkamerad/in, Mitschüler/in I

°**class rep** [ˌklɑːs 'rep] *(kurz für:* **class representative)** Kurs-, Klassensprecher/in

classroom ['klɑːsruːm] Klassenzimmer I

°**clause** [klɔːz] (Teil-, Glied-)Satz

clean [kliːn] sauber II

clean [kliːn] sauber machen, putzen I • **I clean my teeth.** Ich putze mir die Zähne. I

cleaner ['kliːnə] Putzfrau, -mann II

clear [klɪə] klar, deutlich I

clever ['klevə] klug, schlau I

cleverness ['klevənəs] Klugheit, Schlauheit IV

click on sth. [klɪk] etwas anklicken II

climate ['klaɪmət] Klima VI 2 (29)

climate change ['klaɪmət tʃeɪndʒ] (der) Klimawandel VI 2 (29)

°**climax** ['klaɪmæks] Höhepunkt

climb [klaɪm] klettern; hinaufklettern (auf) I • **Climb a tree.** Klettere auf einen Baum. I

clinic ['klɪnɪk] Klinik II

clock [klɒk] (Wand-, Stand-, Turm-) Uhr I

clone [kləʊn] Klon III

close [kləʊs]
1. eng V
2. close (to) nahe (bei, an) III
That was close. Das war knapp. II

close [kləʊz] schließen, zumachen I

closed [kləʊzd] geschlossen II

°**closely** ['kləʊsli]: **Look closely at ...** Sieh dir ... genau an.

°**closing phrase** ['kləʊzɪŋ freɪz] Schlusswort(e) *(am Briefende)*

clothes *(pl)* [kləʊðz, kləʊz] Kleider, Kleidung(sstücke) II

cloud [klaʊd] Wolke II

cloudless ['klaʊdləs] wolkenlos IV

cloudy ['klaʊdi] bewölkt II

club [klʌb] Klub; Verein I

coach [kəʊtʃ] Trainer/in III

coal [kəʊl] Kohle VI 2 (30)

coast [kəʊst] Küste III

coat [kəʊt] Mantel VI 2 (34)

coffee ['kɒfi] Kaffee IV • **coffee to go** Kaffee zum Mitnehmen IV

coin [kɔɪn] Münze V

cola ['kəʊlə] Cola I

cold [kəʊld] kalt I • **be cold** frieren I

cold [kəʊld]
1. Kälte IV
2. Erkältung II
have a cold erkältet sein, eine Erkältung haben II

°**collage** ['kɒlɑːʒ] Collage

collapse [kəˈlæps] zusammenbrechen; einstürzen IV

collect [kəˈlekt] sammeln I

collection [kəˈlekʃn] Sammlung IV

collector [kəˈlektə] Sammler/in II

college ['kɒlɪdʒ] Hochschule, Fachhochschule IV

collocation [ˌkɒləˈkeɪʃn] Kollokation *(Wörter, die oft zusammen vorkommen)* IV

colony ['kɒləni] Kolonie V

colour ['kʌlə] Farbe I • **What colour is ...?** Welche Farbe hat ...? I

colour ['kʌlə] kolorieren, färben; bunt an-, ausmalen III

colour-blind ['kʌləblaɪnd] farbenblind V

colourful ['kʌləfl] farbenfroh, farbenprächtig, farbig V

column ['kɒləm] Säule III

°**combine** [kəmˈbaɪn] kombinieren, verbinden

come [kʌm], **came, come** kommen I • **come home** nach Hause kommen I • **come in** hereinkommen I • **Come on. 1.** Na los, komm. II; **2.** Ach komm! / Na hör mal! II • **come out** rauskommen; veröffentlicht werden *(Film, DVD)* IV

comedian [kəˈmiːdiən] Komiker/in IV

comedy ['kɒmədi] Komödie; Comedy IV

comfortable ['kʌmftəbl] bequem IV • **feel comfortable** sich wohl fühlen VI 3 (51) • **Make yourself comfortable.** Machen Sie es sich bequem. / Mach es dir bequem. IV

comic ['kɒmɪk] Comic-Heft I

command [kəˈmɑːnd] Befehl, Aufforderung V

comment ['kɒment] Kommentar, Bemerkung IV

comment (on sth.) ['kɒment] sich (zu etwas) äußern; einen Kommentar abgeben (zu etwas) V

commit a crime (-tt-) [kəˈmɪt] ein Verbrechen / eine Straftat verüben, begehen V

common ['kɒmən] weit verbreitet, häufig V

Commonwealth ['kɒmənwelθ]: **the Commonwealth** Gemeinschaft der Länder des ehemaligen Britischen Weltreichs III

communicate (with) [kəˈmjuːnɪkeɪt] kommunizieren (mit), sich verständigen (mit) VI 2 (29)

communication [kəˌmjuːnɪˈkeɪʃn] Verständigung VI 2 (31/176)

community [kəˈmjuːnəti]: **community centre** Gemeinschaftszentrum, Gemeindezentrum III • **community hall** Gemeinschaftshalle, -saal, Gemeindehalle, -saal III • **community service** gemeinnützige Arbeit V

commuter [kəˈmjuːtə] Pendler/in V

°**compact fluorescent light bulb** [ˌkɒmpækt flɔːˌresnt ˈlaɪt bʌlb] Kompaktleuchtstofflampe, Energiesparlampe

company [ˈkʌmpəni] Firma, Gesellschaft III

compare [kəmˈpeə] vergleichen IV

compared to [kəmˈpeəd] verglichen mit VI 3 (49)

comparison [kəmˈpærɪsn] Steigerung; Vergleich II • °**make comparisons** Vergleiche anstellen, vergleichen

compete [kəmˈpiːt] konkurrieren, mithalten IV

competition [ˌkɒmpəˈtɪʃn] Wettbewerb, Wettkampf IV

complain (to sb. about sth.) [kəmˈpleɪn] sich beschweren, sich beklagen (bei jm. über etwas) VI 3 (47)

complete [kəmˈpliːt] vollständig, komplett VI 2 (36)

°**complete** [kəmˈpliːt] vervollständigen, ergänzen

°**compromise** [ˈkɒmprəmaɪz] Kompromiss

computer [kəmˈpjuːtə] Computer I

°**computer geek** [giːk] (bes. AE, infml) Computerfreak

concentrate (on) [ˈkɒnsntreɪt] sich konzentrieren (auf) VI 3 (54)

concentration [ˌkɒnsnˈtreɪʃn] Konzentration VI 3 (54)

concert [ˈkɒnsət] Konzert III

conclusion [kənˈkluːʒn] Schluss(folgerung) IV • **draw conclusions** Schlüsse ziehen, schlussfolgern IV

conditions (pl) [kənˈdɪʃnz] Bedingungen, Verhältnisse VI 2 (29)

confidence [ˈkɒnfɪdəns]
1. Selbstvertrauen, Selbstsicherheit VI 1 (6)
2. Zuversicht VI 1 (6)

confident [ˈkɒnfɪdənt]
1. selbstbewusst, (selbst)sicher V
2. zuversichtlich V

conflict [ˈkɒnflɪkt] Konflikt VI 3 (55)

°**confused** [kənˈfjuːzd] verwirrt

connect (to/with) [kəˈnekt] verbinden (mit) V

console [ˈkɒnsəʊl] Konsole, Steuerpult VI 2 (28)

constitution [ˌkɒnstɪˈtjuːʃn] Verfassung VI 3 (47/180)
▶ S.180 Politics

contact sb. [ˈkɒntækt] sich mit jm. in Verbindung setzen; mit jm. Kontakt aufnehmen III

contact [ˈkɒntækt] Kontakt V
contacts (pl) Liste von Bekannten/Kontakten (im Handy, im Mailprogramm) V

contain [kənˈteɪn] enthalten IV

content [ˈkɒntent] Gehalt, Inhalt IV

contestant [kənˈtestənt] Kandidat/Kandidatin (in Fernsehshow), (Wettkampf-)Teilnehmer/in IV

context [ˈkɒntekst] Kontext, Zusammenhang IV

continent [ˈkɒntɪnənt] Kontinent, Erdteil V

continue [kənˈtɪnjuː] fortsetzen; weitermachen (mit) V

control (of/over) [kənˈtrəʊl] Kontrolle (über) VI 1 (12)

control sth. (-ll-) [kənˈtrəʊl] etwas kontrollieren, die Kontrolle über etwas haben VI 3 (49)

conversation [ˌkɒnvəˈseɪʃn] Gespräch, Unterhaltung V

convict [ˈkɒnvɪkt] Sträfling, Strafgefangene(r) V

cook [kʊk] kochen, zubereiten II

cook [kʊk] Koch/Köchin III

cooker [ˈkʊkə] Herd I

cookie [ˈkʊki] (AE) Keks IV

cool [kuːl]
1. kühl II
2. cool I

copy [ˈkɒpi] kopieren II

copy [ˈkɒpi]
1. Kopie II
2. Exemplar III

corner [ˈkɔːnə] Ecke I • **on the corner of Sand Street and London Road** Sand Street, Ecke London Road II

cornflakes [ˈkɔːnfleɪks] Cornflakes I

correct [kəˈrekt] berichtigen, korrigieren II • °**correcting circle** etwa: Korrekturkreis

correct [kəˈrekt] korrekt, richtig III

°**correction** [kəˈrekʃn] Korrektur, Berichtigung

corridor [ˈkɒrɪdɔː] Gang, Korridor VI 3 (51)

°**cos** [kɒz] BE infml für **because**

cost [kɒst], **cost, cost** kosten IV

cost [kɒst] Kosten VI 2 (36)

costume [ˈkɒstjuːm] (Bühnen-)Kostüm V

cotton [ˈkɒtn] Baumwolle IV

could [kəd, kʊd]: **he could ...**
1. er konnte ... II
2. er könnte ... III
▶ S.176 Möglich? Wahrscheinlich? Sicherlich?

count [kaʊnt] zählen II

counter [ˈkaʊntə]
1. Spielstein II
2. Theke, Ladentisch IV

country [ˈkʌntri] Land (auch als Gegensatz zur Stadt) II • **in the country** auf dem Land II

°**county** [ˈkaʊnti] Bezirk, Landkreis

couple [ˈkʌpl] Paar, Pärchen V
a couple of ein paar, einige V
married couple Ehepaar V

course [kɔːs] Kurs, Lehrgang III

course: of course [əv ˈkɔːs] natürlich, selbstverständlich I

court [kɔːt]
1. Platz, Court (für Squash, Badminton) III
2. Gericht(shof) IV

cousin [ˈkʌzn] Cousin, Cousine I

cover [ˈkʌvə]
1. (CD-)Hülle I
°2. **inside cover** Umschlaginnenseite

cow [kaʊ] Kuh II

crash sth. [kræʃ] einen Unfall mit etwas haben IV

crazy [ˈkreɪzi] verrückt III

cream [kriːm] Sahne; Creme IV

cream cheese [ˌkriːm ˈtʃiːz] Frischkäse IV

create [kriˈeɪt] schaffen, erschaffen V

creative [kriˈeɪtɪv] kreativ, schöpferisch VI 1 (15)

credit card [ˈkredɪt kɑːd] Kreditkarte V • **pay by credit card** mit Kreditkarte bezahlen V

creeps [kriːps]: **it gives me the creeps** es ist mir unheimlich; es ist mir nicht geheuer VI 2 (35)

cricket [ˈkrɪkɪt] Kricket (Schlagballspiel) V

crime [kraɪm] Kriminalität; Verbrechen IV

crime series [ˈkraɪm ˌsɪəriːz] Krimiserie IV

crisps (pl) [krɪsps] Kartoffelchips I

criticize (for) [ˈkrɪtɪsaɪz] kritisieren (wegen) VI 3 (49)

crocodile [ˈkrɒkədaɪl] Krokodil II

cross [krɒs] überqueren; (sich) kreuzen II

°**cross** [krɒs] Kreuz, Kreuzchen

crossing [ˈkrɒsɪŋ] (Grenz-)Übergang; (Fußgänger-)Überweg V
crowd [kraʊd] (Menschen-)Menge IV
crowded [ˈkraʊdɪd] überfüllt, voll(gestopft) V
cruel [kruːəl] grausam IV
crush [krʌʃ]: **have a crush on sb.** in jn. verknallt sein III
cry [kraɪ]
  1. weinen IV
  2. schreien, rufen IV
  cry out aufschreien IV
cultural [ˈkʌltʃərəl] kulturell V
culture [ˈkʌltʃə] Kultur IV
cup [kʌp]
  1. Tasse III
  2. Pokal III
  a cup of tea eine Tasse Tee III
cupboard [ˈkʌbəd] (Küchen-)Schrank I
curly [ˈkɜːli] lockig VI 1 (6)
curriculum vitae [kəˌrɪkjələm ˈviːtaɪ] **(CV)** Lebenslauf V
curtain [ˈkɜːtn] Vorhang III
customer [ˈkʌstəmə] Kunde, Kundin II
customer adviser [ədˈvaɪzə] Kundenbetreuer/in, -berater/in V
cut (-tt-) [kʌt], **cut, cut** schneiden III • **cut sth. down** etwas zurückschneiden; (Baum) fällen VI 2 (36) **cut sth. off** etwas abschneiden, abtrennen III • **cut the grass** Rasen mähen IV
CV [siː ˈviː] **(curriculum vitae** [kəˌrɪkjələm ˈviːtaɪ]) Lebenslauf V
cycle [ˈsaɪkl] (mit dem) Rad fahren II • **cycle path** Radweg II
°**cyclist** [ˈsaɪklɪst] Radfahrer/in

D

dad [dæd] Papa, Vati; Vater I
daily [ˈdeɪli] täglich, Tages- IV
dance [dɑːns] tanzen I
dance [dɑːns] Tanz I
dance floor [ˈdɑːns flɔː] Tanzfläche, Tanzboden IV
dancer [ˈdɑːnsə] Tänzer/in II
dancing [ˈdɑːnsɪŋ] Tanzen I
  dancing lessons Tanzstunden, Tanzunterricht I
danger [ˈdeɪndʒə] Gefahr I
dangerous [ˈdeɪndʒərəs] gefährlich II
dark [dɑːk]
  1. dunkel I
  2. dunkelhaarig V
dark [dɑːk] Dunkelheit VI 2 (34)

darkness [ˈdɑːknəs] Dunkelheit VI 3 (54)
date [deɪt]
  1. Datum I
  2. Date, Verabredung III
  date of birth Geburtsdatum V
  to date bis heute V
date sb. [deɪt] mit jm. (aus)gehen; sich (regelmäßig) mit jm. treffen III
daughter [ˈdɔːtə] Tochter I
day [deɪ] Tag I • °**a day out** ein Tagesausflug • **one day** eines Tages I • **days of the week** Wochentage I • **the day she was stolen** der Tag, an dem sie gestohlen wurde V • **that day** an jenem Tag III
dead [ded] tot I
deal [diːl]: **It's a deal!** Abgemacht! III • **make a deal** ein Abkommen / eine Abmachung treffen III
dear [dɪə] Schatz, Liebling I • **Oh dear!** Oje! II
dear [dɪə]: **Dear Jay ...** Lieber Jay, ... I • **Dear Sir/Madam** Sehr geehrte Damen und Herren (Briefbeginn) V
death [deθ] Tod IV
debate [dɪˈbeɪt] debattieren IV
debate [dɪˈbeɪt] Debatte IV
December [dɪˈsembə] Dezember I
decide (on) [dɪˈsaɪd] beschließen; sich entscheiden (für) III
decision [dɪˈsɪʒn] Entscheidung V
  make a decision eine Entscheidung fällen V
deer, pl **deer** [dɪə] Reh, Hirsch II
definite [ˈdefɪnət] fest, bestimmt; endgültig, eindeutig V
°**definition** [ˌdefɪˈnɪʃn] Definition V
degree [dɪˈɡriː] Grad II
deli [ˈdeli] Deli (Lebensmittelgeschäft mit Fastfoodrestaurant) IV
delicious [dɪˈlɪʃəs] köstlich, lecker II
democracy [dɪˈmɒkrəsi] Demokratie VI 3 (47/180)
  ▶ S.180 Politics
democratic [ˌdeməˈkrætɪk] demokratisch V
dentist [ˈdentɪst] Zahnarzt, -ärztin IV
dentist's assistant [ˌdentɪsts əˈsɪstənt] Zahnarzthelfer/in V
department store [dɪˈpɑːtmənt stɔː] Kaufhaus II
departure (dep) [dɪˈpɑːtʃə] Abfahrt; Abflug; Abreise III
depressed [dɪˈprest] deprimiert, niedergeschlagen IV
depressing [dɪˈpresɪŋ] trostlos, deprimierend IV

describe sth. (to sb.) [dɪˈskraɪb] (jm.) etwas beschreiben II
description [dɪˈskrɪpʃn] Beschreibung II
desert [ˈdezət] Wüste V
deserve [dɪˈzɜːv] verdienen (zu Recht bekommen) VI 3 (48)
design [dɪˈzaɪn] entwerfen, gestalten II
design [dɪˈzaɪn] Muster, Entwurf; Design, Gestaltung V
designer [dɪˈzaɪnə] Designer/in V
desk [desk] Schreibtisch I
detail [ˈdiːteɪl] Detail, Einzelheit III
°**detailed** [ˈdiːteɪld] detailliert, ausführlich
detective [dɪˈtektɪv] Detektiv/in I
determined [dɪˈtɜːmɪnd]: **be determined** (fest) entschlossen sein V
device [dɪˈvaɪs] Vorrichtung, Gerät VI 3 (49)
°**diagram** [ˈdaɪəɡræm] Diagramm, Schaubild
dialogue [ˈdaɪəlɒɡ] Dialog IV
diary [ˈdaɪəri] Tagebuch; Terminkalender I • °**keep a diary** ein Tagebuch führen
dice, pl **dice** [daɪs] Würfel II
°**dictate** [dɪkˈteɪt] diktieren
dictionary [ˈdɪkʃənri] Wörterbuch, (alphabetisches) Wörterverzeichnis I
did [dɪd] siehe **do** • **Did you know ...?** Wusstest du ...? I • **we didn't go** [ˈdɪdnt] wir gingen nicht / wir sind nicht gegangen I
die (of) (-ing form: **dying**) [daɪ] sterben (an) II
difference [ˈdɪfrəns] Unterschied III • **make a difference** etwas bewirken, bewegen VI 2 (36)
different (from) [ˈdɪfrənt] verschieden, unterschiedlich; anders (als) I
difficult [ˈdɪfɪkəlt] schwierig, schwer I
dining room [ˈdaɪnɪŋ ruːm] Esszimmer I
dinner [ˈdɪnə] Abendessen, Abendbrot I • **have dinner** Abendbrot essen I
dinosaur [ˈdaɪnəsɔː] Dinosaurier III
direct [dəˈrekt, daɪˈrekt] direkt VI 3 (102) • **direct question** direkte Frage II • **direct speech** direkte Rede, wörtliche Rede IV
direct a film/play [dəˈrekt] bei einem Film/Theaterstück Regie führen VI 1 (12)
directions (pl) [dəˈrekʃnz] Wegbeschreibung(en) II
director [dəˈrektə] Regisseur/in VI 1 (12/173)

dirt [dɜːt] Schmutz, Dreck V
dirt bike ['dɜːt baɪk] Geländemotorrad V
dirty ['dɜːti] schmutzig II
disabled [dɪs'eɪbld] (körper)behindert III
disadvantage [ˌdɪsəd'vɑːntɪdʒ] Nachteil IV
disagree (with) [ˌdɪsə'griː] nicht übereinstimmen (mit); anderer Meinung sein (als) III
disagreement [ˌdɪsə'griːmənt] Uneinigkeit, Streit VI 3 (54)
disappear [ˌdɪsə'pɪə] verschwinden II
discipline ['dɪsəplɪn] Disziplin V
disc jockey (DJ) ['dɪsk dʒɒki, 'diː dʒeɪ] Diskjockey III
disco ['dɪskəʊ] Disko I
discover [dɪ'skʌvə] entdecken; herausfinden II
discovery [dɪ'skʌvəri] Entdeckung VI 2 (32)
discriminate against sb. [dɪ'skrɪmɪneɪt] jn. diskriminieren, jn. benachteiligen IV
discrimination (against) [dɪˌskrɪmɪ'neɪʃn] Diskriminierung (von), Benachteiligung (von) IV
discuss sth. [dɪ'skʌs] etwas besprechen, über etwas diskutieren VI 2 (31/176)
discussion [dɪ'skʌʃn] Diskussion II
written discussion Erörterung VI 2 (37)
disease [dɪ'ziːz] Krankheit V
disgusting [dɪs'gʌstɪŋ] widerlich, ekelhaft VI 3 (49)
dish [dɪʃ] Gericht (Speise) III
dishes ['dɪʃɪz]: **wash the dishes** das Geschirr abwaschen V
dishwasher ['dɪʃwɒʃə] Geschirrspülmaschine I
display [dɪ'spleɪ]: **be on display** ausgestellt sein/werden IV
°**distance** ['dɪstəns] Entfernung
divide sth. (into) [dɪ'vaɪd] etwas (auf)teilen (in) V
divorced [dɪ'vɔːst] geschieden I
get divorced sich scheiden lassen V
DJ ['diː dʒeɪ] Diskjockey III
DJ ['diː dʒeɪ] (Musik/CDs/Platten) auflegen (in der Disko) III
do [duː], **did, done** tun, machen I
Do you like ...? Magst du ...? I
do sth. about sth. etwas unternehmen gegen etwas V • **do an exam** eine Prüfung ablegen IV
do a gig einen Auftritt haben, ein Konzert geben III • **do a good job** gute Arbeit leisten II • **do a**

project ein Projekt machen, durchführen II • **do an exercise** eine Übung machen II • **do badly** schlecht abschneiden (Prüfung) V
do business with Handel treiben mit; Geschäfte machen mit V
do jobs Arbeiten/Aufträge erledigen V • **do research** recherchieren IV • **do sport** Sport treiben I
do well erfolgreich sein, gut abschneiden V • **do work experience** ein Praktikum machen V
doable ['duːəbl] machbar IV
doctor ['dɒktə] Doktor; Arzt/Ärztin II • **to the doctor's** zum Arzt III
°**document** ['dɒkjumənt] Dokument
documentary [ˌdɒkju'mentri] Dokumentarfilm, -beitrag IV
dog [dɒg] Hund I
dollar ($) ['dɒlə] Dollar IV
dolphin ['dɒlfɪn] Delfin V
donate [dəʊ'neɪt] spenden, schenken V
done [dʌn] siehe **do**
don't [dəʊnt]: **Don't listen to Dan.** Hör/Hört nicht auf Dan. I • **I don't like ...** Ich mag ... nicht. / Ich mag kein(e) ... I
door [dɔː] Tür I
doorbell ['dɔːbel] Türklingel I
dormitory ['dɔːmətri] Schlafsaal V
dossier ['dɒsieɪ] Mappe, Dossier (des Sprachenportfolios) I
double ['dʌbl] zweimal, doppelt, Doppel- I • **double glazing** [ˌdʌbl 'gleɪzɪŋ] (Fenster mit) Doppelverglasung VI 2 (28) • **double room** Doppelzimmer V
double-click ['dʌblklɪk] doppelklicken II
down [daʊn] hinunter, herunter, nach unten I • **down there** dort unten II • **fall down** hinfallen II
download [ˌdaʊn'ləʊd] runterladen, downloaden II
downloadable [ˌdaʊn'ləʊdəbl] herunterladbar IV
downstairs [ˌdaʊn'steəz] unten; nach unten I
downtown [ˌdaʊn'taʊn] (AE) (im/in das) Stadtzentrum IV • **the downtown bus** (AE) der Bus in Richtung Stadtzentrum IV
drama ['drɑːmə]
1. Schauspiel, darstellende Kunst I
2. Fernsehspiel; Drama IV
drank [dræŋk] siehe **drink**
draw [drɔː] Unentschieden III
draw [drɔː], **drew, drawn**
1. zeichnen III
2. **draw conclusions** Schlüsse ziehen, schlussfolgern IV • **draw sb.'s**

attention to sth. jn. auf etwas aufmerksam machen; jemandes Aufmerksamkeit auf etwas lenken V
drawing ['drɔːɪŋ] Zeichnung III
drawn [drɔːn] siehe **draw**
dream [driːm] Traum I
dream (of, about) [driːm] träumen (von) III • **dream on** weiterträumen III
dreamer ['driːmə] Träumer/in V
dress [dres] Kleid I
dress [dres] sich kleiden V
dressed [drest]: **get dressed** sich anziehen V
drew [druː] siehe **draw**
drink [drɪŋk] Getränk I
drink [drɪŋk], **drank, drunk** trinken I
drinkable ['drɪŋkəbl] trinkbar, genießbar IV
drive [draɪv], **drove, driven** (ein Auto / mit dem Auto) fahren II
drive [draɪv] (Auto-)Fahrt III
driven ['drɪvn] siehe **drive**
driver ['draɪvə] Fahrer/in II
driverless ['draɪvələs] fahrerlos, führerlos VI 2 (31)
driving licence ['draɪvɪŋ laɪsns] Führerschein V
drop (-pp-) [drɒp]
1. fallen lassen I
2. fallen I
drop sb. off jn. absetzen (aussteigen lassen) IV
drove [drəʊv] siehe **drive**
drug [drʌg] Droge, Rauschgift; Medikament IV
drum [drʌm] Trommel III • **play the drums** Schlagzeug spielen III
drunk [drʌŋk] betrunken IV
siehe **drink**
dry [draɪ] trocken V
dump sb. [dʌmp] (infml) mit jm. Schluss machen VI 1 (12)
during (prep) ['djʊərɪŋ] während IV
dustbin ['dʌstbɪn] Mülltonne II
dusty ['dʌsti] staubig IV
DVD [ˌdiː viː' diː] DVD I
DVD recorder DVD-Rekorder IV

E

each [iːtʃ] jeder, jede, jedes (einzelne) I • **each other** einander, sich (gegenseitig) III
eagle ['iːgl] Adler V
ear [ɪə] Ohr I
earache ['ɪəreɪk] Ohrenschmerzen II
early ['ɜːli] früh I

earn [ɜːn] verdienen *(Geld, Respekt usw.)* V

earring [ˈɪərɪŋ] Ohrring I

earth [ɜːθ] Erde III • **on earth** auf der Erde III

earthquake [ˈɜːθkweɪk] Erdbeben III

east [iːst] Osten; nach Osten; östlich III

eastbound [ˈiːstbaʊnd] Richtung Osten III

easy [ˈiːzi] leicht, einfach I

easy-going [ˌiːziˈɡəʊɪŋ] gelassen, locker III

eat [iːt], **ate, eaten** essen I

eaten [ˈiːtn] *siehe* **eat**

economic [ˌiːkəˈnɒmɪk, ˌekəˈnɒmɪk] Wirtschafts-, wirtschaftliche(r, s) V

editor [ˈedɪtə] Redakteur/in III

education [ˌedʒuˈkeɪʃn] (Schul-)Bildung, Ausbildung; Erziehung IV

effect [ɪˈfekt] (Aus-)Wirkung, Effekt VI 1 (12)

e-friend [ˈiːfrend] Brieffreund/in *(im Internet)* I

e.g. [ˌiːˈdʒiː] *(from Latin:* **exempli gratia***)* z.B. (zum Beispiel) V

egg [eɡ] Ei III

either [ˈaɪðə, ˈiːðə]

  1. not (...) either auch nicht; auch kein VI 1 (8)

  °**2. either ... or ...** entweder ... oder IV

elect sb. sth. [ɪˈlekt] jn. zu etwas wählen IV

election [ɪˈlekʃn] Wahl *(von Kandidaten bei einer Abstimmung)* IV

electric [ɪˈlektrɪk] elektrisch, Elektro- III

electricity [ɪˌlekˈtrɪsəti] Strom, Elektrizität III

electronic [ɪˌlekˈtrɒnɪk] elektronisch III

elementary school [ˌelɪˈmentri skuːl] *(USA)* Grundschule *(für 6- bis 11-Jährige)* IV

elephant [ˈelɪfənt] Elefant I

elevator [ˈelɪveɪtə] *(AE)* Fahrstuhl, Aufzug II

else [els]: **anybody else** (sonst) noch jemand / irgendjemand anderes IV • **anything else** (sonst) noch etwas / irgendetwas anderes IV • **somebody else** (noch) jemand anderes IV • **somewhere else** woanders(hin); sonst irgendwo(hin) IV • **what else?** was (sonst) noch? IV • **What else do you know?** Was weißt du sonst noch? II • **who else?** wer/wen/wem (sonst) noch? IV

e-mail, email [ˈiːmeɪl] E-Mail I

e-mail, email [ˈiːmeɪl] mailen V

embarrassed [ɪmˈbærəst] verlegen; peinlich berührt V

emission [iˈmɪʃn] Emission, (Schadstoff-)Ausstoß VI 2 (29)

empty [ˈempti] leer I

emu [ˈiːmjuː] Emu V

enclose sth. [ɪnˈkləʊz] etwas *(einem Brief)* beilegen V

encourage [ɪnˈkʌrɪdʒ] *(jn.)* ermutigen, ermuntern; *(etwas)* fördern V

°**encyclopedia** [ɪnˌsaɪkləˈpiːdiə] Enzyklopädie, Lexikon

end [end] Ende, Schluss I • **at the end (of)** am Ende (von) I • **in the end** schließlich, zum Schluss III

end [end] enden; beenden III

ending [ˈendɪŋ]

  1. Ende, (Ab-)Schluss *(einer Geschichte, eines Films usw.)* III

  2. Endung IV

endless [ˈendləs] endlos IV

enemy [ˈenəmi] Feind/in II

energetic [ˌenəˈdʒetɪk] dynamisch, tatkräftig, energisch V

energy [ˈenədʒi] Energie; Kraft II

engine [ˈendʒɪn] Motor IV

engineer [ˌendʒɪˈnɪə] Ingenieur/in II

engineering [ˌendʒɪˈnɪərɪŋ] Maschinenbau; Ingenieurswesen V

English [ˈɪŋɡlɪʃ] Englisch; englisch I

English-speaking [ˈɪŋɡlɪʃ ˌspiːkɪŋ] englischsprachig; Englisch sprechend V

enjoy [ɪnˈdʒɔɪ] genießen II

enough [ɪˈnʌf] genug I

enquire (about) [ɪnˈkwaɪə] sich erkundigen (nach); anfragen (wegen) V

enquiry [ɪnˈkwaɪəri] Anfrage, Erkundigung V

enter [ˈentə]

  1. betreten; eintreten (in) III

  2. enter sth. etwas eingeben, eintragen II

  enter a country in ein Land einreisen IV

entry [ˈentri] Eintrag, Eintragung *(in Wörterbuch/Tagebuch)* III

environment [ɪnˈvaɪrənmənt] Umwelt; Umgebung VI 1 (15)

episode [ˈepɪsəʊd] Folge, Episode *(einer Fernsehserie)* IV

equal [ˈiːkwəl] gleich *(Rechte, Bezahlung usw.)* VI 3 (48)

equipment [ɪˈkwɪpmənt] Ausrüstung III

eraser [ɪˈreɪzə, *AE:* ɪˈreɪsər] *(AE)* Radiergummi IV

escape (from sb./sth.) [ɪˈskeɪp] fliehen (vor jm./aus etwas); entkommen III

especially [ɪˈspeʃəli] besonders, vor allem II

essay (about, on) [ˈeseɪ] Aufsatz (über) I

etc. (et cetera) [etˈsetərə] usw. (und so weiter) IV

ethnic [ˈeθnɪk] ethnisch IV

euro (€) [ˈjʊərəʊ] Euro I

even [ˈiːvn] sogar II • **even if** selbst wenn; obwohl IV • **not even** (noch) nicht einmal III

evening [ˈiːvnɪŋ] Abend I • **in the evening** abends, am Abend I • **on Friday evening** freitagabends, am Freitagabend I

event [ɪˈvent] Ereignis; Veranstaltung IV

ever? [ˈevə] je? / jemals? / schon mal? II

every [ˈevri] jeder, jede, jedes I

everybody [ˈevribɒdi] jeder, alle II

everyday *(adj)* [ˈevrideɪ] Alltags-; alltägliche(r, s) III

everyone [ˈevriwʌn] IV *siehe* **everybody**

everything [ˈevriθɪŋ] alles I

everywhere [ˈevriweə] überall I

evil [ˈiːvl] böse *(bösartig, feindselig)*, übel, schlimm VI 2 (35)

exact [ɪɡˈzækt] exakt, genau IV

exactly [ɪɡˈzæktli] genau III

exam [ɪɡˈzæm] Prüfung, Examen IV • **fail an exam** eine Prüfung nicht bestehen; durchfallen IV • **take/do an exam** eine Prüfung ablegen IV

example [ɪɡˈzɑːmpl] Beispiel I **for example** zum Beispiel I

excellent [ˈeksələnt] ausgezeichnet, hervorragend IV

except [ɪkˈsept] außer IV

°**exchange** [ɪksˈtʃeɪndʒ] austauschen

exchange [ɪksˈtʃeɪndʒ] (Schüler-)Austausch III

exchange rate [ɪksˈtʃeɪndʒ reɪt] Wechselkurs V

exchange student [ɪksˈtʃeɪndʒ ˌstjuːdənt] Austauschschüler/in III

excited [ɪkˈsaɪtɪd] aufgeregt, begeistert III

exciting [ɪkˈsaɪtɪŋ] aufregend, spannend II

Excuse me, ... [ɪkˈskjuːz miː] Entschuldigung, ... / Entschuldigen Sie, ... I

exercise [ˈeksəsaɪz]

  1. Übung, Aufgabe I

  2. *(no pl)* (körperliche) Bewegung, Training IV

exercise book [ˈeksəsaɪz bʊk] Schulheft, Übungsheft I

expect [ɪkˈspekt] erwarten III

expensive [ɪk'spensɪv] teuer I
experience [ɪk'spɪərɪəns] erleben, erfahren IV
experience [ɪk'spɪərɪəns] Erlebnis, Erfahrung IV
experiment [ɪk'sperɪmənt] Experiment VI 2 (30)
explain sth. to sb. [ɪk'spleɪn] jm. etwas erklären, erläutern II
explanation [ˌeksplə'neɪʃn] Erklärung II
explode [ɪk'spləʊd] explodieren VI 3 (54)
explore [ɪk'splɔː] erkunden, erforschen I
explorer [ɪk'splɔːrə] Entdecker/in, Forscher/in II
explosion [ɪk'spləʊʒn] Explosion IV
express [ɪk'spres] ausdrücken, äußern V
extra ['ekstrə] zusätzlich I
extracurricular activities (kurz: **extracurriculars**) [ˌekstrəkə'rɪkjələz] schulische Angebote außerhalb des regulären Unterrichts, oft als Arbeitsgemeinschaften IV
eye [aɪ] Auge I
°**e-zine** ['iːziːn] elektronisches Magazin, elektronische Zeitschrift

F

face [feɪs] Gesicht I
facilities (pl) [fə'sɪlətiz] Einrichtungen, Anlagen VI 3 (46)
fact [fækt] Tatsache, Fakt III • **in fact** tatsächlich; in Wirklichkeit; um genau zu sein VI 1 (12)
factory ['fæktri] Fabrik II
fail an exam [feɪl] eine Prüfung nicht bestehen; durchfallen IV
failure (n) ['feɪljə] ungenügend (USA, Schulnote) IV
fair [feə]
1. fair, gerecht II
2. hell (Haut; Haare) V
faithfully ['feɪθfəli]: **Yours faithfully** Mit freundlichen Grüßen (Briefschluss bei namentlich unbekanntem Empfänger) IV
fall [fɔːl], **fell, fallen** fallen, stürzen; hinfallen II • **fall down** hinfallen II • **fall in love (with sb.)** sich verlieben (in jn.) IV • **fall off** herunterfallen (von) II
fallen ['fɔːlən] siehe fall
false [fɔːls] falsch, unecht V
family ['fæməli] Familie I • **family tree** (Familien-)Stammbaum I
famous (for) ['feɪməs] berühmt (für, wegen) II

fan [fæn] Fan I
fancy sb. ['fænsi] (infml) auf jn. stehen V
fantastic [fæn'tæstɪk] fantastisch, toll I
fantasy ['fæntəsi] Fantasy(film, -roman) VI 1 (12)
far [fɑː] weit (entfernt) I • **so far** bis jetzt, bis hierher I
fare [feə] Fahrpreis VI 3 (50)
farm [fɑːm] Bauernhof, Farm II
farmer ['fɑːmə] Bauer/Bäuerin, Landwirt/in; (Fisch-)Züchter/in III
fashion ['fæʃn] Mode II
fashionable ['fæʃnəbl] modisch, schick V
fast [fɑːst] schnell II • **fast food** Fastfood III
fat [fæt] dick IV
father ['fɑːðə] Vater I
fault [fɔːlt]: **It's not my fault.** Es/Das ist nicht meine Schuld. IV
favourite ['feɪvərɪt] Favorit/in; Liebling III; Lieblings- I
February ['februəri] Februar I
fed [fed] siehe feed • **be fed up (with sth.)** [ˌfed_'ʌp] die Nase voll haben (von etwas) III
feed [fiːd], **fed, fed** füttern I
feel [fiːl], **felt, felt** fühlen; sich fühlen; sich anfühlen II • **feel comfortable** sich wohl fühlen VI 3 (51) **Feel free to ask questions.** etwa: Ihr könnt jetzt gern Fragen stellen. V • **How do they feel about ...?** Was halten sie von ...? III • **I feel sick.** Mir ist schlecht. IV
feeling ['fiːlɪŋ] Gefühl III
feet [fiːt] pl von „foot"
fell [fel] siehe fall
felt [felt] siehe feel
felt tip ['felt tɪp] Filzstift I
fence [fens] Zaun IV
ferry ['feri] Fähre III
festival ['festɪvl] Fest, Festival III
few: a few [ə 'fjuː] ein paar, einige II
fiddle ['fɪdl] (infml) Fiedel, Geige III **play the fiddle** Geige spielen III
field [fiːld] Feld, Acker, Weide II; Sportplatz, Spielfeld III • **in the field** auf dem Feld II
FIFA World Cup [ˌfiːfə wɜːld 'kʌp] FIFA-Fußball-WM V
fight (for) [faɪt], **fought, fought** kämpfen (für, um) III • **fight sth.** etwas bekämpfen III
fight [faɪt] Kampf; Schlägerei IV
figure ['fɪgə] Zahl, Ziffer V
°**file** [faɪl] (Akten-)Ordner, Hefter I
file [faɪl]: **background file** etwa: Hintergrundinformation(en) II

grammar file Grammatikanhang I
skills file Anhang mit Lern- und Arbeitstechniken I • **sound file** Tondatei, Soundfile III
fill [fɪl] füllen, ausfüllen V
fill in 1. ausfüllen (Formular) V; °**2.** einsetzen
film [fɪlm] filmen III
film [fɪlm] Film I
film star ['fɪlm stɑː] Filmstar I
final ['faɪnl] letzte(r, s); End- III **final score** Endstand (beim Sport) III
final ['faɪnl] Finale, Endspiel III
finally ['faɪnəli] schließlich, endlich V
financial [faɪ'nænʃl] finanziell, Finanz- V
find [faɪnd], **found, found** finden I **find out (about)** herausfinden (über) I
fine [faɪn]
1. gut, schön; in Ordnung II
2. (gesundheitlich) gut II
I'm/He's fine. Es geht mir/ihm gut. II
finger ['fɪŋgə] Finger I
finish ['fɪnɪʃ] beenden, zu Ende machen; enden II
fire ['faɪə] Feuer, Brand II
firefighter ['faɪəfaɪtə] Feuerwehrmann, -frau IV
fireman ['faɪəmən] Feuerwehrmann II
fireproof ['faɪəpruːf] feuerfest V
fire station ['faɪə steɪʃn] Feuerwache IV
firewoman ['faɪəˌwʊmən] Feuerwehrfrau IV
fireworks (pl) ['faɪəwɜːks] Feuerwerk(skörper) II
first [fɜːst]
1. erste(r, s) I
2. zuerst, als Erstes I
at first zuerst, am Anfang IV
be first der/die Erste sein I
first aid [ˌfɜːst_'eɪd] Erste Hilfe V
first floor [ˌfɜːst flɔː] erster Stock (BE) / Erdgeschoss (AE) IV
fish, pl **fish** [fɪʃ] Fisch I
fish [fɪʃ] fischen, angeln III
°**fishbowl** ['fɪʃbəʊl] Fischglas III
fist [fɪst] Faust IV
fit (-tt-) [fɪt] passen I • **fit in** hineinpassen; sich einfügen, sich anpassen IV
fit [fɪt] fit III
fitness ['fɪtnəs] Fitness V
fitness instructor ['fɪtnəs_ɪnˌstrʌktə] Fitnesstrainer/in V
flash [flæʃ] Lichtblitz III
flat [flæt] Wohnung I

°**flat** [flæt] flach, eben
flavour ['fleɪvə] Geschmack, Geschmacksrichtung II
flew [fluː] *siehe* **fly**
flight [flaɪt] Flug II
flirt [flɜːt] flirten VI 1 (9)
floor [flɔː]
  1. Fußboden I
  2. Stock(werk) IV
  first floor erster Stock *(BE)* / Erdgeschoss *(AE)* IV • **ground floor** *(BE)* Erdgeschoss IV • **on the second floor** im zweiten Stock *(BE)* / im ersten Stock *(AE)* IV
flow chart ['fləʊ tʃɑːt] Flussdiagramm I
flower ['flaʊə] Blume; Blüte III
flown [fləʊn] *siehe* **fly**
flute [fluːt] Querflöte III
fly [flaɪ], **flew, flown** fliegen II
fog [fɒɡ] Nebel II
foggy ['fɒɡi] neblig II
folk (music) [fəʊk] Folk *(englische, schottische, irische oder nordamerikanische Volksmusik des 20. Jahrhunderts)* III
follow ['fɒləʊ] folgen; verfolgen I
  the following ... die folgenden ... II
food [fuːd]
  1. Essen; Lebensmittel I
  2. Futter I
foot [fʊt], *pl* **feet** [fiːt] Fuß I; Fuß *(Längenmaß; ca. 30 cm)* IV
  on foot zu Fuß III
football ['fʊtbɔːl] Fußball I
football boots ['fʊtbɔːl buːts] Fußballschuhe, -stiefel I
football pitch ['fʊtbɔːl pɪtʃ] Fußballplatz, -feld II
football shirt ['fʊtbɔːl ʃɜːt] (Fußball-)Trikot III
footprint ['fʊtprɪnt] Fußabdruck VI 2 (29/175)
for [fə, fɔː] für I • **for ages** ewig, eine Ewigkeit IV • **for a while** für eine Weile, eine Zeit lang V • **for breakfast/lunch/dinner** zum Frühstück/Mittagessen/Abendbrot I • **for example** zum Beispiel I • **for his birthday** zu seinem Geburtstag III • **for lots of reasons** aus vielen Gründen I • **for miles** meilenweit II • **for sale** *(auf Schild)* zu verkaufen IV • **for the first time** zum ersten Mal IV • **for 20 minutes** seit 20 Minuten; 20 Minuten lang IV • **just for fun** nur zum Spaß I • **What for?** Wofür? II **What's for homework?** Was haben wir als Hausaufgabe auf? I
foreground ['fɔːɡraʊnd] Vordergrund II

foreign ['fɒrən] ausländisch, fremd IV • **foreign language** Fremdsprache IV
foreigner ['fɒrənə] Ausländer/in, Fremde(r) VI 3 (54)
forest ['fɒrɪst] Wald II
forever [fər'evə] ewig, für immer IV
forgave [fə'ɡeɪv] *siehe* **forgive**
forget (-tt-) [fə'ɡet], **forgot, forgotten** vergessen III
forgive [fə'ɡɪv], **forgave, forgiven** vergeben, verzeihen IV
forgiven [fə'ɡɪvn] *siehe* **forgive**
forgot [fə'ɡɒt] *siehe* **forget**
forgotten [fə'ɡɒtn] *siehe* **forget**
fork [fɔːk] Gabel III
form [fɔːm]
  1. (Schul-)Klasse I
  2. Form IV
  3. Formular V
  form teacher Klassenlehrer/in I
form [fɔːm] (sich) bilden, formen IV
formal ['fɔːml] formell, förmlich V
former ['fɔːmə] ehemalige(r, s), frühere(r, s) V
fortunately ['fɔːtʃənətli] glücklicherweise VI 1 (12/173)
forum ['fɔːrəm] Forum V
forward ['fɔːwəd]: **look forward to sth.** sich auf etwas freuen IV
fossil fuel [ˌfɒsl 'fjuːəl] fossiler Brennstoff VI 2 (30)
fought [fɔːt] *siehe* **fight**
found [faʊnd] gründen IV
found [faʊnd] *siehe* **find**
fox [fɒks] Fuchs II
free [friː]
  1. frei I
  2. kostenlos I
  free speech Redefreiheit VI 3 (54)
  free time Freizeit, freie Zeit I
  Feel free to ask questions. *etwa:* Ihr könnt jetzt gern Fragen stellen. V
freedom ['friːdəm] Freiheit IV
freezing ['friːzɪŋ] eisig; eiskalt VI 2 (35)
French [frentʃ] Französisch I
French fries [ˌfrentʃ 'fraɪz] *(AE)* Pommes frites IV
fresh [freʃ] frisch IV
Friday ['fraɪdeɪ, 'fraɪdi] Freitag I
fridge [frɪdʒ] Kühlschrank I
friend [frend] Freund/in I • **make friends (with sb.)** Freunde finden; sich anfreunden (mit jm.) V
friendliness ['frendlinəs] Freundlichkeit IV
friendly ['frendli] freundlich II
°**friendship** ['frendʃɪp] Freundschaft I
frog [frɒɡ] Frosch II

from [frəm, frɒm]
  1. aus I
  2. von I
  from all around Wales aus ganz Wales II • **from all over England/ the UK** aus ganz England/aus dem gesamten Vereinigten Königreich III • **from Monday to Friday** von Montag bis Freitag III • **from my point of view** aus meiner Sicht; von meinem Standpunkt aus gesehen II • **I'm from ...** Ich komme aus .../bin aus ... I • **Where are you from?** Wo kommst du her? I
front [frʌnt]: **in front of** vor *(räumlich)* I • **to the front** nach vorn I
front door [ˌfrʌnt 'dɔː] Wohnungstür, Haustür I
°**front inside cover** [ˌfrʌnt ˌɪnsaɪd 'kʌvə] vordere Umschlaginnenseite
fruit [fruːt] Obst, Früchte; Frucht I
fruit salad ['fruːt ˌsæləd] Obstsalat I
fruity ['fruːti] fruchtig V
fuel ['fjuːəl] Brenn-, Treib-, Kraftstoff VI 2 (31/176)
full [fʊl] voll I
fun [fʌn] Spaß I • **have fun** Spaß haben, sich amüsieren I • **Have fun!** Viel Spaß! I • **just for fun** nur zum Spaß I • **Riding is fun.** Reiten macht Spaß. I
funeral ['fjuːnərəl] Trauerfeier, Beerdigung V
funny ['fʌni] witzig, komisch I
furniture *(no pl)* ['fɜːnɪtʃə] Möbel III
  a piece of furniture ein Möbelstück III
future ['fjuːtʃə] Zukunft I

G

gadget ['ɡædʒɪt] (kleines) Gerät, Apparat; technische Spielerei VI 2 (28)
gallery ['ɡæləri] (Bilder-)Galerie V
game [ɡeɪm] Spiel I • **a game of football** ein Fußballspiel II
gangster ['ɡæŋstə] Gangster/in V
°**gap** [ɡæp] Lücke
garage ['ɡærɑːʒ]
  1. Garage II
  2. Autowerkstatt *(oft mit Tankstelle)* V
garbage ['ɡɑːbɪdʒ] *(AE)* Müll, Abfall IV
garden ['ɡɑːdn] Garten I
gardener ['ɡɑːdnə] Gärtner/in IV
gas [ɡæs]
  1. Gas VI 2 (29)
  2. *(AE)* Benzin IV
°**gasifier** ['ɡæsɪfaɪə] Vergaser

gasp [gɑːsp] nach Luft schnappen *(auch: vor Überraschung)* IV

gas station ['gæs steɪʃn] *(AE)* Tankstelle IV

gate [geɪt]
1. Tor; Pforte V
2. Flugsteig III

gave [geɪv] *siehe* **give**

gear *(no pl)* [gɪə]**: camping gear** Campingausrüstung, Campingsachen IV • **sports gear** Sportausrüstung, Sportsachen II

°**geek** [giːk]**: computer geek** *(bes. AE, infml)* Computerfreak

general ['dʒenrəl] allgemeine(r, s) III

generation [ˌdʒenəˈreɪʃn] Generation V

geography [dʒiˈɒgrəfi] Geografie, Erdkunde I

German ['dʒɜːmən] Deutsch; deutsch; Deutsche(r) I

Germany ['dʒɜːməni] Deutschland I

get (-tt-) [get]**, got, got**
1. bekommen, kriegen II
2. holen, besorgen II
3. gelangen, (hin)kommen I
4. get angry/hot/... wütend/heiß/... werden II
5. get off (the train/bus) (aus dem Zug/Bus) aussteigen I • **get on (the train/bus)** (in den Zug/Bus) einsteigen I
6. get up aufstehen I
I didn't get that. *(infml)* Das habe ich nicht mitbekommen. / Ich habe das nicht verstanden. V • **get bored** sich langweilen IV • **get divorced** sich scheiden lassen V • **get dressed** sich anziehen I • **get in trouble** in Schwierigkeiten geraten V • **get involved (in)** sich engagieren (für, bei); sich beteiligen (an) IV • **get married (to sb.)** (jn.) heiraten V • **get ready (for)** sich fertig machen (für), sich vorbereiten (auf) I • **get rid of sb./sth.** jn./etwas loswerden IV • **get sth. off the ground** etwas auf den Weg bringen; etwas auf die Beine stellen III • **get things ready** Dinge fertig machen, vorbereiten I **get tired of sth.** einer Sache überdrüssig werden, die Lust an etwas verlieren IV • **get to know sb.** jn. kennenlernen IV

getting by in English [ˌgetɪŋ ˈbaɪ] *etwa:* auf Englisch zurechtkommen I

gig [gɪg] *(infml)* Gig, Auftritt III
do a gig einen Auftritt haben, ein Konzert geben III

giraffe [dʒəˈrɑːf] Giraffe II

girl [gɜːl] Mädchen I

girlfriend ['gɜːlfrend] (feste) Freundin IV

give [gɪv]**, gave, given** geben I
give a talk (on sth.) einen Vortrag/eine Rede halten (über etwas) V
give up aufgeben IV • **it gives me the creeps** es ist mir unheimlich; es ist mir nicht geheuer VI 2 (35)

given ['gɪvn] *siehe* **give**

°**glad** [glæd] froh

glass [glɑːs] Glas I • **a glass of water** ein Glas Wasser I

glasses *(pl)* ['glɑːsɪz] (eine) Brille I

global ['gləʊbl] global, weltweit VI 2 (29/175)

global warming [ˌgləʊbl ˈwɔːmɪŋ] Erwärmung der Erdatmosphäre, globaler Temperaturanstieg VI 2 (29)

glue [gluː] (auf-, ein)kleben II

glue [gluː] Klebstoff I

glue stick ['gluː stɪk] Klebestift I

go [gəʊ]**, went, gone** gehen I; fahren II • **coffee to go** Kaffee zum Mitnehmen IV • **go abroad** ins Ausland gehen/fahren II • **go by** vergehen, vorübergehen *(Zeit)* V **go by car/train/bike/...** mit dem Auto/Zug/Rad/... fahren II • °**go crazy** durchdrehen, verrückt werden • **go for a walk** spazieren gehen, einen Spaziergang machen II **go home** nach Hause gehen I **go on 1.** weitermachen I; weiterreden III; **2.** angehen *(Licht)* III **go on a trip** einen Ausflug machen II • **go on holiday** in Urlaub fahren II • **go out 1.** weg-, rausgehen I; **2.** miteinander gehen, zusammen sein VI 1 (7/171) • **go to bed** ins Bett gehen I • **go to the cinema** ins Kino gehen II • **go together** zusammenpassen IV • **go up to sb./sth.** auf jn./etwas zugehen V • **go well** gut (ver-)laufen, gutgehen III • **go with** gehören zu, passen zu III • **go wrong** schiefgehen III • **Let's go.** Auf geht's! I • **There you go!** *(infml) etwa:* So, das hätten wir. IV

▶ S.171 Relationships: going out

goal [gəʊl] Tor *(im Sport)* III

goalkeeper ['gəʊlkiːpə] Torwart, Torfrau II

God [gɒd] Gott IV

gold [gəʊld] Gold III

golden ['gəʊldən] golden IV

golf [gɒlf] Golf III

gone [gɒn]
1. weg, fort VI 2 (34)
2. *siehe* **go**

good [gʊd]
1. gut I
2. brav II
be good at sth. gut in etwas sein; etwas gut können III • **Good afternoon.** Guten Tag. *(nachmittags)* I • **Good luck (with ...)!** Viel Glück (bei/mit ...)! I • **Good morning.** Guten Morgen. I

Goodbye. [ˌgʊdˈbaɪ] Auf Wiedersehen. I • **say goodbye** sich verabschieden I

good-looking [ˌgʊdˈlʊkɪŋ] gut aussehend V

got [gɒt] *siehe* **get**

got [gɒt]**: I've got ...** Ich habe ... I **I haven't got a chair.** Ich habe keinen Stuhl. I

govern ['gʌvn] regieren VI 3 (54)

government ['gʌvənmənt] Regierung *(als Schulfach etwa: Staatskunde)* IV

governor ['gʌvənə] Gouverneur/in IV

grab (-bb-) [græb] schnappen, packen III

grade [greɪd]
1. (Schul-)Note, Zensur IV
2. *(AE)* Jahrgangsstufe, Klasse IV

graduate ['grædʒueɪt] *(AE)* den Schulabschluss machen *(an einer amerikanischen Highschool)* V

graffiti [grəˈfiːti] Graffiti V

grain [greɪn] Korn IV

grammar ['græmə] Grammatik I **grammar file** *Grammatikanhang* I

grand [grænd] eindrucksvoll, beeindruckend IV

grandchild ['græntʃaɪld]**,** *pl* **grandchildren** ['-tʃɪldrən] Enkel/in IV

granddaughter ['grændɔːtə] Enkelin II

grandfather ['grænfɑːðə] Großvater I

grandma ['grænmɑː] Oma I

grandmother ['grænmʌðə] Großmutter I

grandpa ['grænpɑː] Opa I

grandparents ['grænpeərənts] Großeltern I

grandson ['grænsʌn] Enkel II

granny ['græni] Oma II

grape [greɪp] Weintraube IV

°**graph** [grɑːf] Graph, Kurve, Schaubild

grass [grɑːs] Rasen IV

great [greɪt] großartig, toll I

great-grandfather [ˌgreɪt ˈgrænfɑːðə] Urgroßvater III

great-grandmother [ˌgreɪt ˈgrænmʌðə] Urgroßmutter III

greedy ['griːdi] gierig, habgierig V

green [griːn] grün I

°**greeting** [ˈgriːtɪŋ] Gruß, Begrüßung I

grew [gruː] *siehe* **grow**

grey [greɪ] grau II

ground [graʊnd] (Erd-)Boden III
get sth. off the ground etwas auf den Weg bringen; etwas auf die Beine stellen III

ground floor [ˌgraʊnd ˈflɔː] *(BE)* Erdgeschoss IV

ground zero [ˌgraʊnd ˈzɪərəʊ] Bodennullpunkt *(Bezeichnung für das zerstörte World Trade Center in New York; ursprünglich: Explosionsstelle einer Bombe oder Rakete über dem Boden)* IV

group [gruːp] Gruppe I • **group word** Oberbegriff II

grow [grəʊ], **grew, grown**
1. wachsen II
2. *(Getreide usw.)* anbauen, anpflanzen II
grow up erwachsen werden; aufwachsen III

grown [grəʊn] *siehe* **grow**

grumble [ˈgrʌmbl] murren, nörgeln I

guess [ges] raten, erraten, schätzen II • **Guess what!** Stell dir vor! II

°**guess** [ges] Vermutung, Schätzung II

guest [gest] Gast I

guide [gaɪd] (Fremden-)Führer/in, Reiseleiter/in IV

guidebook [ˈgaɪdbʊk] Reiseführer *(Buch)* V

guilty [ˈgɪlti] schuldbewusst; schuldig IV

guinea pig [ˈgɪni pɪg] Meerschweinchen I

guitar [gɪˈtɑː] Gitarre I • **play the guitar** Gitarre spielen I

gun [gʌn] (Schuss-)Waffe II

guy [gaɪ] *(infml)* Typ, Kerl IV • **guys** *(pl) (AE, infml)* Leute III

gym [dʒɪm] Sporthalle, Turnhalle IV

H

had [hæd] *siehe* **have**

hair *(no pl)* [heə] Haar, Haare I

hairdresser [ˈheədresə] Friseur/in III
at the hairdresser's beim Friseur III

hairdryer [ˈheədraɪə] Föhn, Haartrockner VI 2 (34)

hairy [ˈheəri] haarig, behaart V

half [hɑːf], *pl* **halves** [hɑːvz]
1. Hälfte III
2. Halbzeit III
the first half die erste Halbzeit III

half [hɑːf]: **half an hour** eine halbe Stunde III • **half past 11** halb zwölf (11.30 / 23.30) I • **three and a half days/weeks** dreieinhalb Tage/Wochen IV

half-pipe [ˈhɑːfpaɪp] Halfpipe *(halbierte Röhre für Inlineskater)* III

half-time [ˌhɑːf ˈtaɪm] Halbzeit(pause) III

hall [hɔːl]
1. Flur, Diele I
2. Halle, Saal III
study hall Zeit zum selbstständigen Lernen in der Schule IV
town hall Rathaus VI 3 (47/180)

hallway [ˈhɔːlweɪ] *(AE)* Korridor, Gang IV

halves [hɑːvz] *pl von „half"*

hamburger [ˈhæmbɜːgə] Hamburger I

hamster [ˈhæmstə] Hamster I

hand [hænd] Hand I • **on the one hand ... on the other hand** einerseits ... andererseits VI 2 (37)

hang [hæŋ], **hung, hung** hängen; *(etwas)* aufhängen V • **hang around** rumhängen, herumlungern VI 3 (50) • **hang out** *(infml)* rumhängen, abhängen III • °**hang sth. up** etwas aufhängen

happen (to) [ˈhæpən] geschehen, passieren (mit) I

happiness [ˈhæpinəs] Glück IV

happy [ˈhæpi] glücklich, froh I
Happy birthday. Herzlichen Glückwunsch zum Geburtstag. I
happy ending Happyend II • **be happy to do sth.** *(fml)* gern bereit sein, etwas zu tun V

harbour [ˈhɑːbə] Hafen II

hard [hɑːd]
1. hart; schwer, schwierig II
2. *(adv)* heftig, kräftig IV
work hard hart arbeiten II

hard-working [ˌhɑːd ˈwɜːkɪŋ] fleißig, tüchtig, hart arbeitend V

harvest [ˈhɑːvɪst] Ernte IV

hat [hæt] Hut II

hate [heɪt] hassen, gar nicht mögen I

have [həv, hæv], **had, had** haben, besitzen II • **have a baby** ein Baby/Kind bekommen II • **have a bath** baden, ein Bad nehmen II • **have a cold** erkältet sein, eine Erkältung haben II • **have a crush on sb.** in jn. verknallt sein III • **Have a good time!** Viel Spaß! / Viel Vergnügen! III • **have a party** eine Party feiern/veranstalten II • **have a sauna** in die Sauna gehen II • **have a shower** (sich) duschen

I • **have a sore throat** Halsschmerzen haben II • **have a temperature** Fieber haben II • **have breakfast** frühstücken II • **have dinner** Abendbrot essen I • **have ... for breakfast** ... zum Frühstück essen/trinken I • **have fun** Spaß haben, sich amüsieren I • **Have fun!** Viel Spaß! I • **have to do** tun müssen I • **Have your say!** *etwa:* Übe dein Mitspracherecht aus! / Rede mit! VI 3 (46) • **Can I have a word with you?** Kann ich mal kurz mit dir reden? VI 3 (55)

have got: I've got ... [aɪv ˈgɒt] Ich habe ... I • **I haven't got a chair.** [ˈhævnt gɒt] Ich habe keinen Stuhl. I

he [hiː] er I

head [hed] Kopf I • °**head of state** Staatsoberhaupt • °**running head** Leitwort *(am Kopf einer Wörterbuchseite)*

headache [ˈhedeɪk] Kopfschmerzen II

heading [ˈhedɪŋ] Überschrift IV

headless [ˈhedləs] kopflos IV

headline [ˈhedlaɪn] Schlagzeile IV

headphones *(pl)* [ˈhedfəʊnz] Kopfhörer III

head teacher [ˌhed ˈtiːtʃə] Schulleiter/in III

health [helθ] Gesundheit; Gesundheitslehre IV

healthy [ˈhelθi] gesund II

hear [hɪə], **heard, heard** hören I

heard [hɜːd] *siehe* **hear**

heart [hɑːt] Herz II

heat [hiːt] heizen, erhitzen VI 2 (28/174)

heat [hiːt] Hitze, Wärme VI 2 (28/174)

heating [ˈhiːtɪŋ] Heizung VI 2 (28)

heaven [ˈhevn] Himmel *(im religiösen Sinn)* IV

heavy [ˈhevi]
1. schwer *(von Gewicht)* VI 2 (34)
2. heftig, stark VI 2 (34)

hedgehog [ˈhedʒhɒg] Igel II

held [held] *siehe* **hold**

helicopter [ˈhelɪkɒptə] Hubschrauber, Helikopter II

Hello. [həˈləʊ] Hallo. / Guten Tag. I

helmet [ˈhelmɪt] Helm II

help [help] helfen I • **Can I help you?** Kann ich Ihnen helfen? / Was kann ich für Sie tun? *(im Geschäft)* I

help [help] Hilfe I

helpful [ˈhelpfl] hilfreich, nützlich IV; hilfsbereit V

helpless [ˈhelpləs] hilflos IV

her [hə, hɜː]
1. ihr, ihre I
2. sie; ihr I
here [hɪə]
1. hier I
2. hierher I
Here you are. Bitte sehr. / Hier bitte. I
hero ['hɪərəʊ], *pl* **heroes** ['hɪərəʊz] Held, Heldin II
hers [hɜːz] ihrer, ihre, ihrs II
herself [hə'self, hɜː'self] sich (selbst) III
Hi! [haɪ] Hallo! I • **Say hi to Dilip for me.** Grüß Dilip von mir. I
hid [hɪd] *siehe* **hide**
hidden ['hɪdn] *siehe* **hide**
hide [haɪd], **hid, hidden** sich verstecken; (etwas) verstecken I
high [haɪ] hoch III
high school ['haɪ skuːl] (USA) Schule für 14- bis 18-Jährige IV
highlight ['haɪlaɪt] Höhepunkt V
°**highlighted** ['haɪlaɪtɪd] hervorgehoben, markiert (mit Textmarker)
highway ['haɪweɪ] (USA) Fernstraße (oft mit vier oder mehr Spuren) IV
hijacker ['haɪdʒækə] (Flugzeug-)Entführer IV
hike [haɪk] wandern IV
hike [haɪk] Wanderung, Marsch IV
hill [hɪl] Hügel II
hilly ['hɪli] hügelig III
him [hɪm] ihn; ihm I
himself [hɪm'self] sich (selbst) III
Hindu ['hɪnduː] Hindu V; Hindu-, hinduistisch VI 1 (13/173)
▶ S.173 Religions
hip hop ['hɪp hɒp] Hiphop III
hippo ['hɪpəʊ] Flusspferd II
his [hɪz]
1. sein, seine I
2. seiner, seine, seins II
Hispanic (n; adj) [hɪ'spænɪk] US-amerikanischer Ausdruck für Menschen mit Wurzeln in spanischsprachigen Ländern, besonders in Mittelamerika IV
historical [hɪ'stɒrɪkl] historisch, alt VI 1 (14)
history ['hɪstri] Geschichte I
hit (-tt-) [hɪt], **hit, hit** schlagen I
hit the windscreen gegen/auf die Windschutzscheibe schlagen/ prallen IV
hit [hɪt] Hit III
hobby ['hɒbi] Hobby I
hockey ['hɒki] Hockey I
hockey pitch ['hɒki pɪtʃ] Hockeyplatz, Hockeyfeld II
hockey shoes ['hɒki ʃuːz] Hockeyschuhe I

hold [həʊld], **held, held**
1. halten II
2. abhalten, veranstalten VI 3 (50)
hold on (to sth.) sich festhalten (an etwas) V • **hold sb. up** jn. aufhalten VI 2 (34) • °**hold sth. up** etwas hochhalten
hole [həʊl] Loch I
holiday ['hɒlədeɪ]
1. Feiertag IV
2. holiday(s) Ferien I
be on holiday in Urlaub sein; Ferien haben/machen II • **go on holiday** in Urlaub fahren II
home [həʊm] Heim, Zuhause I
at home daheim, zu Hause I • **come home** nach Hause kommen I • **get home** nach Hause kommen I • **go home** nach Hause gehen I • **leave home** von zu Hause ausziehen VI 3 (48)
homeless ['həʊmləs] obdachlos IV
home-made [ˌhəʊm'meɪd] hausgemacht, selbstgemacht V
hometown ['həʊmtaʊn] Heimatstadt IV
homework (no pl) ['həʊmwɜːk] Hausaufgabe(n) I • **do homework** die Hausaufgabe(n) machen I • **What's for homework?** Was haben wir als Hausaufgabe auf? I
°**homophobia** [ˌhɒmə'fəʊbiə] Homophobie (ablehnende, feindselige Haltung gegenüber Homosexuellen)
honest ['ɒnɪst] ehrlich V • **I honestly think ...** Ich glaube, ehrlich gesagt, dass ... V
°**honey bee** ['hʌnibiː] Honigbiene
Hooray! [hu'reɪ] Hurra! II
hope [həʊp] hoffen II
hope [həʊp] Hoffnung III
hopeless ['həʊpləs] hoffnungslos, verzweifelt IV
horrible ['hɒrəbl] scheußlich, grauenhaft II
horror film ['hɒrə fɪlm] Horrorfilm VI 1 (14)
horse [hɔːs] Pferd I
hospital ['hɒspɪtl] Krankenhaus II
host [həʊst] (Radio-, Fernseh-) Moderator/in IV
hostel ['hɒstl] Herberge, Wohnheim III
hostess ['həʊstəs] Gastgeberin (in USA auch: Frau, die im Restaurant die Gäste empfängt und an ihren Platz führt) IV
hot [hɒt] heiß I • **hot-water bottle** Wärmflasche II
hotel [həʊ'tel] Hotel II
hotline ['hɒtlaɪn] Hotline II

hour ['aʊə] Stunde II • **a 14-hour flight** ein 14-stündiger Flug, ein 14-Stunden-Flug III • **a 24-hour supermarket** ein Supermarkt, der 24 Stunden geöffnet ist III • **half an hour** eine halbe Stunde III **opening hours** (pl) Öffnungszeiten IV • **work long hours** lange arbeiten V
house [haʊs] Haus I • **at the Shaws' house** im Haus der Shaws/ bei den Shaws zu Hause I
household ['haʊshəʊld] Haushalt; Haushalts- VI 2 (32)
how [haʊ] wie I • **How about ...?** Wie wär's mit ...? III • **How am I doing?** Wie komme ich voran? (Wie sind meine Fortschritte?) III **How are you?** Wie geht es dir/ Ihnen/euch? II • **How do you feel about ...?** Was hältst du von ...? III **How do you know ...?** Woher weißt/kennst du ...? I • **How long ...?** Seit wann ...? / Wie lange ...? IV • **how many?** wie viele? I **how much?** wie viel? I • **How much is ...?** Was kostet ...? / Wie viel kostet ...? I • **how to do sth.** wie man etwas tut / tun kann / tun soll IV
however [haʊ'evə] jedoch, allerdings V
huge [hjuːdʒ] riesig, sehr groß III
human ['hjuːmən] Menschen-, menschlich IV
humour ['hjuːmə] Humor VI 1 (6/171) **sense of humour** (Sinn für) Humor VI 1 (6)
hundred ['hʌndrəd] hundert I
hung [hʌŋ] *siehe* **hang**
hungry ['hʌŋgri] hungrig I • **be hungry** Hunger haben, hungrig sein I
hunt [hʌnt] jagen III
hunt [hʌnt] Jagd III
hunter ['hʌntə] Jäger/in III
hurry ['hʌri] eilen; sich beeilen II **hurry up** sich beeilen I
hurry ['hʌri]: **be in a hurry** in Eile sein, es eilig haben I
hurt [hɜːt], **hurt, hurt** wehtun; verletzen I
hurt [hɜːt] verletzt II
husband ['hʌzbənd] Ehemann II
hutch [hʌtʃ] (Kaninchen-)Stall I

I

I [aɪ] ich I • **I'm** [aɪm] ich bin I **I'm from ...** Ich komme aus ... / Ich bin aus ... I • **I'm ... years old.** Ich

bin ... Jahre alt. I • **I'm sorry.**
Entschuldigung. / Tut mir leid. I
ice [aɪs] Eis II
ice cream [ˌaɪs ˈkriːm] (Speise-)Eis I
ice hockey [ˈaɪs hɒki] Eishockey III
ice rink [ˈaɪs rɪŋk] Schlittschuhbahn
II
icy [ˈaɪsi] eisig; vereist V
idea [aɪˈdɪə] Idee, Einfall I
ideal [aɪˈdiːəl] Ideal, Idealvorstel-
lung V
if [ɪf]
 1. falls, wenn II
 2. ob II
 as if als ob IV • **even if** selbst
 wenn; obwohl IV • **if so** wenn ja;
 wenn dem so ist VI 1 (15)
ill [ɪl] krank II
illegal [ɪˈliːgl] illegal, ungesetzlich
IV
illness [ˈɪlnəs] Krankheit IV
°**imaginary** [ɪˈmædʒɪnəri] imaginär
 (nur in der Vorstellung vorhanden)
 °**imaginary journey** Fantasiereise
imagination [ɪˌmædʒɪˈneɪʃn] Fanta-
sie, Vorstellung(skraft) IV
imagine sth. [ɪˈmædʒɪn] sich etwas
vorstellen III
immediately [ɪˈmiːdiətli] sofort IV
immigrant [ˈɪmɪgrənt] Einwande-
rer/Einwanderin IV
immigrate (to) [ˈɪmɪgreɪt] einwan-
dern, immigrieren (in) VI 3 (54)
immigration (to) [ˌɪmɪˈgreɪʃn] Ein-
wanderung, Immigration (in, nach)
VI 3 (54)
impatient [ɪmˈpeɪʃnt] ungeduldig
VI 1 (13/174)
important [ɪmˈpɔːtnt] wichtig II
 important to sb. wichtig für jn. III
impossible [ɪmˈpɒsəbl] unmöglich
II
impress [ɪmˈpres] beeindrucken V
impressed [ɪmˈprest] beeindruckt
IV
°**impression** [ɪmˈpreʃn] Eindruck V
impressive [ɪmˈpresɪv] beeindruckend V
improve [ɪmˈpruːv] (sich) verbes-
sern VI 3 (49)
in [ɪn] in I • **in 1948** im Jahr 1948
II • **in a friendly/strange/different
way** auf freundliche/seltsame/an-
dere Art und Weise VI 1 (7) • **in ...
Street** in der ...straße I • **in English** auf Englisch I • **in fact** tatsächlich; in Wirklichkeit; um genau
zu sein VI 1 (12) • **in front of** vor
(räumlich) I • **in here** hier drinnen I • **in my opinion** meiner
Meinung nach IV • **in my/your
view** meiner/deiner Ansicht nach

III • **in other places** an anderen
Orten, anderswo III • °**in the
1970s** in den 70er-Jahren *(des 20.
Jahrhunderts)* • **in the afternoon**
nachmittags, am Nachmittag I •
in the country auf dem Land II
in the end schließlich, zum
Schluss III • **in the evening**
abends, am Abend I • **in the field**
auf dem Feld II • **in the morning**
am Morgen, morgens I • **in the
photo** auf dem Foto I • **in the
picture** auf dem Bild I • **in the
sky** am Himmel II • **in there** dort
drinnen I • **in the world** auf der
Welt V • **in time** rechtzeitig II
°**inch** [ɪntʃ] Zoll, Inch (= 2,54 cm)
include [ɪnˈkluːd] (mit) einschlie-
ßen, enthalten V
°**incorrect** [ˌɪnkəˈrekt] falsch
independence [ˌɪndɪˈpendəns] Un-
abhängigkeit V
independent [ˌɪndɪˈpendənt] unab-
hängig V
Indian [ˈɪndiən]
 1. Indianer/in; indianisch IV
 2. Inder/in; indisch V
indirect question [ˌɪndərekt
ˈkwestʃən] indirekte Frage II
°**individual** [ˌɪndɪˈvɪdʒuəl]
einzelne(r, s), individuelle(r, s)
indoors [ɪnˈdɔːz]
 1. drinnen, im Haus V
 2. nach drinnen V
industrial [ɪnˈdʌstriəl] industriell,
Industrie- IV
industry [ˈɪndəstri] Industrie IV
infectious [ɪnˈfekʃəs] ansteckend
VI 2 (32)
infinitive [ɪnˈfɪnətɪv] Infinitiv
(Grundform des Verbs) I
inform [ɪnˈfɔːm] informieren
VI 3 (54)
informal [ɪnˈfɔːml] informell;
umgangssprachlich V
information (about/on) *(no pl)*
[ˌɪnfəˈmeɪʃn] Information(en)
(über) I
insect [ˈɪnsekt] Insekt IV
inside [ˌɪnˈsaɪd]
 1. innen (drin), drinnen I
 2. nach drinnen II
 3. inside the car ins Auto (hinein),
 ins Innere des Autos II
inside [ˌɪnˈsaɪd]: **the inside** das
Innere, die Innenseite V
°**inside cover** [ˌɪnsaɪd ˈkʌvə] Umschlaginnenseite
install [ɪnˈstɔːl] installieren, ein-
richten II
installation [ˌɪnstəˈleɪʃn] Installation, Einrichtung II

instant messages *(pl)* [ˌɪnstənt
ˈmesɪdʒɪz] *Nachrichten, die man im
Internet austauscht (in Echtzeit)* III
instead *(adv)* [ɪnˈsted] stattdessen,
dafür V
instead of *(prep)* [ɪnˈsted_əv] statt,
anstatt, anstelle von V
institution [ˌɪnstɪˈtjuːʃn] Institution,
Einrichtung V
instructions *(pl)* [ɪnˈstrʌkʃnz]
(Gebrauchs-)Anweisung(en),
Anleitung(en) II
instructor [ɪnˈstrʌktə] Ausbilder/in
V
instrument [ˈɪnstrəmənt] Instrument II
insulation [ˌɪnsjuˈleɪʃn] Isolierung,
Wärmedämmung VI 2 (28)
intelligence [ɪnˈtelɪdʒəns] Intelli-
genz VI 3 (54)
intelligent [ɪnˈtelɪdʒənt] intelligent,
klug VI 1 (13)
interactive [ˌɪntərˈæktɪv] interaktiv
IV
interest (in) [ˈɪntrəst] Interesse (an)
IV
°**interest sb.** [ˈɪntrəst] jn. interessie-
ren
interested [ˈɪntrəstɪd]: **be interested
(in)** interessiert sein (an), sich inte-
ressieren (für) III
interesting [ˈɪntrəstɪŋ] interessant I
international [ˌɪntəˈnæʃnəl] international III
internet [ˈɪntənet] Internet I
interrupt [ˌɪntəˈrʌpt] unterbrechen
IV
interview [ˈɪntəvjuː] interviewen,
befragen II
interview [ˈɪntəvjuː] Interview II
 (job) interview Vorstellungsgespräch V
into [ˈɪntə, ˈɪntʊ] in ... (hinein) I
 run into sth./sb. gegen etwas
 fahren / jn. anfahren IV
intolerant [ɪnˈtɒlərənt] intolerant III
introduce sb. to sb. [ˌɪntrəˈdjuːs] jn.
jm. vorstellen; jn. mit jm. bekannt-
machen V • **introduce sth.** etwas
einführen *(Thema, Mode, Methode)*
V
introduction [ˌɪntrəˈdʌkʃn] Einführung, Einleitung III
invent [ɪnˈvent] erfinden VI 2 (31/176)
invention [ɪnˈvenʃn] Erfindung
VI 2 (30)
invitation (to) [ˌɪnvɪˈteɪʃn] Ein-
ladung (zu) I
invite (to) [ɪnˈvaɪt] einladen (zu) I
involved [ɪnˈvɒlvd]: **get involved (in)**
sich engagieren (für, bei); sich beteiligen (an) IV

irregular [ɪˈregjələ] unregelmäßig I
is [ɪz] ist I
island [ˈaɪlənd] Insel II
issue [ˈɪʃuː] Thema, (Streit-)Frage
VI 3 (46)
it [ɪt] er/sie/es I • **It's £1.** Er/Sie/
Es kostet 1 Pfund. I • **It says
here: ...** Hier steht: ... / Es heißt
hier: ... II
IT [ˌaɪ ˈtiː], **information technology**
[tekˈnɒlədʒi] IT, Informationstech-
nologie II
°**italics** [ɪˈtælɪks]: **in italics** kursiv; in
Kursivschrift
its [ɪts] sein/seine; ihr/ihre I
itself [ɪtˈself] sich (selbst) III

J

jacket [ˈdʒækɪt] Jacke, Jackett II
jail [dʒeɪl] Gefängnis IV
January [ˈdʒænjuəri] Januar I
jazz [dʒæz] Jazz I
jealous (of) [ˈdʒeləs] neidisch (auf);
eifersüchtig (auf) III
jeans (pl) [dʒiːnz] Jeans I
Jew [dʒuː] Jude/Jüdin VI 1 (13/173)
► S.173 Religions
jewellery (no pl) [ˈdʒuːəlri] Schmuck
II
Jewish [ˈdʒuːɪʃ] jüdisch IV
► S.173 Religions
job [dʒɒb] Aufgabe, Job I • **do jobs**
Arbeiten/Aufträge erledigen V
job interview Vorstellungsgespräch V
jobless [ˈdʒɒbləs] arbeitslos IV
join sb. [dʒɔɪn] sich jm. anschlie-
ßen; bei jm. mitmachen II • °**join
up (with)** sich zusammentun (mit) V
joke [dʒəʊk] Witz I
joke [dʒəʊk] scherzen, Witze
machen II
journalist [ˈdʒɜːnəlɪst] Journalist/in
IV
journey [ˈdʒɜːni] Reise, Fahrt II
judge (by) [dʒʌdʒ] beurteilen, einschätzen (nach) IV
judo [ˈdʒuːdəʊ] Judo I • **do judo**
Judo machen I
jug [dʒʌg] Krug I • **a jug of milk**
ein Krug Milch I
juice [dʒuːs] Saft I
juicy [ˈdʒuːsi] saftig V
July [dʒuˈlaɪ] Juli I
°**jumble** [ˈdʒʌmbl] gebrauchte
Sachen, Trödel
jumble sale [ˈdʒʌmbl seɪl] Wohl-
tätigkeitsbasar I
jump [dʒʌmp] springen II
June [dʒuːn] Juni I

junior [ˈdʒuːniə] Junioren-, Jugend-
I
just [dʒʌst]
1. (einfach) nur, bloß I
2. einfach III • **I just can't find
them.** Ich kann sie einfach nicht
finden. III
3. gerade (eben), soeben II • **just
then** genau in dem Moment;
gerade dann II
4. just like you genau wie du II
just as ... as genauso ... wie V

K

kangaroo [ˌkæŋgəˈruː] Känguru II
keep [kiːp], **kept, kept** (be)halten;
aufbewahren III • **keep in touch**
in Verbindung bleiben, Kontakt
halten III • **keep (on) doing sth.**
etwas weiter tun; etwas immer
wieder tun VI 2 (35/178) • **keep sb.
away (from)** jn. fernhalten (von)
VI 3 (49) • **keep sth. going** etwas in
Gang halten, etwas aufrechterhal-
ten VI 1 (11) • **keep sth. warm/cool/
open/...** etwas warm/kühl/offen/
... halten II • °**keep a diary** ein
Tagebuch führen
► S.178 (to) keep
kept [kept] siehe **keep**
ketchup [ˈketʃəp] Ketschup V
kettle [ˈketl] (Wasser-)Kessel, Was-
serkocher VI 2 (28)
key [kiː] Schlüssel I • **key word**
Stichwort, Schlüsselwort I
keyboard [ˈkiːbɔːd] Keyboard (elektronisches Tasteninstrument) III;
Tastatur VI 2 (30)
key card [ˈkiː kɑːd] Schlüsselkarte
V
kick [kɪk] treten IV
kid [kɪd] Kind, Jugendliche(r) I
kill [kɪl] töten I
kilogram (kg) [ˈkɪləgræm], **kilo**
[ˈkiːləʊ] Kilogramm, Kilo III
a 90-kilogram bear ein 90 Kilogramm schwerer Bär III
kilometre (km) [ˈkɪləmiːtə] Kilometer III • **a ten-kilometre walk**
eine Zehn-Kilometer-Wanderung
III
kind [kaɪnd] freundlich, nett VI 1 (13)
kind (of) [kaɪnd] Art III • **What
kind of car ...?** Was für ein Auto ...?
III
kind of scary [kaɪnd] (infml) irgendwie unheimlich III
kindergarten [ˈkɪndəgɑːtn] Kindergarten; (USA) Vorschule (für 5- bis
6-Jährige) IV

king [kɪŋ] König I
kiss [kɪs] küssen IV
kiss [kɪs] Kuss IV
kitchen [ˈkɪtʃən] Küche I
kite [kaɪt] Drachen I
knee [niː] Knie I
knew [njuː] siehe **know**
knife [naɪf], pl **knives** [naɪvz]
Messer III
knock (on) [nɒk] (an)klopfen (an) I
know [nəʊ], **knew, known**
1. wissen I
2. kennen I
know about sth. von etwas wissen; über etwas Bescheid wissen II
get to know sb. jn. kennenlernen
IV • **How do you know ...?** Woher
weißt du ...? / Woher kennst du ...?
I • **I don't know.** Ich weiß es nicht.
I • **..., you know.** ..., wissen Sie. / ...,
weißt du. I • **You know what,
Sophie?** Weißt du was, Sophie? I
known [nəʊn] bekannt IV
siehe **know**
koala [kəʊˈɑːlə] Koala V
kph (kilometres per hour) [ˌkeɪ piː
ˈeɪtʃ] km/h (Stundenkilometer,
Kilometer pro Stunde) III

L

label [ˈleɪbl] Marke, Label; Etikett V
°**label** [ˈleɪbl] beschriften, etiket-
tieren
°**ladder** [ˈlædə] (die) Leiter
laid [leɪd] siehe **lay**
lake [leɪk] (Binnen-)See II
lamb [læm] Lamm III
lamp [læmp] Lampe I
land [lænd] Land, Grund und Boden
II • **on land** auf dem Land III
land [lænd] landen II
°**landfill** [ˈlændfɪl] Mülldeponie
lane [leɪn] Gasse, Weg III
language [ˈlæŋgwɪdʒ] Sprache I
laptop [ˈlæptɒp] Laptop V
large [lɑːdʒ] groß II
lasagne [ləˈzænjə] Lasagne I
last [lɑːst] letzte(r, s) I • **the last
day** der letzte Tag I • **last name**
Nachname V • **at last** endlich,
schließlich I
last [lɑːst] halten (fortdauern, von
Bestand sein) VI 1 (9) • **last (for)**
dauern IV
late [leɪt] spät; zu spät I • **be late**
zu spät sein/kommen I • **Sorry,
I'm late.** Entschuldigung, dass ich
zu spät bin/komme. I
later [ˈleɪtə] später I
latest [ˈleɪtɪst] neueste(r, s) III

laugh [lɑːf] lachen I • **laugh at sb.** jn. auslachen, über jn. lachen III **laugh out loud** laut lachen II

laughable ['lɑːfəbl] lächerlich, lachhaft IV

laughter ['lɑːftə] Gelächter II

law [lɔː]
1. Gesetz IV
2. Jura, Rechtswissenschaften VI 1 (12)

lay the table [leɪ], **laid, laid** den Tisch decken I

layout ['leɪaʊt] Layout, Anordnung, Aufbau V

lazy ['leɪzi] faul VI 1 (10)

lead (to sth.) [liːd], **led, led** (zu etwas) führen VI 2 (30)

leader ['liːdə] (An-)Führer/in, Leiter/in III

leaf [liːf], pl **leaves** [liːvz] Blatt (an Pflanzen) V

lean [liːn] sich beugen, sich lehnen IV • **lean over** sich herüberbeugen, -lehnen V

learn [lɜːn] lernen I • **learn sth. about sth.** etwas über etwas erfahren, etwas über etwas herausfinden II

least [liːst] am wenigsten III • **at least** zumindest, wenigstens I

leather ['leðə] Leder III

leave [liːv], **left, left**
1. (weg)gehen; abfahren II
2. verlassen II
3. zurücklassen II
leave home von zu Hause ausziehen VI 3 (48) • **leave school** von der Schule abgehen V • **leave sb. alone** jn. in Ruhe lassen IV **leave sth. out** etwas weglassen/ auslassen IV

leaves [liːvz] pl von „leaf"

led [led] siehe **lead**

left [left] siehe **leave**

left [left] linke(r, s) II • **look left** nach links schauen II • **on the left** links, auf der linken Seite I • **turn left** (nach) links abbiegen II

leg [leg] Bein I

legal ['liːgl] legal IV

legend ['ledʒənd] Legende, Sage V

leisure centre ['leʒə sentə] Freizeitzentrum, -park II

lemonade [ˌleməˈneɪd] Limonade I

lend sb. sth. [lend], **lent, lent** jm. etwas leihen, etwas an jn. verleihen V

lent [lent] siehe **lend**

leotard ['liːətɑːd] Gymnastikanzug; Turnanzug III

less [les] weniger IV

lesson ['lesn] (Unterrichts-)Stunde I • **lessons** (pl) ['lesnz] Unterricht I

let (-tt-) [let], **let, let** lassen II **Let's ...** Lass uns ... / Lasst uns ... I **Let's go.** Auf geht's! I • **Let's look at the list.** Sehen wir uns die Liste an. / Lasst uns die Liste ansehen. I **let sb. do sth.** jm. erlauben, etwas zu tun; zulassen, dass jd. etwas tut III

letter ['letə]
1. Buchstabe I
2. letter (to) Brief (an) II • **letter of application** Bewerbungsschreiben V

lettuce ['letɪs] (Kopf-)Salat II

level ['levl] (Lern-)Stand, Niveau, Grad V

library ['laɪbrəri] Bibliothek, Bücherei I

license plate ['laɪsns pleɪt] (AE) Nummernschild V

lie [laɪ] Lüge VI 3 (47/179) • **tell lies** lügen VI 3 (47/179)

life [laɪf], pl **lives** [laɪvz] Leben I

lifesaver ['laɪfseɪvə] Rettungsschwimmer/in V

lifestyle ['laɪfstaɪl] Lebensstil V

lifetime ['laɪftaɪm] Leben, Lebensdauer V

lift [lɪft] Fahrstuhl, Aufzug II

light [laɪt] Licht III

light [laɪt], **lit, lit** anzünden IV

light bulb ['laɪt bʌlb] Glühbirne VI 2 (36)

like [laɪk] wie I • **just like you** genau wie du II • **What was the weather like?** Wie war das Wetter? II • **like that / like this** so IV

like [laɪk] mögen, gernhaben I **like sth. better** etwas lieber mögen II • **like sth. best** etwas am liebsten mögen III • **I like swimming/dancing/...** Ich schwimme/ tanze/... gern. I • **I'd like ... (= I would like ...)** Ich hätte gern ... / Ich möchte gern ... I • **I'd like to go (= I would like to go)** Ich würde gern gehen / Ich möchte gehen I **I wouldn't like to go** Ich würde nicht gern gehen / Ich möchte nicht gehen I • **Would you like ...?** Möchtest du ...? / Möchten Sie ...? I **°Say what you like about ...** Sag, was du an ... magst

likeable ['laɪkəbl] sympathisch, liebenswert IV

likely ['laɪkli] wahrscheinlich VI 3 (47) • **be likely to be/do sth.** wahrscheinlich etwas sein/tun VI 3 (47/180)

line [laɪn]
1. Zeile II
2. (U-Bahn-)Linie III
3. Leitung (Telefon) IV
4. (AE) Schlange, Reihe (wartender Menschen) IV

link [lɪŋk] verbinden, verknüpfen I

link [lɪŋk] Verbindung, Verknüpfung III

linking word ['lɪŋkɪŋ wɜːd] Bindewort II

lion ['laɪən] Löwe II

lip [lɪp] Lippe VI 1 (10)

list [lɪst] Liste I

list [lɪst] auflisten, aufzählen II

listen (to) ['lɪsn] zuhören; sich etwas anhören I • **listen for sth.** auf etwas horchen, achten III

listener ['lɪsnə] Zuhörer/in II

lit [lɪt] siehe **light**

little ['lɪtl]
1. klein I
2. wenig IV

live [lɪv] leben, wohnen I

live music ['laɪv ˌmjuːzɪk] Livemusik II

lives [laɪvz] pl von „life"

living ['lɪvɪŋ] lebend VI 2 (32)

living room ['lɪvɪŋ ruːm] Wohnzimmer I

lobby ['lɒbi] Eingangshalle IV

local ['ləʊkl] Lokal-, örtlich; am/vom Ort IV

location [ləʊ'keɪʃn] (Einsatz-)Ort, Platz III

lock [lɒk] Schleuse III

lock up [ˌlɒk_'ʌp] abschließen II

lodge [lɒdʒ] Landhaus IV

logical ['lɒdʒɪkl] logisch V

logo ['ləʊgəʊ], pl **logos** Logo, Markenzeichen III

lonely ['ləʊnli] einsam III

long [lɒŋ] lang I • **a long time** lange III • **as long as** (conj) solange, sofern IV • **How long ...?** Seit wann ...? / Wie lange ...? IV **work long hours** lange arbeiten V

look [lʊk]
1. schauen, gucken I
2. look different/great/old anders/toll/alt aussehen I **look after sth./sb.** auf etwas/jn. aufpassen; sich um etwas/jn. kümmern II • **look around** sich umsehen III • **look at** ansehen, anschauen I • **look for** suchen II **look forward to sth.** sich auf etwas freuen IV • **look left/right** nach links/rechts schauen II **look round** sich umsehen I • **look sth. up** etwas nachschlagen III

look up (from) hochsehen, aufschauen (von) II
look [lʊk]
1. (Gesichts-)Ausdruck V
2. Blick V
take a look (at) einen Blick werfen (auf) V
lose [luːz], **lost, lost** verlieren II
lost [lɒst] *siehe* **lose**
lot [lɒt]: **a lot (of)** eine Menge, viel, viele II • **Thanks a lot!** Vielen Dank! I • **He likes her a lot.** Er mag sie sehr. I • **lots more** viel mehr I • **lots of …** eine Menge …, viele …, viel … I
loud [laʊd] laut I
lovable ['lʌvəbl] liebenswert VI 1 (7)
love [lʌv] lieben, sehr mögen II
I'd love to … Ich würde liebend gern … V
love [lʌv]
1. Liebe II
2. Liebes, Liebling III
fall in love (with sb.) sich verlieben (in jn.) IV • **Love …** Liebe Grüße, … *(Briefschluss)* I
lover ['lʌvə] Geliebte(r) V
low [ləʊ] niedrig VI 2 (36)
loyal (to sb.) ['lɔɪəl] loyal (gegenüber jm.) VI 1 (6)
luck [lʌk]: **Good luck (with …)!** Viel Glück (bei/mit …)! I
luckily ['lʌkɪli] zum Glück, glücklicherweise II
lucky ['lʌki]: **be lucky (with)** Glück haben (mit) II
lunch [lʌntʃ] Mittagessen I
lunch break Mittagspause I
lunchtime ['lʌntʃtaɪm] Mittagszeit IV
lyrics (pl) ['lɪrɪks] Liedtext(e), Songtext(e) III

M

machine [məˈʃiːn] Maschine, Gerät III
mad [mæd] verrückt I • **be mad about sth.** verrückt nach/auf etwas sein III
Madam ['mædəm]: **Dear Sir/Madam** Sehr geehrte Damen und Herren *(Briefbeginn)* V
made [meɪd] *siehe* **make**
magazine [ˌmægəˈziːn] Zeitschrift, Magazin I
magical ['mædʒɪkl] zauberhaft, wundervoll V
maid [meɪd] Hausangestellte, Zimmermädchen IV

mail [meɪl] schicken, senden *(per Post oder E-Mail)* I • **mail sb.** jn. anmailen II
mailbox ['meɪlbɒks] Mailbox V
main [meɪn] Haupt- III
majority [məˈdʒɒrəti] Mehrheit IV
make [meɪk], **made, made** machen; bauen I • **make a call** ein Telefongespräch führen II • **make a deal** ein Abkommen / eine Abmachung treffen III • **make a decision** eine Entscheidung fällen V • **make a difference** etwas bewirken, etwas bewegen VI 2 (36) • **make a mess** alles durcheinanderbringen, alles in Unordnung bringen I • **make a point** ein Argument vorbringen III • **make a speech** eine Rede halten IV • °**make comparisons** Vergleiche anstellen, vergleichen • **make friends (with sb.)** Freunde finden; sich anfreunden (mit jm.) V • **make money** Geld verdienen IV • °**make notes** (sich) Notizen machen • **make sb. do sth.** jn. dazu bringen, etwas zu tun V • **make sense** sinnvoll sein, einen Sinn ergeben VI 3 (49) • **make sure that …** sich vergewissern, dass …; dafür sorgen, dass … IV • **be made up (of)** zusammengesetzt sein (aus); bestehen (aus) VI 2 (29) • °**make sth. up** sich etwas ausdenken
°**What makes a game a good game?** Was macht ein Spiel zu einem guten Spiel?
make-up ['meɪkʌp] Make-up II
make-up artist ['ɑːtɪst] Maskenbildner/in V
mall [mɔːl], **shopping mall** *(großes)* Einkaufszentrum III
man [mæn], *pl* **men** [men] Mann I
manager ['mænɪdʒə] Manager/in III; Geschäftsführer/in, Leiter/in V
many ['meni] viele I • **how many?** wie viele? I
map [mæp] Landkarte, Stadtplan II
marathon ['mærəθən] Marathon IV
march [mɑːtʃ] Marsch, Demonstration IV
March [mɑːtʃ] März I
mark [mɑːk] (Schul-)Note, Zensur IV
mark sth. up [ˌmɑːkˈʌp] etwas markieren, kennzeichnen II
°**marked** [mɑːkt] markiert
market ['mɑːkɪt] Markt II
marmalade ['mɑːməleɪd] (Orangen-)Marmelade I
married (to) ['mærɪd] verheiratet (mit) I • **get married (to sb.)** (jn.) heiraten V • **married couple** Ehepaar V

°**marry** ['mæri] heiraten
mass [mæs] Messe (Gottesdienst) VI 1 (13/173)
▶ S.173 Religions
°**mass motoring** ['mæs ˌməʊtərɪŋ] Massenmotorisierung
match [mætʃ] Spiel, Wettkampf I
°**match** [mætʃ]
1. passen zu
2. zuordnen
°**Match the letters and numbers.** Ordne die Buchstaben den Zahlen zu.
match day ['mætʃ deɪ] Spieltag V
mate [meɪt] *(infml)* Freund/in, Kumpel III
material [məˈtɪəriəl] Material V
math [mæθ] *(AE)* Mathematik IV
maths [mæθs] Mathematik I
matter ['mætə]: **It doesn't matter.** Es spielt keine Rolle. / Es macht nichts (aus). VI 3 (49)
matter ['mætə]: **What's the matter?** Was ist los? / Was ist denn? II
mattress ['mætrəs] Matratze V
may [meɪ]
1. dürfen I
2. **they may be at home** sie sind vielleicht zu Hause VI 2 (30/176)
what the future may bring was die Zukunft bringen mag VI 2 (30)
▶ S.176 Möglich? Wahrscheinlich? Sicherlich?
May [meɪ] Mai I
maybe ['meɪbi] vielleicht I
mayor [meə] Bürgermeister/in IV
me [miː] mir; mich I • **Me too.** auch. I • **more than me** mehr als ich II • **That's me.** Das bin ich. I
Why me? Warum ich? I
meal [miːl] Mahlzeit, Essen III
set meal Menü III
mean [miːn] gemein VI 1 (8)
mean [miːn], **meant, meant**
1. bedeuten II
2. meinen *(sagen wollen)* II
What do you mean by …? Was meinst du mit …? IV • **I didn't mean to …** Ich wollte nicht …; Es war nicht meine Absicht, zu … VI 3 (55)
meaning ['miːnɪŋ] Bedeutung III
meant [ment] *siehe* **mean**
meat [miːt] Fleisch I
meaty ['miːti] fleischig; Fleisch-; mit viel Fleisch V
mechanic [məˈkænɪk] Mechaniker/Mechanikerin V
medal ['medl] Medaille III
media (pl) ['miːdiə] Medien III
mediation [ˌmiːdiˈeɪʃn] Vermittlung, Sprachmittlung, Mediation II

medicine ['medsn, 'medɪsn] Medizin, Arznei VI 2 (32)

medium ['miːdiəm] mittel(groß) II

meet [miːt], **met, met**
1. treffen; kennenlernen I
2. sich treffen I
Nice to meet you. Nett, dich kennenzulernen. III

meeting ['miːtɪŋ] Versammlung, Besprechung; Treffen, Begegnung IV

melt [melt] schmelzen VI 2 (35)

member (of) ['membə] Mitglied (in, von) IV • **member of parliament** Parlamentsmitglied, Abgeordnete(r) VI 3 (47/180)
▶ S.180 Politics

men [men] *pl von „man"*

mention sth. (to sb.) ['menʃn] etwas erwähnen (jm. gegenüber) VI 1 (10)

menu ['menjuː]
1. Speisekarte III
2. Menü *(Computer)* III

merry-go-round ['merigəʊraʊnd] Karussell IV

mess [mes]: **be a mess** sehr unordentlich sein; fürchterlich aussehen *(Zimmer)* II • **make a mess** alles durcheinanderbringen, alles in Unordnung bringen I

mess things up [mes] *(infml)* alles durcheinanderbringen, alles vermasseln VI 1 (9)

message ['mesɪdʒ] Nachricht III; Botschaft VI 1 (12)

met [met] *siehe* **meet**

metal ['metl] Metall V

meter ['miːtə] *(Gas-, Strom-)*Zähler VI 2 (35)

°method ['meθəd] Methode, Art und Weise

metre ['miːtə] Meter II

mice [maɪs] *pl von „mouse"*

microphone ['maɪkrəfəʊn] Mikrofon III

microwave ['maɪkrəweɪv] Mikrowelle VI 2 (28)

middle (of) ['mɪdl] Mitte I; Mittelteil II • **in the middle of nowhere** *(infml) etwa:* am Ende der Welt V

middle school ['mɪdl skuːl] *(USA)* Schule für 11- bis 14-Jährige IV

might [maɪt]: **you might need help** du könntest (vielleicht) Hilfe brauchen III
▶ S.176 Möglich? Wahrscheinlich? Sicherlich?

mild [maɪld] mild III

mile [maɪl] Meile *(= ca. 1,6 km)* II
for miles meilenweit II

milestone ['maɪlstəʊn] Meilenstein VI 2 (30)

military ['mɪlətri] militärisch, Militär- V • **military-style fashion** Mode im Militärstil V

milk [mɪlk] Milch I

million ['mɪljən] Million III

millionaire [ˌmɪljə'neə] Millionär/in IV

mime [maɪm] pantomimisch darstellen, vorspielen II

°mime [maɪm] Pantomime

mind [maɪnd]: **I don't mind helping/ working/…** Es macht mir nichts aus zu helfen/zu arbeiten/… V
Do you mind? Stört es Sie? V • **if you don't mind** wenn Sie nichts dagegen haben V • **Mind your own business.** Das geht dich nichts an! / Kümmere dich um deine eigenen Angelegenheiten! II • **Never mind.** *etwa:* Nicht so wichtig. / Ist (doch) egal. / Das willst du gar nicht wissen. IV

mind map ['maɪnd mæp] Mindmap („Gedankenkarte", „Wissensnetz") I

mine [maɪn] meiner, meine, meins II

°mine [maɪn] abbauen, fördern *(Kohle usw.)*

°mine [maɪn] Mine, Bergwerk

mini- ['mɪni] Mini- II

minimum ['mɪnɪməm] Minimum V

minister ['mɪnɪstə]
1. Pastor/in, Pfarrer/in IV
2. prime minister [ˌpraɪm 'mɪnɪstə] Premierminister/in, Ministerpräsident/in VI 3 (47/180)
▶ S.173 Religions
▶ S.180 Politics

minority [maɪ'nɒrəti] Minderheit IV

mints *(pl)* [mɪnts] Pfefferminzbonbons I

minus ['maɪnəs] minus III

minute ['mɪnɪt] Minute I • **Wait a minute.** Warte mal! / Moment mal! II

mirror ['mɪrə] Spiegel II

miss [mɪs]
1. vermissen II
2. verpassen II
3. Miss a turn. Einmal aussetzen. II

Miss White [mɪs] Frau White *(unverheiratet)* I

missing ['mɪsɪŋ]: **be missing** fehlen II

mistake [mɪ'steɪk] Fehler I

mix [mɪks] mischen, mixen III
°mix up durcheinanderbringen
°be mixed up durcheinander/ in der falschen Reihenfolge sein

mix [mɪks] Mix, Mischung III

mixed-race gemischtrassische(r, s) V

mixture ['mɪkstʃə] Mischung III

mobile ['məʊbaɪl] mobil, beweglich V

°mobile ['məʊbaɪl] Mobile

mobile (phone) ['məʊbaɪl] Mobiltelefon, Handy I

mobility [məʊ'bɪləti] Mobilität, Beweglichkeit VI 2 (30)

model ['mɒdl] Modell*(-flugzeug, -schiff usw.)* I; (Foto-)Modell II

modelling ['mɒdəlɪŋ] Arbeit als (Foto-)Modell V

moderator ['mɒdəreɪtə] Vermittler/in, Moderator/in VI 3 (51)

modern ['mɒdən] modern III

mole [məʊl] Maulwurf II

mom [mɒm, *AE:* mɑːm] *(AE)* Mama, Mutti; Mutter III

moment ['məʊmənt] Moment, Augenblick II • **at the moment** im Moment, gerade II

Monday ['mʌndeɪ, 'mʌndi] Montag I • **Monday morning** Montagmorgen I

money ['mʌni] Geld I

monitor ['mɒnɪtə] Bildschirm, Monitor III

monkey ['mʌŋki] Affe II

monster ['mɒnstə] Monster, Ungeheuer III

month [mʌnθ] Monat I

monument ['mɒnjumənt] Denkmal, Monument IV

moon [muːn] Mond II

moped ['məʊped] Moped V

more [mɔː] mehr I • **lots more** viel mehr I • **more boring (than)** langweiliger (als) II • **more quickly (than)** schneller (als) II • **more than** mehr als II • **more than me** mehr als ich II • **no more music** keine Musik mehr I • **not (…) any more** nicht mehr II • **once more** noch einmal III • **one more** noch ein(e), ein(e) weitere(r, s) I

morning ['mɔːnɪŋ] Morgen, Vormittag I • **in the morning** morgens, am Morgen I • **Monday morning** Montagmorgen I • **on Friday morning** freitagmorgens, am Freitagmorgen I

mosque [mɒsk] Moschee III
▶ S.173 Religions

mosquito [mə'skiːtəʊ] Moskito, Stechmücke VI 3 (49)

most [məʊst] (der/die/das) meiste …; am meisten II • **most people** die meisten Leute I • **(the) most boring** der/die/das langweiligste …; am langweiligsten II

mostly ['məʊstli] hauptsächlich, überwiegend V
motel [məʊ'tel] Motel IV
mother ['mʌðə] Mutter I
motorbike ['məʊtəbaɪk] Motorrad V
motorway ['məʊtəweɪ] Autobahn V
mountain ['maʊntən] Berg II
mouse [maʊs], *pl* **mice** [maɪs] Maus I
mouth [maʊθ] Mund I
move [muːv]
1. bewegen; sich bewegen II
Move back one space. Geh ein Feld zurück. II • **Move on one space.** Geh ein Feld vor. II
2. transportieren; verrücken (*Möbel*) V
3. move (to) umziehen (nach, in) II
move in einziehen II • **move out** ausziehen II
movement ['muːvmənt] Bewegung II
movie ['muːvi] Film III
MP3 player [ˌempiː'θriː ˌpleɪə] MP3-Spieler I
Mr ... ['mɪstə] Herr ... I
Mrs ... ['mɪsɪz] Frau ... I
Ms ... [mɪz, məz] Frau ... II
much [mʌtʃ] viel I • **how much?** wie viel? I • **How much is/are ...?** Was kostet/kosten ...? / Wie viel kostet/kosten ...? I • **like/love sth. very much** etwas sehr mögen/ sehr lieben II
muesli ['mjuːzli] Müsli IV
mule [mjuːl] Maultier IV
multi- ['mʌlti] viel-, mehr-; multi-, Multi- III • **multi-coloured** vielfarbig, mehrfarbig IV • **multicultural** multikulturell V • **multimillionaire** Multimillionär/in IV
multiple choice [ˌmʌltɪpl 'tʃɔɪs] Multiple-Choice II
mum [mʌm] Mama, Mutti; Mutter I
murder ['mɜːdə] Mord III
murder ['mɜːdə] (er)morden III
murderer ['mɜːdərə] Mörder/in III
museum [mjuː'ziːəm] Museum I
mushroom ['mʌʃrʊm, -ruːm] Pilz III
music ['mjuːzɪk] Musik I
musical ['mjuːzɪkl] Musical I
musical instrument [ˌmjuːzɪkl 'ɪnstrəmənt] Musikinstrument III
musician [mjuː'zɪʃn] Musiker/in III
Muslim ['mʊzlɪm] Muslim/Muslima, Muslimin V; muslimisch VI 1 (13/173)
▸ S.173 Religions
must [mʌst] müssen I
▸ S.176 Möglich? Wahrscheinlich? Sicherlich?

must *(n)* [mʌst] Muss IV
mustn't do ['mʌsnt] nicht tun dürfen II
my [maɪ] mein/e I • **My name is ...** Ich heiße ... / Mein Name ist ... I **It's my turn.** Ich bin dran / an der Reihe. I
myself [maɪ'self] mir/mich (selbst) III
mystery ['mɪstri] Rätsel, Geheimnis II

N

name [neɪm] Name I • **call sb. names** jn. mit Schimpfwörtern hänseln, jm. Schimpfwörter nachrufen III • **My name is ...** Ich heiße ... / Mein Name ist ... I **What's your name?** Wie heißt du? I
name [neɪm] nennen; benennen II
nanny ['næni] Kindermädchen IV
nation ['neɪʃn] Nation IV
national ['næʃnəl] national, National- III • **National Park** Nationalpark IV
nationality [ˌnæʃə'næləti] Nationalität, Staatsangehörigkeit V
Native American [ˌneɪtɪv ə'merɪkən] amerikanische(r) Ureinwohner/in, Indianer/in IV
natural ['nætʃrəl] Natur-, natürlich IV • **natural history** Naturkunde III; Naturgeschichte IV
nature ['neɪtʃə] Natur V
near [nɪə] in der Nähe von, nahe (bei) I
nearly ['nɪəli] fast, beinahe V
neat [niːt] gepflegt II; ordentlich V **neat and tidy** schön ordentlich II
necessary ['nesəsəri] nötig, notwendig IV
need [niːd] Not; Notwendigkeit V
need [niːd] brauchen, benötigen I **need to do sth.** etwas tun müssen; etwas zu tun brauchen V
needn't do ['niːdnt] nicht tun müssen, nicht zu tun brauchen II
neighbour ['neɪbə] Nachbar/in II
neighbourhood ['neɪbəhʊd] Viertel, Gegend; Nachbarschaft V
nephew ['nefjuː, 'nevjuː] Neffe IV
nervous ['nɜːvəs] nervös, aufgeregt I
network ['netwɜːk] *(Radio-, Fernseh-)* Sendernetz IV; (Wörter-)Netz I
never ['nevə] nie, niemals I **Never mind.** *etwa:* Nicht so wichtig. / Ist (doch) egal. / Das willst du gar nicht wissen. IV

never-ending [ˌnevər'endɪŋ] endlos, unendlich I
new [njuː] neu I
news *(no pl)* [njuːz] Nachrichten II
newspaper ['njuːspeɪpə] Zeitung I
next [nekst]: **be next** der/die Nächste sein I • **next time** das nächste Mal VI 3 (102) • **the next morning/day** am nächsten Morgen/Tag I • **the next photo** das nächste Foto I • **What have we got next?** Was haben wir als Nächstes? I
next to [nekst] neben I
nice [naɪs] schön, nett I • **Nice to meet you.** Nett, dich kennenzulernen. III
niece [niːs] Nichte IV
night [naɪt] Nacht, später Abend I **at night** nachts, in der Nacht I **on Friday night** freitagnachts, Freitagnacht I
nightly ['naɪtli] (all)nächtlich, (all)abendlich VI 3 (50)
°**nightmare** ['naɪtmeə] Albtraum I
nil [nɪl] null III
no [nəʊ] nein I
no [nəʊ] kein, keine I • **no more music** keine Musik mehr I • **no one** niemand IV • **No way!** Auf keinen Fall! / Kommt nicht in Frage! II • **No worries.** *(infml)* Kein Problem! / Ist schon in Ordnung! VI 3 (55)
no-no ['nəʊ nəʊ]: **be a no-no** *(infml)* tabu sein, nicht in Frage kommen VI 2 (34)
nobody ['nəʊbədi] niemand II
nod (-dd-) [nɒd] nicken (mit) II
noise [nɔɪz] Geräusch; Lärm I
noisy ['nɔɪzi] laut, lärmend II
non-violent [ˌnɒn'vaɪələnt] gewaltlos, gewaltfrei IV
°**noon** [nuːn] Mittag, zwölf Uhr mittags
normal ['nɔːml] normal V
north [nɔːθ] Norden; nach Norden; nördlich III
northbound ['nɔːθbaʊnd] Richtung Norden III
north-east [ˌnɔːθ'iːst] Nordosten; nach Nordosten; nordöstlich III
°**northern** ['nɔːðən] Nord-, nördlich
north-west [ˌnɔːθ'west] Nordwesten; nach Nordwesten; nordwestlich III
nose [nəʊz] Nase I
not [nɒt] nicht I • **not (...) any** kein, keine I • **not (...) any more** nicht mehr II • **not (...) anybody** niemand II • **not (...) anything** nichts II • **not (...) anywhere**

nirgendwo(hin) II • **not (...) either** ['aɪðə, 'iːðə] auch nicht; auch kein VI 1 (8) • **not even** (noch) nicht einmal III • **not ... till / not ... until** erst (um); nicht vor III • **not (...) yet** noch nicht II

note [nəʊt]
1. Mitteilung, Notiz I
2. (Geld-)Schein, Banknote V
°**make notes** sich Notizen machen
take notes sich Notizen machen I

nothing ['nʌθɪŋ] nichts II

notice ['nəʊtɪs] bemerken, merken VI 1 (6)

notice ['nəʊtɪs] Mitteilung, Aushang V

notice board ['nəʊtɪs bɔːd] Anschlagtafel, „schwarzes Brett" IV

novel ['nɒvl] Roman V

November [nəʊ'vembə] November I

now [naʊ] nun, jetzt I

nowhere ['nəʊweə] nirgendwo(hin) V • **in the middle of nowhere** (infml) etwa: am Ende der Welt V

°**nuclear fusion** [ˌnjuːkliə 'fjuːʒn] Kernfusion

number ['nʌmbə] Zahl, Ziffer, Nummer I

°**numbered** ['nʌmbəd] nummeriert

number plate ['nʌmbə pleɪt] Nummernschild IV

nun [nʌn] Nonne V; VI 1 (13/173)
▶ S.173 Religions

nurse [nɜːs] Krankenpfleger/in, Krankenschwester V

nut [nʌt] Nuss III

O

o [əʊ] null I

ocean ['əʊʃn] Ozean IV

o'clock [ə'klɒk]: **eleven o'clock** elf Uhr I

October [ɒk'təʊbə] Oktober I

°**odd** [ɒd]: **What word is the odd one out?** Welches Wort passt nicht dazu? / Welches Wort gehört nicht dazu?

of [əv, ɒv] von I • **of the summer holidays** der Sommerferien I

of course [əv 'kɔːs] natürlich, selbstverständlich I

off [ɒf]: **cut sth. off** etwas abschneiden, abtrennen III • **drop sb. off** jn. absetzen (aussteigen lassen) IV **fall off** herunterfallen (von) II **get off (the train/bus)** (aus dem Zug/Bus) aussteigen I • **get sth. off the ground** etwas auf den Weg bringen; etwas auf die Beine stel-

len III • **take off** (infml) sich davonmachen, sich aus dem Staub machen IV • **take sth. off** etwas ausziehen (Kleidung) II; etwas absetzen (Hut, Helm) III • **take 10 c off** 10 Cent abziehen I • **tear sth. off** etwas abreißen IV • **turn sth. off** etwas ausschalten II

offer ['ɒfə] anbieten IV

office ['ɒfɪs] Büro III

official [ə'fɪʃl] offiziell, amtlich, Amts- V

often ['ɒfn] oft, häufig I

Oh dear! [əʊ 'dɪə] Oje! II

Oh well ... [əʊ 'wel] Na ja ... / Na gut ... I

°**OHP** [ˌəʊ_eɪtʃ 'piː] (kurz für: overhead projector [ˌəʊvəhed prə'dʒektə]) Overheadprojektor I

oil [ɔɪl] Öl III

oil-producing ['ɔɪl prəˌdjuːsɪŋ] ölproduzierend V

OK [əʊ'keɪ] okay, gut, in Ordnung I

old [əʊld] alt I • **How old are you?** Wie alt bist du? I • **I'm ... years old.** Ich bin ... Jahre alt. I • **thirteen-year-old** Dreizehnjährige(r) III

old-fashioned [ˌəʊld'fæʃnd] altmodisch III

Olympic Games [əˌlɪmpɪk 'ɡeɪmz] Olympische Spiele IV

on [ɒn]
1. auf I
2. weiter III
3. an, eingeschaltet (Radio, Licht usw.) II
and so on (short: etc. [et'setərə]) und so weiter (usw.) IV • **on and on** immer weiter VI 2 (34) • **be on** gezeigt werden, laufen (im Fernsehen) IV • **be on holiday** in Urlaub sein; Ferien haben/machen II • **go on** angehen (Licht) III • **go on holiday** in Urlaub fahren II • **on 13th June** am 13. Juni I • **on charge** am Ladegerät; am Netz (zum Aufladen) VI 3 (47) • **on earth** auf der Erde III • **on foot** zu Fuß III • **on Friday** am Freitag I • **on Friday afternoon** freitagnachmittags, am Freitagnachmittag I • **on Friday evening** freitagabends, am Freitagabend I • **on Friday morning** freitagmorgens, am Freitagmorgen I • **on Friday night** freitagnachts, Freitagnacht I • **on my/our/... own** allein, selbstständig (ohne Hilfe) IV • **on the beach** am Strand II • **on the board** an die Tafel I • **on the corner of Sand Street and London Road** Sand

Street, Ecke London Road II • **on the left** links, auf der linken Seite I • **on the one hand ... on the other hand** einerseits ... andererseits VI 2 (37) • **on the phone** am Telefon I • **on the plane** im Flugzeug II • **on the radio** im Radio I **on the right** rechts, auf der rechten Seite I • **on the second floor** im zweiten Stock (BE) / im ersten Stock (AE) IV • **on the train** im Zug I • **on TV** im Fernsehen I **straight on** geradeaus weiter II **What page are we on?** Auf welcher Seite sind wir? I

once [wʌns]
1. einst, früher einmal III
2. einmal III
once more / once again noch einmal III

one [wʌn] eins, ein, eine I • **a new one** ein neuer / eine neue / ein neues II • **my old ones** meine alten II • **no one** niemand IV • **one another** einander, sich (gegenseitig) III • **one at a time** einzeln VI 3 (48/181) • **one by one** einer nach dem anderen VI 2 (34) **one day** eines Tages I • **one more** noch ein/e, ein/e weitere(r, s) I

onion ['ʌnjən] Zwiebel III

online [ˌɒn'laɪn] online, Online- III

only ['əʊnli]
1. nur, bloß I; erst III
2. the only guest der einzige Gast I

on-screen [ˌɒn'skriːn] Leinwand- VI 1 (12)

onto ['ɒntə, 'ɒntʊ] auf (... hinauf) III

open ['əʊpən]
1. öffnen, aufmachen I
2. sich öffnen I

open ['əʊpən] offen, geöffnet II **open-air** im Freien; Freilicht- III **open-top bus** oben offener (Doppeldecker-)Bus III

opening hours (pl) ['əʊpənɪŋ ˌaʊəz] Öffnungszeiten IV

°**opening sentence** [ˌəʊpənɪŋ 'sentəns] Einleitungssatz

opera ['ɒprə] Oper III

operation (on) [ˌɒpə'reɪʃn] Operation (an) III

opinion (of) [ə'pɪnjən] Meinung (von, zu) IV • **in my opinion** meiner Meinung nach IV

opportunity [ˌɒpə'tjuːnəti] Gelegenheit, Möglichkeit V

opposite ['ɒpəzɪt] gegenüber (von) II

opposite ['ɒpəzɪt] Gegenteil I

opposite ['ɒpəzɪt] gegenteilige(r, s), entgegengesetzte(r, s) v

or [ɔː] oder I • °**either ... or ...** ['aɪðə ... ɔː, 'iːðə ... ɔː] entweder ... oder

orange ['ɒrɪndʒ] orange(farben) I

orange ['ɒrɪndʒ] Orange, Apfelsine I

orange juice ['ɒrɪndʒ dʒuːs] Orangensaft I

order ['ɔːdə]
1. Reihenfolge III
2. Befehl, Anweisung, Anordnung v
°**word order** Wortstellung

order ['ɔːdə] bestellen v

organ ['ɔːgən] Orgel II

organic [ɔː'gænɪk] organisch, biologisch; Bio- VI 2 (36)

organization [ˌɔːgənaɪ'zeɪʃn] Organisation VI 3 (54)

organize ['ɔːgənaɪz] organisieren v

organized ['ɔːgənaɪzd] (gut) organisiert v

original (n; adj) [ə'rɪdʒɪnl] Original; Original- IV

orphan ['ɔːfn] Waise, Waisenkind v

other ['ʌðə] andere(r, s) I • **the others** die anderen I • **the other way round** anders herum II • **on the one hand ... on the other hand** einerseits ... andererseits VI 2 (37)

Ouch! [aʊtʃ] Autsch! I

our ['aʊə] unser, unsere I

ours ['aʊəz] unserer, unsere, unseres II

ourselves [aʊə'selvz] uns (selbst) III

out [aʊt] heraus, hinaus; draußen II
be out weg sein, nicht da sein I
out of ... aus ... (heraus/hinaus) I
4 out of 5 4 von 5 VI 1 (13) • °**a day out** ein Tagesausflug
▶ S.171 going out, asking sb. out

outback ['aʊtbæk]: **the outback** (Australien) das Hinterland v

outdoor ['aʊtdɔː] im Freien, Außen- III

outdoors [ˌaʊt'dɔːz] draußen, im Freien; nach draußen v

outfit ['aʊtfɪt] Outfit (Kleidung; Ausrüstung) II

outline ['aʊtlaɪn] Gliederung v

outside [aʊt'saɪd]
1. draußen I
2. nach draußen II
3. outside his room vor seinem Zimmer; außerhalb seines Zimmers I

outside [aʊt'saɪd]: **the outside** das Äußere, die Außenseite v

over ['əʊvə]
1. über, oberhalb von I
2. über, mehr als II

3. be over vorbei/zu Ende sein I
all over the world auf der ganzen Welt III • **from all over England/ the UK** aus ganz England/aus dem gesamten Vereinigten Königreich III • **over there** da drüben, dort drüben I • **over to ...** hinüber zu/ nach ... II

°**overhead projector** [ˌəʊvəhed prə'dʒektə] (**OHP** [ˌəʊ_eɪtʃ 'piː]) Overheadprojektor

overhead transparency [ˌəʊvəhed træns'pærənsi] Folie (für Overhead-projektoren) v

overnight [ˌəʊvə'naɪt] über Nacht v

own [əʊn]: **on my/our/... own** allein, selbstständig (ohne Hilfe) IV • **our own pool** unser eigenes Schwimmbad II • °**a statement of your own** eine eigene Aussage I

°**own** [əʊn] besitzen

owner ['əʊnə] Besitzer/in v

ozone layer ['əʊzəʊn leɪə] Ozon-schicht v

P

Pacific: the Pacific (Ocean) [pə,sɪfɪk_'əʊʃn] der Pazifische Ozean, der Pazifik IV

pack [pæk] packen, einpacken II

packaging ['pækɪdʒɪŋ] Verpackung VI 2 (36)

packet ['pækɪt] Päckchen, Packung, Schachtel I • a packet of mints ein Päckchen/eine Packung Pfefferminzbonbons I

paddle ['pædl] paddeln III

paddle ['pædl] Paddel III

pads (pl) [pædz] (Knie- usw.) Schützer (für Inlineskater); Schulterpolster (beim American Football) III

page [peɪdʒ] (Buch-, Heft-)Seite I
What page are we on? Auf welcher Seite sind wir? I

paid [peɪd] siehe **pay**

pain [peɪn] Schmerz(en) IV

painful ['peɪnfl] schmerzhaft; schmerzlich; unangenehm; quälend v

°**painful** ['peɪnfl] schmerzhaft, unangenehm, quälend

paint [peɪnt] malen, anmalen I

painter ['peɪntə] Maler/in II

painting ['peɪntɪŋ] Gemälde IV

pair [peə]: **a pair (of)** ein Paar II

palace ['pæləs] Palast, Schloss III

panic ['pænɪk]: **Don't panic.** Keine Panik. / Bleib ruhig. IV

pants (pl) [pænts] (AE) Hose IV

paper ['peɪpə]
1. Papier I
2. Zeitung II

paragraph ['pærəgrɑːf] Absatz (in einem Text) II

Paralympics (pl) [ˌpærə'lɪmpɪks] olympischer Wettkampf für Behindertensportler/innen III

paramedic [ˌpærə'medɪk] Sanitäter/in II

paraphrase ['pærəfreɪz] umschreiben, anders ausdrücken III

parcel ['pɑːsl] Paket I

parents ['peərənts] Eltern I

park [pɑːk] Park I

parking ['pɑːkɪŋ] (das) Parken IV

park ranger ['reɪndʒə] Ranger sind eine Art Aufseher/in in Nationalparks, die auch Führungen machen und als Wald- und Wildhüter/innen arbeiten IV

parliament ['pɑːləmənt] Parlament III • **member of parliament** Parlamentsmitglied, Abgeordnete(r) VI 3 (47/180)
▶ S.180 Politics

parrot ['pærət] Papagei I

part [pɑːt] Teil I • **take part (in)** teilnehmen (an) IV

particular [pə'tɪkjələ] bestimmte(r, s) v

partner ['pɑːtnə] Partner/in I

party ['pɑːti]
1. (politische) Partei VI 3 (47/180)
2. Party I • **have a party** eine Party feiern/veranstalten II
▶ S.180 Politics

party ['pɑːti] (Partys) feiern IV

pass [pɑːs]
1. (herüber)reichen, weitergeben I
pass round herumgeben I
°**pass sth. on** etwas weitergeben I
2. pass an exam eine Prüfung bestehen IV

passenger ['pæsɪndʒə] Passagier/in v

passion ['pæʃn] Leidenschaft v

°**passport** ['pɑːspɔːt] (Reise-)Pass

past [pɑːst] Vergangenheit II

past [pɑːst] vorbei (an), vorüber (an) II • **half past 11** halb zwölf (11.30 / 23.30) I • **quarter past 11** Viertel nach 11 (11.15 / 23.15) I

pasta (no pl) ['pæstə] Nudeln, Teigwaren IV

path [pɑːθ] Pfad, Weg II • **bridle path** ['braɪdl pɑːθ] Reitweg III

patient ['peɪʃnt] geduldig VI 1 (13)

patrol [pə'trəʊl] Streife, Patrouille IV

pavement ['peɪvmənt] Gehweg, Bürgersteig IV

pay [peɪ] Bezahlung, Lohn v

pay (for sth.) [peɪ], **paid, paid** etwas bezahlen II • **pay by credit card** mit Kreditkarte bezahlen v • **pay cash** bar bezahlen v

PE [ˌpiːˈiː], **Physical Education** [ˌfɪzɪkəl_edʒuˈkeɪʃn] Sportunterricht, Turnen I

pea [piː] Erbse III

peace [piːs] Friede(n) v

peanut [ˈpiːnʌt] Erdnuss VI 1 (6)

pen [pen] Kugelschreiber, Füller I

pence (p) (pl) [pens] Pence (pl von „penny") I

pencil [ˈpensl] Bleistift I

pencil case [ˈpensl keɪs] Federmäppchen I

pencil sharpener [ˈpensl ʃɑːpnə] Bleistiftanspitzer I

penicillin [ˌpenɪˈsɪlɪn] Penizillin VI 2 (32)

penny [ˈpeni] kleinste britische Münze I

people [ˈpiːpl] Menschen, Leute I

pepper [ˈpepə] Pfeffer III

per [pɜː, pə] pro III

per cent (%) [pəˈsent] Prozent III

percentage [pəˈsentɪdʒ] Prozentsatz, prozentualer Anteil v

perfect [ˈpɜːfɪkt] perfekt, ideal, vollkommen IV

°perfume [ˈpɜːfjuːm] Parfüm

perhaps [pəˈhæps] vielleicht VI 1 (8)

period [ˈpɪəriəd]
1. (Unterrichts-/Schul-)Stunde IV
°**2. period of time** Zeitspanne, Zeitraum

person [ˈpɜːsn] Person II

personal [ˈpɜːsənl] persönliche(r, s) III

personality [ˌpɜːsəˈnæləti] Persönlichkeit v

pet [pet] Haustier I

petition [pəˈtɪʃn] Unterschriftensammlung, Petition VI 3 (47)

petrol [ˈpetrəl] Benzin IV

petrol station [ˈpetrəl steɪʃn] Tankstelle IV

pet shop [ˈpet ʃɒp] Tierhandlung I

phone [fəʊn] Telefon I • **on the phone** am Telefon I • **phone call** Anruf, Telefongespräch I • **phone number** Telefonnummer I

phone [fəʊn] anrufen II

photo [ˈfəʊtəʊ] Foto I • **in the photo** auf dem Foto I • **take photos** Fotos machen, fotografieren I

°photocopy [ˈfəʊtəʊkɒpi] Fotokopie

photographer [fəˈtɒɡrəfə] Fotograf/in II

phrase [freɪz] Ausdruck, (Rede-)Wendung I

physics [ˈfɪzɪks] Physik v

piano [piˈænəʊ] Klavier, Piano I
play the piano Klavier spielen I

pick [pɪk]: **pick fruit/flowers** Obst/Blumen pflücken IV • **pick sb. up** jn. abholen III • **pick sth. up** etwas hochheben, aufheben II

picnic [ˈpɪknɪk] Picknick II

picture [ˈpɪktʃə] Bild I • **in the picture** auf dem Bild I

picture sth. [ˈpɪktʃə] sich etwas (bildlich) vorstellen IV

pie [paɪ] Obstkuchen; Pastete II

pie chart [ˈpaɪ tʃɑːt] Tortendiagramm v

piece [piːs]: **a piece of** ein Stück I
a piece of paper ein Stück Papier I

piercing [ˈpɪəsɪŋ] Piercing VI 1 (10)

pig [pɪɡ] Schwein III

pink [pɪŋk] pink(farben), rosa I

pipe [paɪp] Pfeife III

pirate [ˈpaɪrət] Pirat, Piratin I

pitch [pɪtʃ]: **football/hockey pitch** Fußball-/Hockeyplatz, -feld II

pizza [ˈpiːtsə] Pizza I

place [pleɪs] Ort, Platz I • **at someone's place** bei jemandem zu Hause v • **in other places** an anderen Orten, anderswo III • **place of birth** Geburtsort v • **take place** stattfinden IV

°placemat [ˈpleɪsmæt] Set, Platzdeckchen

plan [plæn] Plan I

plan (-nn-) [plæn] planen II

plane [pleɪn] Flugzeug II • **on the plane** im Flugzeug II

planet [ˈplænɪt] Planet II

plant [plɑːnt] Pflanze IV

plant [plɑːnt] pflanzen, einpflanzen IV

plantation [plɑːnˈteɪʃn] Plantage IV

plastic [ˈplæstɪk] Plastik, Kunststoff v

plate [pleɪt] Teller I • **a plate of chips** ein Teller Pommes frites I
license plate (AE) Nummernschild IV • **number plate** Nummernschild IV

platform [ˈplætfɔːm] Bahnsteig, Gleis III

play [pleɪ] spielen I • **play a trick on sb.** jm. einen Streich spielen II
play the drums Schlagzeug spielen III • **play the fiddle** Geige spielen III • **play the guitar** Gitarre spielen I • **play the piano** Klavier spielen I

play [pleɪ] Theaterstück I

player [ˈpleɪə] Spieler/in I

playlist [ˈpleɪlɪst] Titelliste (von zu spielenden Songs) III

please [pliːz] bitte (in Fragen und Aufforderungen) I

plot [plɒt] Handlung (eines Romans, Films) IV

plug [plʌɡ] Stecker III

plus [plʌs] plus III

pm [ˌpiːˈem]: **7 pm** 7 Uhr abends/19 Uhr I

pocket [ˈpɒkɪt] Tasche (an Kleidungsstück) II

pocket money [ˈpɒkɪt ˌmʌni] Taschengeld II

°pod car [ˈpɒd kɑː] „Kabinentaxi" (führerloses, spurgeführtes Personentransportsystem, bestehend aus kleinen unabhängigen Kabinen, mit denen man vollautomatisch an sein Ziel gelangt)

poem [ˈpəʊɪm] Gedicht I

point [pɔɪnt] Punkt II • **make a point** ein Argument vorbringen III
°**point in time** Zeitpunkt • **point of view** Standpunkt II • **from my point of view** aus meiner Sicht; von meinem Standpunkt aus gesehen II • **10.4 (ten point four)** 10,4 (zehn Komma vier) II

point (at/to sth.) [pɔɪnt] zeigen, deuten (auf etwas) II

police (pl) [pəˈliːs] Polizei I

policeman, policewoman [pəˈliːsmən, pəˈliːswʊmən] Polizist, Polizistin II

police officer [pəˈliːs_ˌɒfɪsə] Polizist/in v

police station [pəˈliːs steɪʃn] Polizeiwache, Polizeirevier II

polite [pəˈlaɪt] höflich IV

politeness [pəˈlaɪtnəs] Höflichkeit VI (54)

political [pəˈlɪtɪkl] politisch v
▶ S.180 Politics

politician [ˌpɒləˈtɪʃn] Politiker/in VI 3 (47)
▶ S.180 Politics

politics [ˈpɒlətɪks] Politik VI 1 (15)
▶ S.180 Politics

pollute [pəˈluːt] verschmutzen, verunreinigen VI 2 (31/176)

polluted [pəˈluːtɪd] verseucht, verunreinigt v

pollution [pəˈluːʃn] (Umwelt-)Verschmutzung VI 2 (30)

poltergeist [ˈpəʊltəɡaɪst] Poltergeist I

ponytail [ˈpəʊniteɪl] Pferdeschwanz (Frisur) III

poor [pɔː, pʊə] arm I • **poor Sophie** (die) arme Sophie I

pop (music) [pɒp] Pop(musik) III

popcorn ['pɒpkɔːn] Popcorn II
popular (with) ['pɒpjələ] beliebt (bei) V
popularity [ˌpɒpjuˈlærəti] Beliebtheit, Popularität VI 3 (54)
population [ˌpɒpjuˈleɪʃn] Bevölkerung, Einwohner(zahl) III
pork [pɔːk] Schweinefleisch III
positive ['pɒzətɪv] positiv VI 1 (13)
possibility [ˌpɒsəˈbɪləti] Möglichkeit IV
possible ['pɒsəbl] möglich II
post [pəʊst] Post (Briefe, Päckchen, …) III
post [pəʊst] posten (ins Netz stellen) V
postcard ['pəʊstkɑːd] Postkarte II
postcode ['pəʊstkəʊd] Postleitzahl V
poster ['pəʊstə] Poster I
post office ['pəʊst ˌɒfɪs] Postamt II
potato [pəˈteɪtəʊ], pl **potatoes** Kartoffel I
potato chips [pəˈteɪtəʊ tʃɪps] (AE) Kartoffelchips IV
poultry ['pəʊltri] Geflügel IV
pound (£) [paʊnd] Pfund (britische Währung) I
poverty ['pɒvəti] Armut VI 3 (46)
power ['paʊə]
1. Macht; Stärke V
2. Kraft, Energie, Strom VI 2 (30)
power cut ['paʊə kʌt] Stromabschaltung, Stromausfall VI 2 (35)
power station ['paʊə steɪʃn] Kraftwerk, Elektrizitätswerk VI 2 (31)
practice ['præktɪs] hier: Übungsteil I
practice ['præktɪs] (AE) üben; trainieren II
practise ['præktɪs]
1. üben; trainieren I
°2. ausüben (Religion)
prefer sth. (to sth. else) (-rr-) [prɪˈfɜː] etwas lieber tun/haben (als etwas anderes); etwas (etwas anderem) vorziehen V
pregnant ['pregnənt] schwanger VI 1 (12)
prejudice (against) ['predʒudɪs] Voreingenommenheit (gegen), Vorurteil (gegenüber) IV
prejudiced ['predʒədɪst]: **be prejudiced (against)** voreingenommen sein (gegen), Vorurteile haben (gegenüber) IV
prepare [prɪˈpeə] vorbereiten; sich vorbereiten II • **prepare for** sich vorbereiten auf II
present ['preznt]
1. Gegenwart I
2. Geschenk I

present sth. (to sb.) [prɪˈzent] (jm.) etwas präsentieren, vorstellen I
presentation [ˌpreznˈteɪʃn] Präsentation, Vorstellung I
presenter [prɪˈzentə] Moderator/in II
president ['prezɪdənt] Präsident/in IV
press sth. [pres] etwas drücken; auf etwas drücken IV
pretend [prɪˈtend] so tun, als ob VI 2 (34)
pretty ['prɪti] hübsch I
pretty cool/good/… ['prɪti] ziemlich cool/gut/… II
prevent sth. [prɪˈvent] etwas verhindern V
price [praɪs] (Kauf-)Preis I
priest [priːst] Priester VI 1 (13/173)
► S.173 Religions
primary school ['praɪməri skuːl] Grundschule V
prime minister [ˌpraɪm ˈmɪnɪstə] Premierminister/in, Ministerpräsident/in VI 3 (47/180)
► S.180 Politics
prime time ['praɪm taɪm] Hauptsendezeit IV
print [prɪnt] drucken, abdrucken V
print sth. out etwas ausdrucken II
print: bold print [ˌbəʊld 'prɪnt] Fettdruck III
printer ['prɪntə] Drucker V
prison ['prɪzn] Gefängnis V • **go to prison** ins Gefängnis kommen V
private ['praɪvət] privat IV
private detective [ˌpraɪvət dɪˈtektɪv] Privatdetektiv/in V
prize [praɪz] Preis, Gewinn I
probably ['prɒbəbli] wahrscheinlich II
problem ['prɒbləm] Problem II
process ['prəʊses] Prozess, Verfahren IV
produce [prəˈdjuːs] produzieren, herstellen III
product ['prɒdʌkt] Produkt, Erzeugnis IV
production [prəˈdʌkʃn] Produktion, Herstellung IV
profile ['prəʊfaɪl] Profil, Beschreibung, Porträt V
program ['prəʊgræm] (AE) Programm V
programme ['prəʊgræm] Programm I
project (about, on) ['prɒdʒekt] Projekt (über, zu) I
projector [prəˈdʒektə] Projektor, Beamer V
promise ['prɒmɪs] versprechen II
°pronounce [prəˈnaʊns] aussprechen

pronunciation [prəˌnʌnsiˈeɪʃn] Aussprache I
proof (no pl) [pruːf] Beweis(e) II
protect sb. (from) [prəˈtekt] jn. (be)schützen (vor) III
protest ['prəʊtest] Protest IV
protest [prəˈtest] protestieren IV
Protestant ['prɒtɪstənt] Protestant/-in; protestantisch VI 1 (13/173)
► S.173 Religions
protester [prəˈtestə] Demonstrant/-in, Protestierer/in V
proud (of sb./sth.) [praʊd] stolz (auf jn./etwas) II
province ['prɒvɪns] Provinz III
PS [ˌpiːˈes] **(postscript** ['pəʊstskrɪpt]**)** PS (Nachschrift unter Briefen) III
pub [pʌb] Kneipe, Lokal II
public ['pʌblɪk] Öffentlichkeit VI 3 (48)
public ['pʌblɪk] öffentliche(r, s) III
public transport (no pl) öffentliche Verkehrsmittel, öffentlicher Personennahverkehr III
publish ['pʌblɪʃ] veröffentlichen III
pull [pʊl] ziehen I
pullover ['pʊləʊvə] Pullover II
°pump [pʌmp] pumpen
punctual ['pʌŋktʃuəl] pünktlich V
punish ['pʌnɪʃ] bestrafen V
punishment ['pʌnɪʃmənt] Bestrafung, Strafe V
punk (rock) [pʌŋk] Punk(rock) III
purple ['pɜːpl] violett; lila I
purse [pɜːs] Geldbörse II
push [pʊʃ] drücken, schieben, stoßen I
put (-tt-) [pʊt], **put, put** legen, stellen, (etwas wohin) tun I • **put sth. down** etwas hinlegen IV • **put sth. on** etwas anziehen (Kleidung) II; etwas aufsetzen (Hut, Helm) III
put out a fire ein Feuer löschen IV
°Put up your hand. Heb deine Hand. / Hebt eure Hand.
puzzle ['pʌzl] Rätsel IV
puzzled ['pʌzld] verwirrt II
pyjamas (pl) [pəˈdʒɑːməz] Schlafanzug II
pyramid ['pɪrəmɪd] Pyramide IV

Q

qualification [ˌkwɒlɪfɪˈkeɪʃn] Abschluss, Qualifikation V
quality ['kwɒləti] Qualität IV
quarter ['kwɔːtə]: **quarter past 11** Viertel nach 11 (11.15 / 23.15) I
quarter to 12 Viertel vor 12 (11.45 / 23.45) I

queen [kwiːn] Königin III
question ['kwestʃn] Frage I • **ask questions** Fragen stellen
°questionnaire [ˌkwestʃə'neə] Fragebogen
°question word ['kwestʃn wɜːd] Fragewort
queue [kjuː] Schlange, Reihe *(wartender Menschen)* IV
quick [kwɪk] schnell I
quiet ['kwaɪət] leise, still, ruhig I
quite quickly/well/... [kwaɪt] ziemlich schnell/gut/... II
quiz [kwɪz], *pl* **quizzes** ['kwɪzɪz] Quiz, Ratespiel I
°quotation marks [kwəʊ'teɪʃn mɑːks] Anführungszeichen, -striche

R

rabbit ['ræbɪt] Kaninchen I
rabbit-proof ['ræbɪt pruːf] kaninchen-sicher, kaninchen-fest V
race [reɪs] Rasse V
racial ['reɪʃl] Rassen-, rassisch V
racing car ['reɪsɪŋ kɑː] Rennwagen V
racism ['reɪsɪzəm] Rassismus VI 1 (12)
racist ['reɪsɪst] rassistisch; Rassist/Rassistin V
racket ['rækɪt]: **badminton racket** Badmintonschläger III • **tennis racket** Tennisschläger VI 3 (48)
radio ['reɪdiəʊ] Radio I • **on the radio** im Radio I
raft [rɑːft] Schlauchboot *(wildwassertauglich)* IV
railway ['reɪlweɪ] Eisenbahn II
rain [reɪn] Regen II
rain [reɪn] regnen II
rainforest ['reɪnfɒrɪst] Regenwald V
rainproof ['reɪnpruːf] regendicht, wasserdicht V
rainy ['reɪni] regnerisch II
raise money (for) [reɪz] Geld sammeln (für) IV
ran [ræn] *siehe* **run**
rang [ræŋ] *siehe* **ring**
ranger ['reɪndʒə]: **(park) ranger** *Ranger sind eine Art Aufseher/in in Nationalparks, die auch Führungen machen und als Wald- und Waldhüter/innen arbeiten* IV
rap [ræp] Rap *(rhythmischer Sprechgesang)* I
rap (-pp-) [ræp] rappen III
rapids *(pl)* ['ræpɪdz] Stromschnellen III
rapper ['ræpə] Rapper/in III
rate [reɪt] bewerten V

rate [reɪt] Rate, Quote V • **exchange rate** Wechselkurs V
°ration ['ræʃn] Ration
°rationing ['ræʃənɪŋ] Rationierung
ray [reɪ] Strahl V • **ultraviolet rays** ultraviolette Strahlen V
RE [ˌɑːr_'iː], **Religious Education** [rɪˌlɪdʒəs_edʒu'keɪʃn] Religion, Religionsunterricht I
Re: ... [riː] Betreff: ... IV
reach [riːtʃ] erreichen IV • **reach for sth.** nach etwas greifen V
reach out (for sth.) die Hand/Hände ausstrecken (nach etwas); greifen (nach etwas) V
react (to) [ri'ækt] reagieren (auf) V
reaction (to) [ri'ækʃn] Reaktion (auf) VI 2 (31/176)
read [riːd], **read, read** lesen I
read on weiterlesen III • °**read out** vorlesen • °**Read out loud.** Lies laut vor. • °**Read the poem to a partner.** Lies das Gedicht einem Partner/einer Partnerin vor.
read [red] *siehe* **read**
reader ['riːdə] Leser/in II
ready ['redi] bereit, fertig I • **get ready (for)** sich fertig machen (für), sich vorbereiten (auf) I • **get things ready** Dinge fertig machen, vorbereiten I
real [rɪəl] echt, wirklich I • **real late** *(AE, infml)* wirklich spät, richtig spät III • **real-life** im wirklichen Leben, aus dem wirklichen Leben VI 1 (8)
realistic [ˌrɪə'lɪstɪk] realistisch, wirklichkeitsnah III
reality [ri'æləti] Realität, Wirklichkeit IV
realize ['rɪəlaɪz]
1. verwirklichen, realisieren VI 2 (33)
2. sich *(einer Sache)* bewusst sein/werden VI 2 (33)
really ['rɪəli] wirklich I
reason ['riːzn] Grund, Begründung I • **for lots of reasons** aus vielen Gründen I
rebuild [ˌriː'bɪld], **rebuilt, rebuilt** wiederaufbauen V
rebuilt [ˌriː'bɪlt] *siehe* **rebuild**
receipt [rɪ'siːt] Quittung V
receive [rɪ'siːv] erhalten, empfangen V
recent ['riːsnt] vor kurzem *(geschehen, entstanden usw.)* VI 3 (51)
recently ['riːsntli] neulich, vor kurzem; in letzter Zeit V
receptionist [rɪ'sepʃənɪst] Rezeptionist/in; Empfangsdame V
°recognize ['rekəgnaɪz] erkennen

recommend sth. (to sb.) [ˌrekə'mend] (jm.) etwas empfehlen VI 1 (14)
record ['rekɔːd] Schallplatte III
record [rɪ'kɔːd] *(Musik)* aufnehmen, aufzeichnen III
recorded message [rɪˌkɔːdɪd 'mesɪdʒ] (automatische) Telefonansage IV
recorder [rɪ'kɔːdə] Blockflöte III
recording [rɪ'kɔːdɪŋ] Aufnahme, Aufzeichnung III
recycle [ˌriː'saɪkl] wiederverwerten, wiederverwenden VI 2 (36)
recycled [ˌriː'saɪkld] wiederverwertet, wiederverwendet, recycelt II
recycling [ˌriː'saɪklɪŋ] Wiederverwertung, Recycling II
red [red] rot I
reduce [rɪ'djuːs] verringern, vermindern, reduzieren VI 2 (34)
reef [riːf] Riff V
refer to (-rr-) [rɪ'fɜː] sich beziehen auf III
reference ['refrəns] Referenz, Empfehlung V
reflex ['riːfleks] Reflex IV
reggae ['regeɪ] Reggae III
rehearsal [rɪ'hɜːsl] Probe *(am Theater)* I
rehearse [rɪ'hɜːs] proben *(am Theater)* I
relations *(pl)* [rɪ'leɪʃnz] Beziehungen IV
relationship [rɪ'leɪʃnʃɪp] Beziehung V
relax [rɪ'læks] (sich) entspannen, sich ausruhen II
relaxed [rɪ'lækst] locker, entspannt III
release [rɪ'liːs]
1. herausbringen, auf den Markt bringen *(CD, Film usw.)* III
2. freilassen *(Gefangene)*; freisetzen, ablassen *(Gas)* VI 2 (29)
reliable [rɪ'laɪəbl] zuverlässig, verlässlich V
religion [rɪ'lɪdʒn] Religion VI 1 (13)
▶ S.173 Religions
religious [rɪ'lɪdʒəs] religiös; gläubig VI 1 (13/173)
▶ S.173 Religions
remember sth. [rɪ'membə]
1. sich an etwas erinnern I
2. sich etwas merken I
3. **remember sb./sth.** *einer Person/Sache* gedenken V
°**Remember ...** Denk dran, ...
remind sb. (of/about sth.) [rɪ'maɪnd] jn. (an etwas) erinnern V
remote control [rɪˌməʊt kən'trəʊl] *(infml auch:* **remote***)* Fernbedienung; Fernsteuerung VI 2 (28)
rent [rent] mieten, pachten V

repair [rɪ'peə] reparieren V

repair [rɪ'peə] Reparatur VI 3 (51)

repeat sth. [rɪ'pi:t] etwas wiederholen V

repeat [rɪ'pi:t] Wiederholung (einer Fernsehsendung) IV

report (on) [rɪ'pɔ:t] Bericht, Reportage (über) I

report (to sb.) [rɪ'pɔ:t] (jm.) berichten II

reporter [rɪ'pɔ:tə] Reporter/in IV

represent [ˌreprɪ'zent] repräsentieren, vertreten III

republic [rɪ'pʌblɪk] Republik V

request [rɪ'kwest] Bitte V

rerun ['ri:rʌn] (AE) Wiederholung (einer Fernsehsendung) IV

research (no pl) [rɪ'sɜ:tʃ, 'ri:sɜ:tʃ] Recherche; Nachforschung(en) IV • do research recherchieren IV

reservation [ˌrezə'veɪʃn] Reservierung V

respect [rɪ'spekt] achten, respektieren V

responsibility [rɪˌspɒnsə'bɪləti] Verantwortung VI 3 (54)

responsible [rɪ'spɒnsəbl] verantwortlich; verantwortungsbewusst VI 2 (34)

rest [rest] Rest II

restaurant ['restrɒnt] Restaurant II

result [rɪ'zʌlt] Ergebnis, Resultat I

°retell [ˌri:'tel], retold, retold nacherzählen

°retold [ˌri:'təʊld] siehe retell

return [rɪ'tɜ:n] zurückkehren IV

return ticket [rɪ'tɜ:n ˌtɪkɪt] Rückfahrkarte II

reunification [ˌri:ˌju:nɪfɪ'keɪʃn] Wiedervereinigung V

reunify [ˌri:'ju:nɪfaɪ] wiedervereinigen V

review [rɪ'vju:] besprechen, rezensieren (Buch, Film) VI 1 (12/173)

review [rɪ'vju:] (Buch-, Film-)Kritik, Besprechung, Rezension VI 1 (12)

reviewer [rɪ'vju:ə] Rezensent/in, Kritiker/in VI 1 (12/173)

revise [rɪ'vaɪz]
1. überarbeiten III
2. wiederholen III

revision [rɪ'vɪʒn] Wiederholung (des Lernstoffs) I

revolution [ˌrevə'lu:ʃn] Revolution VI 2 (30)

°rewrite [ˌri:'raɪt], rewrote, rewritten umschreiben, neu schreiben

°rewritten [ˌri:'rɪtn] siehe rewrite

°rewrote [ˌri:'rəʊt] siehe rewrite

rhino ['raɪnəʊ] Nashorn II

rice [raɪs] Reis IV

rich [rɪtʃ] reich II

rid [rɪd]: get rid of sb./sth. jn./ etwas loswerden IV

ridden ['rɪdn] siehe ride

riddle ['rɪdl] Rätsel III

ride [raɪd], rode, ridden reiten I • go riding ['raɪdɪŋ] reiten gehen I • ride a bike Rad fahren I

ride [raɪd] Ritt V • (bike) ride (Rad-)Fahrt, (Rad-)Tour II • take a ride eine Fahrt machen III

rider ['raɪdə] Reiter/in IV

riding boots (pl) ['raɪdɪŋ bu:ts] Reitstiefel III

riding hat ['raɪdɪŋ hæt] Reitkappe, Reiterhelm III

right [raɪt] Recht IV

right [raɪt] richtig I • all right [ɔ:l 'raɪt] gut, in Ordnung II • it's all right with her es ist ihr recht; sie ist einverstanden V • be right Recht haben I • That's right. Das ist richtig. / Das stimmt. I • You need a school bag, right? Du brauchst eine Schultasche, stimmt's? / nicht wahr? I

right [raɪt] rechte(r, s) II • look right nach rechts schauen II • on the right rechts, auf der rechten Seite I • turn right (nach) rechts abbiegen II

right [raɪt]: right after lunch direkt/ gleich nach dem Mittagessen I right now jetzt sofort; jetzt gerade I • right behind you direkt/genau hinter dir I

rim [rɪm] Rand, Kante IV

ring [rɪŋ] Ring II

ring [rɪŋ], rang, rung klingeln, läuten II

ringtone ['rɪŋtəʊn] Klingelton III

rip sb. off (-pp-) [ˌrɪp_'ɒf] (infml) jn. übers Ohr hauen, jn. abzocken VI 2 (35)

rise [raɪz], rose, risen (auf)steigen IV

risen ['rɪzn] siehe rise

river ['rɪvə] Fluss II

road [rəʊd] Straße I • Park Road [ˌpɑ:k 'rəʊd] Parkstraße I

rock [rɒk] Fels, Felsen II

rock (music) [rɒk] Rock(musik) III

rode [rəʊd] siehe ride

role [rəʊl] Rolle III

°role model ['rəʊl mɒdl] Vorbild

role play ['rəʊl pleɪ] Rollenspiel II

roll [rəʊl] Brötchen I

Roman ['rəʊmən] römisch; Römer, Römerin II

°romance [rəʊ'mæns] Romanze

romantic [rəʊ'mæntɪk] romantisch; Liebes- VI 1 (12)

room [ru:m, rʊm] Raum, Zimmer I

rose [rəʊz] siehe rise

round [raʊnd] rund II

round [raʊnd] um ... (herum); in ... umher II • the other way round anders herum II

route [ru:t] Strecke, Route IV

royal ['rɔɪəl] königlich III

rubber ['rʌbə] Radiergummi I

rubbish ['rʌbɪʃ] (Haus-)Müll, Abfall II

rucksack ['rʌksæk] Rucksack III

rude [ru:d] unhöflich, unverschämt II

rudeness ['ru:dnəs] Unhöflichkeit, Unverschämtheit VI 3 (54)

rugby ['rʌgbi] Rugby V

rule [ru:l] Regel, Vorschrift III

ruler ['ru:lə] Lineal I

run [rʌn] (Wett-)Lauf II

run (-nn-) [rʌn], ran, run
1. laufen, rennen I
2. verlaufen (Straße; Grenze) IV
3. run sth. etwas leiten (Hotel, Firma usw.) V
run into sth./sb. gegen etwas fahren / jn. anfahren IV

rung [rʌŋ] siehe ring

runner ['rʌnə] Läufer/in II

°running head [ˌrʌnɪŋ 'hed] Leitwort (am Kopf einer Wörterbuchseite)

running shoes ['rʌnɪŋ ʃu:z] Laufschuhe III

running track ['rʌnɪŋ træk] Laufbahn (Sport) III

rush hour ['rʌʃ_aʊə] Hauptverkehrszeit III

S

sad [sæd] traurig II

saddle ['sædl] Sattel III

sadness ['sædnəs] Traurigkeit IV

safe (from) [seɪf] sicher, in Sicherheit (vor) II

safe [seɪf] Safe V

safety ['seɪfti] Sicherheit IV

said [sed] siehe say

sail [seɪl] segeln II

salad ['sæləd] Salat (als Gericht oder Beilage) I

sale [seɪl] Verkauf; Schlussverkauf IV • for sale (auf Schild) zu verkaufen IV

salmon ['sæmən], pl salmon Lachs III

salt [sɔ:lt] Salz III

same [seɪm]: the same ... der-/die-/dasselbe ...; dieselben ... I • be the same gleich sein I • look the same gleich aussehen I

sandal ['sændl] Sandale II

sandwich ['sænwɪtʃ, 'sænwɪdʒ] Sandwich, *(zusammengeklapptes)* belegtes Brot I

sang [sæŋ] *siehe* **sing**

sat [sæt] *siehe* **sit**

Saturday ['sætədeɪ, 'sætədi] Samstag, Sonnabend I

sauna ['sɔːnə] Sauna II • **have a sauna** in die Sauna gehen II

sausage ['sɒsɪdʒ] (Brat-, Bock-) Würstchen, Wurst I

save [seɪv]
1. retten II
2. sparen II
3. (ab)speichern *(Daten, Telefonnummern)* V

saw [sɔː] *siehe* **see**

saxophone ['sæksəfəʊn] Saxophon III

say [seɪ], **said, said** sagen I • **It says here: ...** Hier steht: ... / Es heißt hier: ... II • **say goodbye** sich verabschieden I • **Say hi to your parents for me.** Grüß deine Eltern von mir. I • **say sorry** sich entschuldigen II

°**scale** [skeɪl] Maßstab

scan (-nn-) [skæn]
°1. (ein)scannen
2. **scan a text** einen Text schnell nach bestimmten Wörtern/Informationen absuchen II

scared [skeəd] verängstigt II • **be scared (of)** Angst haben (vor) I

scary ['skeəri] unheimlich; gruselig I

scene [siːn] Szene I

scenery ['siːnəri] *(schöne)* Landschaft IV

schedule [*AE*: 'skedʒuːl, *BE*: 'ʃedjuːl] *(AE)*
1. Stundenplan IV
2. Fahrplan IV

school [skuːl] Schule I • **at school** in der Schule I

school bag ['skuːl bæg] Schultasche I

school subject ['sʌbdʒɪkt] Schulfach I

science ['saɪəns] Naturwissenschaft I

science fiction [,saɪəns 'fɪkʃn] Sciencefiction VI 1 (14)

scientist ['saɪəntɪst] (Natur-)Wissenschaftler/in VI 2 (29)

score [skɔː] Spielstand; Punktestand III • **final score** Endstand *(beim Sport)* III • **What's the score?** Wie steht es? *(beim Sport)* III

score (a goal) [skɔː] ein Tor schießen, einen Treffer erzielen III

scrapbook ['skræpbʊk] Sammelalbum IV

scream [skriːm] schreien, kreischen IV

screen [skriːn] Leinwand; Bildschirm V

sea [siː] Meer, *(die)* See I

search (for) [sɜːtʃ] suchen (nach) II

search engine ['sɜːtʃ ,endʒɪn] Suchmaschine IV

sea snake ['siː sneɪk] Seeschlange V

second [sekənd] Sekunde VI 2 (30)

second [sekənd] zweite(r, s) I
second-hand [,sekənd 'hænd] gebraucht; aus zweiter Hand III

secondary school ['sekəndri skuːl] weiterführende Schule V

secret ['siːkrət] Geheimnis V

secret ['siːkrət] geheim V

secretly ['siːkrətli] heimlich V

section ['sekʃn] Abschnitt, Teil, (Themen-)Bereich III

sector ['sektə] Sektor, Bereich V

security [sɪ'kjʊərəti] Sicherheit(svorkehrungen) IV

see [siː], **saw, seen**
1. sehen I
2. **see sb.** jn. besuchen, jn. aufsuchen II
See? Siehst du? I • **See you.** Tschüs. / Bis bald. I • **Wait and see!** Wart's ab! III

seem (to be/to do) [siːm] (zu sein/ zu tun) scheinen IV

seen [siːn] *siehe* **see**

see-through ['siːθruː] durchsichtig IV

segregate ['segrɪgeɪt] trennen *(nach Rasse, Religion, Geschlecht)* IV

segregation [,segrɪ'geɪʃn] (Rassen-)Trennung IV

sell [sel], **sold, sold** verkaufen I
be sold out ausverkauft sein, vergriffen sein III

semester [sɪ'mestə] Semester *(Schulhalbjahr in den USA)* IV

semi-final [,semi'faɪnl] Halbfinale III

send [send], **sent, sent** senden, schicken II

sense [sens] Sinn VI 1 (6/171) • **make sense** sinnvoll sein, einen Sinn ergeben VI 3 (49) • **sense of humour** (Sinn für) Humor VI 1 (6)

sensible ['sensəbl] vernünftig VI 3 (49)

sensitive ['sensətɪv] sensibel VI 3 (49/181)

sent [sent] *siehe* **send**

sentence ['sentəns] Satz I

sentimental [,sentɪ'mentl] sentimental VI 1 (14)

separate ['seprət] getrennt, separat IV

September [sep'tembə] September I

series, *pl* series ['sɪəriːz] (Sende-)Reihe, Serie II

serious ['sɪəriəs] ernst, ernsthaft IV **Seriously?** Im Ernst? IV

servant ['sɜːvənt] Diener/in, Bedienstete(r) IV

serve [sɜːv] bedienen *(Kunden)* V

service ['sɜːvɪs]
1. Dienst(leistung), Service V
2. Gottesdienst VI 1 (13/173)
▶ S.173 Religions

set [set] Reihe, Set, Satz V • **set of rules** Reihe von Regeln, Regelwerk V

set (-tt-) [set], **set, set:**
1. **set a trap (for sb.)** (jm.) eine Falle stellen II
2. **the film/novel is set in ...** der Film/Roman spielt in ... VI 1 (12)

set meal [,set 'miːl] Menü III

settle ['setl] sich niederlassen, siedeln; besiedeln V • **settle down** sich eingewöhnen III

°**several** ['sevrəl] einige; mehrere V

sew (on) [səʊ], **sewed, sewn** (an)nähen IV

sewn [səʊn] *siehe* **sew**

sex [seks] Geschlecht V

°**shade** [ʃeɪd] Schatten V

shadow ['ʃædəʊ] Schatten III

shake [ʃeɪk], **shook, shaken** schütteln; zittern IV

shaken ['ʃeɪkən] *siehe* **shake**

shame [ʃeɪm]: **It's a shame.** Es ist ein Jammer/eine Schande. V

shampoo [ʃæm'puː] Shampoo VI 3 (55)

share sth. (with) [ʃeə] sich etwas teilen (mit) I

she [ʃiː] sie I

sheep, *pl* sheep [ʃiːp] Schaf II

sheep station Schaffarm *(in Australien)* V

sheet [ʃiːt] Blatt, Bogen *(Papier)* V

shelf [ʃelf], *pl* **shelves** [ʃelvz] Regal(brett) I

shift [ʃɪft] Schicht *(bei der Arbeit)* IV • **on his shift** in seiner Schicht IV

shine [ʃaɪn], **shone, shone** scheinen *(Sonne)* II

shiny ['ʃaɪni] glänzend V

ship [ʃɪp] Schiff I

shirt [ʃɜːt] Hemd I

shiver ['ʃɪvə] zittern II

shock [ʃɒk] Schock, Schreck v

shocked [ʃɒkt] schockiert v

shocking ['ʃɒkɪŋ] schockierend, erschreckend, schrecklich v

shoe [ʃuː] Schuh I

shone [ʃɒn] *siehe* **shine**

shook [ʃʊk] *siehe* **shake**

shoot [ʃuːt], **shot, shot** (er)schießen v

shop [ʃɒp] Laden, Geschäft I

shop (-pp-) [ʃɒp] einkaufen (gehen) I • **shop for sth.** etwas einkaufen v

shop assistant ['ʃɒp‿ə‚sɪstənt] Verkäufer/in I

shopping ['ʃɒpɪŋ] (das) Einkaufen I **go shopping** einkaufen gehen I

shopping list ['ʃɒpɪŋ lɪst] Einkaufsliste I

shopping mall ['ʃɒpɪŋ mɔːl] *(großes)* Einkaufszentrum III

shop window [‚ʃɒp 'wɪndəʊ] Schaufenster II

short [ʃɔːt] kurz I; klein *(Person)* IV

shorts *(pl)* [ʃɔːts] Shorts, kurze Hose I

shot [ʃɒt] *siehe* **shoot**

shot [ʃɒt]
1. Schuss III
°**2.** Szene *(beim Filmen)*
winning shot Siegtreffer, Siegesschuss III

should [ʃəd, ʃʊd]**: we should ...** wir sollten ... IV • **You should have closed the window.** Du hättest das Fenster schließen sollen. VI 3 (55/182) • **I shouldn't have said that.** Ich hätte das nicht sagen sollen. VI 3 (55/182)
▶ S.176 Möglich? Wahrscheinlich? Sicherlich?
▶ S.182 should + have + past participle

shoulder ['ʃəʊldə] Schulter I

shout [ʃaʊt] schreien, rufen I **shout at sb.** jn. anschreien I

show [ʃəʊ] Show, Vorstellung I

show [ʃəʊ], **showed, shown** zeigen I

shower ['ʃaʊə] Dusche I • **have a shower** (sich) duschen I • **take a shower** (sich) duschen VI 2 (36)

shown [ʃəʊn] *siehe* **show**

shut up [‚ʃʌt‿'ʌp], **shut, shut** *(infml)* den Mund halten II

shy [ʃaɪ] schüchtern, scheu II

sick [sɪk]**: I feel sick.** Mir ist schlecht. IV

side [saɪd] Seite II

sidewalk ['saɪdwɔːk] *(AE)* Gehweg, Bürgersteig IV

sights *(pl)* [saɪts] Sehenswürdigkeiten III

sign [saɪn] Schild; Zeichen III

sign [saɪn] unterschreiben, unterzeichnen VI 3 (47)

silence ['saɪləns] Stille; Schweigen III

silent ['saɪlənt] still, lautlos; schweigend v • **silent letter** „stummer" Buchstabe *(nicht gesprochener Buchstabe)* II

silly ['sɪli] albern, dumm III

similar (to sb./sth.) ['sɪmɪlə] (jm./ etwas) ähnlich v

simple ['sɪmpl] simpel, einfach v

since [sɪns]
1. da (ja), weil IV
2. since April 4th seit dem 4. April IV • **since then** seitdem IV

sincerely [sɪn'sɪəli]**: Yours sincerely** Mit freundlichen Grüßen *(Briefschluss bei namentlich bekanntem Empfänger)* v

sing [sɪŋ], **sang, sung** singen I °**sing along** mitsingen

singer ['sɪŋə] Sänger/in II

single ['sɪŋgl] ledig, alleinstehend I

single ['sɪŋgl] Single III

single (ticket) ['sɪŋgl] einfache Fahrkarte *(nur Hinfahrt)* III **single room** Einzelzimmer v

sink [sɪŋk] Spüle, Spülbecken I

sir [sɜː] Sir *(höfliche Anrede für einen Unbekannten (z. B. einen Kunden) oder einen Vorgesetzten* IV • **Dear Sir/Madam** Sehr geehrte Damen und Herren *(Briefbeginn)* v

sister ['sɪstə] Schwester I

sister city ['sɪstə sɪti] *(AE)* Partnerstadt IV

sit (-tt-) [sɪt], **sat, sat** sitzen; sich setzen I • **sit down** sich hinsetzen II • **Sit with me.** Setz dich zu mir. / Setzt euch zu mir. I

situation [‚sɪtʃu'eɪʃn] Situation, Lage VI 1 (8)

size [saɪz] Größe I

skate [skeɪt] Inliner/Skateboard fahren I; Schlittschuh laufen, eislaufen II

skateboard ['skeɪtbɔːd] Skateboard I

skates *(pl)* [skeɪts] Inliner I

sketch [sketʃ] Sketch I

ski [skiː] Ski III

ski [skiː] Ski laufen/fahren III

skill [skɪl] Fähigkeit, Fertigkeit v

skills file ['skɪlz faɪl] *Anhang mit Lern- und Arbeitstechniken* I `

skim a text (-mm-) [skɪm] einen Text überfliegen *(um den Inhalt grob zu erfassen)* III

skin [skɪn] Haut IV

skirt [skɜːt] Rock II

ski slope ['skiː sləʊp] Skipiste III

sky [skaɪ] Himmel II • **in the sky** am Himmel II

skydiving ['skaɪdaɪvɪŋ] Fallschirmspringen v

skyscraper ['skaɪskreɪpə] Wolkenkratzer IV

slang [slæŋ] Slang, Jargon v

slave [sleɪv] Sklave, Sklavin II

sledge [sledʒ] Schlitten III

sleep [sliːp] Schlaf III

sleep [sliːp], **slept, slept** schlafen I

sleeping bag ['sliːpɪŋ bæg] Schlafsack v

sleepless ['sliːpləs] schlaflos IV

sleepover ['sliːpəʊvə] Schlafparty III

slept [slept] *siehe* **sleep**

slice [slaɪs] Scheibe; (Kuchen-)Stück v

slide [slaɪd] Dia; Folie *(in Präsentationsprogrammen)* v

slogan ['sləʊgən] Slogan, Parole v

slow [sləʊ] langsam II

slum [slʌm] Slum, Elendsviertel v

small [smɔːl] klein II

smart [smɑːt] clever, schlau IV

smell [smel] riechen II

smell [smel] Geruch II

smile [smaɪl] lächeln I • **smile at sb.** jn. anlächeln II

smile [smaɪl] Lächeln II

smoke [sməʊk] rauchen II

smoke [sməʊk] Rauch II

snack [snæk] Snack, Imbiss II

snake [sneɪk] Schlange I

snow [snəʊ] Schnee II

snowball ['snəʊbɔːl] Schneeball IV

snowshoe ['snəʊʃuː] Schneeschuh III

snowshoeing ['snəʊʃuːɪŋ] Schneeschuhwandern III

snowstorm ['snəʊstɔːm] Schneesturm VI 2 (35)

so [səʊ]
1. also; deshalb, daher I • **So?** Und? / Na und? II
2. so sweet so süß I • **so far** bis jetzt, bis hierher I
3. so that sodass, damit III
4. I think so. Ich glaube (ja). I **I don't think so.** Das finde/glaube ich nicht. I • **Do you really think so?** Meinst du wirklich? / Glaubst du das wirklich? II • **if so** wenn ja; wenn dem so ist VI 1 (15)

soap [səʊp]
1. *(infml)* Seife I
2. *(infml)* Seifenoper IV

soap opera ['səʊp‿ɒprə] *(infml auch:* **soap***)* Seifenoper IV soccer ['sɒkə] Fußball IV

social ['səʊʃl] sozial, Sozial-, gesellschaftlich V

social worker ['səʊʃl ˌwɜːkə] Sozialarbeiter/in V

sock [sɒk] Socke, Strumpf I

soda ['səʊdə] (AE) Limonade IV

sofa ['səʊfə] Sofa I

soft [sɒft] weich IV • **soft drink** alkoholfreies Getränk IV

software ['sɒftweə] Software II

solar ['səʊlə] Solar-, Sonnen- VI 2 (30)

sold [səʊld] siehe **sell** • **be sold out** ausverkauft sein, vergriffen sein III

soldier ['səʊldʒə] Soldat/in IV

solve [sɒlv] lösen; aufklären V

some [səm, sʌm] einige, ein paar I **some cheese/juice/money** etwas Käse/Saft/Geld I

somebody ['sʌmbədi] jemand I **Find/Ask somebody who ...** Finde/ Frage jemanden, der ... II

somehow ['sʌmhaʊ] irgendwie V

someone ['sʌmwʌn] IV siehe **somebody**

something ['sʌmθɪŋ] etwas I **something to eat** etwas zu essen I

sometimes ['sʌmtaɪmz] manchmal I

somewhere ['sʌmweə] irgendwo(hin) II

son [sʌn] Sohn I

song [sɒŋ] Lied, Song I

soon [suːn] bald I • **as soon as** sobald, sowie II

sooner ['suːnə] eher, früher V

sore [sɔː]: **be sore** wund sein, wehtun II • **have a sore throat** Halsschmerzen haben II

sorry ['sɒri]: **(I'm) sorry.** Entschuldigung. / Tut mir leid. I • **Sorry, I'm late.** Entschuldigung, dass ich zu spät bin/komme. I • **Sorry?** Wie bitte? I • **say sorry** sich entschuldigen II

sound [saʊnd] klingen, sich (gut usw.) anhören I

sound [saʊnd] Laut; Klang I

sound file ['saʊnd faɪl] Tondatei, Soundfile III

soundtrack ['saʊndtræk] Filmmusik, Soundtrack VI 1 (12)

soup [suːp] Suppe II

source [sɔːs] (Informations-, Text-) Quelle IV

south [saʊθ] Süden; nach Süden; südlich III

southbound ['saʊθbaʊnd] Richtung Süden III

south-east [ˌsaʊθˈiːst] Südosten; nach Südosten; südöstlich III

south-west [ˌsaʊθˈwest] Südwesten; nach Südwesten; südwestlich III

°souvenir [ˌsuːvəˈnɪə] Andenken, Souvenir

space [speɪs] **1.** Platz, Raum V °**2.** Weltraum **Move back one space.** Geh ein Feld zurück. II • **Move on one space.** Geh ein Feld vor. II

spaghetti [spəˈɡeti] Spaghetti II

spat [spæt] siehe **spit**

speak (to) [spiːk], spoke, spoken sprechen (mit), reden (mit) II **speak out** seine Meinung (offen) sagen VI 3 (47)

special ['speʃl] besondere(r, s) III **What's special about ...?** Was ist das Besondere an ...? III • **special effects** (pl) [ˌspeʃl ɪˈfekts] Spezialeffekte VI 1 (12)

°speculate (about) ['spekjuleɪt] Vermutungen anstellen (über), spekulieren (über)

speech [spiːtʃ] Rede IV • **free speech** Redefreiheit VI 3 (54) **make a speech** eine Rede halten IV

°speech bubble ['spiːtʃ bʌbl] Sprechblase

spell [spel] buchstabieren I

spelling ['spelɪŋ] (Recht-)Schreibung, Schreibweise I

spend [spend], spent, spent: **spend money (on)** Geld ausgeben (für) II • **spend time (on)** Zeit verbringen (mit) II

spent [spent] siehe **spend**

spicy ['spaɪsi] würzig, scharf gewürzt III

spit (at sb.) (-tt-) [spɪt], spat, spat (jn. an)spucken IV

splash [splæʃ] spritzen IV

spoke [spəʊk] siehe **speak**

spoken ['spəʊkən] siehe **speak**

spoon [spuːn] Löffel III

sport [spɔːt] Sport; Sportart I **do sport** Sport treiben I

sports gear (no pl) ['spɔːts ɡɪə] Sportausrüstung, Sportsachen II

sports hall ['spɔːts hɔːl] Sporthalle III

sportsman, -woman ['spɔːtsmən, -ˌwʊmən] Sportler/in IV

sporty ['spɔːti] sportlich V

spot (-tt-) [spɒt] entdecken III

spray [spreɪ] sprühen; besprühen IV

spring [sprɪŋ] **1.** Frühling I **2.** Quelle V

spy [spaɪ] Spion/in I

square [skweə] Platz (in der Stadt) II

square km (sq km) [skweə] Quadratkilometer III

squeeze [skwiːz] drücken; (aus-)pressen III

squirrel ['skwɪrəl] Eichhörnchen II

stadium ['steɪdiəm] Stadion III

stage [steɪdʒ] Bühne I

stairs (pl) [steəz] Treppe; Treppenstufen I

stamp [stæmp] Briefmarke I

stand [stænd], stood, stood **1.** stehen; sich (hin)stellen II **stand up** aufstehen II **2.** aushalten, ertragen V • **I can't stand him.** Ich kann ihn nicht ausstehen. V

star [stɑː]: **the film stars ...** der Film hat ... in der Hauptrolle / in den Hauptrollen VI 1 (12)

star [stɑː] **1.** Stern II **2.** (Film-, Pop-)Star I

start [stɑːt] starten, anfangen, beginnen (mit) I • **start a business** ein Unternehmen gründen V

start [stɑːt] Start, Anfang, Beginn II

state [steɪt] Staat III

statement ['steɪtmənt] Aussage, Feststellung III

station ['steɪʃn] **1.** Bahnhof I • **at the station** am Bahnhof I **2.** (radio/pop) station (Radio-/ Pop-)Sender III • **fire station** Feuerwache IV • **gas station** (AE) Tankstelle IV • **petrol station** Tankstelle IV • **power station** Kraftwerk, Elektrizitätswerk VI 2 (31) **sheep station** Schaffarm (in Australien) V

statue ['stætʃuː] Statue II

stay [steɪ] bleiben; wohnen, übernachten II • **stay behind** zurückbleiben, daheimbleiben IV • **stay in touch** in Kontakt bleiben VI 1 (8) **stay out** draußen bleiben, wegbleiben III

stay [steɪ] Aufenthalt V

steak [steɪk] Steak III

steal [stiːl], stole, stolen stehlen II

°steam engine ['stiːm ˌendʒɪn] Dampfmaschine

°steampowered ['stiːm ˌpaʊəd] dampfgetrieben, dampfbetrieben

steel [stiːl] Stahl III

steel drum [ˌstiːl ˈdrʌm] Steeldrum III

step [step]
1. Stufe IV
2. Schritt I

stereo [ˈsteriəʊ] Stereo; Stereoanlage VI 2 (34)

stew [stjuː] Eintopf(gericht) III

stick out of sth. [stɪk]**, stuck, stuck** aus etwas herausragen, herausstehen III

still [stɪl]
1. (immer) noch I
2. trotzdem, dennoch V

°**still** [stɪl] Standfoto

stole [stəʊl] *siehe* **steal**

stolen [ˈstəʊlən] gestohlen V *siehe* **steal**

stomach [ˈstʌmək] Magen II

stomach ache [ˈstʌmək ˌeɪk] Magenschmerzen, Bauchweh II

stone [stəʊn] Stein II

stood [stʊd] *siehe* **stand**

stop (-pp-) [stɒp]
1. aufhören I
2. anhalten I
Stop that! Hör auf damit! / Lass das! I

store [stɔː] (ein)lagern, aufbewahren V

store [stɔː]**: department store** Kaufhaus II

storm [stɔːm] Sturm; Gewitter II

stormy [ˈstɔːmi] stürmisch II

story [ˈstɔːri] Geschichte, Erzählung I

straight [streɪt]
°1. gerade, aufrecht
2. glatt *(Haare)* VI 1 (6/171)
3. **straight on** geradeaus weiter II
straight towards sb. direkt auf jn. zu IV

straighten sth. up [ˌstreɪtn_ˈʌp] etwas aufräumen, etwas in Ordnung bringen V

strange [streɪndʒ] seltsam, sonderbar; fremd III

strawberry [ˈstrɔːbəri] Erdbeere II

street [striːt] Straße I • **at 7 Hamilton Street** in der Hamiltonstraße 7 I

strength [streŋθ] Stärke, Kraft V

stress [stres]
1. Stress V
2. Betonung III

stressed [strest]
1. gestresst V
°2. betont

stressful [ˈstresfl] anstrengend, stressig V

strict [strɪkt] streng III

strike [straɪk] Streik III • **be on strike** streiken, sich im Streik befinden III • **go on strike** streiken, in den Streik treten III

strong [strɒŋ] stark II

structure [ˈstrʌktʃə] Struktur; Gliederung III

structure [ˈstrʌktʃə] strukturieren, aufbauen II

stuck [stʌk] *siehe* **stick**

student [ˈstjuːdənt] Schüler/in; Student/in I

studio [ˈstjuːdiəʊ] Studio I

study [ˈstʌdi] studieren; sorgfältig durchlesen; lernen IV

study hall [ˈstʌdi hɔːl] *Zeit zum selbstständigen Lernen in der Schule* IV

study skills *(pl)* [ˈstʌdi skɪlz] Lern- und Arbeitstechniken I

stuff [stʌf] Zeug, Kram II

stupid [ˈstjuːpɪd] blöd, dumm III

stupidity [stjuːˈpɪdəti] Dummheit VI 3 (54)

style [staɪl] Stil V • **military-style fashion** Mode im Militärstil V

subject [ˈsʌbdʒɪkt] Schulfach I

subject line [ˈsʌbdʒɪkt laɪn] Betreffzeile V

suburb [ˈsʌbɜːb] Vorort V

subway [ˈsʌbweɪ]**: the subway** *(AE)* die U-Bahn II

succeed (in sth.) [səkˈsiːd] Erfolg haben, erfolgreich sein (mit etwas, bei etwas) IV

success [səkˈses] Erfolg III

successful [səkˈsesfl] erfolgreich III

such (a) [sʌtʃ] so (ein/e), solch (ein/e); solche V

suddenly [ˈsʌdnli] plötzlich, auf einmal I

suffix [ˈsʌfɪks] Nachsilbe, Suffix VI 3 (54)

sugar [ˈʃʊgə] Zucker II

suggest sth. (to sb.) [səˈdʒest] (jm.) etwas vorschlagen IV

suggestion [səˈdʒestʃən] Vorschlag IV

suit [suːt] Anzug; (Damen-)Kostüm IV

suitable [ˈsuːtəbl] geeignet, passend V

suitcase [ˈsuːtkeɪs] Koffer II

sum sth. up (-mm-) [ˌsʌm_ˈʌp] etwas zusammenfassen V

°**summarize** [ˈsʌməraɪz] zusammenfassen

summary [ˈsʌməri] Zusammenfassung IV

summer [ˈsʌmə] Sommer I

sun [sʌn] Sonne II

Sunday [ˈsʌndeɪ, ˈsʌndi] Sonntag I

sung [sʌŋ] *siehe* **sing**

sunglasses *(pl)* [ˈsʌnglɑːsɪz] (eine) Sonnenbrille I

sunny [ˈsʌni] sonnig II

sunscreen [ˈsʌnskriːn] Sonnenschutzmittel V

supermarket [ˈsuːpəmɑːkɪt] Supermarkt II

supper [ˈsʌpə] Abendessen IV

support [səˈpɔːt] unterstützen IV
support a team eine Mannschaft unterstützen; Fan einer Mannschaft sein III

supporter [səˈpɔːtə] Anhänger/in, Fan III

suppose [səˈpəʊz] annehmen, vermuten II

sure [ʃʊə, ʃɔː] sicher I • **make sure that ...** sich vergewissern, dass ...; dafür sorgen, dass ... IV

surely [ˈʃʊəli, ˈʃɔːli] doch wohl; doch sicher VI 3 (49/181)
▶ S.181 surely

surf [sɜːf] surfen IV • **surf the internet** im Internet surfen II

surfboard [ˈsɜːfbɔːd] Surfbrett II

surfer [ˈsɜːfə] Surfer/in IV

surfing [ˈsɜːfɪŋ]**: go surfing** wellenreiten gehen, surfen gehen II

surprise [səˈpraɪz] Überraschung II

surprise sb. [səˈpraɪz] jn. überraschen III

surprised (at sth.) [səˈpraɪzd] überrascht (über etwas) III

surprising [səˈpraɪzɪŋ] überraschend, erstaunlich III

surrounded by [səˈraʊndɪd] umgeben von; umstellt von V

survey (on) [ˈsɜːveɪ] Umfrage, Untersuchung (über) II

survival [səˈvaɪvl] Überleben II

survive [səˈvaɪv] überleben II

suspense [səˈspens] Spannung V

swam [swæm] *siehe* **swim**

swap sth. (for sth.) (-pp-) [swɒp] etwas (ein)tauschen (für etwas/ gegen etwas) IV

°**sway** [sweɪ] *hier:* hin- und herwiegen

sweat [swet] schwitzen IV

sweat [swet] Schweiß IV

sweatshirt [ˈswetʃɜːt] Sweatshirt I

sweet [swiːt] süß I

sweetheart [ˈswiːthɑːt] Liebling, Schatz II

sweets *(pl)* [swiːts] Süßigkeiten I

swim (-mm-) [swɪm]**, swam, swum** schwimmen I • **go swimming** schwimmen gehen I

swimmer [ˈswɪmə] Schwimmer/in II

swimming pool ['swɪmɪŋ puːl]
Schwimmbad, Schwimmbecken I
swimming trunks *(pl)* ['swɪmɪŋ
trʌŋks] Badehose III
swimsuit ['swɪmsuːt] Badeanzug III
swipe a card [swaɪp] eine Karte
durchziehen *(an Tür, Eingang)*
VI 2 (34)
swum [swʌm] *siehe* **swim**
syllable ['sɪləbl] Silbe I
°**symbol** ['sɪmbl] Symbol
synagogue ['sɪnəgɒg] Synagoge III
▶ S.173 Religions
synonym ['sɪnənɪm] Synonym
(Wort mit gleicher oder sehr ähnlicher Bedeutung) IV
system ['sɪstəm] System IV

T

table ['teɪbl] Tisch I
table tennis ['teɪbl tenɪs] Tischtennis I • **table tennis bat** Tischtennisschläger III
taboo [tə'buː] tabu; Tabu V
take [teɪk], **took, taken**
  1. nehmen I
  2. (weg-, hin)bringen I
  3. dauern, *(Zeit)* brauchen III
  I can take it. Ich halt's aus. / Ich
  kann's aushalten. IV • **I'll take it
  from here.** *etwa:* Ich übernehme
  das jetzt. / Ich komme jetzt allein
  klar. IV • **take action** handeln;
  etwas unternehmen VI 3 (50)
  take a break eine Pause machen
  IV • **take an exam** eine Prüfung
  ablegen IV • **take a look (at)**
  einen Blick werfen (auf) V • **take
  a ride** eine Fahrt machen III
  take a shower duschen VI 2 (36)
  take notes sich Notizen machen I
  take off *(infml)* sich davonmachen, sich aus dem Staub machen
  IV • **take someone's advice** auf jemandes Rat hören V • **take sth.
  off** etwas ausziehen *(Kleidung)* II;
  etwas absetzen *(Hut, Helm)* III
  take 10 c off 10 Cent abziehen I
  take sth. out etwas herausnehmen I • **take sth. over** etwas
  übernehmen; etwas in seine Gewalt bringen IV • **take part (in)**
  teilnehmen (an) IV • **take photos**
  Fotos machen, fotografieren I
  take place stattfinden IV • **take
  sb./sth. seriously** jn./etwas ernst
  nehmen VI 3 (48) • **take sb.
  through sth.** etwas mit jm. (genau) durchgehen VI 2 (34) • °**Take
  turns.** Wechselt euch ab.

taken ['teɪkən] *siehe* **take**
talent ['tælənt] Talent, Begabung III
talk [tɔːk]
  1. Gespräch IV
  2. Vortrag, Rede V
  give a talk (on sth.) einen Vortrag/
  eine Rede halten (über etwas) V
talk (to sb. about sth.) [tɔːk] (mit
  jm. über etwas) reden, sich (mit jm.
  über etwas) unterhalten I
tall [tɔːl] hoch *(Bäume, Türme usw.)*;
  groß *(Person)* IV
tank [tæŋk] Tank III
target ['tɑːgɪt] Ziel; Zielscheibe
  VI 2 (29)
tattoo [tə'tuː] Tattoo, Tätowierung
  VI 1 (10)
taught [tɔːt] *siehe* **teach**
tax [tæks] *(die)* Steuer VI 3 (49)
taxi ['tæksi] Taxi III
tea [tiː] Tee *(auch: leichte Nachmittags- oder Abendmahlzeit)* I
tea bag ['tiː bæg] Teebeutel IV
teach [tiːtʃ], **taught, taught** unterrichten, lehren I
teacher ['tiːtʃə] Lehrer/in I
team [tiːm] Team, Mannschaft I
tear [tɪə] Träne IV
tear sth. off [teə], **tore, torn** etwas
  abreißen IV
teaspoon ['tiːspuːn] Teelöffel III
technical ['teknɪkl] technisch V
technician [tek'nɪʃn] Techniker/in V
technology [tek'nɒlədʒi] Technologie V
teddy bear ['tedi beə] Teddybär III
teen [tiːn] Teenager-, Jugend- III
teenager ['tiːneɪdʒə] Teenager,
  Jugendliche(r) II
teeth [tiːθ] *pl von „tooth"*
°**telegraph** ['telɪgrɑːf] Telegraf
telephone ['telɪfəun] Telefon I
  telephone number Telefonnummer I
television (TV) ['telɪvɪʒn] Fernsehen
  I
tell (about) [tel], **told, told** erzählen
  (von), berichten (über) I • **Tell me
  your names.** Sagt mir eure Namen.
  I • **tell lies** lügen VI 3 (47/179) **tell
  sb. the way** jm. den Weg beschreiben II • **tell sb. to do sth.** jn. auffordern, etwas zu tun; jm. sagen,
  dass er/sie etwas tun soll II
temperature ['temprətʃə] Temperatur II • **have a temperature** Fieber haben II
temple ['templ] Tempel VI 1 (13/173)
  ▶ S.173 Religions
tennis ['tenɪs] Tennis I
tennis racket Tennisschläger
  VI 3 (48)

tense [tens] (grammatische) Zeit,
  Tempus III
tent [tent] Zelt IV
term [tɜːm] Trimester II
terrible ['terəbl] schrecklich, furchtbar I
terrified ['terɪfaɪd]: **be terrified (of)**
  schreckliche Angst haben (vor) IV
°**territory** ['terətri] Revier, Gebiet,
  Territorium
terrorist ['terərɪst] Terrorist/in IV
terrorist ['terərɪst] terroristisch,
  Terror- IV
test [test] Klassenarbeit, Test, Prüfung II
test testen, prüfen VI 2 (32)
text [tekst] Text I
text message ['tekst ˌmesɪdʒ] SMS III
text sb. [tekst] jm. eine SMS schicken III
than [ðæn, ðən] als II • **more than**
  mehr als II • **more than me** mehr
  als ich II
Thank you. ['θæŋk juː] Danke
  (schön). I • **Thanks.** [θæŋks]
  Danke. I • **Thanks a lot!** Vielen
  Dank! I • **Thanks very much!**
  Danke sehr! / Vielen Dank! II
  thanks to penicillin dank Penizillin; wegen Penizillin VI 2 (32)
that [ðət, ðæt]
  1. das (dort) I
  2. jene(r, s) I
  that day an jenem Tag III • **That's
  me.** Das bin ich. I • **That's right.**
  Das ist richtig. / Das stimmt. I
  That's up to you. Das liegt bei dir./
  Das kannst/musst du (selbst) entscheiden. III • **that's why** deshalb, darum I • **That way ...** So .../
  Auf diese Weise ... III
that [ðət, ðæt] der, die, das; die
  (Relativpronomen) III
that [ðət, ðæt] dass I • **so that**
  sodass, damit III
that far/good/bad/... [ðæt] so weit/
  gut/schlecht/... I
the [ðə, ði] der, die, das; die I
theatre ['θɪətə] Theater II
their [ðeə] ihr, ihre *(Plural)* I
theirs [ðeəz] ihrer, ihre, ihrs *(Plural)*
  II
them [ðəm, ðem] sie; ihnen I
theme park ['θiːm pɑːk] Themenpark *(Freizeitpark mit Attraktionen
  zu einem bestimmten Thema)* IV
themselves [ðəm'selvz] sich (selbst)
  III
then [ðen]
  1. dann, danach I
  2. damals VI 2 (32)
  since then seitdem IV

there [ðeə]
1. da, dort I
2. dahin, dorthin I
down there dort unten II • **in there** dort drinnen I • **over there** da drüben, dort drüben I • **there are** es sind (vorhanden); es gibt I
there's es ist (vorhanden); es gibt I • **there isn't a ...** es ist kein/e ...; es gibt kein/e ... I • **There you go!** *(infml)* etwa: So, das hätten wir. IV
up there dort oben III
thermometer [θə'mɒmɪtə] Thermometer II
these [ði:z] diese, die (hier) I
they [ðeɪ] sie *(Plural)* I
thick [θɪk] dick VI 1 (7/171)
thief [θi:f], *pl* **thieves** [θi:vz] Dieb/in II
thin [θɪn] dünn VI 1 (7)
thing [θɪŋ] Ding, Sache I • **What was the best thing about ...?** Was war das Beste an ...? I
think [θɪŋk], **thought, thought** glauben, meinen, denken I • **I think so.** Ich glaube (ja). I • **I don't think so.** Das finde/glaube ich nicht. I • **think about 1.** nachdenken über II; **2.** denken über, halten von II • **think of 1.** denken über, halten von II; **2.** denken an; sich ausdenken II
third [θɜ:d] dritte(r, s) I
thirsty ['θɜ:sti] durstig I • **be thirsty** Durst haben, durstig sein I
this [ðɪs]
1. dies (hier) I
2. diese(r, s) I
like this so IV • **This is Isabel.** Hier spricht Isabel. / Hier ist Isabel. *(am Telefon)* II • **This is where ...** Hier ... V • **this morning/afternoon/evening** heute Morgen/Nachmittag/Abend I • **this way 1.** hier entlang, in diese Richtung II; **2.** so; auf diese Weise III
those [ðəʊz] die (da), jene (dort) I
though [ðəʊ] obwohl V
thought [θɔ:t] *siehe* **think**
thought [θɔ:t] Gedanke IV
thoughtful ['θɔ:tfl] nachdenklich; aufmerksam, rücksichtsvoll VI 3 (102)
thousand ['θaʊznd] tausend I
threw [θru:] *siehe* **throw**
thriller ['θrɪlə] Thriller VI 1 (12)
throat [θrəʊt] Hals, Kehle II • **have a sore throat** Halsschmerzen haben II
through [θru:] durch II
throw [θrəʊ], **threw, thrown** werfen I • **throw up** sich übergeben IV

thrown [θrəʊn] *siehe* **throw**
Thursday ['θɜ:zdeɪ, 'θɜ:zdi] Donnerstag I
°**tick** [tɪk] Häkchen
°**tick** [tɪk] ein Häkchen machen, ankreuzen
ticket ['tɪkɪt]
1. Eintrittskarte I
2. Fahrkarte II
all-day ticket Tagesfahrkarte III
return ticket Rückfahrkarte II
single ticket einfache Fahrkarte *(nur Hinfahrt)* III
ticket agent ['tɪkɪt ˌeɪdʒənt] *Ange*stellte(r) in Kartenvorverkaufsstelle IV
ticket machine ['tɪkɪt məˌʃi:n] Fahrkartenautomat III
ticket office ['tɪkɪt ˌɒfɪs] Kasse *(für den Verkauf von Eintrittskarten)*; Fahrkartenschalter IV
tide [taɪd] Gezeiten, Ebbe und Flut II • **the tide is in** es ist Flut II • **the tide is out** es ist Ebbe II
tidy ['taɪdi] aufräumen I
tidy ['taɪdi] ordentlich, aufgeräumt II
tie (-ing form: **tying**) [taɪ] binden IV
tie [taɪ] Krawatte, Schlips IV
tiger ['taɪgə] Tiger II
tight [taɪt] fest IV
tights (pl) [taɪts] Strumpfhose III
till [tɪl] bis *(zeitlich)* I • **not ... till** erst (um); nicht vor III
time [taɪm]
1. Zeit; Uhrzeit I • **What's the time?** Wie spät ist es? I • **a long time** lange III • **in time** rechtzeitig II • **time of day** Tageszeit V
2. time(s) Mal(e); -mal II • **for the first time** zum ersten Mal IV
next time das nächste Mal VI 3 (102) • **one at a time** einzeln VI 3 (48/181) • **two at a time** zwei auf einmal *(zur selben Zeit)* VI 3 (48)
timeline ['taɪmlaɪn] Zeitstrahl III
timetable ['taɪmteɪbl]
1. Stundenplan I
2. Fahrplan III
timing ['taɪmɪŋ]: **bad timing** schlechtes Timing III
tip [tɪp]
1. Spitze IV
2. Tipp III
tired ['taɪəd] müde I • **be tired of sth.** genug von etwas haben, etwas satt haben IV • **get tired of sth.** einer Sache überdrüssig werden, die Lust an etwas verlieren IV
title ['taɪtl] Titel, Überschrift I

to [tə, tu]
1. zu, nach I • **an e-mail to** eine E-Mail an I • **to Jenny's** zu Jenny I • **to the doctor's** zum Arzt III
to the front nach vorn I • **I've never been to Bath.** Ich bin noch nie in Bath gewesen. II • **write to** schreiben an I
2. quarter to 12 Viertel vor 12 (11.45 / 23.45) I • **from Monday to Friday** von Montag bis Freitag I • **to date** bis heute V • **to this day** bis heute, bis zum heutigen Tag V
3. something to eat etwas zu essen I • **try to do** versuchen, zu tun I • **we know what to do** wir wissen, was wir tun müssen; wir wissen, was zu tun ist III
4. um zu I
toast [təʊst] Toast(brot) I
toaster ['təʊstə] Toaster VI 2 (28)
tobacco [tə'bækəʊ] Tabak II
today [tə'deɪ] heute I; heutzutage V
toe [təʊ] Zeh I
together [tə'geðə] zusammen I
go together zusammenpassen IV
toilet ['tɔɪlət] Toilette I
told [təʊld] *siehe* **tell**
tolerant ['tɒlərənt] tolerant III
tomato [tə'mɑ:təʊ], *pl* **tomatoes** Tomate II
tomorrow [tə'mɒrəʊ] morgen I
tomorrow's weather das Wetter von morgen II
°**tongue-twister** ['tʌŋtwɪstə] Zungenbrecher
tonight [tə'naɪt] heute Nacht, heute Abend I • **tonight's programme** das Programm von heute Abend; das heutige Abendprogramm II
tonne [tʌn] Tonne *(Gewichtseinheit)* VI 2 (29)
too [tu:]: **from Bristol too** auch aus Bristol I • **Me too.** Ich auch. I
too much/big/... [tu:] zu viel/groß/ ... I
took [tʊk] *siehe* **take**
tool [tu:l] Werkzeug IV
tooth [tu:θ], *pl* **teeth** [ti:θ] Zahn I
toothache ['tu:θeɪk] Zahnschmerzen II
toothless ['tu:θləs] zahnlos IV
top [tɒp]
1. Spitze, oberes Ende I • **at the top (of)** oben, am oberen Ende, an der Spitze (von) I
2. Top, Oberteil I
topic ['tɒpɪk] Thema, Themenbereich I • **topic sentence** *Satz, der in das Thema eines Absatzes einführt* II

tore [tɔː] *siehe* **tear**

torn [tɔːn] *siehe* **tear**

tornado [tɔːˈneɪdəʊ] Tornado, Wirbelsturm II

tortoise [ˈtɔːtəs] Schildkröte I

touch [tʌtʃ] berühren, anfassen II

touch [tʌtʃ]: **keep in touch** in Verbindung bleiben, Kontakt halten III • **stay in touch** in Kontakt bleiben VI 1 (8)

tour [tʊə] Tour, Rundgang I • **tour of the house** Rundgang durch das Haus I

tourism [ˈtʊərɪzəm] Tourismus V

tourist [ˈtʊərɪst] Tourist/in II **tourist information** Fremdenverkehrsamt II

towards [təˈwɔːdz] auf ... zu II; in Richtung VI 2 (30) • °**feel ... towards sb.** sich ... fühlen gegenüber jm.

towel [ˈtaʊəl] Handtuch IV

tower [ˈtaʊə] Turm I

town [taʊn] Stadt I

town council [ˈkaʊnsl] Stadtrat *(Gremium)* VI 3 (47/180)
▶ S.180 Politics

town councillor [ˈkaʊnsələ] Stadtrat/-rätin VI 3 (47/180)
▶ S.180 Politics

town hall [taʊn ˈhɔːl] Rathaus VI 3 (47/180)
▶ S.180 Politics

track [træk]
1. Stück, Titel, Track *(auf einer CD)* III
2. running track Laufbahn *(Sport)* III

tractor [ˈtræktə] Traktor V

trade [treɪd] Handel VI 3 (47)

tradition [trəˈdɪʃn] Tradition IV

traditional [trəˈdɪʃənl] traditionell III

traffic [ˈtræfɪk] Verkehr II

traffic jam [ˈtræfɪk dʒæm] (Verkehrs-)Stau IV

trail [treɪl]
1. (Lehr-)Pfad IV
°**2.** Route, Weg

train [treɪn] Zug I • **on the train** im Zug I

train [treɪn] trainieren III • **train as ...** eine Ausbildung machen zu ... V

trainers *(pl)* [ˈtreɪnəz] Turnschuhe II

training [ˈtreɪnɪŋ] *(berufliche)* Ausbildung V

training session [ˈtreɪnɪŋ ˌseʃn] Trainingsstunde, -einheit III

train times *(pl)* [ˈtreɪn taɪmz] (Zug-)Abfahrtszeiten IV

tram [træm] Straßenbahn III

translate [trænsˈleɪt] übersetzen III

translation [trænsˈleɪʃn] Übersetzung III

transparency [trænsˈpærənsi] Folie *(für Overheadprojektoren)* V

transport *(no pl)* [ˈtrænspɔːt] Verkehrsmittel III • **public transport** *(no pl)* öffentliche Verkehrsmittel, öffentlicher Personennahverkehr III

trap [træp] Falle II

trash [træʃ] *(AE)* Abfall, Müll V

travel *(BE: -ll-)* [ˈtrævl] reisen II

travel agent [ˈtrævl ˌeɪdʒənt] Reisebürokaufmann/-kauffrau V • **travel agent's** Reisebüro V

Travelcard [ˈtrævlkɑːd] Tagesfahrkarte *(der Londoner Verkehrsbetriebe)* III

tree [triː] Baum I

trendy [ˈtrendi] modisch, schick III

trick [trɪk]
1. (Zauber-)Kunststück, Trick I • **do tricks** (Zauber-)Kunststücke machen I
2. Streich II • **play a trick on sb.** jm. einen Streich spielen II

trick sb. [trɪk] jn. reinlegen V **trick sb. into doing sth.** jn. mit einer List / einem Trick dazu bringen, etwas zu tun V

tricky [ˈtrɪki] verzwickt, heikel V

trip [trɪp] Reise; Ausflug I • **go on a trip** einen Ausflug machen II

trombone [trɒmˈbəʊn] Posaune III

trouble [ˈtrʌbl] Schwierigkeiten, Ärger II • **be in trouble** in Schwierigkeiten sein; Ärger kriegen II **get in trouble** in Schwierigkeiten geraten V

trousers *(pl)* [ˈtraʊzəz] Hose II

truck [trʌk] Last(kraft)wagen, LKW V

true [truː] wahr II

trumpet [ˈtrʌmpɪt] Trompete III

trust [trʌst] trauen, vertrauen V

truth [truːθ] Wahrheit VI 3 (47)

try [traɪ]
1. versuchen I
2. probieren, kosten I
try and do sth. / try to do sth. versuchen, etwas zu tun I • **try on** anprobieren *(Kleidung)* I

T-shirt [ˈtiːʃɜːt] T-Shirt I

tube [tjuːb]: **the Tube** *(no pl)* die Londoner U-Bahn III

Tuesday [ˈtjuːzdeɪ, ˈtjuːzdi] Dienstag I

tune [tjuːn] Melodie III

tunnel [ˈtʌnl] Tunnel II

turkey [ˈtɜːki] Truthahn, Pute/Puter III

turn [tɜːn]
1. sich umdrehen II • **turn left/ right** (nach) links/rechts abbiegen II • **turn to sb.** sich jm. zuwenden; sich an jn. wenden II
2. turn sth. on etwas einschalten I **turn sth. off** etwas ausschalten II **turn sth. up/down** etwas lauter/ leiser stellen III; etwas höher/ niedriger stellen *(Heizung usw.)* VI 2 (29)

turn [tɜːn]: **(It's) my turn.** Ich bin dran / an der Reihe. I • **Miss a turn.** Einmal aussetzen. II • °**Take turns.** Wechselt euch ab. • **Whose turn is it?** Wer ist dran / an der Reihe? II

turtle [ˈtɜːtl] Wasserschildkröte V

TV [tiːˈviː] Fernsehen I • **on TV** im Fernsehen I • **watch TV** fernsehen I

TV listings *(pl)* [ˈlɪstɪŋz] das Fernsehprogramm IV

twenty-four seven (24/7) rund um die Uhr, sieben Tage die Woche VI 2 (35)

twice [twaɪs] zweimal III

°**twilight** [ˈtwaɪlaɪt] Dämmerung, Zwielicht

twin [twɪn]: **twin brother** Zwillingsbruder I • **twins** *(pl)* Zwillinge I **twin towers** Zwillingstürme IV **twin town** Partnerstadt I

type [taɪp] *(infml)* Typ III

typical (of) [ˈtɪpɪkl] typisch (für) V

U

ultraviolet (UV) [ˌʌltrəˈvaɪələt] ultraviolett V • **ultraviolet rays** ultraviolette Strahlen V

unattractive [ˌʌnəˈtræktɪv] unattraktiv; wenig verlockend VI 1 (6/170)

unbelievable [ˌʌnbɪˈliːvəbl] unglaublich IV

uncle [ˈʌŋkl] Onkel I

unconscious [ʌnˈkɒnʃəs] bewusstlos II

uncool [ˌʌnˈkuːl] *(infml)* uncool III

under [ˈʌndə] unter I • **under age** minderjährig V

underground [ˈʌndəɡraʊnd]: **the underground** die U-Bahn II

°**underline** [ˌʌndəˈlaɪn] unterstreichen

°**underlined** [ˌʌndəˈlaɪnd] unterstrichen

understand [ˌʌndəˈstænd], **understood, understood** verstehen, begreifen I

understandable [ˌʌndə'stændəbl] verständlich IV
understood [ˌʌndə'stʊd] *siehe* **understand**
unfair [ˌʌn'feə] unfair, ungerecht III
unforgettable [ˌʌnfə'getəbl] unvergesslich V
unforgiveable [ˌʌnfə'gɪvəbl] unverzeihlich V
unfortunately [ʌn'fɔːtʃənətli] leider, unglücklicherweise VI 1 (12)
unfriendly [ʌn'frendli] unfreundlich III
unhappy [ʌn'hæpi] unglücklich III
unhealthy [ʌn'helθi] ungesund III
uniform ['juːnɪfɔːm] Uniform I
unit ['juːnɪt] Kapitel, Lektion I
unite [ju'naɪt] vereinen, vereinigen, verbinden V
united [ju'naɪtɪd]: **the United Kingdom (UK)** [juˌnaɪtɪd 'kɪndəm] das Vereinigte Königreich *(Großbritannien und Nordirland)* III • **the United States (US)** [juˌnaɪtɪd 'steɪts] die Vereinigten Staaten (von Amerika) III
university [ˌjuːnɪ'vɜːsəti] Universität IV
unless [ən'les] es sei denn; wenn ... nicht VI 3 (48)
unlike [ˌʌn'laɪk] anders als; im Gegensatz zu VI 1 (6)
unpopular [ʌn'pɒpjələ] unbeliebt, unpopulär VI 1 (15)
unsafe [ʌn'seɪf] nicht sicher, gefährlich III
untidy [ʌn'taɪdi] unordentlich III
until [ən'tɪl] bis III • **not ... until** erst (um); nicht vor III
unwanted [ˌʌn'wɒntɪd] unerwünscht, ungewollt V
up [ʌp] hinauf, herauf, nach oben I
up (the hill) (den Hügel) hinauf II
up there dort oben III • **go up to sb./sth.** auf jn./etwas zugehen V
That's up to you. Das liegt bei dir./ Das kannst/musst du (selbst) entscheiden. III
°**update** [ˌʌp'deɪt] aktualisieren, auf den neuesten Stand bringen
uprising ['ʌpraɪzɪŋ] Aufstand V
upset (about) [ˌʌp'set] aufgebracht, gekränkt, mitgenommen (wegen) III
upset sb. (-tt-) [ʌp'set], **upset, upset** jn. ärgern, kränken, aus der Fassung bringen III
upstairs [ˌʌp'steəz] oben; nach oben I
us [əs, ʌs] uns I
use [juːz] benutzen, verwenden I; verbrauchen *(Energie)* VI 2 (29)

use [juːs] Gebrauch, Benutzung, Verwendung V
°**used** [juːzd] gebraucht
used to ['juːst tə]: **I used to be excited ...** Früher war ich (immer) aufgeregt ... V
useful ['juːsfl] nützlich III
useless ['juːsləs] nutzlos, unbrauchbar V
usually ['juːʒuəli] meistens, gewöhnlich, normalerweise I

V

vacation [və'keɪʃn, *AE:* veɪ'keɪʃn] *(AE)* Urlaub, Ferien III
valley ['væli] Tal II • **valley floor** Talboden II
valuable ['væljuəbl] wertvoll; nützlich IV
valuables *(pl)* ['væljuəblz] Wertgegenstände, Wertsachen V
vampire ['væmpaɪə] Vampir/in VI 1 (12)
vandalism ['vændəlɪzəm] Vandalismus, Zerstörungswut V
vandalize ['vændəlaɪz] mutwillig beschädigen, mutwillig zerstören V
vegetable ['vedʒtəbl] *(ein)* Gemüse III • **vegetable oil** Pflanzenöl IV
vegetarian [ˌvedʒə'teəriən] vegetarisch; Vegetarier/in IV
°**verse** [vɜːs] Strophe, Vers
°**version** ['vɜːʒn, 'vɜːʃn] Version
very ['veri] sehr I • **like/love sth. very much** etwas sehr mögen/ sehr lieben II • **Thanks very much!** Danke sehr! / Vielen Dank! II
vet [vet] Tierarzt/-ärztin V
vet's assistant [ˌvets_ə'sɪstənt] Tierarzthelfer/in V
victim ['vɪktɪm] Opfer III
video ['vɪdiəʊ] Video III
view [vjuː] Aussicht, Blick II • **in my/your view** meiner/deiner Ansicht nach III • **point of view** Standpunkt II • **from my point of view** aus meiner Sicht; von meinem Standpunkt aus gesehen II
°**view** [vjuː] betrachten; *(im Fernsehen/Kino)* anschauen
viewer ['vjuːə] Zuschauer/in IV
village ['vɪlɪdʒ] Dorf I
violence ['vaɪələns] Gewalt, Gewalttätigkeit IV
violent ['vaɪələnt] gewalttätig; gewaltsam IV
virus ['vaɪrəs] Virus I

visibility [ˌvɪzə'bɪləti] Sicht(weite) IV
visit ['vɪzɪt] besuchen, aufsuchen II
visit ['vɪzɪt] Besuch II
visitor ['vɪzɪtə] Besucher/in, Gast I
visual ['vɪʒuəl] visuell; optisch V
vocabulary [və'kæbjələri] Vokabelverzeichnis, Wörterverzeichnis I
voice [vɔɪs] Stimme I
volleyball ['vɒlibɔːl] Volleyball I
°**volt** [vəʊlt, vɒlt] Volt
volunteer [ˌvɒlən'tɪə] Freiwillige(r) IV
volunteer [ˌvɒlən'tɪə] sich freiwillig melden, sich bereit erklären IV
volunteer with ehrenamtliche Arbeit leisten für/bei V
vote [vəʊt] zur Wahl gehen, wählen V • **vote for sb.** für jn. stimmen IV
°**vote** [vəʊt] Abstimmung
vowel sound ['vaʊəl saʊnd] Vokallaut II

W

wait (for) [weɪt] warten (auf) I
I can't wait to see ... ich kann es kaum erwarten, ... zu sehen I
Wait a minute. Warte mal! / Moment mal! II • **Wait and see!** Wart's ab! III
waiter ['weɪtə] Kellner II
waiting room ['weɪtɪŋ ruːm] Wartezimmer IV
waitress ['weɪtrəs] Kellnerin II
wake [weɪk], **woke, woken:**
1. wake sb. (up) jn. (auf)wecken III
2. wake up aufwachen III
walk [wɔːk] (zu Fuß) gehen I
walk on weitergehen III
walk [wɔːk] Spaziergang II • **go for a walk** spazieren gehen, einen Spaziergang machen II
wall [wɔːl] Wand; Mauer II
walrus ['wɔːlrəs] Walross III
want [wɒnt] (haben) wollen I
want to do tun wollen I • **want sb. to do sth.** wollen, dass jd. etwas tut IV
war [wɔː] Krieg IV
wardrobe ['wɔːdrəʊb] Kleiderschrank I
warm [wɔːm] warm II
warm-hearted [ˌwɔːm'hɑːtɪd] warmherzig V
warn sb. (about sth.) [wɔːn] jn. (vor etwas) warnen III
was [wəz, wɒz]: **I/he/she/it was** *siehe* **be**
wash [wɒʃ] waschen I; (auf-) wischen *(Fußboden)* II • **I wash**

my face. Ich wasche mir das Gesicht. • **wash the dishes** das Geschirr abwaschen V

waste [weɪst] Verschwendung VI 3 (47)

waste (on) [weɪst] verschwenden, vergeuden (für) III

watch [wɒtʃ] beobachten, sich *etwas* ansehen; zusehen I
°**watch for sth.** auf etwas achten, nach etwas Ausschau halten
watch TV fernsehen I

watch [wɒtʃ] Armbanduhr I

water ['wɔːtə] Wasser I

waterproof ['wɔːtəpruːf] wasserdicht, wasserfest V

wave [weɪv] winken II

wave [weɪv] Welle V

way [weɪ]
1. Weg II • **ask sb. the way** jn. nach dem Weg fragen II • **on the way (to)** auf dem Weg (zu/nach) II • **tell sb. the way** jm. den Weg beschreiben II
2. Richtung II • **the other way round** anders herum II • **the wrong way** in die falsche Richtung II • **this way** hier entlang, in diese Richtung II • **which way?** in welche Richtung? / wohin? II
3. Art und Weise III • **in a friendly/strange/different way** auf freundliche/seltsame/andere Art und Weise VI 1 (7) • **that way/this way** so; auf diese Weise III • **the way you ...** so wie du ..., auf dieselbe Weise wie du ... IV
4. by the way übrigens; nebenbei (bemerkt) III • **No way!** Auf keinen Fall! / Kommt nicht in Frage! II

we [wiː] wir I

weak [wiːk] schwach II

weakness ['wiːknəs] Schwäche, Schwachpunkt V

wear [weə], **wore, worn** tragen, anhaben *(Kleidung)* I

weather ['weðə] Wetter II

weatherproof ['weðəpruːf] wetterfest V

webcam ['webkæm] Webcam, Internetkamera I

website ['websaɪt] Website II

°**wedding** ['wedɪŋ] Hochzeit, Trauung

Wednesday ['wenzdeɪ, 'wenzdi] Mittwoch I

week [wiːk] Woche I • **days of the week** Wochentage I • **a two-week holiday** ein zweiwöchiger Urlaub III

weekend [ˌwiːk'end] Wochenende I
at the weekend am Wochenende I

welcome ['welkəm]
1. Welcome (to Bristol). Willkommen (in Bristol). I
2. You're welcome. Gern geschehen. / Nichts zu danken. I

welcome sb. (to) ['welkəm] jn. begrüßen, willkommen heißen (in) I
They welcome you to ... Sie heißen dich in ... willkommen I

well [wel]
1. gut II • **do well** erfolgreich sein, gut abschneiden V • **go well** gut (ver)laufen, gutgehen III • **You did well.** Das hast du gut gemacht. II
Oh well ... Na ja ... / Na gut ... I
Well, ... Nun, ... / Also, ... I
2. *(gesundheitlich)* gut; gesund, wohlauf II

well-behaved [ˌwelbɪ'heɪvd] artig, gut erzogen V

well-paid [ˌwel'peɪd] gut bezahlt V

Welsh [welʃ] walisisch; Walisisch II

went [went] *siehe* **go**

were [wə, wɜː]: **we/you/they were** *siehe* **be**

west [west] Westen; nach Westen; westlich III

westbound ['westbaʊnd] Richtung Westen III

western ['westən] westlich, West III

western ['westən] Western VI 1 (14)

wet [wet] nass, feucht V

wetsuit ['wetsuːt] Surfanzug, Taucheranzug V

whale [weɪl] Wal(fisch) V

what [wɒt]
1. was I
2. welche(r, s) I
we know what to do wir wissen, was wir tun müssen; wir wissen, was zu tun ist III • **What about ...? 1.** Was ist mit ...? / Und ...? I;
2. Wie wär's mit ...? I • **What an interesting life!** Was für ein interessantes Leben! III • °**What are the pages about?** Wovon handeln die Seiten? I • **What are you talking about?** Wovon redest du? I • **What colour is ...?** Welche Farbe hat ...? I • **What else do you know ...?** Was weißt du sonst noch ...? II • **What for?** Wofür? II
What have we got next? Was haben wir als Nächstes? I • **What kind of car ...?** Was für ein Auto ...? III • **What page are we on?** Auf welcher Seite sind wir? I • **What's for homework?** Was haben wir als

Hausaufgabe auf? I • **What's for lunch?** Was gibt es zum Mittagessen? III • **What's the matter?** Was ist los? / Was ist denn? II
What's the time? Wie spät ist es? I • **What's wrong with you?** Was fehlt dir? II • **What's your name?** Wie heißt du? I • **What was the weather like?** Wie war das Wetter? II

whatever [wɒt'evə] was (auch) immer IV

wheel [wiːl] Rad III • **big wheel** Riesenrad III

wheelchair ['wiːltʃeə] Rollstuhl I

when [wen] wann I • **When's your birthday?** Wann hast du Geburtstag? I

when [wen]
1. wenn I
2. als I

whenever [wen'evə] wann (auch) immer IV

where [weə]
1. wo I
2. wohin I
This is where ... Hier ... V
Where are you from? Wo kommst du her? I

wherever [weər'evə] wo(hin) (auch) immer IV

whether ['weðə] ob VI 1 (9)

which [wɪtʃ] welche(r, s) I • **Which picture ...?** Welches Bild ...? I
which way? in welche Richtung? / wohin? II

which [wɪtʃ] der, die, das; die *(Relativpronomen)* II

while *(conj)* [waɪl] während III

while [waɪl] Weile V • **for a while** für eine Weile, eine Zeit lang V

whisky ['wɪski] Whisky II

whisper ['wɪspə] flüstern I

whistle ['wɪsl] pfeifen II

whistle ['wɪsl] (Triller-)Pfeife; Pfiff III

white [waɪt] weiß I

whiteboard ['waɪtbɔːd] Weißwandtafel, Whiteboard VI 2 (28)

who [huː]
1. wer I
2. wen / wem II

who [huː] der, die, das; die *(Relativpronomen)* III

whoever [huː'evə] wer (auch) immer; wen/wem (auch) immer IV

whole [həʊl] ganze(r, s), gesamte(r, s) III

whole-grain ['həʊlɡreɪn] Vollkorn IV

whose [huːz] deren, dessen *(Relativpronomen)* V

whose? [hu:z] wessen? II
Whose are these? Wem gehören diese? II • **Whose turn is it?** Wer ist dran? / Wer ist an der Reihe? II

why [waɪ] warum I • **Why me?** Warum ich? I • **that's why** deshalb, darum I • **Why not tell her ...?** Warum erzählst/sagst du ihr nicht ...? VI 1 (9)
▶ S.172 'Why not' + Infinitiv

°**wide** [waɪd] breit

wife [waɪf], *pl* **wives** [waɪvz] Ehefrau II

wild [waɪld] wild II

will [wɪl]: **you'll be cold (= you will be cold)** du wirst / ihr werdet frieren II

win (-nn-) [wɪn], **won, won** gewinnen I

win [wɪn] Sieg III

wind [wɪnd] Wind I

window ['wɪndəʊ] Fenster I

windproof ['wɪndpru:f] winddicht V

windscreen ['wɪndskri:n] Windschutzscheibe III

windy ['wɪndi] windig I

wine [waɪn] Wein IV

wing [wɪŋ] Flügel IV

winner ['wɪnə] Gewinner/in, Sieger/in II

winning shot [ˌwɪnɪŋ 'ʃɒt] Siegtreffer, Siegesschuss III

winter ['wɪntə] Winter I

wish [wɪʃ] wünschen V • **wish for sth.** sich etwas wünschen VI 3 (47)

wish [wɪʃ] Wunsch VI 3 (47) • **Best wishes** *etwa:* Alles Gute / Mit besten Grüßen *(als Briefschluss)* IV

with [wɪð]
1. mit I
2. bei I
be with sb. mit jm. zusammen sein IV • **go with** gehören zu, passen zu III • **Sit with me.** Setz dich zu mir. / Setzt euch zu mir. I

within [wɪ'ðɪn] innerhalb (von) V

without [wɪ'ðaʊt] ohne I

wives [waɪvz] *pl von „wife"* II

woke [wəʊk] *siehe* **wake**

woken ['wəʊkən] *siehe* **wake**

wolf [wʊlf], *pl* **wolves** [wʊlvz] Wolf II

woman ['wʊmən], *pl* **women** ['wɪmɪn] Frau I

won [wʌn] *siehe* **win**

wonder ['wʌndə] sich fragen, gern wissen wollen II

°**wonderful** ['wʌndəfl] wunderbar

won't [wəʊnt]: **you won't be cold (= you will not be cold)** du wirst

nicht frieren / ihr werdet nicht frieren II

wood [wʊd] Holz II

woodpecker ['wʊdpekə] Specht II

woods *(pl)* [wʊdz] Wald, Wälder II

word [wɜ:d] Wort I • **Can I have a word with you?** Kann ich mal kurz mit dir reden? VI 3 (55) • **word building** Wortbildung II • **word field** Wortfeld III • °**word order** Wortstellung

wore [wɔ:] *siehe* **wear**

work [wɜ:k]
1. arbeiten I
2. funktionieren III
work hard hart arbeiten II • **work long hours** lange arbeiten V • **work on sth.** an etwas arbeiten I • **work out** gut ausgehen IV • **work sth. out** etwas herausarbeiten, herausfinden IV

work [wɜ:k] Arbeit I • **at work** bei der Arbeit / am Arbeitsplatz I

worker ['wɜ:kə] Arbeiter/in II

work experience *(no pl)* ['wɜ:kɪkˌspɪəriəns] Praktikum; Arbeits-, Praxiserfahrung(en) V • **do work experience** ein Praktikum machen V

worksheet ['wɜ:kʃi:t] Arbeitsblatt I

workshop ['wɜ:kʃɒp] Workshop, Werkstatt III

world [wɜ:ld] Welt I • **all over the world** auf der ganzen Welt III • **in the world** auf der Welt V

world war [ˌwɜ:ld 'wɔ:] Weltkrieg V

worldwide [ˌwɜ:ld'waɪd] weltweit; auf der ganzen Welt V

worn [wɔ:n] *siehe* **wear**

worried ['wʌrid]: **be worried (about)** beunruhigt sein, besorgt sein (wegen/um) IV

worry ['wʌri] Sorge, Kummer II
No worries. *(infml)* Kein Problem!/ Ist schon in Ordnung! VI 3 (55)

worry (about) ['wʌri] sich Sorgen machen (wegen, um) I • **Don't worry.** Mach dir keine Sorgen. I • **worry sb.** jn. beunruhigen, jm. Sorgen machen V

worse [wɜ:s] schlechter, schlimmer II

worst [wɜ:st]: **(the) worst** am schlechtesten, schlimmsten; der/ die/das schlechteste, schlimmste II

would [wəd, wʊd]: **you would ...** du würdest ... III • **I'd like ... (= I would like ...)** Ich hätte gern ... / Ich möchte gern ... I • **Would you like ...?** Möchtest du ...? / Möchten Sie ...? I • **I'd like to go (= I would**

like to go) ich würde gern gehen / ich möchte gehen I • **I wouldn't like to go** ich würde nicht gern gehen / ich möchte nicht gehen I • **I'd love to ... (= I would love to ...)** Ich würde liebend gern ... V

write [raɪt], **wrote, written** schreiben I • **write down** aufschreiben I • °**write sth. out** etwas ausschreiben • **write to** schreiben an I • °**write sth. up** etwas (schriftlich) ausarbeiten

writer ['raɪtə] Schreiber/in; Schriftsteller/in II

written ['rɪtn] *siehe* **write**

written discussion Erörterung VI 2 (37)

wrong [rɒŋ] falsch, verkehrt I • **be wrong 1.** falsch sein I; **2.** sich irren, Unrecht haben II • **go wrong** schiefgehen III • **the wrong way** in die falsche Richtung II • **What's wrong with you?** Was fehlt dir? II

wrote [rəʊt] *siehe* **write**

X

X-ray ['eks reɪ] Röntgenstrahl; Röntgenbild VI 2 (32)

Y

yard [jɑ:d] Hof II • **in the yard** auf dem Hof II

yawn [jɔ:n] gähnen II

year [jɪə]
1. Jahr I
2. Jahrgangsstufe I
thirteen-year-old Dreizehnjährige(r) III

yellow ['jeləʊ] gelb I

yes [jes] ja I

yesterday ['jestədeɪ, 'jestədi] gestern I • **yesterday morning/afternoon/ evening** gestern Morgen/Nachmittag/Abend I • **yesterday's homework** die Hausaufgaben von gestern II

yet [jet]: **not (...) yet** noch nicht II **yet?** schon? II

yoga ['jəʊgə] Yoga I

you [ju:]
1. du; Sie I
2. man III
3. ihr I • **you two** ihr zwei I
4. dir; dich; euch I
You bet! *(infml)* Aber klar! / Und ob! IV • **There you go!** *(infml)* *etwa:* So, das hätten wir. IV

young [jʌŋ] jung I
your [jɔː]
 1. dein/e I
 2. Ihr I
 3. euer/eure I
yours [jɔːz]
 1. deiner, deine, deins II
 2. Ihrer, Ihre, Ihrs II
 3. eurer, eure, eures II
 Yours faithfully Mit freundlichen Grüßen *(Briefschluss bei namentlich unbekanntem Empfänger)* V

Yours sincerely Mit freundlichen Grüßen *(Briefschluss bei namentlich bekanntem Empfänger)* V
yourself [jəˈself, jɔːˈself] dir/dich (selbst) III • **about yourself** über dich selbst III
yourselves [jəˈselvz, jɔːˈselvz] euch (selbst) III
youth [juːθ]
 1. Jugend III
 2. *(pl* **youths** [juːðz]*)* Jugendliche(r) V

Z

zebra [ˈzebrə] Zebra II
zero [ˈzɪərəʊ] null I
zone [zəʊn] Zone, Bereich III
zoo [zuː] Zoo IV

First names
(Vornamen)

Abraham ['eɪbrəhæm]
Adam ['ædəm]
Adisa [ə'di:sə]
Adrian ['eɪdriən]
Afra ['æfrə]
Alexander [,ælɪg'za:ndə]
Alexis [ə'leksɪs]
Ally ['æli]
Amy ['eɪmi]
Andrew ['ændru:]
Arnie ['a:ni]
Arnold ['a:nəld]
Barbara ['ba:brə]
Baz, Bazza [bæz], ['bæzə]
Belinda [bə'lɪndə]
Brad [bræd]
Caitlin ['keɪtlɪn]
Carla ['ka:lə]
Celia ['si:liə]
Charles [tʃa:lz]
Chaz [tʃæz]
Dani ['dæni]
Daniel ['dænjəl]
David ['deɪvɪd]
Davina [də'vi:nə]
Dayamayee [,daɪəmaɪ'i:]
Diana [daɪ'ænə]
Diane [daɪ'æn]
Earl [3:l]
Edward ['edwəd]
Elizabeth [i'lɪzəbəθ]
Ella ['elə]
Ethan ['i:θn]
Fay [feɪ]
Fran [fræn]
Gary ['gæri]
George [dʒɔ:dʒ]
Hailey ['heɪli]
Hanif ['hænɪf]
Harita [hə'ri:tə]
Helen ['helən]
Holly ['hɒli]
Jake [dʒeɪk]
James [dʒeɪmz]
Jean [dʒi:n]
Jeannie ['dʒi:ni]
Jérôme [dʒə'rəʊm]
Jess [dʒes]
Jill [dʒɪl]
Jody ['dʒəʊdi]
Joseph ['dʒəʊzɪf]
Josh [dʒɒʃ]
Judy ['dʒu:di]
Julia ['dʒu:liə]
Julian ['dʒu:liən]
Julie ['dʒu:li]
Juno ['dʒu:nəʊ]
Kate [keɪt]
Katy ['keɪti]
Kristen ['krɪstən]
Laura ['lɔ:rə]
Laurie ['lɒri]
Layla ['leɪlə]

Leo ['li:əʊ]
Lisa ['li:sə], ['li:zə]
Lucy ['lu:si]
Maggie ['mægi]
Margaret ['ma:grət]
Mary ['meəri]
Matty ['mæti]
Megan ['megən]
Mel [mel]
Melinda [mə'lɪndə]
Michael ['maɪkəl]
Minty ['mɪnti]
Morpheus ['mɔ:fiəs]
Murat [mu:'ra:t]
Nadia ['na:diə]
Nathan ['neɪθən]
Neil [ni:l]
Neo ['ni:əʊ]
Parminder [pa:'mɪndə]
Patricia [pə'trɪʃə]
Paulie ['pɔ:li]
Penelope [pə'neləpi]
Petra ['petrə]
Robert ['rɒbət]
Roger ['rɒdʒə]
Rose [rəʊz]
Rosie ['rəʊzi]
Ruby ['ru:bi]
Saci ['sæʃi]
Sanjay [,sʌn'dʒeɪ], ['sændʒeɪ]
Sarah ['seərə]
Sean [ʃɔ:n]
Seb [seb]
Sharon ['ʃærən]
Sherman ['ʃ3:mən]
Stephenie ['stefəni]
Tina ['ti:nə]
Toby ['təʊbi]
Tony ['təʊni]
Tyler ['taɪlə]
Zooey ['zəʊi]

Family names
(Familiennamen)

Alexie [ə'leksi]
Beckham ['bekəm]
Blair [bleə]
Blanchett ['bla:ntʃɪt]
Boateng ['bwa:teŋ]
Broun [braʊn]
Clooney ['klu:ni]
Dee [di:]
Deschanel [,deɪʃə'nel]
Fleming ['flemɪŋ]
Ford [fɔ:d]
Fry [fraɪ]
Gee [dʒi:]
Gordon-Levitt [,gɔ:dn 'levɪt]
Halse Anderson
    [,hæls_'ændəsən]
Kennedy ['kenədi]
Lee [li:]
Lincoln ['lɪŋkən]
Livingstone ['lɪvɪŋstən]
Lloyd [lɔɪd]

Martin ['ma:tɪn]
McBeath [mək'bi:θ]
McCormick [mə'kɔ:mɪk]
McKenzie [mə'kenzi]
Mead [mi:d]
Meyer ['maɪə]
Miller ['mɪlə]
Minton ['mɪntən]
Mitchell ['mɪtʃəl]
Munslow ['mʌnsləʊ]
Nagra ['na:grə]
Neck [nek]
Nutt [nʌt]
Patel [pə'tel]
Pattinson ['pætɪnsən]
Petrakis [pə'tra:kɪs]
Pitt [pɪt]
Presley ['presli], ['prezli]
Pym [pɪm]
Roberts ['rɒbəts]
Sandburg ['sændb3:g]
Shrimpton ['ʃrɪmptən]
Simons ['saɪmənz]
Smith [smɪθ]
Stephenson ['sti:vnsən]
Stewart ['stju:ət]
Thompson ['tɒmpsən]
Volta ['vəʊltə]
Webber ['webə]
Wilde [waɪld]
Wilson ['wɪlsn]
Worth [w3:θ]

Place names
(Ortsnamen)

Antalya [æn'tæljə]
Arizona [,ærɪ'zəʊnə]
Banff [bænf]
Bavaria [bə'veəriə] *Bayern*
Belfast [,bel'fa:st]
Birmingham ['b3:mɪŋəm]
Brighton ['braɪtn]
Bristol ['brɪstl]
Broughton ['brɔ:tn]
Brussels ['brʌslz] *Brüssel*
California [,kælə'fɔ:niə]
Cambridge ['keɪmbrɪdʒ]
Canterbury ['kæntəbəri]
Cape Breton [,keɪp 'bretən]
Cardiff ['ka:dɪf]
Cashel ['kæʃl]
Chicago [ʃɪ'ka:gəʊ]
Colorado [,kɒlə'ra:dəʊ]
Delhi ['deli]
Dover ['dəʊvə]
Dublin ['dʌblɪn]
Edinburgh ['edɪnbərə]
Fort William [,fɔ:t 'wɪljəm]
Glasgow ['gla:zgəʊ]
Hamilton ['hæmltən]
Helsinki [hel'sɪŋki]
Hexham ['heksəm]
Hobart ['həʊba:t]
Holborn ['həʊbən]
Hove [həʊv]

Huddersfield ['hʌdəzfi:ld]
Iveragh Peninsula
    [,aɪvrə pə'nɪnsjʊlə]
Kent [kent]
Kerry ['keri]
Launceston ['lɒnsəstən]
Liverpool ['lɪvəpu:l]
London ['lʌndən]
Majorca [mə'jɔ:kə]
Malaga ['mæləgə]
Manchester ['mæntʃɪstə]
Marineland [mə'ri:nlænd]
Marseille [ma:'seɪ]
Melbourne ['melbən]
Michigan ['mɪʃɪgən]
Milson's Point
    [,mɪlsənz 'pɔɪnt]
Mt. Cameron
    [,maʊnt 'kæmrən]
Newton ['nju:tn]
Niagara Falls [naɪ,ægərə 'fɔ:lz]
Norton ['nɔ:tən]
Nova Scotia [,nəʊvə 'skəʊʃə]
Ontario [ɒn'teəriəʊ]
Ottawa ['ɒtəwə]
Oxford ['ɒksfəd]
Peterborough ['pi:təbərə]
Piccadilly [,pɪkə'dɪli]
Rearden ['rɪədn]
Rosebrook ['rəʊzbrʊk]
San Francisco
    [,sæn frən'sɪskəʊ]
Spokane [spəʊ'kæn]
St Pauls [sənt 'pɔ:lz]
Stranraer [stræn'ra:]
Sunderland ['sʌndələnd]
Sydney ['sɪdni]
Tasmania [tæz'meɪniə]
Tianjin [ti,æn'dʒɪn]
Torbay [,tɔ:'beɪ]
Toronto [tə'rɒntəʊ]
Toulouse [tu:'lu:z]
Venice ['venɪs] *Venedig*
Victoria [vɪk'tɔ:riə]
Washington ['wɒʃɪŋtən]
Wellington ['welɪŋtən]
Wellpinit ['welpɪnɪt]
Westport ['westpɔ:t]
York [jɔ:k]

Other names
(Andere Namen)

Arsenal ['a:snəl]
Aviator ['eɪvieɪtə]
Beluga [bə'lu:gə]
Boeing ['bəʊɪŋ]
Celtic Tiger [,keltɪk 'taɪgə]
Galadriel [gə'la:driəl]
Matrix ['meɪtrɪks]
Meatrix ['mi:trɪks]
Moopheus ['mu:fiəs]
St Ambrose ['æmbrəʊz]
Titanic [taɪ'tænɪk]
Vatican ['vætɪkən]
Volpi Cup ['vɒlpi kʌp]

Country/Continent	Adjective	Person	People
Africa [ˈæfrɪkə] *Afrika*	African [ˈæfrɪkən]	an African	the Africans
America [əˈmerɪkə] *Amerika*	American [əˈmerɪkən]	an American	the Americans
Asia [ˈeɪʃə, ˈeɪʒə] *Asien*	Asian [ˈeɪʃn, ˈeɪʒn]	an Asian	the Asians
Australia [ɒˈstreɪliə] *Australien*	Australian [ɒˈstreɪliən]	an Australian	the Australians
Austria [ˈɒstriə] *Österreich*	Austrian [ˈɒstriən]	an Austrian	the Austrians
Belgium [ˈbeldʒəm] *Belgien*	Belgian [ˈbeldʒən]	a Belgian	the Belgians
Canada [ˈkænədə] *Kanada*	Canadian [kəˈneɪdiən]	a Canadian	the Canadians
China [ˈtʃaɪnə] *China*	Chinese [ˌtʃaɪˈniːz]	a Chinese	the Chinese
Croatia [krəʊˈeɪʃə] *Kroatien*	Croatian [krəʊˈeɪʃn]	a Croatian	the Croatians
the Czech Republic [ˌtʃek rɪˈpʌblɪk] *Tschechien, die Tschechische Republik*	Czech [tʃek]	a Czech	the Czechs
Denmark [ˈdenmɑːk] *Dänemark*	Danish [ˈdeɪnɪʃ]	a Dane [deɪn]	the Danes
Egypt [ˈiːdʒɪpt] *Ägypten*	Egyptian [iˈdʒɪpʃn]	an Egyptian	the Egyptians
England [ˈɪŋglənd] *England*	English [ˈɪŋglɪʃ]	an Englishman/-woman	the English
Europe [ˈjʊərəp] *Europa*	European [ˌjʊərəˈpiːən]	a European	the Europeans
Finland [ˈfɪnlənd] *Finnland*	Finnish [ˈfɪnɪʃ]	a Finn [fɪn]	the Finns
France [frɑːns] *Frankreich*	French [frentʃ]	a Frenchman/-woman	the French
Georgia [ˈdʒɔːdʒə] *Georgien*	Georgian [ˈdʒɔːdʒən]	a Georgian	the Georgians
Germany [ˈdʒɜːməni] *Deutschland*	German [ˈdʒɜːmən]	a German	the Germans
(Great) Britain [ˈbrɪtn] *Großbritannien*	British [ˈbrɪtɪʃ]	a Briton [ˈbrɪtn]	the British
Greece [griːs] *Griechenland*	Greek [griːk]	a Greek	the Greeks
Holland [ˈhɒlənd] *Holland, die Niederlande*	Dutch [dʌtʃ]	a Dutchman/-woman	the Dutch
Hungary [ˈhʌŋgəri] *Ungarn*	Hungarian [hʌŋˈgeəriən]	a Hungarian	the Hungarians
India [ˈɪndiə] *Indien*	Indian [ˈɪndiən]	an Indian	the Indians
Ireland [ˈaɪələnd] *Irland*	Irish [ˈaɪrɪʃ]	an Irishman/-woman	the Irish
Italy [ˈɪtəli] *Italien*	Italian [ɪˈtæliən]	an Italian	the Italians
Japan [dʒəˈpæn] *Japan*	Japanese [ˌdʒæpəˈniːz]	a Japanese	the Japanese
Malaysia [məˈleɪʒə, məˈleɪziə] *Malaysia*	Malaysian [məˈleɪʒn, məˈleɪziən]	a Malaysian	the Malaysians
the Netherlands [ˈneðələndz] *die Niederlande, Holland*	Dutch [dʌtʃ]	a Dutchman/-woman	the Dutch
New Zealand [ˌnjuː ˈziːlənd] *Neuseeland*	New Zealand [ˌnjuː ˈziːlənd]	a New Zealander	the New Zealanders
Nigeria [naɪˈdʒɪəriə] *Nigeria*	Nigerian [naɪˈdʒɪəriən]	a Nigerian	the Nigerians
Norway [ˈnɔːweɪ] *Norwegen*	Norwegian [nɔːˈwiːdʒən]	a Norwegian	the Norwegians
Pakistan [ˌpækɪˈstæn, ˌpɑːkɪˈstɑːn] *Pakistan*	Pakistani [ˌpækɪˈstæni, ˌpɑːkɪˈstɑːni]	a Pakistani	the Pakistanis
the Philippines [ˈfɪlɪpiːnz] *die Philippinen*	Philippine [ˈfɪlɪpiːn]	a Filipino [ˌfɪlɪˈpiːnəʊ]/ Filipina [ˌfɪlɪˈpiːnə]	the Filipinos/ Filipinas
Poland [ˈpəʊlənd] *Polen*	Polish [ˈpəʊlɪʃ]	a Pole [pəʊl]	the Poles
Portugal [ˈpɔːtʃʊgl] *Portugal*	Portuguese [ˌpɔːtʃuˈgiːz]	a Portuguese	the Portuguese
Russia [ˈrʌʃə] *Russland*	Russian [ˈrʌʃn]	a Russian	the Russians
Scotland [ˈskɒtlənd] *Schottland*	Scottish [ˈskɒtɪʃ]	a Scotsman/-woman, a Scot [skɒt]	the Scots, the Scottish
Slovakia [sləʊˈvɑːkiə, sləʊˈvækiə] *die Slowakei*	Slovak [ˈsləʊvæk]	a Slovak	the Slovaks
Slovenia [sləʊˈviːniə] *Slowenien*	Slovenian [sləʊˈviːniən], Slovene [ˈsləʊviːn]	a Slovene, a Slovenian	the Slovenes, the Slovenians
Spain [speɪn] *Spanien*	Spanish [ˈspænɪʃ]	a Spaniard [ˈspænɪəd]	the Spaniards
Sweden [ˈswiːdn] *Schweden*	Swedish [ˈswiːdɪʃ]	a Swede [swiːd]	the Swedes
Switzerland [ˈswɪtsələnd] *die Schweiz*	Swiss [swɪs]	a Swiss	the Swiss
Tanzania [ˌtænzəˈniːə] *Tansania*	Tanzanian [ˌtænzəˈniːən]	a Tanzanian	the Tanzanians
Turkey [ˈtɜːki] *die Türkei*	Turkish [ˈtɜːkɪʃ]	a Turk [tɜːk]	the Turks
the United Kingdom (the UK) [juˌnaɪtɪd ˈkɪŋdəm, juːˈkeɪ] *das Vereinigte Königreich (Großbritannien und Nordirland)*	British [ˈbrɪtɪʃ]	a Briton [ˈbrɪtn]	the British
the United States of America (the USA) [juˌnaɪtɪd ˌsteɪts‿əv‿əˈmerɪkə, juːˌesˈeɪ] *die Vereinigten Staaten von Amerika*	American [əˈmerɪkən]	an American	the Americans
Wales [weɪlz] *Wales*	Welsh [welʃ]	a Welshman/-woman	the Welsh

Infinitive	Simple past form	Past participle	
(to) **be**	**was/were**	**been**	sein
(to) **beat**	**beat**	**beaten**	schlagen; besiegen
(to) **become**	**became**	**become**	werden
(to) **begin**	**began**	**begun**	beginnen, anfangen (mit)
(to) **bet**	**bet**	**bet**	wetten
(to) **bite** [aɪ]	**bit** [ɪ]	**bitten** [ɪ]	beißen
(to) **blow**	**blew**	**blown**	wehen, blasen
(to) **break** [eɪ]	**broke**	**broken**	(zer)brechen; kaputt gehen
(to) **bring**	**brought**	**brought**	(mit-, her)bringen
(to) **build**	**built**	**built**	bauen
(to) **buy**	**bought**	**bought**	kaufen
(to) **catch**	**caught**	**caught**	fangen; erwischen
(to) **choose** [uː]	**chose** [əʊ]	**chosen** [əʊ]	(aus)wählen; (sich) aussuchen
(to) **come**	**came**	**come**	kommen
(to) **cost**	**cost**	**cost**	kosten
(to) **cut**	**cut**	**cut**	schneiden
(to) **do**	**did**	**done** [ʌ]	tun, machen
(to) **draw**	**drew**	**drawn**	zeichnen; ziehen
(to) **drink**	**drank**	**drunk**	trinken
(to) **drive** [aɪ]	**drove**	**driven** [ɪ]	*(ein Auto)* fahren
(to) **eat**	**ate** [et, eɪt]	**eaten**	essen
(to) **fall**	**fell**	**fallen**	(hin)fallen, stürzen
(to) **feed**	**fed**	**fed**	füttern
(to) **feel**	**felt**	**felt**	(sich) fühlen; sich anfühlen
(to) **fight**	**fought**	**fought**	kämpfen
(to) **find**	**found**	**found**	finden
(to) **fly**	**flew**	**flown**	fliegen
(to) **forget**	**forgot**	**forgotten**	vergessen
(to) **forgive**	**forgave**	**forgiven**	vergeben, verzeihen
(to) **get**	**got**	**got**	bekommen; holen; werden; (hin)kommen
(to) **give**	**gave**	**given**	geben
(to) **go**	**went**	**gone** [ɒ]	gehen, fahren
(to) **grow**	**grew**	**grown**	wachsen; anbauen, anpflanzen
(to) **hang**	**hung**	**hung**	hängen; *(etwas)* aufhängen
(to) **have (have got)**	**had**	**had**	haben, besitzen
(to) **hear** [ɪə]	**heard** [ɜː]	**heard** [ɜː]	hören
(to) **hide** [aɪ]	**hid** [ɪ]	**hidden** [ɪ]	(sich) verstecken
(to) **hit**	**hit**	**hit**	schlagen
(to) **hold**	**held**	**held**	halten; abhalten, veranstalten
(to) **hurt**	**hurt**	**hurt**	wehtun; verletzen
(to) **keep**	**kept**	**kept**	(be)halten
(to) **know** [nəʊ]	**knew** [njuː]	**known** [nəʊn]	wissen; kennen
(to) **lay** the table	**laid**	**laid**	den Tisch decken
(to) **lead** [iː]	**led**	**led**	führen
(to) **leave**	**left**	**left**	(weg)gehen; abfahren; verlassen; zurücklassen
(to) **lend**	**lent**	**lent**	(ver)leihen

Infinitive	Simple past form	Past participle	
(to) **let**	let	let	lassen
(to) **light**	lit	lit	anzünden
(to) **lose** [uː]	lost [ɒ]	lost [ɒ]	verlieren
(to) **make**	made	made	machen; bauen; bilden
(to) **mean** [iː]	meant [e]	meant [e]	bedeuten; meinen
(to) **meet**	met	met	(sich) treffen
(to) **pay**	paid	paid	bezahlen
(to) **put**	put	put	legen, stellen, *(wohin)* tun
(to) **read** [iː]	read [e]	read [e]	lesen
(to) **ride** [aɪ]	rode	ridden [ɪ]	reiten; *(Rad)* fahren
(to) **ring**	rang	rung	klingeln, läuten
(to) **rise** [aɪ]	rose	risen [ɪ]	(auf)steigen
(to) **run**	ran	run	rennen, laufen; verlaufen *(Straße, Grenze)*; leiten *(Hotel, Firma)*
(to) **say** [eɪ]	said [e]	said [e]	sagen
(to) **see**	saw	seen	sehen; besuchen, aufsuchen
(to) **sell**	sold	sold	verkaufen
(to) **send**	sent	sent	schicken, senden
(to) **set** a trap	set	set	eine Falle stellen
(to) **sew** [əʊ]	sewed	sewn	nähen
(to) **shake**	shook	shaken	schütteln; zittern
(to) **shine**	shone [ɒ]	shone [ɒ]	scheinen *(Sonne)*
(to) **shoot**	shot	shot	(er)schießen
(to) **show**	showed	shown	zeigen
(to) **shut** up	shut	shut	den Mund halten
(to) **sing**	sang	sung	singen
(to) **sit**	sat	sat	sitzen; sich setzen
(to) **sleep**	slept	slept	schlafen
(to) **speak**	spoke	spoken	sprechen
(to) **spend**	spent	spent	*(Zeit)* verbringen; *(Geld)* ausgeben
(to) **spit**	spat	spat	spucken
(to) **stand**	stood	stood	stehen; sich (hin)stellen
(to) **steal**	stole	stolen	stehlen
(to) **stick**	stuck	stuck	herausragen, herausstehen
(to) **swim**	swam	swum	schwimmen
(to) **take**	took	taken	nehmen; (weg-, hin)bringen; dauern, *(Zeit)* brauchen
(to) **teach**	taught	taught	unterrichten, lehren
(to) **tear off** [eə]	tore	torn	abreißen
(to) **tell**	told	told	erzählen, berichten
(to) **think**	thought	thought	denken, glauben, meinen
(to) **throw**	threw	thrown	werfen
(to) **understand**	understood	understood	verstehen
(to) **upset**	upset	upset	ärgern, kränken, aus der Fassung bringen
(to) **wake** up	woke	woken	aufwachen; wecken
(to) **wear** [eə]	wore [ɔː]	worn [ɔː]	tragen *(Kleidung)*
(to) **win**	won [ʌ]	won [ʌ]	gewinnen
(to) **write**	wrote	written	schreiben

Getting ready for a test 1 Revision ▸ pp. 20–23

1 Outdoor holidays ▸ p. 20
a)
1 Do ... prefer	6 fit
2 Have ... got	7 Has ... got
3 Is	8 do ... need
4 Do ... know	9 does ... cost
5 goes	

b) (Individuelle Lösungen)

2 A holiday by the sea is more exciting ▸ p. 20
(Mögliche Lösungen)

1 ... is more/less exciting than ...
 ... is/isn't as exciting as ...
2 ... is more comfortable than ...
3 ... is cooler than ...
4 ... are more crowded than ...
5 ... is less expensive than ...
6 ... is more interesting than ...
7 ... is more exciting than ...
8 ... is better than ...
9 ... are higher than ...

3 SPEAKING Likes and dislikes ▸ p. 20
(individuelle Lösungen)

4 WORDS A teenage magazine ▸ p. 21
a) **music:** playlist, sound file, label, release, CD, MP3, tune, instruments, melody
cinema & TV: cable, anchorwoman, prime time, repeat (n.), soap opera, series, news
books: comic, novel, narrator, poem, cover, author, pages   **computer:** menu, link, install, save, download, freeze, screen, keyboard
sports: athletics, ballet, train, pitch, soccer, match, team, coach **theatre:** stage, scene, rehearsal, actor(s), plot, make-up, costumes

b)
1 rehearsals	4 install
2 compete	5 repeat
3 released	6 concert

5 WORDS Talking about religions ▸ p. 21
a)
| 1 English |
| 2 cathedral |
| 3 palace |
| 4 technician |
| 5 bell |
| 6 believe |

b)
| 1 Muslim |
| 2 Protestant |
| 3 synagogue |
| 4 priest |
| 5 bell |
| 6 believe |

6 WORDS The world of soap opera ▸ p. 22
a)
| 1 father |
| 2 uncle |
| 3 granddaughter |
| 4 wife |
| 5 lover |
| 6 ex-husband |

b)
| 1 divorced |
| 2 love |
| 3 relationship |
| 4 baby |
| 5 father |
| 6 single |

7 Tell me it isn't true ▸ p. 22
1 isn't	5 can't go
2 don't have/ haven't got	6 aren't/are not
3 doesn't like	7 don't know
4 doesn't care	8 doesn't mean

8 I'd never fall in love ... ▸ p. 23
1 with	6 From
2 from	7 about
3 by	8 by
4 about	9 by
5 about	10 with

9 Teenage mums ▸ p. 23
1 Although	5 However,
2 especially	6 Instead of
3 really	7 of course
4 Perhaps	

10 SPEAKING Expressing opinions ▸ p. 23
a) wie vorgegeben
b) (Individuelle Lösungen)

Getting ready for a test 1 Practice Test ▸ pp. 24–26

1 LISTENING
What can we do this weekend? ▸ p. 24
(Mögliche Lösung)
Helen rings up her friend Tina to discuss some plans for the weekend. They agree to spend time together on Saturday evening and

Helen makes lots of suggestions, like going to the theatre, playing a computer game, listening to music or watching TV. Tina disagrees with every idea. She thinks the theatre is boring and doesn't like computer games. She doesn't want to listen to music or watch TV either because she thinks there will be only repeats. In the end, Helen is fed up and suggests something completely different: she will stay at home, watch TV and read and Tina can do whatever she likes. Helen ends the phone call without waiting for Tina's reaction.

2 SPEAKING Holiday plans ▸ p. 24
b) (Indiviuelle Lösungen)

3 LISTENING Living together ▸ p. 25
1 D 4 A
2 C 5 D
3 D 6 C

4 LISTENING Radio adverts ▸ p. 25
1 True 4 True
2 False 5 True
3 False 6 False

5 SPEAKING Too young to be a mum? ▸ p. 26
1–6 (Individuelle Lösungen)

6 PRESENTATION My lifestyle ▸ p. 26
(Individuelle Lösungen)

Getting ready for a test 2 Revision ▸ pp. 38–41

1 WORDS Mobility ▸ p. 38
a) **air:** airport, flight, plane, gate, (to) land, helicopter, wing
railway: carriage, platform, train, the Tube, underground, line, station
road: cab, (to) cycle, (to) drive, motorway, petrol station, rush hour, traffic jam, bike, wheel, taxi, bus
sea: ferry, boat, harbour, ship, anchor, coastguard

b) 1 went 4 broke down
2 picked 5 drive
3 travel 6 ask

2 London's underground ▸ p. 38
1 opened 5 came
2 was 6 travelled
3 have been added 7 has grown
4 were pulled 8 appeared

3 Customers' mails ▸ p. 38
1 I always try to sit **at the top** so I can enjoy the view.
2 I was in a terrible traffic jam **yesterday**. It took one hour to drive from Piccadilly to Tower Bridge! I don't think that I'll go into London by car **again**.
3 ... , so I **sold** my car a long time ago.
4 ... if you **ask** them.

5 ..., the last bus had left **early**.
6 ... always use the Tube **on Saturdays** when we go shopping.

4 WORDS After the accident ▸ p. 39
1 unconscious 6 hurts
2 operation 7 headache
3 alcohol 8 threw up
4 drunk 9 sweat
5 healthy 10 ambulance

5 Reporting what people said ▸ p. 39
1 He told me I had had an accident.
2 He said that Julie was still unconscious.
3 He added that we would have to have an operation.
4 He asked if we had drunk any alcohol before the accident.
5 He asked if Julie and I had had a cold recently.
6 He wanted to know if I felt any pain.
7 He told me that I had thrown up after the accident.

6 STUDY SKILLS Writing ▸ p. 39
1 23-year-old truck driver (who)
2 one of the worst accidents (what)
3 driving at over 80 miles per hour (why/how)
4 hit by broken glass (how/why)
5 in the late afternoon (when)
6 St Pauls and Eastville Park (where)

7 WORDS For a greener world ▸ p. 40

a)
1 sun
2 wind
3 waste
4 pollute
5 solar power
6 trees

b)
1 F
2 B
3 A
4 E
5 D
6 G
7 C

8 Our green holiday ▸ p. 40

1 So did you enjoy your holiday?
2 Where did you stay?
3 How did you find out about it?
4 So what was special about it?
5 And was it organic?
6 Anyway, what else did you do?
7 How far away was it?
8 And did you have good weather?

9 Ben's blog ▸ p. 41

1 I didn't take the bus because it uses too much energy.
2 Unfortunately, they didn't have any.
3 I didn't choose the big, red apples from Italy.

4 I wasn't allowed to buy organic ones just because they're a bit more expensive!
5 I couldn't find a second-hand clothes shop anywhere!
6 I just wasn't able to find one made in this country.

10 WRITING A written discussion ▸ p. 41

a) B , D , A , C

b) (Mögliche Lösungen)

B: You often hear people say that …; So the question is: …

D: On the one hand …; First, …; Second, …

A: On the other hand …; First, …; Second, …

C: After looking at both sides, I think …; For me…

Other possible phrases: Lots of people think …; One/Another argument for/against … is …; Other people disagree. They think that …; To sum up (the main points) …; Finally, I think …

Getting ready for a test 2 Practice Test ▸ pp. 42–44

1 LANGUAGE ▸ p. 42

1 B
2 A
3 A
4 C
5 B
6 C
7 C
8 B
9 A
10 A
11 C
12 A

2 WRITING ▸ p. 43

a) A dialogue (Individuelle Lösungen)
b) An email (Individuelle Lösungen)

3 WRITING A report ▸ p. 43
(Individuelle Lösungen)

4 WRITING A shopping survey ▸ p. 44
(Individuelle Lösungen)

5 WRITING A letter to a newspaper ▸ p. 44
(Individuelle Lösungen)

6 WRITING Opinions ▸ p. 44
(Individuelle Lösungen)

Getting ready for a test 3 Revision ▸ pp. 56–58

1 WORDS Getting involved ▸ p. 56

1 protest
2 speech
3 have
4 part
5 create
6 raise
7 volunteered
8 march
9 vote

2 READING Which event? ▸ p. 56

a) RSPCA Volunteer Information Day
b) Ella: Queen's Park project week;
Adam: Film and discussion

3 Are you going to work in the holidays?
► *p. 57*

a) 1 Are you going to …
  2 … I'm going to look …
  3 … Sam and I are going to work …
  4 … we aren't/we're not going to do …
  5 … we're going to spend …
  6 … is he going to show …
  7 … he isn't going to spend …
  8 … are you going to look …
  9 I'm not going to work …

b) (Individuelle Antworten)

4 WORDS Paraphrasing ► *p. 57*
  1 e: Partei   4 d: Moderator
  2 f: Untertitel   5 c: Ziel
  3 b: Abgeordnete/r 6 a: Wirtschaft

5 EVERYDAY ENGLISH
  Making suggestions ► *p. 57*
a) 1B, 2A, 3A, 4B, 5B, 6B
b) (Individuelle Lösungen)

6 WORDS Politics ► *p. 58*
  1 elect a new   5 discriminates
    government   against
  2 represent   6 the majority
  3 citizen   7 illegal
  4 responsibility   8 criticize

7 READING ► *p. 58*
a)–c) (Individuelle Tabellen/
Schülereinschätzungen)

Getting ready for a test 3 **Practice Test** ► *pp. 59–62*

1 READING Events ► *p. 59*
Jill: F Megan: A Ben: C Ethan: D
Sally: E

2 MEDIATION An advertisement ► *p. 60*
(Mögliche Lösungen)
1 Ich werde in einem internationalen
  Jugendcamp arbeiten und kostenlos in
  einem Dorf wohnen, wo Jugendliche auch
  aus vielen anderen Ländern untergebracht
  sind.
2 Ich werde hauptsächlich das Tages- und
  Abendprogramm organisieren.
3 Die angeforderten Voraussetzungen sind:
  man muss zwischen 17 und 20 Jahren alt
  sein, sollte gut mit 11 bis 15-Jährigen
  umgehen können, sollte organisiert und
  energiegeladen sein und gut in der Gruppe
  arbeiten können.
4 Man verdient 25 Pfund pro Woche.
5 Andere Vergünstigungen sind:
  Übernahme der Anreisekosten, kostenlose
  Unterkunft und Verpflegung (Frühstück
  sowie zwei heiße Mahlzeiten am Tag), die
  Chance mit Leuten aus anderen Ländern in
  Kontakt zu kommen.

3 MEDIATION
Helping a visitor to Germany ► *p. 60*
(Mögliche Lösungen)
Mit Cartoons in die Politik einsteigen
You could go to the youth club in Böllstraße,
where they're going to show a DVD which
introduces the programmes of the main
political parties and uses funny drawings to
explain the different areas of politics. It starts
at 7.30 pm and lasts about 45 minutes. After
that they're going to have a discussion,
followed by live music.

Live-Polit-Talk mit Studiogästen
You could also go to a live talk show where
people from different European countries are
going to discuss Europe's future. The show
starts at 6.30 pm at the Fernsehzentrum Köln
and ends at about 8 pm. The discussion will be
translated into English.

4 READING Notices, short ads and signs

▶ *p. 61*

6	False	12	False
7	False	13	True
8	True	14	False
9	False	15	True
10	True	16	False
11	False	17	True

5 READING ▶ *p. 62*

1 a) False b) False c) True
d) Not in the text

2 Ⓐ

3 Ⓑ

4 (Mögliche Lösungen)
a) Will Black wants free recycling at all schools because that would give them a reason to do it as much as possible.
b) Barbara McKenzie believes public transport for students should be cheaper because they cannot afford high fares while they're at school.
c) Jack Smith says that there's so much negative stuff about young people in the media and that many of them are working hard for lasting change.

5 (Mögliche Lösung)
This statement is false because the text says the UK Youth Parliament's main sitting this year will be at the University of Ulster. There might be another meeting later in the year in the House of Commons.

Unit 3 **Part Ⓐ**

P3 **EVERYDAY ENGLISH** **SPEAKING Solving conflicts** ▶ *p. 55*

c) 👥 *You're sharing a room with your partner, but one of you has annoyed the other.*
Choose one of these ideas to start the conversation, or use your own ideas.

- I hate your music! Can't you play something else?
- Did you leave my MP3 player on? The battery is dead.
- When you smoke your cigarettes outside you stand near the window. But the smell comes into the room.
- You're always on the phone and your conversations are very loud.
- Can you leave the room when you're speaking on the phone?
- You and your friends are talking very loudly. I need to get up early to go to the airport.
- It's very cold with the window open. Do you really need that much fresh air?
- You haven't washed for 3 days and you're starting to smell.
- Do you have to practise playing the trumpet in the room?
- Your trainers smell really, really bad.

Illustrationen

Silke Bachmann, Hamburg (S. 52; 103 TF 5 (u. 117)); **Roland Beier**, Berlin (S. 54; 81; 83; 124; 125; 127; 129; 130; 132–182); **Carlos Borrell**, Berlin (Umschlaginnenseite 2); **Cornelsen Verlag GmbH**; Berlin (S. 114 unten li.); **Gareth Evans**, Berlin (S. 73 oben, unten li. (u. 131 unten)); **Dylan Gibson**, Pitlochry (S. 103 TF 1 (u. 105)); **Karin Mall**, Berlin (S. 29; 72 (u. 131 oben u. Mitte); 73 Mitte re., unten re.); **Alfred Schüssler**, Frankfurt/Main (S. 51 re.; 75)

Bildquellen

action press, Hamburg (S. 114 unten re.: REX FEATURES LTD.); **Alamy**, Abingdon (Inhaltsverz. (u. 28 unten li.): Jeff Greenberg, Inhaltsverz. Juno film still re.: PHOTOS 12, Inhaltsverz. (u. 46 Bild D): David Levenson; S. 7 oben lesbian couple: Image Source Pink (RF); S. 15 oben Tyler und Chaz (M): GlowImages (RF); S. 25 oben 2. v. li.: Wedding Day; S. 26 oben re.: Catchlight Visual Services, unten: Image Source; S. 28 oben li. (M): Cultura RM, unten li.: Jeff Greenberg; S. 41 unten: British Retail Photography; S. 46 Bild F (u. 126 oben): Beyond Fotomedia GmbH; S. 51 li.: DBURKE; S. 90 Bild G: Somos Images (RF); S. 112 oben: David Lyons; S. 123 re.: vario images; S. 125 unten: Horizon International Images Limited); **The Associated Press**, New York (S. 62: PA Wire); **The Bridgeman Art Library** (S. 122 unten re.: George Washington (oil on canvas), Stuart, Gilbert (1755–1828) / Sterling & Francine Clark Art Institute, Williamstown, USA); **www.carbonfootprint. com** (Inhaltsverz. footprint (u. 29)); **CBC** (S. 50: stills from news report "The mosquito". Copyright © CBC Vancouver); **Cinetext**, Frankfurt/Main (Inhaltsverz. Juno poster (u. 13): 20th Century Fox; S. 98: Delphi); **Corbis**, Düsseldorf (Inhaltsverz. (u. 6 Ed): moodboard (RF); S. 10 unten: cultura (RF); S. 20: Biscuit Eight LLC (RF); S. 80 oben: Monalyn Gracia (RF); S. 86: Matilda Hartman; S. 88 unten: Asia Images/Alex Mares-Manton; S. 89 oben: Image Source (RF); S. 92: Blend Images / Jose Luis Pelaez, Inc. (RF); S. 122 unten li., oben re.: Corbis); **Corel Library** (S. 138 oben); **Cornelsen Verlag GmbH**, Berlin (Inhaltsverz. film still review (u. 13); S. 14); **ddp images**, Hamburg (S. 49: AP Photo/Compound Security Systems); **Deutsches Museum**, München (S. 30 li.); **Philip Devlin**, Berlin (S. 89 unten); **Education Photo**, Guildford (S. 28 unten re.: educationphotos.co.uk/walmsley); **Financial Times**, London (S. 126 unten); **Ellen Forney** (S. 16–18: From THE ABSOLUTELY TRUE DIARY OF A PART-TIME INDIAN by Sherman Alexie. Copyright © 2007 by Sherman Alexie. Illustrations copyright 2007 by Ellen Forney. By permission of LITTLE, BROWN & COMPANY); **Fotex**, Hamburg (S. 8 li.: Susa); **Fotolia**, New York (S. 9 oben:

martins; S. 99 Mitte li.: Dustin Lyson, unten li.: Phototom); **Getty Images**, München (Inhaltsverz. (u. 6 Toby): A J James (RF), Inhaltsverz. (u. 6 Minty): Thinkstock (RF); S. 10 oben: DreamPictures; S. 21: Lisa Zador; S. 32 unten: SSPL; S. 76: Fuse (RF); S. 87 oben: Winston Davidian (RF); S. 95 unten: Pieter Folkens; S. 103 TF 6 Wulff (u. 123 li.): AFP; S. 111; S. 138 unten cover (M): Terry Vine); **GRACE** (S. 103 TF 3 (u. 113 unten): Produced by Free Range Studios, www.freerangestudios.com, in conjunction with GRACE/Sustainable Table, www.sustainabletable.org. Copyright © 2003 GRACE. Reproduced and distributed with the permission of GRACE); **Hachette**, London (S. 34: from "The Carbon Diaries" by Saci Lloyd, first published in the UK by Hodder Children's, an imprint of Hachette Children's Books, 338 Euston Road, London NW1 3BH); **iStockphoto**, Calgary (Inhaltsverz. (u. 7 Peanut): Don Bayley; S. 6 oben gay couple: Libby Chapman, oben Hintergrund blond girl: mammamaart, oben Hintergrund group of friends: mandygodbehear, oben girl with headphones: Skip ODonnell; S. 7: Chris Schmidt; S. 9 Mitte: asiseeit; S. 15 Alexis (M): Zlata Zubenko, Hailey (M): MoniqueRodriguez; S. 25 oben li.: Adam James; S. 26 oben li.: Lone Elisa Plougmann; S. 28 unten li.: Jeff Greenberg; S. 28 oben li. (M): Šarūnas Babilas; S. 29 oben re.: Ian Bracegirdle; S. 32 oben: muratseyit; S. 33 unten smart: Danylchenko Iaroslav; S. 36 unten li.: Nicholas Homrich, organic food: Dan Moore; S. 37: matteo; S. 40 oben: Robert Byron; S. 41 oben: Borut Trdina; S. 44: Sally Llanes; S. 48 (M): Sascha Burkard; S. 61: kelvin wakefield; S. 84: Morgan Lane Studios; S. 99 unten re.: ranplett; S. 103 TF 2 (u. 112 unten): Mikhail Bistrov; S. 104 oben re.: mocker_bat; S. 115: Shelly Perry; S. 116 unten 2. v. li.: poco_bw, 2. v. re.: 4FR; S. 136 oben: james steidl); **ITN Source** (S. 31 unten: still from "Bang goes the theory – The Human Power Station". Courtesy of ITN Source); **Brent Martin**, Cambridge, NZ (S. 33 oben); **Masterfile**, Düsseldorf (S. 28 oben re.: SimplyMui); **www.offthemark. com** (S. 80 Mitte: Cartoon copyrighted by Mark Parisi); **Photofusion**, London (Inhaltsverz. (u. 46 Bild B): Janine Wiedel; S. 46 Bild A: Joanne OBrien); **Photolibrary**, London (Inhaltsverz. (u. 46 Bild C): INC SUPERSTOCK, Inhaltsverz. (u. 6 Bex): Design Pics Inc (RF); S. 88 oben: age fotostock / Saxpixcom Saxpixcom); **Picture-Alliance**, Frankfurt/Main (S. 11: chromorange; S. 31 Mitte li.: dpa; S. 33 unten map (M): dieKLEINERT.de; S. 36 unten re.: dpa; S. 91: dpa; 103 TF 6 Obama (u. 122 oben li.): dpa; S. 104 unten li.: abaca; S. 114 oben: dpa); **Picture-Desk**, London (S. 12 oben li.: THE KOBAL COLLECTION/ WATERMARK, unten: THE KOBAL COLLECTION/ FILM COUNCIL/BEND IT FILMS, oben re.: THE